# The Economics of
# Property Rights

# The Economics of Property Rights

Edited by

**Eirik G. Furubotn**
*Texas A&M University*

**Svetozar Pejovich**
*Ohio University*

**Ballinger Publishing Company** ● Cambridge, Mass.
*A Subsidiary of J.B. Lippincott Company*

Library of Congress Cataloging in Publication Data
Furubotn, Eirik Grundtvig, 1923–      comp.
   The economics of property rights.
   CONTENTS: Cheung, S. The Structure of a contract and the theory of a
non-exclusive resource. —Demsetz, H. Toward a theory of property rights.
—McKean, R. Products liability: implications of some changing property rights.
[etc.]
   1. Property—Addresses, essays, lectures. 2. Property and socialism—Addresses,
essays, lectures. I. Pejovich, Svetozar, joint comp. II. Title.
HB701.F86                    333.3'23                    73-14644
ISBN 0-88410-251-3

Library of Congress Catalog Card Number: 73-14644

International Standard Book Number: 0-88410-251-3

International Standard Book Number: 0-88410-278-5  PBK

Printed in the United States of America

# Table of Contents

# List of Figures

# List of Tables

# Foreword

The fields of economics, as identified in the Directory of the American Economic Association, do not include a field on "Property, Entitlements, or Rights." Economic theory, as taught in our colleges at every level, has essentially been an analytical apparatus applicable to private property rights. Government, nonprofit, cooperative, mutually "owned," communal property rights or entitlements are almost ignored analytically, as if they did not exist or were no different in their effects than stereotyped private property rights. True, there were some efforts to compare economic "systems," but these were essentially descriptive, with slight if any analytical derivations of implied consequences of differences in types of rights.

Systematic differences in behavior or results among governmental, nonprofit, mutual, and private property organizations may be regarded as obvious and hardly worth deriving from theory, or as nonexistent! Studies of differences and attempts to establish existence of systematic differences either by empirical studies or as theoretical deductions have recently, I believe, been motivated by the conviction that systematic differences exist and can be explained consistently with economic theory. The behavior constraints installed in the theoretical apparatus must not be confined to private property constraints, or the opportunity set open to individuals must not be confined to the tradeoffs and options that exist only under private property rights, as is the case with the standard budget constraint.

During the past decade or so, a rise of interest in this problem has become noticeably productive, though, as yet, no well-explicated or organized formulation of the constraints operative under these other entitlements has been achieved. Significant progress has been made with relatively obvious and "literary" revisions of the constraint away from private property toward other rights and entitlements.

Because of the absence of a field of property rights or entitlements, it has been easy to overlook the significant advances in this area. The editors of this collection have therefore enabled the profession at large to have a convenient and fairly representative sampling of articles devoted to this topic. The presentation is by no means complete. Benjamin Ward and Evsey Domar, to name a couple, are also significant, but they were probably omitted because of their already established status.

Perhaps noteworthy is the interest of the so-called communist, or socialist, bloc economists to make the market operate more effectively in socialist countries. The intense interest and desire to achieve the results of the capitalist or free enterprise market performance is impressive. They keep saying, "Don't try to tell us how to make planning work. We know more about its difficulties than you do. Tell us how to make markets more common in our economies." Unfortunately, the reply proferred was, "You have to introduce more private property rights to make markets work the way you think they should work. Unless you do, you will find that the market allocation will also seem to be perverse or deficient." That reply is an unsubstantiated proposition, not yet derivable from economic theory nor fully validated by sufficient evidence. Yet I believe that factually it is true and will before too long be derivable as theory is developed. The socialists may well be the first to derive it and substantiate it. Collections of essays like this one may help Western economists win the race.

**A. Alchian**

# Preface

The development of the modern theory of property rights represents one of the most important advances in economic thinking that has occurred in the post-war period. Moreover, in the last decade, particularly, the volume of technical literature in the area has been increasing rapidly. Yet, despite its clear significance, property rights analysis is still not as widely known as it should be; and a major objective of the present book is to change this condition. Specifically, it is hoped to enlarge interest in and understanding of the economics of property rights by bringing together in one volume a broad collection of readings that can be of use to both students and professional economists.

The selections made cover applications of property rights analysis to widely different types of problems. But, in presenting such a diverse group of papers, it becomes possible to give an indication of the great scope and flexibility of the new approach and to reveal some of the potential research opportunities that exist in the field. The collection includes a number of fundamental papers on the economics of property rights, but attention is also given to less familiar articles dealing with somewhat specialized topics. While limitations of space have made it necessary to omit many important works, the basic intention has been to reprint useful and representative papers from as many significant subareas as possible. With this organization, the collection should be able to serve as supplementary reading for courses in such different specialties as price theory, comparative economic systems, regulation of industry, economic development, etc.

In the course of our research on the subject of property rights, as well as in the work of preparing this collection of essays, we have received support, encouragement, and valuable critical commentary from a number of scholars. In particular, we owe thanks to Ronald Coase, Harold Demsetz, Henry Manne, Gordon Tullock, and, most especially, to Armen Alchian whom we consider to be the founding father of the new property rights analysis. We should also like to thank the agencies that have provided financial support for the different phases of our research and writing; grateful acknowledgment is made for the assistance given by the National Science Foundation, the Earhart Foundation, the American Enterprise Institute, and the American Council of Learned Societies.

**Eirik G. Furubotn**
College Station, Texas

**Svetozar Pejovich**
Athens, Ohio

**Part I**

# Property Rights and Economic Theory: Some Basic Issues

**Chapter One**

# Introduction: The New Property Rights Literature[1]

In the last decade or so, a significant body of literature has grown up around the central idea that property rights concepts must be incorporated into economic analysis and given serious attention. According to the proponents of the new approach, the scope and content of property rights assignments over resources affect the way that people behave in a world of scarcity. In other words, individuals respond to economic incentives, and the pattern of incentives present at any time is influenced by the prevailing property rights structure. On this logic, it is clear that careful specification of the institutional setting of an economic problem is essential. Moreover, it also follows that generalization of traditional microeconomic theory is both feasible and necessary; by making appropriate adjustments for different property rights configurations, the applicability of classical marginalism can be extended greatly.

To achieve the important objective of generalization, the property rights analysis introduces several crucial changes into the standard theory of production and exchange. Of particular interest is the new interpretation given to the role of the individual decision-maker within an organization. The business manager, for example, is no longer regarded as a passive agent who automatically obeys orders from higher authorities; rather, he is assumed to seek his own interests and to maximize utility subject to the limits established by the existing organizational structure. In general, the property rights approach reflects the perspectives of methodological individualism, and considers both the individual's and the organization's position in the choice process.

Another shift in viewpoint is found in the assumptions made about the possible variations in property rights structures. Explicit account is taken of the fact that many different patterns of property rights can exist in human societies. Thus, contrary to conventional theory, models need not be confined to

1. This brief explanation of the nature of property rights analysis follows the discussion developed in Furubotn and Pejovich (1972c).

those implying profit maximization and the special set of ownership conditions that Alchian and Demsetz (1972) have indicated as necessary for the emergence of the *classical capitalist firm*. By considering the effects of various property rights assignments on the penalty-reward system, detailed analysis of the interrelations between institutional arrangements and economic behavior becomes feasible. This last condition is important, of course, because it means that economic activity taking place in quite varied socioeconomic environments can be discussed in terms of a single analytical framework.

Also contributing to a more flexible and comprehensive theory of production and exchange is the recognition by the property rights literature that transactions costs are positive in virtually all cases of practical significance. That is, the costs incurred by individuals in defining, policing, negotiating, and enforcing resource rights and contractual agreements are nonzero, and may often be very large indeed. The existence of a structure of transactions costs within an economy does not, however, affect the relevance of the basic market logic; the concept of economic efficiency remains, but it becomes possible to explain the conditions under which markets should or should not be extended into new areas.[2]

Although relatively few of the property rights studies have a strongly formal character, the assumptions underlying the new approach fit smoothly into the conventional optimization framework. Conceptually, the situation is this. In each application, it is necessary to define the particular utility function that reflects the decision-maker's preferences, and to determine the actual set of options that is attainable by the decision maker. Then, the formal problem emerges as the familiar one of maximizing the utility function subject to the constraint imposed by the opportunity set (i.e., the set of alternatives established by the existing penalty-reward system). Of course, the usefulness of any such model depends on how skillfully the specification is made of the objective function and the opportunity set.

Broadly speaking, the property rights approach can be understood as an attempt to avoid the overly abstract analytical treatment of traditional microeconomic theory by focusing on optimization problems that have substantial empirical input. Thus, in the cases studied, the prevailing property relations and the exchange, policing and enforcement costs of contractual activities tend to be spelled out in some detail. Similarly, the utility function is associated with a particular decision-maker, and specific empirical content is introduced into the function. In this way, it becomes possible to consider the probable behavior of the decision-maker within the business firm, the government bureau, or any comparable collective agency. Attention is concentrated on the objectives of the individual, not on those of the organization. The latter comes into the analysis as a limiting factor or constraint; different property rights assignments lead to different penalty-reward structures and, hence, determine the choices that are open

2. See, for example, Demsetz (1964, pp. 11–26).

to decision-makers. An important shift of viewpoint is evident here. Consider, for example, the discussion of the modern corporation. Instead of treating the firm as the unit of analysis and assuming that the owners' interests are given exclusive attention via the process of profit maximization, the utility maximizing model emphasizes individual adjustment to the economic environment and seeks to explain the firm's allocation and use of resources by observing individual actions within the organization.

The rejection of profit maximization as the fundamental behavioral postulate explaining the actions of decision-makers in a capitalist economy represents a simple yet important step. For, the shift to utility as the maximand opens up new possibilities for studying different patterns of managerial behavior, and permits greater insight into the way firms operate when faced with different institutional conditions. This is so because regardless of the number, character, or diversity of the goals established by an individual decision-maker, the goals can always be conceived as arguments in some type of utility function. At the same time, the institutional background translates into a corresponding set of constraints and, as noted, the utility function can be maximized subject to these. Since the property rights theorists tend to reject "satisficing" hypotheses, each decision-maker is assumed to be motivated by self-interest and to move efficiently toward the most preferred operating position open. It follows, therefore, that under the analytic conditions envisioned, classical marginalism is not rejected; the standard techniques are merely extended to new applications.

Insofar as the new generalization of conventional microeconomics turns on the concept of property rights, it is essential that the meaning of the latter term be fully grasped. Fortunately, the literature provides a clear definition. Property rights are understood as the *sanctioned behavioral relations* among men that arise from the existence of goods and pertain to their use. These relations specify the norms of behavior with respect to goods that each and every person must observe in his daily interactions with other persons, or bear the cost of nonobservance. The term "good" is used here for anything that yields utility or satisfaction to a person. Thus, and this point is important, the concept of property rights in the context of the new approach applies to *all* scarce goods. The concept encompasses both the rights over material things (to sell my typewriter) as well as "human" rights (the right to vote, to publish, etc.). The prevailing system of property rights in the community is, then, the sum of economic and social relations with respect to scarce resources in which individual members stand to each other.

The means through which the prevailing property rights assignments in an economy affect the allocation of resources is *exchange*. Indeed, trade generates contractual agreements, not so much to exchange goods, but to exchange bundles of property rights to do things with those goods. Since an individual cannot ordinarily transfer to others more rights to an asset than he himself possesses, the *extent* of exchange and the *terms* of trade are, obviously, not independent of the existing property rights assignments in the community. In other words, the volumes of goods exchanged and their terms of trade must depend on the bundles of rights that can be transferred legally. For example, the value of an automobile to a person will increase, and he will be willing to pay more for it, as the bundle of rights he acquires stipulates fewer restrictions on the use of the vehicle and on his freedom to resell the car at any time in the open market.

As the basic definition suggests, the categories of property rights are many. Certainly, however, the *right of ownership*, which is actually a subcategory of the general concept of property rights, is the best known. By general agreement, the right of ownership in an asset consists of three elements: (a) the right to use the asset (usus), (b) the right to appropriate returns from the asset (usus fructus), and (c) the right to change the asset's form and/or substance (abusus). This last element, the right to bear the consequences from changes in the value of an asset, is the fundamental component of the right of ownership. It implies that the owner has the legal freedom to transfer all rights (e.g., to sell a house), or some rights (e.g., to rent the house), in the asset to others at a mutually agreed-upon price. Although our definition suggests that the right of ownership is an *exclusive* right, ownership is not, and can hardly be expected to be, an *unrestricted* right. The right of ownership is an exclusive right in the sense that it is limited *only* by those restrictions that are explicitly stated in the law. Such restrictions may range from the substantial to the minor. For example, on one hand, there is the serious case where an individual's right of ownership in an asset cannot be transferred for a price higher than the ceiling price established by the government; on the other, there is the situation where a land owner is constrained from building a fence within two feet of the property line.

In general, then, it is important to recognize that the attenuation of private property rights in an asset[3], via the imposition of restrictive measures, affects the owner's expectations about the uses to which he can put the asset, the value of the asset to the owner and to others and, consequently, the terms of trade. Granting these interrelations, the significance of attenuation is clear; whatever specific form it takes, attenuation implies the existence of limitations on the owner's rights to change the form, place, or substance of an asset, and to transfer all of his rights in it to others at a mutually acceptable price.

It follows from what has been said that an asset or commodity can be defined not only by its technical properties but also by the particular set of legal restrictions governing the use and exchange of the item. Two physically identical houses constitute effectively different commodities when the property rights attached to them are different and will, presumably, have different market values. Generalizing on this theme, the situation in an idealized capitalistic economy can be conceived as follows. At any moment of time, there is a legally sanctioned

---

3. It should be noted that the state's ownership rights in assets are also subject to attenuation.

structure of property rights in existence, and each individual in the system possesses definite property rights over certain economic goods and services. In other words, each individual has an initial endowment composed of quantities of various "effective commodities" (specific commodities plus associated property rights). Assuming there are $m$ decision-makers and $n$ distinct "effective commodities,"[4] the system's initial allocation can be described by a matrix $A$, where any element in the matrix, $a_{ij}$, indicates the quantity of the effective commodity $j$ held by individual $i$ (and $a_{ij} \geqslant 0$).

  Since an extensive network of interlocking markets exists in an enterprise economy, institutional conditions are favorable to trade, and the $m$ individuals here can be expected to exchange commodities (and "bundles" of property rights) in an effort to increase their respective utility levels. A complex production-exchange process will ensue, and, assuming that this activity takes place over a finite time period, the result will be a reconstituted commodity matrix at the end of that period. Through trade, each person will secure a new set of commodities and achieve equilibrium at a higher level of utility than was possible in the pre-trade situation $(A)$. The new matrix—say, $B$—will reflect different holdings of effective commodities by the $m$ trade participants. Each row vector in $B$, as $(b_{i1}, b_{i2}, ..., b_{in})$, represents the set of commodities an individual $i$ possesses at the conclusion of the period's activities. Thus, given each person's utility function, $u_i = f_i(b_{i1}, b_{i2}, ..., b_{in})$, $i = 1, 2, ..., m$, the general distribution of welfare $(u_1, u_2, ..., u_m)$ implied by allocation $B$ is determinate. It is in this way that the possession of various bundles of rights in resources can be said to enter the utility functions of individuals. Moreover, when the usual neoclassical assumptions are made concerning competition, continuity, the shapes of the system's production and utility functions, etc., the equilibrium position described by matrix $B$ is Pareto optimal. Maximizing behavior by the decision-makers insures that transactions will be undertaken until there are no incentives for futher exchange and the situation is such that one individual cannot gain without harming another.[5]

  Once emphasis is placed on the structure of property rights, it becomes obvious that any change in the law affecting the conditions of ownership alters the set of effective commodities in the system and produces a new distribution of welfare. In formal terms, the original matrix $A$ is replaced by another—say, $G$—that involves the redefined commodities plus those that are unchanged by the legal adjustments. The reestablished (initial) set of effective commodities $(1, 2, ..., s)$ is possessed by the $m$ individuals present and, as before, the production-

---

  4. Just as identical physical goods located at different points in space (or time) can be regarded as distinct items, so also can two goods having different property rights assignments.

  5. In the usual welfare analysis, such factors as property rights assignments, transactions costs, etc., are given little if any systematic attention. See Mishan (1960). Some thoughts on the general influence of the institutional structure on welfare are found in Samuelson (1950) and Graaff (1967).

exchange process will lead to revised commodity holdings on the part of the community. The new situation can be symbolized by a $m \times s$ matrix $H$. The latter, of course, yields a distribution of welfare $(u'_1, u'_2, \ldots, u'_m)$ that will, in general, be different from the distribution based on matrix $B$.

But what occurs here is not a movement in utility space from one point on the original welfare frontier to another. The shift from the legal-economic situation summarized by $A, B$ to that summarized by $G, H$ implies the emergence of a *new* welfare frontier. Since the legal restrictions on an owner's freedom to transfer property rights to others and on his freedom to use resources in particular ways are determined by the system of property relations extant, the latter structures must directly affect the productive capabilities of the economy and the position of the welfare frontier.[6] Thus, if matrix $G$ represents a system where property rights have been attenuated significantly relative to the situation under $A$ (e.g., through prohibition of interregional movement of commodities), it follows that greater allocative inefficiency and/or other difficulties will exist in that system. It is also clear that the associated welfare frontier must lie within the frontier of the "less attenuated" economy over at least part of its range.

The intimate connection between property rights and welfare is not brought out in the conventional theory because no real attention is given to the question. Usually, the property rights structure of an economy is either ignored or specified in some highly simplified fashion.[7] In the real world, though, the regulations pertaining to property are crucially important in determining the welfare potentialities of the system; as the elementary general equilibrium model suggests, property rights assignments exert systemwide influence on the allocation of resources, the composition of output, the distribution of income, etc. It is also true that the sharpness of specification of property rights and their development over time affect welfare. The logic of competition (i.e., the heeding of alternative uses) indicates that a more complete and definite specification of individual property rights diminishes uncertainty and tends to promote efficient allocation and use of resources. Dynamic questions are more complex. At this stage, the way in which the specification process unfolds is not entirely clear; nevertheless, it seems plausible to say that either a reduction of the costs of transaction, or an increase in the value of a given commodity will result in fuller specification of property rights in that commodity and, hence, in an improvement in the accuracy of private accounting calculations.

6. North (1972) argues that the state has often traded inefficient property rights arrangements (e.g., licences to operate in closed markets) for revenue, and in doing so has retarded economic growth.

7. The standard competitive model envisions a special system where one particular set of private property rights governs the use of *all* resources, and where the exchange, policing, and enforcement costs of contractual activities are zero. In the simplest version, individuals begin each period with quantities of productive services and no consumer goods. They, then, exchange services for money and use the money to obtain desired commodities. The static character of conventional microeconomic theory has tended to prevent extensive analysis of asset-holding and the role of property rights structures.

The purpose of the property rights approach is to achieve a generalization of the standard theory of production and exchange by considering the interconnectedness of ownership rights, incentives, and economic behavior. If the approach is to justify the hopes held out for it, however, it must satisfy two key conditions. That is, the new theory must demonstrate that: (a) the content of property rights affects the allocation and use of resources in *specific* and *predictable* ways; and (b) the logic of economics can explain the long-term *development* of property rights, including the nature of the changes in their content. The importance of these points is obvious. Without the assurance that prediction is possible, there is no way of constructing analytically significant and empirically refutable propositions about the effects of various property rights assignments on the level and character of economic activity in the community. Similarly, the dynamics of the property rights structure must be understood. The system of property relations cannot be taken as given from without, or as a type of human discovery that is unrelated to the contemporaneous economic situation. Economists have to offer a testable theory of the development of property rights. Ideally, such a theory will throw light on the linkages between the system of laws and economic decisions and, in this way, contribute to the establishment of an institutional environment favorable to efficiency and progress.

This book, which is a collection of essays, is organized around the set of problems just discussed. Part I is concerned with the question of the extent to which the development of legal institutions, and the norms that regulate the quality of economic life in a community, can be deduced theoretically. Part II attempts to provide evidence that a systematic relationship exists between property rights assignments on the one hand, and economic behavior and the level and character of economic activity on the other. Included here are topics in the theory of the firm—an area where perhaps the greatest advances have been made by the property rights approach. Attention is given to transactions costs, attenuation of ownership rights, legal restraint on economic activity, externalities, and related considerations. Part III deals with the effects of various forms of state ownership in resources on the behavior of decision-makers. The fact that property rights analysis can be applied fruitfully to such diverse problems as those of the socialist firm, corruption, and bureaucratic behavior gives some indication of the great power and flexibility of the new approach. Finally, Part IV offers a brief overview of the state of property rights research. It must be recognized, of course, that work in this area is still in its initial stage. Some important contributions have been made but a great many questions remain to be explored. The three readings presented in this section represent a sample of current efforts to achieve a general theory of economic organization.

## THE DEVELOPMENT OF PROPERTY RIGHTS

Turning to the topic of Part I, we are confronted with a series of inter-related questions: Can the logic of economics explain the development of property rights? Is the development of property rights determined endogenously within the economic system? Does the creation and specification of property rights take place in response to the desire of individual decision-makers for more utility? The basic issue, then, concerns the existence of interconnections between the law system and economic life in its various aspects. Merely to state the problem in this way is sufficient to suggest its difficulty. Nevertheless, property rights theorists have been able to sketch the broad outlines of a behavioral theory explaining the development of property institutions. And the latter construction can be summarized as follows.

Assuming that individuals or groups in society are motivated by self-interest and seek constantly to increase their utility levels, they will, presumably, try to exclude others from exploiting an existing good whenever it appears advantageous to do so. That is, whenever their own expected benefits appear to exceed the expected costs of defining, negotiating, policing, and enforcing the "claim." Of course, to exclude some people from free access to a good *means to specify property rights in that good*. Analogously, any change in the specification of the current regulations governing the use of a good means a change in the content of the prevailing property rights assignments. Thus, new property rights are created, and existing ones are changed because certain individuals and groups believe it profitable to restructure the system and are willing to bear the costs of bringing about such change.

An adequate theory of this process must accomplish two objectives. First, it has to establish what the factors are that affect the cost-benefit ratio associated with an economic activity. Second, it must indicate the general mechanism through which changes in the cost-benefit conditions are translated into the development of property rights. Relative to the former question, the factors that have been stressed in the property rights literature as being responsible for changes in cost-benefit calculations include such things as: technical progress, the opening up of new markets, the introduction of new products, and changes in resource endowments. In other words, a dynamic economy generates new price configurations and provides opportunities for the restructuring of property rights.

In considering how shifts in the data work themselves out, property rights theorists have pointed to the central role of *contractual agreements*, As mentioned earlier, trade permits the exchange of "bundles" of rights authorizing the recipients to do things with the goods that are traded. A contractual agreement is vitally important here because it represents the *means* by which the bundles of rights are exchanged. Of course, the prevailing property rights structure must determine the content of contractual agreements—i.e., the specific bundle of rights that can be transferred via the exchange of goods and services. But if contractual stipulations are constrained in specific ways by existing property rights assignments, a qualitative change in the content of contractual agreements must presuppose a change in the property rights structure (e.g., changes in the liability assignments for accidental damages) or the development of new rights (e.g., limited liability). Otherwise, new contractual stipulations would not be enforceable.

It also follows that any changes in the economy affecting private cost-benefit calculations tend to create opportunities for individuals or groups to capture profits by engaging in activities that were not previously considered profitable (e.g., high seas shipping). To engage in these new activities, however, requires the formation of some definite contractual agreements that allow the participants to claim the potential benefits foreseen. Moreover, if the prevailing property relations are poorly attuned to the new contractual agreements and are unable to enforce them, legal arrangements and/or the constraints of custom must change in order to permit the enforcement of the new stipulations. For example, revised institutional arrangements had to appear when the concept of risk spreading via insurance became the basis for commercial activity. In general, then, if individuals are to appropriate the potential gains from innovative ventures, it may be necessary to change the content of contractual agreements; but the acceptance of changes in contractual forms must lead to a new or modified set of property rights assignments. *Changes in property rights are triggered by the interaction between the prevailing property rights structure and man's search for ways of achieving more utility.* On this interpretation, the development of property rights can be deduced theoretically.

The chapters by Cheung and Demsetz deal with questions of the type just discussed. Thus, these writers endeavor to explain *why* property rights develop, *what* the factors are that change economic conditions and create incentives for people to define new rights or redefine the old, and *how* changes in the prevailing economic environment are translated into the restructuring of property rights. In addition, and quite appropriately, the problem of resource allocation in the absence of property rights is discussed by Cheung. The analysis here elucidates three main questions: What procedures are used to allocate a non-owned good among competing claimants? What is the private (and social) cost of "purchasing" a non-owned asset? And, what are the implications of an absence of property rights in a resource for its rate of consumption and reproduction?

# Chapter Two

# The Structure of a Contract and the Theory of a Non-Exclusive Resource

S. Cheung

Reprinted from the *Journal of Law and Economics* 13 (April 1970): 49–70, by permission of publisher and author.

The process of arriving at a useful concept of analysis is not only slow and painful but also may go astray and attain nothing useful. Someone begins with one example or observation, followed by a theory which is intuitively plausible. A theoretical term associated with a vague concept is coined. Examples of a seemingly different type emerge, which call for another theory. The process goes on. As examples and theories continue to accumulate, the different categories under the same heading of analysis serve only to confuse, and each associated theory becomes ad hoc. Such has been the fate of the concept of "externality."[1]

    A more useful approach, I think, is via contractual conditions. The example chosen for illustration is marine fisheries, where the fishing right is taken as non-exclusive, and where most economists agree that externalities exist in several directions.[2] In the absence of exclusive rights to the use of the fishing ground,[3] the right to contract so as to stipulate its use does not exist. This implies the absence of contractual stipulations governing resource use which would exist if the fishing ground were private property, thereby altering the constraint of competition and affecting resource allocation in a number of ways. The alleged "externalities" in fisheries are thus attributable to the absence of the right to contract.

    1. For a fairly comprehensive count, see Mishan (1965). Note, however, that the number of "externalities" has increased rapidly in the subsequent four years.
    2. See, for example, Turvey (1964) and Smith (1969).
    3. What resource in marine fisheries is non-exclusive—the ocean bed, the water, or the fish? The answer is that any productive resource is multi-dimensional, and the term "fishing ground" is chosen to include all of them. This term is used synonymously with "fishery resource" or "fishing rights" in this paper.

## PROPERTY RIGHTS AND CONTRACTING

Combining resources of several owners for production involves partial or out-right transfers of property rights through a contract.[4] A contract for the partial transfer of rights, such as leasing or hiring—embodies a *structure*. The stipulations, or terms, which constitute the structure of the contract are, as a rule, designed to specify (a) the distribution of income among the participants and (b) the conditions of resource use. Under transferable rights, these stipulations are consistent with, or determined by, competition in the marketplace. As shown elsewhere (Cheung 1969a), the choice of contracts is determined by transaction costs, natural (economic) risks, and legal (political) arrangements. However, the familiar market prices are but one among many of the contractual terms (indeed, in share contracts, prices are not explicitly specified).

With private property rights governing the use of *all* resources, the postulate of wealth maximization implies that the contractual stipulations are designed to maximize the return to all resources subject to the constraint of competition. Assume away the costs of transactions, the contractual stipulations for every resource use will be so designed that they are consistent with the equi-marginal principle. In general, the structure of the contract will be such that the marginal gain and cost are equal. In specific details, however, the elements constituting gains and costs are multiple, and the marginal equalities of a constrained maximization are several. Since to satisfy one particular marginal equality, one or more contractual stipulations, implicitly or explicitly, are required, pages of stipulations in one contract can be found.

Two questions immediately arise. First, given the contractual stipulations, do we know that the required marginal equalities are satisfied? And second, what bearing do these stipulations have on the actual outcome of income distribution and resource allocation?

The answer to the first is that we know at least whether the stipulations are *consistent* with the requisite marginal equalities. The stipulations of a contract may be inconsistent with marginal equality of resource use (for example, a contract stipulating only a lump-sum charge without quantity stipulation); or the contract may not exist, implicitly or explicitly, as in the case of the use of a non-exclusive right. A defective contract, or the absence of a contract, does not necessarily imply economic inefficiency, and can be traced either to the presence of transaction costs, the existing legal arrangements, or the lack of foresight and the costs of information.[5] The second question—the relation between a set of stipulations and the actual outcome—is one of contractual enforcement. While one may

---

4. If only outright transfers exist for all resources, then only owner production will exist, and contractual stipulations on resource use will be absent. Partial transfers, such as leasing and hiring, are emphasized here because (a) they lead more directly to the problems involved and (b) they serve to illustrate more clearly the function of a contract.

    5. See Coase (1960), Stigler (1961), and Demsetz (1964).

argue that non-enforceable stipulations will not be present in a contract, for our present purpose it suffices to point out that the absence of a contract will lead to different resource use than when an enforceable contract exists.

But the main point here is that a contract may encompass a large set of stipulations, governing a set of marginal equalities associated with various aspects of resource use. If outright transfers exist for all resources engaged in production, the owner alone is responsible for the decision aspects. If partial transfers exist, then the contracting parties mutually negotiate the terms. For any production process, multiple contracts may exist. Given the form of contract, the stipulations would be more complex the more complex the physical attributes of inputs and outputs.

It has become increasingly clear to me that the mushrooming of alleged "externalities" is attributable to either (a) the absence of the right to contract, (b) the presence of a contract but with incomplete stipulations, or (c) the presence of stipulations that are somehow inconsistent with some marginal equalities. Among these cases, however, differences are only a matter of degree. Since the conceivable number of different contractual stipulations is very large, the rapid growth rate in the literature in recognizing "new" externalities is natural.

As an example, let us examine marine fisheries, wherein the right to use the fishing ground is said to be non-exclusive and hence the right to contract is absent. The assumed condition of a lack of exclusive right to use the resource, free of institutional regulations, does not, of course, correspond to the real world where rules and regulations established by governments and unions are numerous.[6] The issue of regulation versus voluntary contractual arrangements in the marketplace will be discussed briefly in the section on "The Nature of the Problem."

Fish, like rice or any other growing (biological) asset, require "planting" as well as "harvesting." Different physical attributes of such resources, however, will lead to different degrees of emphasis on the alternative options of choice. In general, decisions will be made on the product to be produced, the method of production, the amount and type of investment over time, the financial maturity of the catch, and the intensity and method of harvesting. With private property rights, these decisions will result in stipulations mutually negotiated by the contracting parties (for example, the fishing-ground owner, the boat owner, and the fisherman). Although the stipulations differ when the forms of contract differ, the implied resource use may not.

In the absence of exclusive rights governing the use of the fishing ground, not only will the intensity of its use be affected but also the costs of policing (enforcing) the income generated by other private investment inputs will

6. The literature is immense. See Christy and Scott (1965); Crutchfield and Zellner (1962); "Expert Meeting on the Economic Effects of Fishery Regulations, Ottawa, 1961" (1962); McDougal and Burke (1962); Sinclair (1960); "International Technical Conference on the Conservation of the Living Resources of the Sea" (1956). Rules imposed by boat and fisherman unions can best be obtained from the unions themselves.

be higher. Higher policing costs will affect decisions pertaining to planting and financial maturity. For example: if the right to the use of land is non-exclusive, the cost of policing *private* fertilizers applied to land for the production of corn will be higher than if the land use is exclusive and is subject to contractual stipulation and enforcement. That is, if private landownership obtained, the owner could enter a contract with labor and fertilizer owners, and restrict nonparticipants from interfering in any undesirable way. The right to contract is also the *right to exclude*. The same applies to the non-exclusive fishing ground, despite the different physical atrributes of fish and corn. Some implications are:

1. The choice of product will be constrained by the higher costs of guarding private investment inputs, generated by the non-exclusive use of the resource. This implies that a product, the physical attributes of which entail relatively low costs of policing private investment inputs, will be preferred by the users of the non-exclusive resource. In Tripolitania, for example, potentially lucrative almond trees are reported to have been forsaken for cattle-raising owing to the "common ownership" of land.[7] This can be explained by the fact that the cost of policing investment in a tree, perenially "attached" to the common land, is high, whereas cattle are driven home at night. The change in product as described results in a different composition of investment inputs; but the total value of investment may rise or fall. Furthermore, the collectable rent—a residual under non-exclusive land-ownership—will decline even before its dissipation under competition, owing to the choice of a product differing from that chosen to maximize rent under private property.

Does the lack of exclusivity in the fishing ground significantly affect the choice of product in marine fisheries? One impression is that it does not, since the fishing ground appears to be amenable to concurrent uses, or the existing types of marine product might be the most valuable choices. Still, there may be too many of some fish and too few of another, or the product choice in aquaculture may be affected.[8] The issue is an empirical one.

2. Given the product, some types of investment input will predictably decline when a private fishing ground becomes non-exclusive. For example, privately owned paddy-field fisheries will receive more intensive feeding than if the same fish were placed in a common lake.[9] The phenomenon is again due to the higher cost of policing private feeding inputs, on account of the non-exclusive use of the common lake. In marine fisheries, the rate of return to this type of invest-

---

7. See Bottomley (1963).

8. See Scott (1968).

9. But investment of this type may not be reduced to zero. While no definitive solution for this is offered here, let me suggest an approach to the problem. Assume that the cost of policing private investment is so high as to be prohibitive. Let $p$ be the marginal rate of return on investment and $r$ be the rate of interest. If the return to investment is non-exclusive, then given $n$ identical people, an individual will invest if $p/n \geqslant r$. It is, of course, possible that investment of this type be reduced to zero even if $n$ is quite small. However, the number of individuals should be treated as a variable partly dependent on $p$.

ment appears negligible, hence unimportant. But the same may not be true for all marine products.

3. The physical attributes of marine fisheries, together with policing costs, also affect the value at maturity (size of catch) of the growing asset. Should the fishing ground be exclusively owned and its products costlessly enforced as private, the financial maturity of fisheries and the implied rate of rotation (that is, the mesh size) would be so chosen as to maximize wealth.[10] Similarly, the time shape of the income stream of harvesting will differ from that of maximizing wealth under non-exclusive rights.[11] These factors, while significant in marine fisheries, do not appear so for cattle-raising in common pastures, since the cost of policing cattle is lower. That is, the cost of policing privately raised fish in a "common" ocean is higher than that of raising cattle in common pastures.

The several changes in decisions pertaining to planting and financial maturity discussed above are only some of the more prominent effects of the absence of exclusive rights in one of the factors of production. While an exhaustive list is not attempted here, our discussion shows that since a contract embodies a structure, the absence of the right to contract, as with a non-exclusive resource, will affect resource allocation in a variety of ways. And since production decisions are usually several, so are the marginal equalities affected: the marginal mesh size, marginal feeding inputs, marginal product choice, and so forth. According to the current practice, these decision aspects affected by the absence of a contract are treated as different types of externalities.

While, in the section on "Harvesting: The Dissipation of Rent," I shall support the existing conclusion of the dissipation of rent under the non-exclusive use of a resource, I shall not endorse the traditionally accepted analysis through which this dissipation takes place. This section has shown that the effects pertaining to planting and financial maturity, if they occur, will in themselves reduce the collectable rent. And it is not difficult to conceive of a situation in which, by harvest time, there is nothing worthwhile to harvest. But marine fisheries have better luck.

## HARVESTING: PRIVATE PROPERTY RIGHTS AND THE MARGIN OF DAMAGE

We now turn to analyze the intensity of fishery "harvesting" in two hypothetical worlds, one with private property in all resources and one with a non-exclusive fishing ground. The harvesting issue is singled out here because the existing theoretical solution has been fundamental in recent economic analysis of marine fisheries and of the "common pool." Furthermore, externality is said to

10. Although the "tree-cutting" problem is well known, I refer here to an early solution by Martin Faustmann (1849), which is resurrected in Gaffney (1960).
11. The best exposition of "time shape" and wealth maximization is still found in Fisher (1961, ch. 5 and 6).

exist in its purest form: the catch of one fisherman depends not only on his own input but also on the inputs of other competing fishermen. In this section we discuss the private-property world, and the common pool in the next. The simple manipulation of the law of diminishing returns serves to demonstrate further the function of contracting and the ambiguity of the concept of externality.

Consider two private factor inputs in fishery production: the fishing ground and fisherman labor (assume that fish grow by themselves and ignore biomass value, hence harvesting is the only consideration). The rent derivable from the fishing ground is thus the integral of the difference between the marginal product of labor and the wage rate. To maximize rent (income) under private ownership,[12] the rate of change of rent with respect to labor is required to be set at zero, implying that the marginal product of labor equals the wage rate.

The above equilibrium condition can be viewed in terms of the gain from adding labor to fishery harvesting and the damage the incremental labor inflicts on the productivity of the existing (intramarginal) labor input. Viewing the marginal gain per infinitesimal unit of labor added as its average product (its contribution) minus the wage rate (its alternative earning), we write

$$\Omega(L) = \frac{Q}{L} - W$$

On the other hand, "external" to the labor being added, the productivity of all existing (intramarginal) labor declines. This decline in productivity, or the *marginal damage* the increment labor imposes on the productivity of the existing labor, is the amount of existing labor times the rate of change of the average product of each labor unit. That is,

$$\Lambda(L) = L \frac{d(Q/L)}{dL} = L \left( \frac{L(\partial Q/\partial L) - Q}{L^2} \right) = \frac{\partial Q}{\partial L} - \frac{Q}{L}$$

To maximize rent of the fishing ground, the marginal gain of adding labor must equal the associated marginal damage, that is, $\Omega(L) + \Lambda(L) = 0$.

In this simple model we see that the effects of an action are independent of the system of property rights. To prohibit damage entirely is, insofar as diminishing returns holds (as in our model), to prohibit output entirely. What counts is whether the incremental gain can more than offset the associated damage. And it is one main function of contracting to stipulate the margin of damage that is to be allowed. Private property in the fishing ground grants its owner the

---

12. Throughout this chapter, the word "rent" is used synonymously with "income," the flow of returns to any private resource right. For constrained maximization, it is viewed as an annuity.

right to contract and stipulate. The absence of such a right, as in marine fisheries, will affect the margin of damage.

What, then, is an externality? Does it exist always? If so, why is it treated as a special problem? Does it exist only when the marginal gain from an action is not equal to the marginal damage it causes? If so, should we view an externality as becoming less "external" when the inequality diminishes? Does it exist only when the damage is so great that rental income (in our example) is reduced to zero? If so, what is the conceptual difference between a zero rent and a negligibly small rent? In the simple case presented, indeed it is impossible to draw a dividing line such that externality can be meaningfully identified. *Every economic action has effects.* Nor is it illuminating to view the damage as external or internal to a firm, for the firm is but a holder of contracts.[13] The same applies to all decisions on resource use. It follows that the classification of various kinds of "externalities," if at all useful, is ad hoc theorizing, a cumbersome way to treat a general problem. The problem is general because for every gain there is a cost.

Because the above conclusion appears abrupt, let me retreat for a moment to discuss, by way of illustration, several types of economic effects caused by actions of individual decision units. The first type includes actions which produce trivial effects *and* which are transacted (with contracts) "smoothly" in the market. The traditional term for this appears to be "perfect competition"—with perhaps "constant cost for the industry." Note, however, that the same trivial action may no longer be trivial without contracting (for example, to acquire an apple without payment).

The second type includes effects which are trivial and are not transacted with contracts. Examples for this are to say "sorry" for minor damages done among individuals, or be gentle to the neighbor's dog. Let me refer to this type of behavior as "customs." According to J.S. Mill (1857), when an activity is a customary practice and "not of a varying convention, political economy has no laws of distribution to investigate."[14] While the persuasiveness of Mill may yield peace of mind, subsequent economists have frequently employed "custom" as an excuse to avoid analysis.[15] Even a practice that is truly customary may reflect the existence of costs in contracting. Furthermore, the effect of an action which resolves into a custom under one property right arrangement may be taken as a crime under another.

Third, there are actions which produce significant effects and which are transacted in the marketplace. Examples given have been cases of rising sup-

---

13. I believe this accords with R.H. Coase, "The Nature of the Firm," *Economica* 4 (1937): 386, reprinted in Stigler and Boulding, eds. (1952). Not every holder of contracts is a firm. The associated complexity is not yet relevant here.

14. Mill was commenting on the terms of a share contract.

15. Some asserted "customs" are, in fact, market practices in which the contractual terms are not obvious. See Cheung (1969, ch. 3 and 4).

ply,[16] or of interactions among large and perhaps oligopolistic producers. Such actions have been termed "pecuniary external economies or diseconomies,"[17] and do not necessarily entail specifiable economic waste.[18]

Fourth, there are actions which produce significant effects but contractual arrangements are absent—so significant, indeed, that "customs" simply will not bail them out. The classic example is a factory polluting the environment. This type of effect is traditionally termed "technological external economies or diseconomies."[19] Since these effects occur to consumption as well as production activities, in many cases it is difficult to see their "technological" attributes.[20]

Consider finally a fifth type of action, the effects of which may be trivial or significant, and which are governed by contracts. However, for some reasons certain marginal conditions required for the standard constrained maximization are not satisfied. Referring to our earlier exposition of fishery harvesting, such a case would arise if the marginal gain, $\Omega(L)$, from an increment of labor is either greater or smaller than the associated marginal damage, $\Lambda(L)$. The traditional term for this, I think, is "market imperfection."

In the above five paragraphs I have, as perceived in the light of contracting, sketched my impression of the literature relating to externalities. The arbitrariness of the division should be self-evident. What is trivial is at best a matter of degree, and the economic significance of the same actions varies under different circumstances. Similarly, "perfection" or "imperfection" is difficult if not impossible to define. And to call some effects of actions "externalities" and some—"internalities" (?)—is to me incomprehensible.

It would be ambiguous enough if "externalities" were confined to effects that are economically significant but with respect to which the rights of actions are not clearly delineated and thus not transacted in the market place. However, such a classification would have the merit of not doing much harm. But—perhaps prompted by the obvious non-existence of internalities—the concept of externality has been extended to virtually all economic activities,[21] with end-

16. See Jacob Viner, "Cost Curves and Supply Curves," in *Zeitschrift fur Nationalokonomie* (1931), reprinted in Stigler and Boulding, eds. (1952); Joan Robinson, "Rising Supply Price," *Economica* 8 (1941), reprinted in Stigler and Boulding, eds. (1952); and Howard S. Ellis and William Fellner, "External Economies and Diseconomies," *American Economic Review* 33 (1943), reprinted in Stigler and Boulding, eds. (1952).

17. See Viner, *supra* note 16; and Scitovsky (1954).

18. The best exposition on this point appears to be McKean (1958).

19. See Viner, *supra* note 16; and Scitovsky, *supra* note 16.

20. Francis M. Bator has a somewhat different classification. See his "The Anatomy of Market Failure" (1958). Bator's classification would be incomplete if compared with the present count of externalities.

21. See, for example, Buchanan and Stubblebine (1962). See also Mishan, *supra* note 1.

less divisions of types.[22] And the many associated theories serve only to confuse.

The issue at stake is not merely a semantic one. And I do not propose to refine the concept of externality. I propose to discard the concept entirely. The change in view through the analysis of contracting is not a redundant way of treating the same class of problems, for this change in view leads to different—and I believe more fruitful—questions. Why do market contracts not exist for certain effects of actions? Because of the absence of exclusive rights, or because transaction costs are prohibitive? Why do exclusive rights not exist for certain actions? Because of the legal institutions, or because policing costs are prohibitive? Why do some conceivably more efficient stipulations not exist in the structure of a contract? And what implications for resource allocation and income distribution can we deduce from all this?

## HARVESTING: THE DISSIPATION OF RENT

As we turn now to analyze the intensity of fishery harvesting—with the fishing ground as a non-exclusive resource—we should keep in mind that we refer to only one of several decision aspects affected by the absence of a contract.

The puzzle at stake is, I believe, one of the sources of the stream of externalities. My main concern in this section, however, is to correct an error in the existing solution. Thus the externality issue will be put aside until the next section.

Ever since F.H. Knight's exposition[23] of A.C. Pigou's (1920) example of good and bad roads, which in a tilted mirror image is seen in H. Scott Gordon's (1954) analysis of the common fishing ground, models of fishery harvesting have followed the conclusion that, in equilibrium, the *average* product of fishing effort (or labor) equals the wage rate (or the marginal factor cost).[24] Hence economic waste results, since the marginal product of labor in fishing is lower than of that employed elsewhere. The equalization of the average product of labor to the wage rate leads to the dissipation of rent for the fishing ground tautologically.

Obvious as it appears at first sight, two puzzles remain in the dissipation of rent. First, individual decisions are, by definition, made at the margin: how is it possible that the marginal product of fisherman labor be lower than the

22. Vernon L. Smith, *supra* note 2, for example, has classified mesh externalities, stock externalities, and crowding externalities for fisheries alone. Classification according to physical attributes can be traced back to J.E. Meade's "creation of atmosphere." See Meade (1952). The frequency of new classifications in recent doctoral dissertations is striking. See, for example, Schall (1969).

23. Frank H. Knight, "Some Fallacies in the Interpretation of Social Cost," *Quarterly Journal of Economics* (1924) reprinted in Stigler and Boulding (1952).

24. See, for example, Scott (1955), Scott, "Optimal Utilization and the Control of Fisheries," in Turvey and Wiseman, eds. (1956), and Crutchfield (1956).

wage rate (in the social sense) if *no* fisherman (that is, a decision unit) will apply labor to fishing when its marginal product to *any fisherman* is less than the wage rate? Second, just what does a fisherman maximize if exclusive right to the fishing ground is absent? Failure to answer these questions satisfactorily renders the average-product argument, hence the dissipation of rent, an asserted and not a derived result.[25] In what follows I offer an analysis which answers these questions, and the associated solution yields some implications different from those of the existing analysis.

Before proceeding to the formal analysis, an introductory summary will help. Under private ownership of the fishing ground, the right to the rent (income) is exclusive, and a contractual arrangement will make rent a private cost of fishery production. With non-exclusive fishing rights and without collusion among fishermen, rent becomes a residual, with every decision-making unit—a fisherman or a fishing firm—maximizing the portion left behind by others. Behavior is thus consistent with wealth maximization subject to the wage constraint *and* the absence of contractual constraint on other people's use of the fishing ground. With independent maximization, the marginal product of each fisherman is equal to his wage rate. In the absence of both legal and contractual restrictions on the use of the fishing ground, a fisherman will enter the industry so long as the residual (that is, earnings in excess of his alternative wage) for him is positive. With each new entrant, however, the marginal product for all fishermen will fall, and, following the equimarginal rule, each of them will *curtail* their fishing effort (or labor input). The process is thus analogous to Cournot's duopoly solution *with free entry*, with ocean rent replacing monopoly rent, average product of labor in place of demand for product, and a positive wage rate in place of the assumed zero cost of production.[26] Assume that fisherman labor is homogeneous and supply to the industry perfectly elastic, the complete dissipation of rent in equilibrium implies that the *number* of individual fishermen (or firms) approaches infinity, with each committing a trifling amount of fishing effort.

To illustrate geometrically, let us turn to Figure 2-1. In this figure, output per unit of labor is measured along the vertical axis, and labor (or fishing effort) along the horizontal axis. The amount of fishing ground (or fishery resource) is held constant. For simplicity, the linear $Q/L$ and $(\partial Q/\partial L)_\alpha$ are the average and marginal product curves respectively, with $W$ representing the wage rate, or marginal factor cost of labor, $\partial(WL)/\partial L$. If there is only one individual decision unit—say, Alpha—to decide the harvesting labor input, the result will be

25. In Gordon's exposition, *supra* note 24, fishing grounds with different fertility are explicit. I find his analysis of the dissipation of rent unclear, particularly if only one homogeneous fishing ground exists.

26. Criticisms of Cournot's duopoly solution, however, are not applicable here because we are concerned with a large number of entrants, and, by the nature of a non-exclusive resource, collusion of any kind among firms does not exist. For two criticisms of Cournot's duopoly solution, see Stigler (1968, pp. 36–37).

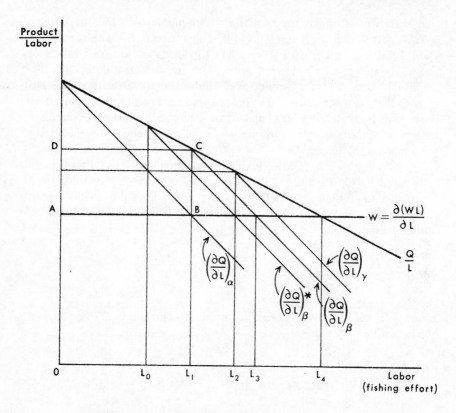

**Figure 2-1.** The Dissipation of Rent

the same as with private property rights governing the use of the fishing ground, with one or many private owners. The owner(s) may employ his (their) own labor, or hire any amount of laborers. In any case, equilibrium is at $B$, where $(\partial Q/\partial L)_\alpha = \partial(WL)/\partial L$, a condition implied by the maximization of rent subject to the constraints of private property rights. The maximum rent is represented by the area $ABCD$, with $OL_1$ of labor employed, or one-half of $OL_4$—the amount of labor input with which rent will be dissipated.

Under non-exclusive rights to the fishing ground, there exists no contract stipulating the input $L_1$, and other individuals will freely compete to obtain the rent (now a residual). For a second individual, say Beta, the marginal product of his first unit of labor, with Alpha already supplying $QL_1$, will be $CL_1$. Beta's marginal product curve will be $(\partial Q/\partial L)_\beta$, and for constrained maximization he will supply labor from $L_1$ to $L_3$, such that $(\partial Q/\partial L)_\beta = \partial(WL)/\partial L$. With Beta's entry, the marginal product of labor for Alpha falls, and he will curtail his fishing effort. The curtailment by Alpha leads to a higher marginal product of labor for Beta, and the latter will accordingly increase his fishing effort. The rule has it that, with two individuals, the equilibrium labor input will be $OL_2$, or two-thirds of $OL_4$, with Alpha supplying $OL_0$ and Beta supplying $L_0L_2$. With the adjustment, Beta's marginal product curve will be $(\partial Q/\partial L)_\beta$. The total rent will be less and will be split equally between the two. However, with labor input $OL_2$, the marginal product curve for Gamma, a third individual, is $(\partial Q/\partial L)_\gamma$, and he will enter to share in the residual.[27] The process goes on. Equilibrium is reached when the residual is exhausted, which implies that the number of fishermen approaches infinity, with each supplying a trifling amount of fishing effort. The model is instantaneous and timeless.

Algebraically, let the production function be $Q = Q(L,Z)$, where $L$ is labor and $Z$ is a *fixed* amount of fishing ground. For any individual fisherman $i$, the residual to maximize will be $R_i = q_i - WL_i$, where $q_i$ is the output of this fisherman, $L_i$ is his labor input and $W$ is the wage rate. Letting the total amount of *other* fishermen's labor be $L^*$, we write

$$q_i(L_i) = \frac{L_i}{L^* + L_i} Q(L^* + L_i),$$

assuming that each individual decision unit operates identically. From these we obtain $\partial q_i/\partial L_i = W$, and

$$\frac{\partial q_i}{\partial L_i} = \frac{L^*Q(L^* + L_i)}{(L^* + L_i)^2} + \frac{L_i}{L^* + L_i} \frac{\partial Q(L^* + L_i)}{\partial L_i}$$

Assume that there are $N$ identical individuals, such that the total labor is $L_N$, then in equilibrium $L_i = L_N/N$, and $L^* = [(N - 1)/N] L_N$. Therefore,

$$\frac{\partial q_i}{\partial L_i} = \frac{N - 1}{N} \frac{Q(L_N)}{L_N} + \frac{1}{N} \frac{\partial Q(L_N)}{\partial L_N} = W.$$

When the number of fishermen (or fishing firms) approaches infinity, we have

$$\lim_{N \to \infty} \left( \frac{N - 1}{N} \frac{Q(L_N)}{L_N} + \frac{1}{N} \frac{\partial Q(L_N)}{\partial L_N} \right) = \frac{Q(L_\infty)}{L_\infty} = W$$

where $L_\infty = \lim_{N \to \infty} L_N$, and where $Q(L_\infty)$ is the total social product of fish.

27. If the reader finds it difficult to accept that the marginal product curve for a single decision unit is negatively sloping and not horizontal, he may think of a situation where a single unit can hire in fishing labor and be a large firm, or where the fishing ground is small.

From the social point of view, the equality of the would-be average product of labor under private exploitation of the fishing ground and the wage rate implies that rent is entirely dissipated, and the corresponding (would-be) marginal product of labor being lower than the wage rate (marginal social opportunity cost) implies economic waste—if all costs associated with defining and policing private property in the fishing ground are ignored. Note that similar results can be obtained for share contracting between boat owner and fisherman,[28] which is of some interest since we are informed that share contracts between boat owners and fishermen predominate in marine fisheries.[29]

Strange as the above results may seem to be, the analysis is consistent with maximization by the equimarginal rule, at the same time producing a condition that the social average product is equal to the wage rate. The main feature in which this analysis differs from the traditional average-product argument is in the curtailment of fishing input by one decision unit when the number of competitors increases. The implication is important: if the number of competing fishermen is reduced or restricted, each fisherman will capture part of the ocean rent even though none has an exclusive right to the fishing ground.

But in the real world the observed number of fishermen is finite. To explain this we relax some of the hypothetical specifications which I have implicitly or explicitly employed in the analysis. First, the fishermen are not identical and their supply to the industry is not infinitely elastic. Leaving aside the various meanings of a homogeneous factor, one may point out that not all fishermen are equally productive, and that their alternative earnings are not the same. In other words, their comparative advantages in fishing are not equal. Thus, not all decision units will commit the same trifling amounts of inputs. Second, the cost structure of fishery harvesting has been neglected. The costs of entry will reduce the number of fishermen. And the production function is not necessarily linear homogeneous. There is the possibility of economies of scale, in the minimum boat size, gear size,

---

28. Let the production function be $Q = Q(L,H,Z)$ where $Z$ is fixed. Let the shares received by owners of Labor ($L_i$) and boat ($H_i$) be

$$q_{L_i} = \frac{L_i W_L Q (L^* + L_i, H^* + H_i)}{(L^* + L_i) W_L + (H^* + H_i) W_H}$$

and

$$q_{H_i} = \frac{H_i W_H Q (L^* + L_i, H^* + H_i)}{(L^* + L_i) W_L + (H^* + H_i) W_H}$$

where $W$ is the respective factor price. From the Lagrangian for each individual, then the marginal product of his input equals the factor price. When the number of sharing pairs approaches infinity, we obtain $Q = L_\infty W_L + H_\infty W_H$, and rent is dissipated.

29. See H. Zoeteweij, "Fisherman's Remuneration," in Turvey and Wiseman (1956).

and distance of travel for operation. And third, institutional arrangements designed to restrict entry, such as fisherman and boat unions and legal regulations, will impose constraints on competition.

So finite they are. Still, the implications of the model remain. The following are worth noting. First, other things being equal, the total outlay per decision unit will be lower with non-exclusive rights over the fishing ground than if it were private property. This may be observed in boat sizes being voluntarily kept small, and the number of days per year engaged in fishing few. Conversely, an effective restriction on entry will result in an increase in outlay per decision unit.

Second, there exist incentives to fishermen to restrict the *number* of decision units who have access to the fishing right. That is, even if each decision unit is free to commit the amount of fishing effort, the "rent" captured by each will be larger the smaller the number of decision units. Could that explain the prevalence of boat and fisherman unions in marine fisheries? An interesting case for further study is the recent issuance of licenses to fishing boats in British Columbia. Implied by our model is that such a license, if transferable, will yield a market price representing the present value of the ocean rent to be captured.

A third implication is more complex. Consider three alternative arrangements. The first arrangement is a group of individuals forming a tribe, a clan or a union so as to exclude "outsiders" from competing for the use of a non-exclusive resource. In this arrangement each "insider" is free to use the resource as he pleases and derive income therefrom. According to our analysis, the fewer the insiders, the greater will be the rent captured by each. On the other hand, the cost of exclusion (for example, bloodshed) for each insider is a rising function of the number of outsiders excluded. In equilibrium, the number of insiders is determined when the gains and costs of excluding outsiders are equal at the margin.

The second arrangement involves not only the exclusion of outsiders, but, as in some cooperatives, there is central regulation of the amounts of work and income for the insiders. The third arrangement is private property rights governing all resources, where the property rights are exclusively delineated and enforced, and where resource use is guided by contracting in the marketplace.

All three arrangements are costly. While it appears that these costs are lowest for the first type and highest for the third, the gains from each arrangement are in a reverse order. Weighing these gains and costs, the choice of property right arrangements becomes predictable. Thus the analysis points to the possibility of a theory of property right formation. Such a theory, however, is not intended here.

## THE NATURE OF THE PROBLEM

In this concluding section, I discuss generally the nature of the problem in light of the suggested contractual approach. The economic problem of marine fisheries is not unique, although the physical attributes of the fish and the legal arrangements for that industry yield certain characteristic features.

If an idea must have an origin, then the growth of the concept of "externality" can be traced back to Pigou's analysis of the divergences between social and private net product (1932, ch. 9), although Pigou did not use either the term externality or a similar term. At a time when "economic efficiency" began to be understood in terms of the fulfillment of some marginal equalities, it was natural as well as important to think of situations under which certain marginal equalities may not hold. In imagination Pigou excelled. However, he had weaknesses.

One of Pigou's weaknesses, shown in his discussion of social and private net product, is that he took assertions of fact for granted, accepting claims of deficient contractual arrangements without demanding evidence.[30] The manifestation of this is that, years later, when someone came up with the example of an apple orchard and honey production, it was universally accepted as a clear case of resource misallocation requiring government intervention. No one, however, has ever investigated the actual contractual arrangements between the apple grower and the beekeeper, or even suggested that a contract might exist.[31]

Another weakness in Pigou's analysis is the lack of any thorough attempt to generalize the various kinds of possible "divergence." Pigou seems to say that each kind differs from the others, but with no convincing reason as to why they differ.[32] The ambiguity has since remained a tradition in the externality literature, and the nature of the problem remained obscure. Indeed, one wonders what the state of the art would be had Pigou taken advantage of Knight's exposition on "Some Fallacies in the Interpretation of Social Cost," published in 1924, in the subsequent revisions of his book. Commenting on Pigou's example of good and bad roads, where "excessive" use of the good road is said to result in a lower marginal value for the users, Knight wrote:

> The [conclusion] does in fact indicate what would happen *if no one owned the superior* [road]. But under private appropriation and self-

---

30. This charge is based on my checking of all the references cited in A.C. Pigou (1932) on pp. 174, 175, 178, 181, and 182, where deficient lease contracts in agriculture are said to be evident.

31. However, Demsetz (1964) at 15, wrote: "Coase would probably point out, it is possible for beekeepers and apple growers to strike a bargain over how many trees are to be planted." Another alternative, of course, is that the apple growers keep the bees themselves, or purchase the beekeepers' resource ownerships outright. A similar neglect of contractual arrangements is found in the literature of economic development, where technological externalities are frequently said to exist for the training of workers in poor countries. "Undertraining" is alleged on ground that future returns are not capturable by the trainers. However, even casual conversation with teenage apprentices in Southeast Asia reveals the existence of complex training contract.

32. Although Pigou frequently referred to "kinds" or "classes" or divergences of social and private products, I have been unable to count them separately, or even to determine where one discussion begins and where it ends.

seeking exploitation of the [roads] the course of events is very different. It is in fact the social function of ownership to prevent this excessive [use of the superior road]. Professor Pigou's logic in regard to the roads is, as logic, quite unexceptionable. Its weakness is one frequently met with in economic theorizing, namely, that the assumptions diverge in essential respects from the facts of real economic situations. . . . If the roads are assumed to be subject to private appropriation and exploitation, precisely the ideal situation which would be established by the imaginary tax will be brought about through the operation of ordinary economic motives. (Pp. 163–164)

The associated analysis is not flawless,[33] but the argument is sound. There was an interval of several years in which Pigou could have revised his analysis on social and private product,[34] by incorporating Knight's "social function of ownership" to his various cases of "divergences." However, Pigou did not do so.

Some thirty years later,[35] R.H. Coase published "The Problem of Social Cost."[36] Although the contribution of this paper is justly well known, the reader may find the following statement of Coase's thesis unfamiliar. Commenting on Pigou, Coase (1960) wrote:

Pigou seems to make a distinction between the case in which no contract is possible (the second class) and that in which the contract is unsatisfactory (the first class). . . . But the reason why some activities are not the subject of contracts is exactly the same as the reason why some contracts are commonly unsatisfactory—it would cost too much to put the matter right. Indeed, the two cases are really the same since the contracts are unsatisfactory because they do not cover certain activities. (Pp. 38–39)

The *problem* of social cost, therefore, arises either in the absence of exclusive rights (hence the absence of the right to contract), or where the right to contract

33. See the previous section. Also, Knight should be more specific about the kind of investment he has in mind when he speaks of "excessive investment in superior situations" (p. 163). A comment on the "imaginary tax" will come later.

34. After 1924, The Economics of Welfare was revised in 1928 and in 1931. It is, of course, possible that Pigou never knew of Knight's article.

35. The term "external economies or diseconomies" began, perhaps, with Marshall, and it was used frequently in the 1930s and early 1940s for the derivation of cost and supply curves. The works of both Marshall and Pigou were influential. (See Stigler and Bouldings, eds. [1952, Pt. 2]. In the 1950s, however, external effects became popular in the literature of economic development. In fact, it was the main issue of the debate of balanced versus unbalanced growth and of investment criteria. The general theme is that, in order to achieve rapid economic growth, certain external effects should be maximized. The associated literature is immense. Externalities constitute a new trend in the 1960s.

36. Also important is Coase's earlier (1959) work, "The Federal Communications Commission."

exists "but where contracts are peculiarly difficult to draw up and an attempt to describe what the parties have agreed to do or not to do . . . would necessitate a lengthy and highly involved document. . ." (P. 16). It is, therefore, strange that recent discussions of externality are almost invariably associated with Coase's work.[37]

Let us discuss the problem further. The transfer of property rights among individual owners through contracting in the marketplace requires that the rights be exclusive. An exclusive property right grants its owner a *limited* authority to make a decision on resource use so as to derive income therefrom. To define this limit requires measurement and enforcement. Any property is multidimensional and exclusivity is frequently a matter of degree. But without some enforced or policed exclusivity to a right of action, the right to contract so as to exchange is absent.

The absence of exclusivity in property may be due to the absence of recognition by legal institutions of that exclusivity, or to the costs of delineating and policing the limit of the right being prohibitively high. The general issue is thus whether contractual arrangements and exclusive rights exist so that gains and costs of actions are weighed in the market; if not, whether alternative legal arrangements or government regulations are economically desirable.

The costs associated with the formation of property and of the subsequent contracts may be viewed in two stages. At one stage, without exchange, there are costs of defining and policing exclusivity. These costs vary, among other things, according to the physical attributes of the resource in question. In our example of marine fisheries, the difficulty of assessing, quantifying, identifying and policing private fishing rights is evident. Even the branding of cattle is costly. At this stage also, these costs also depend on the size of holding: it may cost less per unit of holding if the entire fishing ground is owned by one individual, or a group of individuals through the issuance of stock;[38] it may cost more per unit of holding if all the land in the world is owned by one man. If the individual is left to make the decision, then the degree of exclusivity and the size of holding chosen, among other things, will be such that the marginal cost of enforcing exclusivity equals the associated marginal gain.

At a second stage, there are costs associated with negotiating and enforcing contracts for the exchange or transfer of property rights. At least two reasons may be offered for the difficulty of separating the costs of this second stage from the first. One reason is that the income derivable from an exclusive right, or the *gain* of enforcing it, depends on the existence of transferability in the marketplace, for without transfer the highest-valued option may not be realized.

---

37. See, for a few examples, Buchanan (1962), Buchanan and Stubblebine (1962), Wellisz (1964), Mishan (1965), and Plott (1966).
    38. Note that monopoly in the fishery market is not necessarily implied. There may still exist a large number of fishing firms, potentially or actually, renting the fishing rights.

This implies that the lower the costs of contracting for transfer, the higher will be the gain of enforcing exclusivity. A second reason is that the *cost* of enforcing exclusivity also depends on the existence of transfer and its associated costs. The preferred size of resource-holding so as to lower policing cost, for example, can be chosen insofar as the market exchange permits. For these reasons it is convenient, although somewhat arbitrary, to lump the costs at the two stages into one broad term, namely, transaction costs. As in the case of joint products, only *marginal* costs are relevant.

In modern societies, private property rights require the recognition and enforcement of law. There are reasons to believe that the existence of government lowers transaction costs. But history has repeatedly demonstrated that market response is much quicker than legal response to changing economic conditions.[39] What was not worthwhile to enforce as private yesterday may be so today: changes in supply and demand conditions, technological innovations, and improved methods of organization may lower the transaction costs.[40]

In the case of marine fisheries, it is an empirical question whether the enforcement of private property is economically worthwhile. International conflicts of interest make the problem almost unmanageable. Still, economic theory predicts that since nonmigratory marine products cost less to police, private property will be instituted earlier in these than in migratory products. Such has been the case with oyster beds, which in some states in America are recognized and enforced as private by law. Could the lag in government response alone account for the absence of property rights over the oyster beds in the remaining states, and similarly in other nonmigratory and aquacultural products?

Finally, let us consider the issue of resource allocation channeled through the market versus government regulations. For any imaginary divergence between private and social costs, there exists an imaginery market contract through which the divergence will be eliminated. As emphasized in the first section, a contract entails a structure of stipulations. It follows that in many cases a single regulation, such as an imaginary tax, will not serve the same function as a contract.[41] To replace an imaginary contract, an imaginary *set* of regulations is required. Of course, some imaginary contracts—imaginable while ignoring transaction costs and information problems—are farflung and may have no resemblance in the real world.[42] But so are many "ideal" government regulations.

---

39. The Japanese experience is notable. See Takekoshi (1967). Note, in particular, the duration of various land systems before and after the Taika reforms (chs. 4, 5, and 10), and that decades had passed before Meiji (1868) legally recognized some "grey" market activities existing in Tokugawa agriculture (chs. 81, 82, and 83).

40. See, as a case in point, North (1968).

41. That an imaginery tax may not fully correct an imaginary divergence between private and social costs is seen in Plott (1966), and Davis and Whinston (1962).

42. An imaginery contract for the "ideal" pricing of a "public" good—or a good amenable to concurrent consumption—would fall into this category. Needless to say, public goods have given rise to still another type of externality. See, for example, Buchanan (1966b).

To evaluate economic efficiency by comparing imaginary contracts and regulations is futile, for in so doing any divergence between private and social costs is simply imagined away. Nor is it fruitful to compare the "imaginary" and the "actual," for Demsetz would rightly charge the "grass is greener" fallacy.[43] It is the "actual" compared with the "actual" that is relevant. The question is whether, given the same effects of an action, actual market contracts or realizable government regulations involve lower transaction costs so that a higher net gain or a lower net loss will result. And while facts and measurements are hard to come by, they still require theoretical interpretation.

The effectiveness of the market in weighing the gains and costs of some action is evident. The existence of a great variety of contracts in free markets suggests what an unmanageable situation it would be if all contractual stipulations were replaced by government regulations.[44] Elsewhere I wrote:

> For any resource, a number of individuals compete for ownership. Each potential buyer or user possesses some knowledge not only of alternative uses of the resource, but also of different transaction costs associated with different [contractual] arrangements by which the resource may enter into production. Assume away information problems that may exist in competitive trading in the marketplace; the resource will find that owner whose use of the resource yields the highest value. *Competition* for and *transferability* of the ownership right in the marketplace thus perform two main functions for contracting. First, competition conglomerates knowledge from all potential owners—the knowledge of alternative contractual arrangements and uses of the resource; and transferability of property rights ensures that the most valuable knowledge will be utilized. Second, competition among potential contract participants and a resource owner's ability to transfer the right to use his resource reduce the cost of enforcing the stipulated terms in a contract. This is because competing parties will stand by to offer or accept similar terms. In sum, competition *in the marketplace* reduces the costs of finding and pursuing the most valuable option in which a resource may be contracted for production. While transaction cost determines, it is also determined. [Cheung 1969a, p. 64]

43. See Demsetz (1969).
44. A striking case is the experience of the People's Republic of China. On the one hand, the important role of contracts similar to those developed in the market was recognized; on the other hand, the property right constraints and regulations were at odds with market contracts. The result was the existence of a variety of contracts supervised by the government, involving great complexities and inconsistencies. See the informative *Chung Hwa Jen Min Kung Ho Kuo Min Fa Chi Pen Wen Ti* (A Textbook of Civil Law of the People's Republic of China, in Chinese, 1958). See also: Pfeffer (April–June 1963, July–September 1963), "Contracts in China Revisited, with a Focus on Agriculture, 1949–63," 1966; Hsiao (1965).

But the above quotation ignores the possibility that transaction costs may be so high as to result in the absence of exclusive rights and of contracting among individuals. Gains and costs of an action are thus not weighed in the market. Is it likely, then, that government action or regulation will actually be more efficient? The question is difficult, and no answer to it will be attempted here.[45]

Let me conclude. In light of the analysis of contracting, this section has discussed the problem of the divergence of private and social costs. Externality, on the other hand, seems to center on different cases of "divergence" and to ignore the economic problem involved. The concept of externality is vague because every economic action has effects; it is confusing because classifications and theories are varied, arbitrary, and ad hoc. For these reasons, theories generated by the concept of externality are not likely to be useful.

45. But see Coase (1960, pp. 19–28).

## Chapter Three

# Toward a Theory of Property Rights

H. Demsetz

Reprinted from the *American Economic Review* 57 (May 1967): 347-359, by permission of publisher and author.

When a transaction is concluded in the marketplace, two bundles of property rights are exchanged. A bundle of rights often attaches to a physical commodity or service, but it is the value of the rights that determines the value of what is exchanged. Questions addressed to the emergence and mix of the components of the bundle of rights are prior to those commonly asked by economists. Economists usually take the bundle of property rights as a datum and ask for an explanation of the forces determining the price and the number of units of a good to which these rights attach.

I seek to fashion here some of the elements of an economic theory of property rights. This article is organized into three parts. The first part discusses briefly the concept and role of property rights in social systems. The second part offers some guidance for investigating the emergence of property rights. The third part sets forth some principles relevant to the coalescing of property rights into particular bundles and to the determination of the ownership structure that will be associated with these bundles.

## THE CONCEPT AND ROLE OF PROPERTY RIGHTS

In the world of Robinson Crusoe property rights play no role. Property rights are an instrument of society and derive their significance from the fact that they help a man form those expectations which he can reasonably hold in his dealings with others. These expectations find expression in the laws, customs, and mores of a society. An owner of property rights possesses the consent of fellow men to allow him to act in particular ways. An owner expects the community to prevent others from interfering with his actions, provided that these actions are not prohibited in the specifications of his rights.

It is important to note that property rights convey the right to benefit or harm oneself or others. Harming a competitor by producing superior products may be permitted, while shooting him may not. A man may be permitted to benefit himself by shooting an intruder but be prohibited from selling below a price floor. It is clear, then, that property rights specify how persons may be benefited and harmed, and, therefore, who must pay whom to modify the actions taken by persons. The recognition of this leads easily to the close relationship between property rights and externalities.

Externality is an ambiguous concept. For our purposes here, the concept includes external costs, external benefits, and pecuniary as well as nonpecuniary externalities. No harmful or beneficial effect is external to the world. Some person or persons always suffer or enjoy these effects. What converts a harmful or beneficial effect into an externality is that the cost of bringing the effect to bear on the decisions of one or more of the interacting persons is too high to make it worthwhile, and this is what the term shall mean here. "Internalizing" such effects refers to a process, usually a change in property rights, that enables these effects to bear (in greater degree) on all interacting persons.

A primary function of property rights is that of guiding incentives to achieve a greater internalization of externalities. Every cost and benefit associated with social interdependencies is a potential externality. One condition is necessary to make costs and benefits externalities. The cost of a transaction in the rights between the parties (internalization) must exceed the gains from internalization. In general, transacting cost can be large relative to gains because of "natural" difficulties in trading or they can be large because of legal reasons. In a lawful society the prohibition of voluntary negotiations makes the cost of transacting infinite. Some costs and benefits are not taken into account by users of resources whenever externalities exist, but allowing transactions increases the degree to which internalization takes place. For example, it might be thought that a firm which uses slave labor will not recognize all the costs of its activities, since it can have its slave labor by paying subsistence wages only. This will not be true if negotiations are permitted, for the slaves can offer to the firm a payment for their freedom based on the expected return to them of being free men. The cost of slavery can thus be internalized in the calculations of the firm. The transition from serf to free man in feudal Europe is an example of this process.

Perhaps one of the most significant cases of externalities is the extensive use of the military draft. The taxpayer benefits by not paying the full cost of staffing the armed services. The costs which he escapes are the additional sums that would be needed to acquire men voluntarily for the services or those sums that would be offered as payment by draftees to taxpayers in order to be exempted. With either voluntary recruitment, the "buy-him-in" system, or with a "let-him-buy-his-way-out" system, the full cost of recruitment would be brought to bear on taxpayers. It has always seemed incredible to me that so many economists can recognize an externality when they see smoke but not when they see the draft. The familiar smoke example is one in which negotiation costs may be too high (because of the large number of interacting parties) to make it worthwhile to internalize all the effects of smoke. The draft is an externality caused by forbidding negotiation.

The role of property rights in the internalization of externalities can be made clear within the context of the above examples. A law which establishes the right of a person to his freedom would necessitate a payment on the part of a firm or of the taxpayer sufficient to cover the cost of using that person's labor if his services are to be obtained. The costs of labor thus become internalized in the firm's or taxpayer's decisions. Alternatively, a law which gives the firm or the taxpayer clear title to slave labor would necessitate that the slaveowners take into account the sums that slaves are willing to pay for their freedom. These costs thus become internalized in decisions although wealth is distributed differently in the two cases. All that is needed for internalization in either case is ownership which includes the right of sale. It is the prohibition of a property right adjustment, the prohibition of the establishment of an ownership title that can thenceforth be exchanged, that precludes the internalization of external costs and benefits.

There are two striking implications of this process that are true in a world of zero transaction costs. The output mix that results when the exchange of property rights is allowed is efficient and the mix is independent of who is assigned ownership (except that different wealth distributions may result in different demands).[1] For example, the efficient mix of civilians and military will result from transferable ownership no matter whether taxpayers must hire military volunteers or whether draftees must pay taxpayers to be excused from service. For taxpayers will hire only those military (under the "buy-him-in" property right system) who would not pay to be exempted (under the "let-him-buy-his-way-out" system). The highest bidder under the let-him-buy-his-way-out property right system would be precisely the last to volunteer under a buy-him-in system.[2]

We will refer back to some of these points later. But for now, enough groundwork has been laid to facilitate the discussion of the next two sections.

---

1. These implications are derived by Coase (1960).
2. If the demand for civilian life is unaffected by wealth redistribution, the assertion made is correct as it stands. However, when a change is made from a buy-him-in system to a let-him-buy-his-way-out system, the resulting redistribution of wealth away from draftees may significantly affect their demand for civilian life; the validity of the assertion then requires a compensating wealth change. A compensating wealth change will not be required in the ordinary case of profit maximizing firms. Consider the farmer-rancher example mentioned by Coase. Society may give the farmer the right to grow corn unmolested by cattle or it may give the rancher the right to allow his cattle to stray. Contrary to the Coase example, let us suppose that if the farmer is given the right, he just breaks even, i.e., with the right to be compensated for corn damage, the farmer's land is marginal. If the right is transferred to the rancher, the farmer, not enjoying any economic rent, will not have the wherewithal to pay the rancher to reduce the number of head of cattle raised. In this case, however, it will be profitable for the rancher to buy the farm, thus merging cattle-raising with farming. His self-interest will then lead him to take account of the effect of cattle on corn.

## THE EMERGENCE OF PROPERTY RIGHTS

If the main allocative function of property rights is the internalization of beneficial and harmful effects, then the emergence of property rights can be understood best by their association with the emergence of new or different beneficial and harmful effects.

Changes in knowledge result in changes in production functions, market values, and aspirations. New techniques, new ways of doing the same things, and doing new things—all invoke harmful and beneficial effects to which society has not been accustomed. It is my thesis in this section that the emergence of new property rights takes place in response to the desires of the interacting persons for adjustment to new benefit-cost possibilities.

The thesis can be restated in a slightly different fashion: property rights develop to internalize externalities when the gains of internalization become larger than the cost of internalization. Increased internalization, in the main, results from changes in economic values, changes which stem from the development of new technology and the opening of new markets, changes to which old property rights are poorly attuned. A proper interpretation of this assertion requires that account be taken of a community's preferences for private ownership. Some communities will have less well-developed private ownership systems and more highly developed state ownership systems. But, given a community's tastes in this regard, the emergence of new private or state-owned property rights will be in response to changes in technology and relative prices.

I do not mean to assert or to deny that the adjustments in property rights which take place need to be the result of a conscious endeavor to cope with new externality problems. These adjustments have arisen in Western societies largely as a result of gradual changes in social mores and in common law precedents. At each step of this adjustment process, it is unlikely that externalities per se were consciously related to the issue being resolved. These legal and moral experiments may be hit-and-miss procedures to some extent but in a society that weights the achievement of efficiency heavily, their viability in the long run will depend on how well they modify behavior to accommodate to the externalities associated with important changes in technology or market values.

A rigorous test of this assertion will require extensive and detailed empirical work. A broad range of examples can be cited that are consistent with it: the development of air rights, renters' rights, rules for liability in automobile accidents, etc. In this part of the discussion, I shall present one group of such examples in some detail. They deal with the development of private property rights in land among American Indians. These examples are broad ranging and come fairly close to what can be called convincing evidence in the field of anthropology.

The question of private ownership of land among aboriginals has held a fascination for anthropologists. It has been one of the intellectual battlegrounds in the attempt to assess the "true nature" of man unconstrained by the "artificialities" of civilization. In the process of carrying on this debate, information has been uncovered that bears directly on the thesis with which we are now concerned. What appears to be accepted as a classic treatment and a high point of this debate is Eleanor Leacock's memoir on *The Montagnes "Hunting Territory" and the Fur Trade* (1954). Leacock's research followed that of Frank G. Speck (1915, pp. 491–495) who had discovered that the Indians of the Labrador Peninsula had a long-established tradition of property in land. This finding was at odds with what was known about the Indians of the American Southwest and it prompted Leacock's study of the Montagnes who inhabited large regions around Quebec.

Leacock clearly established the fact that a close relationship existed, both historically and geographically, between the development of private rights in land and the development of the commercial fur trade. The factual basis of this correlation has gone unchallenged. However, to my knowledge, no theory relating privacy of land to the fur trade has yet been articulated. The factual material uncovered by Speck and Leacock fits the thesis of this paper well, and in doing so, it reveals clearly the role played by property right adjustments in taking account of what economists have often cited as an example of an externality—the overhunting of game.

Because of the lack of control over hunting by others, it is in no person's interest to invest in increasing or maintaining the stock of game. Overly intensive hunting takes place. Thus a successful hunt is viewed as imposing external costs on subsequent hunters—costs that are not taken into account fully in the determination of the extent of hunting and of animal husbandry.

Before the fur trade became established, hunting was carried on primarily for purposes of food and the relatively few furs that were required for the hunter's family. The externality was clearly present. Hunting could be practiced freely and was carried on without assessing its impact on other hunters. But these external effects were of such small significance that it did not pay for anyone to take them into account. There did not exist anything resembling private ownership in land. And in the *Jesuit Relations*, particularly Le Jeune's record of the winter he spent with the Montagnes in 1633–34 and in the brief account given by Father Druilletes in 1647–48, Leacock finds no evidence of private land holdings. Both accounts indicate a socioeconomic organization in which private rights to land are not well developed.

We may safely surmise that the advent of the fur trade had two immediate consequences. First, the value of furs to the Indians was increased considerably. Second, and as a result, the scale of hunting activity rose sharply. Both consequences must have increased considerably the importance of the externalities associated with free hunting. The property right system began to change, and it changed specifically in the direction required to take account of the economic effects made important by the fur trade. The geographical or distributional evidence collected by Leacock indicates an unmistakable correlation between early centers of fur trade and the oldest and most complete development of the private hunting territory.

> By the beginning of the eighteenth century, we begin to have clear evidence that territorial hunting and trapping arrangements by individual families were developing in the area around Quebec. . . . The earliest references to such arrangements in this region indicates a purely temporary allotment of hunting territories. They [Algonkians and Iroquois] divide themselves into several bands in order to hunt more efficiently. It was their custom . . . to appropriate pieces of land about two leagues square for each group to hunt exclusively. Ownership of beaver houses, however, had already become established, and when discovered, they were marked. A starving Indian could kill and eat another's beaver if he left the fur and the tail. (P. 15).

The next step toward the hunting territory was probably a seasonal allotment system. An anonymous account written in 1723 states that the "principle of the Indians is to mark off the hunting ground selected by them by blazing the trees with their crests so that they may never encroach on each other. . . . By the middle of the century these allotted territories were relatively stabilized" (Leacock 1954, p. 15).

The principle that associates property right changes with the emergence of new and reevaluation of old harmful and beneficial effects suggests in this instance that the fur trade made it economic to encourage the husbanding of fur-bearing animals. Husbanding requires the ability to prevent poaching and this, in turn, suggests that socioeconomic changes in property in hunting land will take place. The chain of reasoning is consistent with the evidence cited above. Is it inconsistent with the absence of similar rights in property among the southwestern Indians?

Two factors suggest that the thesis is consistent with the absence of similar rights among the Indians of the southwestern plains. The first of these is that there were no plains animals of commercial importance comparable to the fur-bearing animals of the forest, at least not until cattle arrived with Europeans. The second factor is that animals of the plains are primarily grazing species whose habit is to wander over wide tracts of land. The value of establishing boundaries to private hunting territories is thus reduced by the relatively high cost of preventing the animals from moving to adjacent parcels. Hence both the value and cost of establishing private hunting lands in the Southwest are such that we would expect little development along these lines. The externality was just not worth taking into account.

The lands of the Labrador Peninsula shelter forest animals whose habits are considerably different from those of the plains. Forest animals confine their territories to relatively small areas so that the cost of internalizing the effects of husbanding these animals is considerably reduced. This reduced cost, together with the higher commercial value of fur-bearing forest animals, made it productive to establish private hunting lands. Frank G. Speck finds that family proprietorship among the Indians of the Peninsula included retaliation against trespass.

Animal resources were husbanded. Sometimes conservation practices were carried on extensively. Family hunting territories were divided into quarters. Each year the family hunted in a different quarter in rotation, leaving a tract in the center as a sort of bank, not to be hunted over unless forced to do so by a shortage in the regular tract.

To conclude our excursion into the phenomenon of private rights in land among the American Indians, we note one further piece of corroborating evidence. Among the Indians of the Northwest, highly developed private family rights to hunting lands had also emerged—rights which went so far as to include inheritance. Here again we find that forest animals predominate and that the West Coast was frequently visited by sailing schooners whose primary purpose was trading in furs.[3]

## THE COALESCENCE AND OWNERSHIP OF PROPERTY RIGHTS

I have argued that property rights arise when it becomes economic for those affected by externalities to internalize benefits and costs. But I have not yet examined the forces which will govern the particular form of right ownership. Several idealized forms of ownership must be distinguished at the outset. These are communal ownership, private ownership, and state ownership.

By communal ownership, I shall mean a right which can be exercised by all members of the community. Frequently the rights to till and to hunt the land have been communally owned. The right to walk a city sidewalk is communally owned. Communal ownership means that the community denies to the state or to individual citizens the right to interfere with any person's exercise of com-

---

3. The thesis is consistent with the development of other types of private rights. Among wandering primitive peoples the cost of policing property is relatively low for highly portable objects. The owning family can protect such objects while carrying on its daily activities. If these objects are also very useful, property rights should appear frequently, so as to internalize the benefits and costs of their use. It is generally true among most primitive communities that weapons and household utensils, such as pottery, are regarded as private property. Both types of articles are portable and both require an investment of time to produce. Among agriculturally-oriented peoples, because of the relative fixity of their location, portability has a smaller role to play in the determination of property. The distinction is most clearly seen by comparing property in land among the most primitive of these societies, where crop rotation and simple fertilization techniques are unknown, or where land fertility is extremely poor, with property in land among primitive peoples who are more knowledgeable in these matters or who possess very superior land. Once a crop is grown by the more primitive agricultural societies, it is necessary for them to abandon the land for several years to restore productivity. Property rights in land among such people would require policing costs for several years during which no sizable output is obtained. Since to provide for sustenance these people must move to new land, a property right to be of value to them must be associated with a portable object. Among these people it is common to find property rights to the crops, which, after harvest, are portable, but not to the land. The more advanced agriculturally based primitive societies are able to remain with particular land for longer periods, and here we generally observe property rights to the land as well as to the crops.

munally owned rights. Private ownership implies that the community recognizes
the right of the owner to exclude others from exercising the owner's private rights.
State ownership implies that the state may exclude anyone from the use of a right
as long as the state follows accepted political procedures for determining who may
not use state-owned property. I shall not examine in detail the alternative of state
ownership. The object of the analysis which follows is to discern some broad
principles governing the development of property rights in communities oriented
to private property.

It will be best to begin by considering a particularly useful example
that focuses our attention on the problem of land ownership. Suppose that land
is communally owned. Every person has the right to hunt, till, or mine the land.
This form of ownership fails to concentrate the cost associated with any person's
exercise of his communal right on that person. If a person seeks to maximize the
value of his communal rights, he will tend to overhunt and overwork the land
because some of the costs of his doing so are borne by others. The stock of game
and the richness of the soil will be diminished too quickly. It is conceivable that
those who own these rights, i.e., every member of the community, can agree to
curtail the rate at which they work the lands if negotiating and policing costs are
zero. Each can agree to abridge his rights. It is obvious that the costs of reaching
such an agreement will not be zero. What is not obvious is just how large these
costs may be.

Negotiating costs will be large because it is difficult for many persons
to reach a mutually satisfactory agreement, especially when each hold-out has the
right to work the land as fast as he pleases. But, even if an agreement among all
can be reached, we must yet take account of the costs of policing the agreement,
and these may be large also. After such an agreement is reached, no one will privately own the right to work the land; all can work the land but at an agreed upon
shorter workweek. Negotiating costs are increased even further because it is not
possible under this system to bring the full expected benefits and expected costs
of future generations to bear on current users.

If a single person owns land, he will attempt to maximize its present
value by taking into account alternative future time streams of benefits and costs
and selecting that one which he believes will maximize the present value of his
privately owned land rights. We all know that this means that he will attempt to
take into account the supply-and-demand conditions that he thinks will exist
after his death. It is very difficult to see how the existing communal owners can
reach an agreement that takes account of these costs.

In effect, an owner of a private right to use land acts as a broker
whose wealth depends on how well he takes into account the competing claims
of the present and the future. But with communal rights there is no broker, and
the claims of the present generation will be given an uneconomically large weight
in determining the intensity with which the land is worked. Future generations
might desire to pay present generations enough to change the present intensity of

land usage. But they have no living agent to place their claims on the market. Under a communal property system, should a living person pay others to reduce the rate at which they work the land, he would not gain anything of value for his efforts. Communal property means that future generations must speak for themselves. No one has yet estimated the costs of carrying on such a conversation.

The land ownership example confronts us immediately with a great disadvantage of communal property. The effects of a person's activities on his neighbors and on subsequent generations will not be taken into account fully. Communal property results in great externalities. The full costs of the activities of an owner of a communal property right are not borne directly by him, nor can they be called to his attention easily by the willingness of others to pay him an appropriate sum. Communal property rules out a "pay-to-use-the-property" system and high negotiation and policing costs make ineffective a "pay-him-not-to-use-the-property" system.

The state, the courts, or the leaders of the community could attempt to internalize the external costs resulting from communal property by allowing private parcels owned by small groups of persons with similar interests. The logical groups in terms of similar interests, are, of course, the family and the individual. Continuing with our use of the land ownership example, let us initially distribute private titles to land randomly among existing individuals and, further, let the extent of land included in each title be randomly determined.

The resulting private ownership of land will internalize many of the external costs associated with communal ownership, for now an owner, by virtue of his power to exclude others, can generally count on realizing the rewards associated with husbanding the game and increasing the fertility of his land. This concentration of benefits and costs on owners creates incentives to utilize resources more efficiently.

But we have yet to contend with externalities. Under the communal property system the maximization of the value of communal property rights will take place without regard to many costs, because the owner of a communal right cannot exclude others from enjoying the fruits of his efforts and because negotiation costs are too high for all to agree jointly on optimal behavior. The development of private rights permits the owner to economize on the use of those resources from which he has the right to exclude others. Much internalization is accomplished in this way. But the owner of private rights to one parcel does not himself own the rights to the parcel of another private sector. Since he cannot exclude others from their private rights to land, he has no direct incentive (in the absence of negotiations) to economize in the use of his land in a way that takes into account the effects he produces on the land rights of others. If he constructs a dam on his land, he has no direct incentive to take into account the lower water levels produced on his neighbor's land.

This is exactly the same kind of externality that we encountered with communal property rights, but it is present to a lesser degree. Whereas no one had an incentive to store water on any land under the communal system, private owners now can take into account directly those benefits and costs to their land that accompany water storage. But the effects on the land of others will not be taken into account directly.

The partial concentration of benefits and costs that accompany private ownership is only part of the advantage this system offers. The other part, and perhaps the most important, has escaped our notice. The cost of negotiating over the remaining externalities will be reduced greatly. Communal property rights allow anyone to use the land. Under this system it becomes necessary for all to reach an agreement on land use. But the externalities that accompany private ownership of property do not affect all owners, and, generally speaking, it will be necessary for only a few to reach an agreement that takes these effects into account. The cost of negotiating an internalization of these effects is thereby reduced considerably. The point is important enough to elucidate.

Suppose an owner of a communal land right, in the process of plowing a parcel of land, observes a second communal owner constructing a dam on adjacent land. The farmer prefers to have the stream as it is, and so he asks the engineer to stop his construction. The engineer says, "Pay me to stop." The farmer replies, "I will be happy to pay you, but what can you guarantee in return?" The engineer answers, "I can guarantee you that I will not continue constructing the dam, but I cannot guarantee that another engineer will not take up the task because this is communal property; I have no right to exclude him." What would be a simple negotiation between two persons under a private property arrangement turns out to be a rather complex negotiation between the farmer and everyone else. This is the basic explanation, I believe, for the preponderance of single rather than multiple owners of property. Indeed, an increase in the number of owners is an increase in the communality of property and leads, generally, to an increase in the cost of internalizing.

The reduction in negotiating cost that accompanies the private right to exclude others allows most externalities to be internalized at rather low cost. Those that are not are associated with activities that generate external effects impinging upon many people. The soot from smoke affects many homeowners, none of whom is willing to pay enough to the factory to get its owner to reduce smoke output. All homeowners together might be willing to pay enough, but the cost of their getting together may be enough to discourage effective market bargaining. The negotiating problem is compounded even more if the smoke comes not from a single smoke stack but from an industrial district. In such cases, it may be too costly to internalize effects through the marketplace.

Returning to our land ownership paradigm, we recall that land was distributed in randomly sized parcels to randomly selected owners. These owners now negotiate among themselves to internalize any remaining externalities. Two market options are open to the negotiators. The first is simply to try to reach a contractual agreement among owners that directly deals with the external effects at issue. The second option is for some owners to buy out others, thus changing the parcel size owned. Which option is selected will depend on which is cheaper. We have here a standard economic problem of optimal scale. If there exist constant returns to scale in the ownership of different sized parcels, it will be largely a matter of indifference between outright purchase and contractual agreement if only a single, easy-to-police, contractual agreement will internalize the externality. But, if there are several externalities, so that several such contracts will need to be negotiated, or if the contractual agreements should be difficult to police, then outright purchase will be the preferred course of action.

The greater diseconomies of scale are to land ownership, the more contractual arrangement will be used by the interacting neighbors to settle these differences. Negotiating and policing costs will be compared to costs that depend on the scale of ownership, and parcels of land will tend to be owned in sizes which minimize the sum of these costs.[4]

The interplay of scale economies, negotiating cost, externalities, and the modification of property rights can be seen in the most notable "exception" to the assertion that ownership tends to be an individual affair: the publicly held corporation. I assume that significant economies of scale in the operation of large corporations is a fact and, also, that large requirements for equity capital can be satisfied more cheaply by acquiring the capital from many purchasers of equity shares. While economies of scale in operating these enterprises exist, economies of scale in the provision of capital do not. Hence, it becomes desirable for many "owners" to form a joint-stock company.

But if all owners participate in each decision that needs to be made by such a company, the scale economies of operating the company will be overcome quickly by high negotiating cost. Hence a delegation of authority for most decisions takes place and, for most of these, a small management group becomes the de facto owners. Effective ownership, i.e., effective control of property, is thus legally concentrated in management's hands. This is the first legal modification, and it takes place in recognition of the high negotiating costs that would otherwise obtain.

The structure of ownership, however, creates some externality difficulties under the law of partnership. If the corporation should fail, partnership law commits each shareholder to meet the debts of the corporation up to the limits of his financial ability. Thus, managerial de facto ownership can have considerable external effects on shareholders. Should property rights remain unmodified, this externality would make it exceedingly difficult for entrepreneurs to acquire equity capital from wealthy individuals. (Although these individuals have recourse to reimbursements from other shareholders, litigation costs will be high.) A second legal modification, limited liability, has taken place to reduce the

---

4. Compare this with the similar rationale given by R.H. Coase to explain the firm in "The Nature of the Firm" (1937, pp. 386–405).

effect of this externality.[5] De facto management ownership and limited liability combine to minimize the overall cost of operating large enterprises. Shareholders are essentially lenders of equity capital and not owners, although they do participate in such infrequent decisions as those involving mergers. What shareholders really own are their shares and not the corporation. Ownership in the sense of control again becomes a largely individual affair. The shareholders own their shares, and the president of the corporation and possibly a few other top executives control the corporation.

To further ease the impact of management decisions on shareholders, that is, to minimize the impact of externalities under this ownership form, a further legal modification of rights is required. Unlike partnership law, a shareholder may sell his interest without first obtaining the permission of fellow shareholders or without dissolving the corporation. It thus becomes easy for him to get out if his preferences and those of the management are no longer in harmony. This "escape hatch" is extremely important and has given rise to the organized trading of securities. The increase in harmony between managers and shareholders brought about by exchange and by competing managerial groups helps to minimize the external effects associated with the corporate ownership structure. Finally, limited liability considerably reduces the cost of exchanging shares by making it unnecessary for a purchaser of shares to examine in great detail the liabilities of the corporation and the assets of other shareholders; these liabilities can adversely affect a purchaser only up to the extent of the price per share.

The dual tendencies for ownership to rest with individuals and for the extent of an individual's ownership to accord with the minimization of all costs is clear in the land ownership paradigm. The applicability of this paradigm has been extended to the corporation. But it may not be clear yet how widely applicable this paradigm is. Consider the problems of copyright and patents. If a new idea is freely appropriable by all, if there exist communal rights to new ideas, incentives for developing such ideas will be lacking. The benefits derivable from these ideas will not be concentrated on their originators. If we extend some degree of private rights to the originators, these ideas will come forth at a more rapid pace. But the existence of the private rights does not mean that their effects on the property of others will be directly taken into account. A new idea makes an old one obsolete and another old one more valuable. These effects will not be directly taken into account, but they can be called to the attention of the originator of the new idea through market negotiations. All problems of externalities are closely analogous to those which arise in the land ownership example. The relevant variables are identical.

What I have suggested in this article is an approach to problems in property rights. But it is more than that. It is also a different way of viewing traditional problems. An elaboration of this approach will, I hope, illuminate a great number of social-economic problems.

5. Henry G. Manne discusses this point in a forthcoming book about the American corporate system.

# Part II

# Private Property Rights and Economic Behavior

## Chapter Four

# Two Essential Concepts: Transaction Costs and Attenuation

To consider the problem of efficient allocation of resources in the real world, it is necessary, inter alia, to have substantial information about the actual institutional structure of the economy and the conditions under which transactions take place. Unfortunately, however, these requirements are normally given no more than perfunctory attention in economic analysis. Indeed, major limitations of the conventional theory of production and exchange are traceable to the highly simplified assumptions made in this area. The standard competitive model presupposes the existence of only one idealized set of property rights and assumes that this set of relations governs the use of all resources. Moreover, the exchange, policing, and enforcement costs of contractual activities are taken to be zero. While this conception of the business environment need not prevent some useful analysis, it does have the effect of narrowing significantly the range of phenomena that can be explained.

The cases that fall outside the scope of traditional economic theory can be said to arise because: (a) actual market solutions are inconsistent with those indicated by the marginal equivalences for the general social optimum, and (b) traditional theory fails to account for the effects of various types and degrees of attenuation of private property rights in resources. The term "externality" is associated with the first point, while the second suggests situations where firms do not pursue the profit maximization objective and show different behavior from the classical firm. Property rights scholars have addressed themselves to both types of problems.

The concept of externality is central to the theory of economic policy, but only recently have concerted attempts been made to give the notion rigorous analytical definition.[1] According to the argument advanced by Coase, Buchanan, and others, proper assessment of all the social costs associated with externalities

1. Fundamental papers here are those by Buchanan and Stubblebine (1962), Coase (1960), and Demsetz (1964).

requires recognition that *two* parties are always involved in an externality situation. For social policy, the fundamental issue reduces to this: at any moment of time, there is a legally sanctioned structure of property rights in force. Consequently, if the existing structure is to be modified by social action designed to reduce or eliminate the effects of an externality, taxes must be imposed on those who will gain from the proposed legal change, and compensation paid to those who will suffer capital loss or loss of satisfaction as a result of the new law. Presumably, agreement on the terms of the tax-compensation scheme can be reached through a political process, but the basic mechanism here is one of "trade." For example, in the classic case of the factory smoke nuisance, gains from trade are possible for A and B if B gives up some or all of his rights to operate a smoke-producing factory in exchange for appropriate monetary compensation. As in other trading situations, the benefits obtained by A are purchased from B at a "price." If the actions are voluntary, both parties move to preferred positions on a "contract curve" where Pareto equilibrium holds.

The role of transactions costs was not made explicit in the preceding illustration, but all exchange involves such costs and their magnitudes influence the economic outcomes obtained.[2] In general, the property rights approach places great emphasis on the idea that externalities are associated with the costs of defining, exchanging, policing, or enforcing property rights. Whenever the private terms of exchange fail to account for some harmful or beneficial effects to the contractual parties or to others, the market solution will appear inconsistent with the social value of the bundle of property rights that is exchanged. And such private-social divergences tend to arise because of high transactions costs or because of the existence of legal restraints on the use and exchange of resources.

Certain conclusions of this line of reasoning are worth considering. First, transactions costs are found to contribute to greater use of *nonmarket* forms of exchange and, thus, to prices that diverge from the social values of the goods traded. Second, the model shows that there is no basis for believing that all existing externalities should be corrected. Insofar as the existence of a large class of externalities is explained by high transactions costs, it follows that making contractual stipulations more complete must be a costly undertaking. Therefore, any indiscriminate attempt to do something about externalities, either through the market mechanism or the political process, may well result in an excess of net social costs over net social benefits. Third, it is apparent that once nonzero transactions costs are recognized, a question of major importance is: How do alternative property rights assignments affect the use of resources and the output mix? This last topic has extensive theoretical ramifications and technical discussion of the issues is still taking place.

2. Government intervention may be required if transactions costs are so high as to prevent private exchange in the manner just suggested. When the impact of transactions costs is recognized, it becomes clear that the initial assignment of property rights, including the assignment of liability for damages, does matter.

The concept of attenuation of private property rights lies at the heart of the modern theory of the firm. Indeed, concern with attenuation became inevitable when the goals of the firm were re-examined. Since empirical evidence indicated that the behavior of many types of firms deviated from the profit maximizing ideal upon which the standard theory of the firm rests, the question that arose was whether the standard theory could be extended so as to include models that were not based on profit maximization. The answer, of course, was yes, and the new theory developed accordingly. What is required is that the concept of income or wealth maximization be replaced by that of utility maximization, and that the analysis takes into account the effects of changes in the content of property rights in resources on the actions of decision-makers. Under these conditions, the behavior of managers becomes the key for understanding the allocation and use of resources by corporations, government bureaus, and other organizations. Ideally, the objective is to introduce greater empirical content into the theory of the firm.

More concretely, it is necessary to develop a refutable theory by identifying those elements in the institutional structure that affect the cost to managers of attenuating the nominal ownership rights in existence. In other words, managers can, at some cost, engage in discretionary behavior and divert a portion of the organization's resources to their own ends. But by appropriating pecuniary or nonpecuniary benefits for themselves, the managers necessarily infringe on the interests of the owners and must reckon with a greater or lesser reaction from the owners. Relative to the owners of the classical capitalist firm, the owners of a modern corporation have reduced ability to revise or terminate the membership of the production team. Thus, the owners' bundle of property rights in the corporation is attenuated compared to that of the classical firm. Operationally, this attenuation of stockholders' rights in the firm takes the form of a reduced ability of the owners to control the decisions made by the managers.[3] It should be noted, however, that the attenuation of the stockholders' property rights and the "rule of management" result not from legal restraints on private property rights, but from the costs to the owners of detecting and policing managerial decisions and of enforcing wealth maximizing behavior.

The greater the dispersion of stock ownership in the firm, the higher will be the costs to stockholders of reassigning decision-making authority, and the easier it will be for management to substitute other objectives for the goal of wealth maximization. But management's efforts to gain advantage will be constrained by the managers' own estimates of the costs stockholders face in monitoring managerial performance and by the level of risk managers are willing to assume. The precise position of the managerial constraint depends on various factors, including the nature of the institutional structure. In any event, though,

---

3. This is significant, of course, because the managers' decisions affect the present value of the firm.

certain limits exist on the possible attenuation of the stockholders' property rights in the firm. The transfer of wealth from stockholders to managers has to be equal to or less than the cost to stockholders of enforcing a return to optimal behavior. Or, alternatively, the owners' freedom to sell shares in a market that reflects the capitalized value of current managerial decisions sets a limit on the power of managers to pursue their own objectives at the expense of profit.

The preceding discussion relates to the modern capitalist corporation that is free to conduct its operations so as to seek a profit. The property rights analysis, however, is also applicable to other types of organizations, including the regulated firm and the not-for-profit firm. These firms, of course, have different property rights arrangements than those of the standard corporation and exhibit correspondingly different behaviors. The attenuation of the bundle of property rights that defines ownership of the regulated firm takes a specific form: there is legal restraint on the owners' right to the residual. By contrast, the attenuation of ownership in the not-for-profit firm goes even further; the crucial determining characteristic here is this: no one can claim the right to appropriate the residual. In these respective cases, the logic of the property rights analysis suggests that the managers will enjoy substantial freedom to divert the organization's resources to their own uses, and that, in general, managerial behavior will be tolerated that would be repressed under competition.

The articles reprinted in this section are directly related to the themes just considered. Although different in style and specific content, each of the various contributions is concerned with the fundamental question of how alternative property rights structures and transactions costs affect economic behavior. Detailed commentary on the papers is not necessary, but a few brief remarks will be made concerning their contents. First, McKean shows that when transactions costs are positive, the way in which property rights are assigned must influence the allocation of resources and the composition of output. The articles by Manne, Williamson, and Alchian consider different aspects of the phenomenon of property rights attenuation. Williamson and Alchian focus on the corporation and discuss the conditions under which stockholders may be abused and how the interests of the stockholders can be protected. Coase's careful study of the Federal Communications Commission explores the implications of establishing legal restraints on an owner's right to profits. Finally, Pauly and Redisch analyze the interesting case of the not-for-profit hospital where individuals are able to derive benefits from capital that is not owned by them.

## Chapter Five

# Products Liability: Implications of Some Changing Property Rights

## R. McKean

Reprinted from the *Quarterly Journal of Economics* (November 1970) 84: 611–626, by permission of publisher and author.

The use of products, from tractors to glass shower doors, often results in accidents and damages, sometimes to the purchaser and sometimes to bystanders. Who should be liable for these costs has for many years been a subject of much concern. Politicians and officials have become increasingly aroused about the safety of items ranging from Corvairs to "shamburgers," leading in part to complaints about liability assignment (though mainly to advocacy of product specifications). In the legal profession, this subject of who is or should be liable has been labeled "products liability" and has caused concern, particularly because of its connection to individuals' notions of equity or fairness. In economics, since accidental damages are a special case of externalities, the subject is also of great concern, especially because of the connection between externalities—those interdependencies that are not mutually, voluntarily accepted—and economic efficiency.

The existence of any externality is related to the rules for and costs of assigning and exchanging property rights. The basic things that we exchange are not products' physical features as such but rather packages of rights to do things with those features. *If* all rights were clearly defined and assigned, *if* there were zero transaction costs, and *if* people agreed to abide by the results of voluntary exchange, there would be no externalities. Accidental damage is no exception. Wherever it results in an externality, this is related to the rules for and costs of assigning and exchanging rights. In this instance, one of the principal rights involved[1] is the right not to be liable for damages or, to look at the other side of the coin, the obligation to pay for damages. As is the case with other rights, this one exists as some sort of expectation, not as a certainty.

The right to avoid liability, like the right to resell one's land, is a feature of an asset that has value. Alternative right assignments may have different impacts on equity (as conceived of by each individual) and, since there are trans-

---

1. Others would include rights to use items for various purposes and with varying degrees of care.

action costs, different impacts on production processes and costs, insurance carried, the allocation of resources among uses, and the options open to consumers. In this article I shall discuss some of those impacts of different right assignments pertaining to liability for damage. The coverage will not include "safety legislation," e.g., requiring that all cars be equipped with safety belts. Such legislation is a big topic in itself, and while requiring certain behavior affects right-assignment, the discussion here will be confined to requiring right-reassignments that affect behavior. First, however, I shall sketch out some of the background concerning products liability.

## DEVELOPMENTS CONCERNING PRODUCTS LIABILITY

After the development of industrial societies, one of the most important conditions for the existence of products liability was that privity, or a direct contractual relationship, had to exist.[2] In other words, a manufacturer might be liable to the wholesaler, the wholesaler to the retailer, and the retailer to his customer, but the manufacturer was not liable to remote customers or to third parties because he had no contractual relationship with them. For the most part this requirement of privity was upheld in England and the United States throughout the nineteenth century. In one famous case, *Winterbottom* v. *Wright* (1842), in which a coach with a defective wheel had overturned, Lord Abinger said: "There is no privity of contract between these parties; and if the plaintiff can sue, every passenger, or even any person passing along the road, who was injured by the upsetting of the coach, might bring a similar action. Unless we confine the operation of such contracts as this to the parties who entered into them, the most absurd and outrageous consequences, to which I can see no limit, would ensue" (M & W 109, 152 Eng. Rep. 402 [Exch. 1842]).

### Evolution of Sales Law

In connection with certain products and activities, quite a few exceptions to the privity rule developed, especially late in the nineteenth and early in the twentieth centuries (Feezer 1925). There is a long history of special concern about foods and about "inherently or imminently dangerous" or "ultrahazardous" products, e.g., explosives. In developing special rules for these categories, the courts may have been groping for changes in rights that would yield more gain than cost, as gauged by the judges (Coase 1960). Concern about liability for in-

---

2. Only the high spots will be reviewed here. For more detail see such articles as Noel (1957) or Prosser (1960).
  This section will be nonanalytical, but I hope that the background will be of interest to economists. The AEA-AALS Committee arranged for the study in the hope of stimulating interest among economists in the evolving legal framework and its analysis (and to stimulate lawyers to be more concerned with the *economic* implications of that framework).

juries from these products rose whenever people became more impressed with the hazards. For instance, concern about foods soared after the publication of Upton Sinclair's work.[3]

The big breakthrough, however, was the decision in the famous case of the collapsing automobile, *MacPherson* v. *Buick Motor Company* (212 N.Y. 382, 111 N.E. 1050 [1916]). This 1916 decision held the manufacturer liable, in the absence of privity, for injuries resulting from the use of a product, whether or not inherently dangerous, if there is evidence of "negligence" in the manufacture or assembly of the product. Afterward, this position was adopted in case after case and state after state. The ruling was applied, not just to special categories, such as food, beverages, firearms, and explosives, but to such varied items as a sanitary napkin (*La Frumento* v. *Kotex Co.*, 131 Misc. 314, 226 N.Y. Supp. 750 [N.Y.C. City Ct. 1928]), an inflammable celluloid comb (*Farley* v. *Edward E. Tower Co.*, 271 Mass. 230. 171 N.E. 639 [1930]), and a defective bar stool (*Okker* v. *Chrome Furniture Mfg. Co.*, 26 N.J. Super. 295, 97 A. 2d 699 [1953]). The product usually had to pose significant danger to life and limb, and the courts sometimes refused to make awards for minor hazards, such as a defective high heel or coffee-can key[4] (*Timpson* v. *Marshall, Meadows and Stewart, Inc.*, 198 Misc. 1034, 101 N.Y.S. 2d 583 [Sup. Ct. 1950]; *Boyd* v. *American Can Co.*, 249 App. Div. 644, 291 N.Y.S. 205 [2d Dept. 1936]). Nonetheless, there was unquestionably a shift toward making producers liable in a wider range of circumstances.

Other extensions of producers' liability were brought about by means of special ad hoc devices. It is often difficult to prove negligence on the part of a manufacturer, but in some instances the courts applied the doctrine of *res ipsa loquitur*: let the matter speak for itself. If a sealed bottle of soft drink was found to contain a cockroach, it seemed highly unlikely that anyone, after the bottling was done, had opened the container and inserted the insect. The courts were prepared to assume that the production process did involve negligence. Similarly, if a sealed unit in a machine caused damage, the courts often concluded that the matter spoke for itself. Another device for getting around the privity requirement was to regard the wife as an agent for her husband so that, even if he has no direct contractual relationship with the seller, the latter may be liable if the husband suffers injuries while using the product.

These devices are often criticized as being tortured or "artificial" attempts to move toward strict producer liability, but with uncertainty one might without being illogical judge these rules to be better than the alternatives. The courts were uneasy about proceeding to strict liability lest it yield more harm than good, yet they felt that these small steps with comparatively unambiguous cut-off points would yield more good than harm. Similarly one might be uneasy about

---

3. Upton Sinclair "said later that he had aimed at the public's heart, and by accident hit it in the stomach" (C.C. Regier, "The Struggle for Federal Food and Drugs Legislation," *Law and Contemporary Problems* 3 (1933): 9, cited by Prosser (1960, p. 1106).

4. For a discussion and other citations see Noel (1957).

permitting automobiles to proceed in the face of a red traffic light whenever drivers deem it safe, yet feel confident that allowing *right* turns on a red light would yield more good than harm.

Express warranty and especially implied warranty have been extended by recent interpretations of the law, further reflecting the shift toward "let the seller beware." There may now be an implied warranty of fitness for a particular purpose as distinct from the item's ordinary purpose. For this warranty to hold, the seller must have reason to know that purpose, but it is not necessary for the buyer to have informed the seller; the buyer must be relying on the seller's judgment in selecting *or furnishing* the goods (formerly the seller was liable only if he selected the goods); and purchase by trade name no longer means that the seller's judgment is not being relied upon. The course of dealing and trade usage may generate implied warranties, e.g., may give the seller "reason to know" the particular purpose to which goods are put in a particular locality (Neuman 1960–61). Advertising directly to consumers can generate warranties to them. In *Baxter* v. *Ford Motor Co.*, the manufacturer was held to be liable because a windshield advertised as shatterproof did in fact shatter when struck by a stone (168 Wash. 456, 12 P. 2d 409).

### Shifts Toward Strict Liability Under Tort

Strict liability under tort can be roughly defined as liability simply because a wrong was done, not because a contract was unfulfilled. No attribution of negligence is necessary (though the presence of a "defect," which may simply substitute another word for negligence, is necessary), and no contract need be involved. To many observers it seems that products liability has been evolving rapidly toward strict liability under tort. The following are typical comments: "With privity on the wane, *caveat venditor* will be the rule, not *caveat emptor*; the time has come to hold a requiem for this . . . anachronism" (Jaeger 1963, p. 1). "It seems safe to predict that strict liability for products will soon be the established law in this country" (Wade 1965, pp. 5–25).

A crucial case was that of *Henningsen* v. *Bloomfield Motors, Inc.* in 1960 (32 N.J. 358, 161 A. 2d 84).[5] Mrs. Henningsen suffered injuries when the car suddenly turned right and ran into a wall, presumably due to a defective steering gear. Without any evidence of negligence, the court held Chrysler as well as the dealer liable, saying: "an implied warranty that it [the product] is reasonably suitable for use as such accompanies it into the hands of the ultimate purchaser. Absence of agency . . . is immaterial" (32 N.J. 384, 161 A. 2d 84). There had been earlier and unsuccessful attempts to put automobiles under the heading of "deadly and dangerous instrumentalities" or to apply the rules for "ferocious animals" to the "devil wagon" (*Lewis* v. *Amorous*, 3 Ga. App. 50, 55; 59 S.E. 338, 340 [1907] ), but the Henningsen case appeared to eliminate the require-

5. See Prosser (1966).

ments for privity or negligence with respect to *all* products, and to cast doubt on the effectiveness of disclaimers. Within a few years the Henningsen precedent was applied to a wide variety of products, including a glass door, shotgun, dental chair, and hula skirt. Liability to bystanders, and other extensions of manufacturer liability, have been established more recently (*Time Magazine*, May 23, 1969, p. 66).

Even strict tort liability, however, would still require that there be a defect in the product. The issues about proof of injury and defect, abnormal use (a manufacturer will not be held liable simply because he produces a hammer with which someone manages to hit his head), intervening conduct, and knowledge of the defect will still exist and relieve the producer of liability in many circumstances (Prosser 1960). Thus the full development of strict liability under tort would simply go further to raise the probability that the producer would be held liable. It would reassign certain property rights in a probabilistic sense.

### Moves Toward Other Liability Assignments

Some writers appear to have in mind more than strict tort liability, however, for they urge or foresee more comprehensive compensation of victims than would occur under strict liability. One writer explicitly supports eliminating the requirement of a defect (Cowan 1965). For some situations, compulsory accident insurance has been urged, assigning the liability to a large group of potential victims without regard to fault. Automobile accidents especially—with the high court costs and long delays, the difficulties of determining fault, and the large financial consequences—have given rise to proposals such as the Keeton-O'Connell plan (1965). Debate about these liability assignments may lead in turn to serious consideration of social accident insurance under which the taxpayers would be liable.

## IMPLICATIONS OF ALTERNATIVE ASSIGNMENTS OF LIABILITY

I shall attempt not to identify optimal policies, but simply to discuss some of the consequences of alternative products-liability arrangements.[6] (Indeed, while each individual can identify the policies *he* prefers, there is no criterion of optimality that *all* members of a group are compelled by logic to accept.) These consequences will be mainly certain costs generated by the alternative arrangements—costs in terms of the price tags that are implicit in a predominantly voluntary exchange system and that would help direct one toward Pareto-optimal policies. Such costs may not be relevant from the standpoint of every individual, but I believe that the value judgments of many persons would cause these costs to be pertinent to their choosing among products-liability arrangements.

6. See also Blum and Calven (1965); Calabreisi (1968), and Williamson, Olson, and Ralston (1967) for other pertinent analyses.

Let us examine a spectrum of possibilities from customer liability without fault to taxpayer liability without fault.

### Caveat Emptor

As a starter, what would be the consequences of complete caveat emptor—of having customers watch out for themselves and bear the losses that occur during the use of a product? As Coase (1960) has shown, that arrangement would lead to economic efficiency—to the production of safety features, caution in using products, and so on, by those parties having a comparative advantage in accident prevention—*if* there were zero transaction costs, and *if* people agreed to accept the results of voluntary exchanges. Purchasers of products would hire producers to include safety features and hire themselves to be careful as long as these actions paid. What about third parties who were injured? If owners of products were liable, they would modify their choices of products and hire bystanders to be careful as long as the gains outweighed the costs. Bargaining would lead to economic efficiency in producing safety features, warnings, instructions to users, instructions to bystanders, caution in using products, caution in standing or walking nearby, and so on. (Or, another possible arrangement would be to make the third parties liable for injuries to themselves. In this case, the third parties could costlessly get together and pay as much as it would be worth to them to have safer products or more cautious use of them.)

Transaction costs, it might be noted, include the costs of negotiation, contracting, and enforcement, which therefore include the costs of acquiring information about the features of products and about contract violations. If we are to consider products-liability issues in a world of zero transaction costs, however (and in my view it is useful to *start out* that way), that world cannot mean zero information costs in the sense of complete certainty about everything; for in those circumstances there would be no defects, carelessness, chance, accidents, or questions of liability.[7]

In actuality, of course, there are heavy transaction costs. Sometimes one may judge that alternative assignments of rights would bring roughly equivalent results, but often transaction costs vary markedly with different right assignments.[8] With customer liability, however, note that *certain* transaction costs are

---

7. Another condition for applying the Coase theorem, according to some, is that there be perfect competition, which may seem inconsistent with the existence of products-liability issues (since they often involve brand names, differentiated products, and warranties on such products). In the zero-transaction-cost case, however, monopolists would be hired by consumers to act like competitors. Also, homogeneity of products *to customers* does not necessarily imply that retailers, wholesalers, and manufacturers of particular items cannot be identified. In any event, one can discuss the implications of right assignments for costs and Pareto-optimal *changes* without assuming conditions that would lead to overall Pareto-optimality; "second-best" complications raise doubts, but they raise the same doubts about *any* partial equilibrium analysis.

8. For example, if one knew that group A would nearly always buy certain rights from group B, he could reduce transaction costs by assigning these rights to group A in the first place (see Demsetz (1966, p. 66).

in fact *comparatively* low. The costs of hiring producers to make safer products and issue warnings and instructions are relatively low, for the market is a mechanism through which customers are able to bid for safer products, instructions, and so on. If one is injured, financially or physically, by defective merchandise, he feels after the event that he has been at the mercy of producers and completely without influence on the design of products. (Moreover, caveat emptor may strike one as being inequitable—but for the present let us confine our attention to costs and economic efficiency.) Nonetheless, as disappointments occur to thousands of customers, they turn to rival products or producers—unless upon reflection they prefer the lower price plus that risk to higher prices with reduced risks; and producers find it profitable to make a larger percentage of their products relatively safe, to issue instructions and warnings, to carry liability insurance, and to have broader warranties or more generous returned-goods policies. Hence, while disappointments and injuries never cease, users are able in the aggregate to register their preferences by turning to competitors and bidding more for the goods that they prefer.

Transaction costs become higher if they deal with producers whose profits are regulated or who are sheltered from entry (even through the purchase of existing enterprises), since such producers will be less responsive to consumers' willingness to pay. Such costs will be still higher if one buys from a government agency and tries to hire this producer to offer a safer or otherwise modified product. If a publicly owned highway or reservoir strikes you as being dangerous, the threat of your turning to competitors will not influence the design of the output. Hiring these producers to alter their products takes the comparatively expensive form of organizing pressure groups.

Customer liability would hold another kind of transaction cost in check: the cost of information about what degree of product safety in particular uses is economical. The buyer is in a better position than anyone else to know the exact use to which he plans to put a product and what alternative qualities, or degrees of safety, in the product would mean to his costs and gains. The customer, if he is liable, has an extra incentive to acquire and make appropriate use of information. To get the information, he must deal not with thousands of individuals, but with the seller and a few other identifiable persons. Now the result will *not* be zero information cost or complete information or zero mistakes. All that is being asserted is that customer liability tends to keep *part* of the information costs relatively low.

On the other hand, caveat emptor may keep other types of information cost comparatively high. The manufacturers do know more than anyone else about the nature of their products, and unless they probe and offer consumers numerous alternative amounts of information, customers may never know how much information they would be willing to pay for. This could be especially serious with enterprises that do not count heavily on repeat business and customer goodwill. With any arrangement, many resources will go into acquiring and providing information about products. At present, buyers utilize consumer reports, producer brochures, telephone enquiries, conversations with friends and salesmen, advertisements that convey information, engineers' and other experts' services, and directories and the Yellow Pages to help them find out where to make enquiries. But useful information about products is very costly. How difficult it is to inspect many modern products; how little one discovers about color TV sets or psychiatric treatment or new plumbing fixtures even after investigation. With high costs, potential buyers settle for relatively little information and either forego exchanges that might be mutually advantageous or accept risks that would be rejected—*if* information costs were lower. One may judge that overall costs— information, transaction, foregone-exchange, and accident costs—could be reduced by directing government,[9] or inducing producers, to provide additional information.

The amount of information that it is economical to generate and the costs of generating information will be different for different products. For example, producers surely provide all the information that customers are willing to pay for in the case of simple familiar products like ordinary tools and supplies. When one considers new, changing, or complex products like new drugs or power tools, however, it may take years of transactions before customers can determine what kind of extra information can be offered and how much various amounts will cost. For complex secondhand items, great effort to gather information will still leave enormous uncertainty. Information about items that one does not buy frequently—e.g., swimming pools, gas furnaces, specialized medical-care equipment, food at unknown restaurants, a house in an unfamiliar city—is also comparatively expensive per unit of the product purchased. (In addition, the consequences of a bad outcome or of nonoptimal calculations by consumers may be particularly serious for certain products, which may bring forth value judgments that consumers should be protected against themselves.) Thus different treatment, e.g., liability assignments, for different product categories (such as "ultrahazardous" or "highly complex" products) may make sense even though it might be foolish in some ideal world with zero transaction costs.

Caveat emptor would also keep another transaction cost relatively low—that of hiring the users to be careful in employing the product. For the user is most frequently the buyer of the product or an acquaintance or a member of his family. Thus if he is liable for losses, he has to obtain the cooperation not of thousands of strangers, but of himself and a few individuals with whom he has direct personal contact, in seeing that an appropriate degree of care is exercised. This does not mean that he will be as careful as it is humanly possible to be; it merely means that he will choose by weighing the costs of extra care, such as loss of time, against the gains, such as the reduced risk of suffering uncompensated losses or injuries.

9. It should be remembered, however, that governments are often inefficient providers of useful information; the incentives of those who write government pamphlets will not reflect a premium placed on gaining customers' goodwill.

With customer liability it is costly—as it would also be with either victim or producer liability—for bystanders to register their bids. It would be very expensive for potential third-party victims to acquire information about the myriad contingencies, and then to get together and bid for safer products, better instructions, more warnings, greater care by the user, and so on. Again, one may judge that total costs could be reduced by reassigning rights so as to elicit safer products, more warnings, and more careful use from the standpoint of bystanders. (And, with regard to fairness, rather than efficiency, *most* people would probably say that product users or producers, or perhaps taxpayers, should compensate injured bystanders.)

Incidentally, when third-party effects or any externalities are large and one sees no way of reducing the costs of voluntary negotiations, one may judge that the use of compulsion would cut total costs. When people are denied options, e.g., when producers are forbidden to produce items that do not have specified safety features, there is no objective evidence about the magnitude of certain costs and gains, since there is no way to see how much people would be willing to pay for options denied or items they are forced to take. Nonetheless, one must sometimes make judgments about these costs and gains. For instance, I understand that in the early days of television, each receiving set emitted signals that interfered with the reception of other sets in the vicinity. Bargaining among set owners to hire each other to install shielding or to watch television only at designated times would have been extremely expensive. The government ordered producers to install shielding on all future sets, thus compelling even isolated set owners to buy this extra feature. Most of us would probably agree in this instance that this action was preferable to doing nothing, i.e., we would judge that the gains exceeded the costs.

On balance, customer liability probably does bring relatively low transaction costs for many product categories. Wherever this is so, bargaining under customer liability would effect additional Pareto-optimal exchanges in comparison with other liability assignments. There are nonetheless several major reasons that might make one oppose caveat emptor.

1. One might believe that he could negotiate through the political process for liability assignments that would yield more equitable (i.e., distributional impacts that one prefers) outcomes, yet that high negotiation costs preclude making tax-subsidy arrangements that would yield an equally desirable wealth distribution *and* economic efficiency.

2. One might attach value to certain political procedures or arrangements per se (e.g., for ideological reasons) and simply not care much about costs that are relevant to Pareto-optimal steps.

3. One might attach value to preventing people from taking the risks they would voluntarily choose to take.

4. One might still believe that customer liability leads to less economic efficiency than other arrangements, since the issue is in doubt once transaction costs are recognized. It is in doubt because we do not know exactly what informa-

tion, negotiation, and enforcement costs would be with some other assignment of rights (or compulsory product specifications). Since some of these costs will be in doubt, one must in the end make personal judgments in deciding what arrangement he believes would be efficient. One individual, or a majority of individuals, may judge that total costs could be reduced by departing from customer liability.

### Producer Liability with Defect

What are the consequences of moving further toward producer liability—of reducing the chances that the purchaser will be held liable and increasing the chances that the producer will face liability? (And this, to repeat, is what seems to have happened.) In my judgment the effects would not have great quantitative significance but would be along the following lines. I would expect more court cases and court costs, since under complete customer liability, the product owner is not compensated, and there is no court determination of the extent of injury, the presence of defects, or the existence of negligence. There would now be higher costs of hiring purchasers to exercise care, for this would now require myriad special contracts with prohibitive enforcement costs, and those higher transaction costs would result in the existence of more externalities, i.e., accident rates would rise.[10] Producers would turn increasingly to liability insurance, and since it would not be economical to adjust the premiums continuously or precisely, producers might, up to certain thresholds, find it efficient to neglect safety features (Williamson, Olson, and Ralston [1967]), diluting the shift toward safer products that is noted below.

With the customer facing a lower probability of being liable, relatively hazardous designs would be less unattractive to him, and the demand curve for such products would rise relative to the demand curve for comparatively safe products. With the producer facing a higher probability of being liable and with his either carrying liability insurance or paying damages, relatively hazardous designs would be more costly, and the supply curve for such products would decrease. On the basis of this shift in liability assignment by itself, there is no presumption that the quantity of hazardous products sold would change, and while the consumer would pay a higher price to the producer, he would simply be forced to buy insurance from the producer instead of having the option of insuring

10. Some people argue that removing liability from users, thus reducing the monetary cost of their having accidents, would not induce those persons to have additional painful and perhaps fatal accidents. To be sure, if more carelessness meant a 100 percent probability of having a serious accident, prospective pain would be deterrent enough, but what more carelessness really means is ordinarily a *modest* increase in the probability of having *some* sort of accident. We trade such increased chances of having an accident for a saving of money or time every day. If carelessness is made to cost less, more will be taken. (Admittedly, the costs that people associate with extremely low risks are unclear. For instance, they may treat a trivial chance, and a still lower chance, of a large loss as being equivalent. There is all the more reason, it seems to me, to expect people to respond to clearly perceived costs in money or time.)

himself. The only thing that would happen to the consumer's position is that he would be denied the opportunity of taking the risk. Since that option would be preferred by some consumers, especially by the poor, this would mean in effect a rise in the price of hazardous products relative to the price of "safe" products, resulting in the end in some shift toward safer products and working to the detriment of the poor.

The shift in liability assignment would decrease efficiency, however, if there were a net increase in transaction costs. (As noted above, producer liability would surely raise the costs of hiring users to be careful and raise some, though not all, information costs.) If this happened, the supply curve would decrease still further, resulting in higher prices for hazardous relative to safer products and in a net shift from hazardous to safer products.

### Producer Liability Without Defect

Let us turn now to a rather extreme arrangement that has been mentioned in recent years—producer liability *without fault or defect*. The manufacturer would simply be held liable for all injuries occurring with the use of his product, regardless of circumstances. As in the other cases, if there were zero transaction costs, producers could hire purchasers to be careful, third parties could hire users to be careful and producers to issue safer products, and purchasers could hire manufacturers to provide various safety features. Each would take these actions as long as the extra gain exceeded the extra cost, and resource use would end up at an efficient point. With transaction costs, however, manufacturer liability without fault or defect would alter resource allocation, and, unless the transactions costs could be measured, it would be uncertain which liability assignment would lead to an efficient point.

I conjecture that costs would be affected in the following ways and that the changes would be important quantitatively. The cost of hiring thousands of purchasers or third parties to exercise care would be enormous, and therefore these persons would now find it relatively inexpensive to be careless. Accident rates would rise. Insurance premiums would become high except on relatively safe products, increasing the net price of hazardous products relative to the price of safe products. As in the preceding case, there would be a shift away from the comparatively hazardous product lines toward the safer products. The net impact on accident costs is not clear, but total costs would rise, because accident prevention would not be produced by those having a comparative advantage in doing so. Court costs per case would decline in comparison with the fault system, but the number of claims would rise; and, unlike the case of caveat emptor, disputes and court costs would not be nil, because even if fault did not have to be established, the fact and extent of injury would have to be determined. (Otherwise, claims would be infinitely large.) Consumers would face a narrower range of choice—a significant sacrifice, but one that is impossible to quantify in any generally valid fashion. As far as this particular sacrifice is concerned, poor people would be hardest hit, because their options would now be to buy relatively expensive safe products, or hazardous products plus high producer-insurance costs, or nothing at all.

The higher accident prevention costs would be borne largely by the customers and potential customers in each industry in the form of higher prices and restricted choice (though I would predict legislative intervention in an effort to check the rising costs). Some of the burden might be passed on to customers in other industries, as people shifted their purchases, and input rents might be reshuffled somewhat. Whether or not one regarded these changes in wealth distribution as being equitable would depend upon the precise impacts and upon one's value judgments.

### Taxpayer Liability

Many persons believe that it would be more equitable to spread the burdens more widely, e.g., to spread the burden of aircraft accidents over input owners in, and customers of, airlines or aircraft manufacturers or both. As far as equity is concerned, however, such redistributions still seem rather arbitrary. Why not put the burden on taxpayers in general?

One way to do this would be to have government compensate people for all injuries without regard to fault. Of course a claim that an injury had occurred would have to be checked; so there would still be this sort of administrative cost. Note, however, that neither purchasers nor producers (nor third parties) would now have to worry about being liable, so that carelessness in design and use of products would become relatively inexpensive to these persons. With the customer not liable, hazardous products would be less unattractive. As the cost of selling unsafe or defective products went down from producers' standpoints, they would expand supplies. Thus both the demand curve and the supply curve of relatively hazardous products would increase, and, without government regulations, there would be a shift toward the use of dangerous products. As the cost of failing to inspect products or of employing products carelessly went down from purchasers' standpoints, they would take more of these actions. If officials or taxpayers thought of hiring these persons to behave differently, ordinary bargaining would be prohibitively expensive.

It is virtually certain that voters and their representatives would find this situation unsatisfactory. Costs would soar too high. Liability insurance, warnings, and disclaimers—in this extreme arrangement and without governmental regulation—would practically disappear. To make taxpayer liability workable, government would have to draw up a network of specifications for products, regulations of their use, and required instructions and warnings. Some "unavoidably unsafe products" might be banned altogether. Producers would inevitably face penalties (a kind of liability) for violating the requirements. Again, consumers would find their choice restricted, this time by law; they would be unable to buy relatively cheap, albeit relatively unsafe, products if they preferred them. Some new kind of penalties for negligence in using products, and perhaps for carelessness by bystanders, would be devised. Administrative and enforcement costs would be high. In the end there would be increased sacrifices in general, and these burdens would be shifted around according to the complex factors that determine tax incidence. One cannot say that social accident insurance would be a "bad" policy, but he can say with confidence that it would not amount to a "free lunch."

In short, as with property right assignments in general, different liability assignments would often bring about significant differences in resource use because of differential transaction costs. It is important to know more about the variation of transaction costs under alternative institutions and about the implications for wealth distribution and resource allocation of different right or liability assignments.

**Chapter Six**

# The Parable of the Parking Lots

H. Manne

Reprinted from the *Public Interest* No. 23 (Spring 1971); 10–15, by permission of publisher and author. Copyright by National Affairs Inc., 1971.

In a city not far away there was a large football stadium. It was used from time to time for various events, but the principal use was for football games played Saturday afternoons by the local college team. The games were tremendously popular, and people drove hundreds of miles to watch them. Parking was done in the usual way. People who arrived early were able to park free on the streets, and latecomers had to pay to park in regular and improvised lots.

There were, at distances ranging from five to twelve blocks from the stadium, approximately twenty-five commercial parking lots, all of which received some business from Saturday afternoon football games. The lots closer to the stadium naturally received more football business than those further away, and some of the very close lots actually raised their price on Saturday afternoons. But they did not raise the price much, and most did not change prices at all. The reason was not hard to find.

For something else happened on football afternoons. A lot of people who during the week were students, lawyers, school teachers, plumbers, factory workers, and even stockbrokers went into the parking lot business. It was not a difficult thing to do. Typically a young boy would put up a crude, homemade sign saying, "Parking $3." He would direct a couple of cars into his parents' driveway, tell the driver to take the key, and collect the three dollars. If the driveway was larger or there was yard space to park in, an older brother, an uncle, or the head of the household would direct the operation, sometimes asking drivers to leave their keys so that shifts could be made if necessary.

Some part-time parking lot operators who lived very close to the stadium charged as much as $5 to park in their driveways. But as the residences-turned-parking-lots were located further from the stadium (and incidentally closer to the commercial parking lots), the price charged at game time declined. In fact, houses at some distance from the stadium charged less than the adjacent commercial lots. The whole system seemed to work fairly smoothly, and though traffic just after a big game was terrible, there were no significant delays parking cars or retrieving parked cars.

But one day the owner of a chain of parking lots called a meeting of all the commercial parking lot owners in the general vicinity of the stadium. They formed an organization known as the Association of Professional Parking Lot Employers, or APPLE. And they were very concerned about the Saturday parking business. One man who owned four parking lots pointed out that honest parking lot owners had heavy capital investments in their businesses, that they paid taxes, and that they employed individuals who supported families. There was no reason, he alleged, why these lots should not handle all the cars coming into the area for special events like football games. "It is unethical," he said, "to engage in cutthroat competition with irresponsible fender benders. After all, parking cars is a profession, not a business." This last remark drew loud applause.

Thus emboldened he continued, stating that commercial parking lot owners recognize their responsibility to serve the public's needs. Ethical car parkers, he said, understand their obligations not to dent fenders, to employ only trustworthy car parkers, to pay decent wages, and generally to care for their customers' automobiles as they would the corpus of a trust. His statement was hailed by others attending the meeting as being very statesmanlike.

Others at the meeting related various tales of horror about nonprofessional car parkers. One homeowner, it was said, actually allowed his fifteen-year-old son to move other peoples' cars around. Another said that he had seen an $8,000 Cadillac parked on a dirt lawn where it would have become mired in mud had it rained that day. Still another pointed out that a great deal of the problem came on the side of the stadium with the lower-priced houses, where there were more driveways per block than on the wealthier side of the stadium. He pointed out that these poor people would rarely be able to afford to pay for damage to other peoples' automobiles or to pay insurance premiums to cover such losses. He felt that a professional group such as APPLE had a duty to protect the public from their folly in using those parking spaces.

Finally another speaker reminded the audience that these "marginal, fly-by-night" parking lot operators generally parked a string of cars in their driveways so that a driver had to wait until all cars behind his had been removed before he could get his out. This, he pointed out, was quite unlike the situation in commercial lots where, during a normal business day, people had to be assured of ready access to their automobiles at any time. The commercial parking lots either had to hire more attendants to shift cars around, or they had to park them so that any car was always accessible, even though this meant that fewer cars could park than the total space would actually hold. "Clearly," he said, "driveway parking constitutes unfair competition."

Emotions ran high at this meeting, and every member of APPLE pledged $1 per parking space for something mysteriously called a "slush fund." It was never made clear exactly whose slush would be bought with these funds, but several months later a resolution was adopted by the city council requiring licensing for anyone in the parking lot business.

The preamble to the new ordinance read like the speeches at the earlier meeting. It said that this measure was designed to protect the public against unscrupulous, unprofessional, and undercapitalized parking lot operators. It required, inter alia, that anyone parking cars for a fee must have a minimum capital devoted to the parking lot business of $25,000, liability insurance in an amount not less than $500,000, bonding for each car parker, and a special driving test for these parkers (which incidentally would be designed and administered by APPLE). The ordinance also required, again in the public's interest, that every lot charge a single posted price for parking and that any change in the posted price be approved in advance by the city council. Incidentally, most members were able to raise their fees by about 20 percent before the first posting.

Then a funny thing happened to drivers on their way to the stadium for the next big game. They discovered city police in unusually large numbers informing them that it was illegal to pay a non-licensed parking lot operator for the right to park a car. These policemen also reminded parents that if their children were found in violation of this ordinance, it could result in a misdemeanor charge being brought against the parents and possible juvenile court proceedings for the children. There were no driveway parking lots that day.

Back at the commercial parking lots, another funny thing occurred. Proceeding from the entrance of each of these parking lots within twelve blocks of the stadium were long lines of cars waiting to park. The line got larger as the lot was closer to the stadium. Many drivers had to wait so long or walk so far that they missed the entire first quarter of the big game.

At the end of the game it was even worse. The confusion was massive. The lot attendants could not cope with the jam-up, and some cars were actually not retrieved until the next day. It was even rumored about town that some automobiles had been lost forever and that considerable liabilities might result for some operators. Industry spokesmen denied this, however.

Naturally there was a lot of grumbling, but there was no agreement on what had caused the difficulty. At first, everyone said there were merely some "bugs" in the new system that would have to be ironed out. But the only bug ironed out was a Volkswagen which was flattened by a careless lot attendant in a Cadillac Eldorado.

The situation did not improve at subsequent games. The members of APPLE did not hire additional employees to park cars, and operators near the stadium were not careful to follow their previous practice of parking cars in such a way as to have them immediately accessible. Employees seemed to become more surly, and the number of dented-fender claims mounted rapidly.

Little by little, too, cars began appearing in residential driveways again. For instance, one enterprising youth regularly went into the car wash business on football afternoons, promising that his wash job would take at least two hours. He charged $5, and got it—even on rainy days—in fact, especially on rainy days. Another homeowner offered to take cars on consignment for three hours to sell them at prices fixed by the owner. He charged $4 for this "service," but his subterfuge was quickly squelched by the authorities. The parking situation remained "critical."

Political pressures on the city council began to mount to "do something" about the inordinate delays in parking and retrieving cars on football afternoons. The city council sent a stern note of warning to APPLE, and APPLE appointed a special study group recruited from the local university's computer science department to look into the matter. This group reported that the managerial and administrative machinery in the parking lot business was archaic. What was needed, the study group said, was less goose quills and stand-up desks and more computers and conveyor belts. It was also suggested that all members of APPLE be hooked into one computer so that cars could really be shifted to the most accessible spaces.

Spokesmen for the industry took up the cry of administrative modernization. Subtle warnings appeared in the local papers suggesting that if the industry did not get its own house in order, heavy-handed regulation could be anticipated. The city council asked for reports on failures to deliver cars and decreed that this would include any failure to put a driver in his car within five minutes of demand without a new dent.

Some of the professional operators actually installed computer equipment to handle their ticketing and parking logistics problems. And some added second stories to their parking lots. Others bought up additional space, thereby raising the value of vacant lots in the area. But many simply added a few additional car parkers and hoped that the problem would go away without a substantial investment of capital.

The commercial operators also began arguing that they needed higher parking fees because of their higher operating costs. Everyone agreed that costs for operating a parking lot were certainly higher than before the licensing ordinance. So the city council granted a request for an across-the-board 10 percent hike in fees. The local newspaper editorially hoped that this would ease the problem without still higher fees being necessary. In a way, it did. A lot of people stopped driving. They began using city buses, or they chartered private buses for the game. Some stayed home and watched the game on TV. A new study group on fees was appointed.

Just about then several other blows fell on the parking lot business. Bus transportation to the area near the stadium was improved with a federal subsidy to the municipal bus company. And several new suburban shopping centers caused a loss of automobile traffic in the older areas of town. But most dramatic of all, the local university, under severe pressure from its students and faculty, dropped intercollegiate football altogether and converted the stadium into a park for underprivileged children.

The impact of these events on the commercial parking lots was swift. Income declined drastically. The companies that had borrowed money to finance the expansion everyone wanted earlier were hardest hit. Two declared bankruptcy, and many had to be absorbed by financially stronger companies. Layoffs among car parkers were enormous, and APPLE actually petitioned the city council to guarantee the premiums on their liability insurance policies so that people would not be afraid to park commercially. This idea was suggested to APPLE by recent Congressional legislation creating an insurance program for stock brokers.

A spokesman for APPLE made the following public statement: "New organizations or arrangements may be necessary to straighten out this problem. There has been a failure in both the structure of the industry and the regulatory scheme. New and better regulation is clearly demanded. A sound parking lot business is necessary for a healthy urban economy." The statement was hailed by the industry as being very statesmanlike, though everyone speculated about what he really meant.

Others in the industry demanded that the city bus service be curtailed during the emergency. The city council granted every rate increase the lots requested. There were no requests for rate decreases, but the weaker lots began offering prizes and other subtle or covert rebates to private bus companies who would park with them. In fact, this problem became so serious and uncontrollable that one owner of a large chain proclaimed that old-fashioned price competition for this business would be desirable. This again was hailed as statesmanlike, but everyone assumed that he really meant something else. No one proposed repeal of the licensing ordinance.

One other thing happened. Under pressure from APPLE, the city council decreed that henceforth no parking would be allowed on any streets in the downtown area of town. The local merchants were extremely unhappy with this, however, and the council rescinded the ordinance at the next meeting, citing a computer error as the basis for the earlier restriction.

The ultimate resolution of the "new" parking problem is not in sight. The parking lot industry in this town not very far from here is now said to be a depressed business, even a sick one. Everyone looks to the city council for a solution, but things will probably limp along as they are for quite a while, picking up with an occasional professional football game and dropping low with bad weather.

\* \* \*

MORAL: If you risk your lot under an apple tree, you may get hit in the head.

## Chapter Seven

# The Federal Communications Commission

R. Coase

Reprinted from the *Journal of Law and Economics* 2 (October 1959): 1–40, by permission of publisher and author.

In the United States no one may operate a broadcasting station unless he first obtains a license from the Federal Communications Commission. These licenses are not issued automatically but are granted or withheld at the discretion of the Commission, which is thus in a position to choose those who shall operate radio and television stations. How did the Commission come to acquire this power?

About the turn of the century, radio began to be used commercially, mainly for ship-to-shore and ship-to-ship communication.[1] This led to various proposals for legislation. Some of these were concerned with the promotion of safety at sea, requiring the installation of radio equipment on ships, the employment of skilled operators, and the like. Others, and it is these in which we are interested, were designed to bring about government control of the operations of the industry as a whole.

The reason behind such proposals can be seen from a letter dated March 30, 1910, from the Department of the Navy to the Senate Committee on Commerce, which described "clearly and succinctly," according to the Committee, the purpose of the bill to regulate radio communication which was then under discussion. The Department of the Navy explained that each radio station

> considers itself independent and claims the right to send forth its electric waves through the ether at any time that it may desire, with the result that there exists in many places a state of chaos. Public business is hindered to the great embarrassment of the Navy Department. Calls of distress from vessels in peril on the sea go unheeded or are drowned out in the etheric bedlam produced by numerous stations all trying to communicate at once. Mischievous and irresponsible operators seem to take great delight in impersonating other stations

1. This short account of the development of radio regulation does not call for extensive documentation, but sources are given for all quotations and in other cases where they might be difficult to identify. I found the following books and the references contained therein particularly helpful: Warner (1948) and Schmeckebier (1932).

and in sending out false calls. It is not putting the case too strongly to state that the situation is intolerable, and is continually growing worse. (S. Rep. No. 659, 61st Cong., 2d Sess. 4 [1910])

The letter went on to point out that the Department of the Navy, in cooperation with other government departments,

> has for years sought the enactment of legislation that would bring some sort or order out of the turbulent condition of radio communication, and while it would favor the passage of a law placing all wireless stations under the control of the Government, at the same time recognizes that such a law passed at the present time might not be acceptable to the people of this country. (Ibid.)

The bill to which this letter referred was passed by the Senate but was not acted upon by the House of Representatives. Toward the end of 1911 the same bill was reintroduced in the Senate. A subcommittee concluded that it "bestowed too great powers upon the departments of government and gave too great privileges to military and naval stations, while it did not accurately define the limitations and conditions under which commercial enterprises could be conducted (S. Rep. No. 698, 62d Cong., 2d Sess. 3 [1912]). In consequence, a substitute bill was introduced, and this secured the approval both of the Senate and of the House of Representatives and became law on August 13, 1912. The Act provided that anyone operating a radio station must have a license issued by the Secretary of Commerce. This license would include details of the ownership and location of the station, the wave length or wave lengths authorized for use, the hours for which the station was licensed for work, etc. Regulations, which could be waived by the Secretary of Commerce, required the station to designate a normal wave length (which had to be less than 600 or more than 1,600 meters), but the station could use other wave lengths, provided that they were outside the limits already indicated. Amateurs were not to use a wave length exceeding 200 meters. Various other technical requirements were included in the Act. The main difference between the bill introduced in 1910 and the Act as passed was that specific regulations were set out in the Act, whereas originally power had been given to the Secretary of Commerce to make regulations and to prevent interference to "signals relating to vessels in distress or of naval and military stations by private and commercial stations"; power to make regulations was also given to the President.[2]

It was not long before attempts were made to change the law. The proposal that the Secretary of Commerce should have power to make regulations

2. Mention should also be made of one bill (S. 5630, 62d Cong. [1912]) which gave the task of regulating radio communication to the Interstate Commerce Commission and another (H.R. 23716, 62d Cong. [1912]) which provided for government ownership of wireless telegraphs.

was revived. A bill was even introduced to create a Post Office monopoly of electrical communications. In 1917 and 1918, bills were introduced which would have given control of the radio industry to the Department of the Navy. Indeed, the 1918 bill was described, quite accurately, by Josephus Daniels, the Secretary of the Navy, as one which "would give the Navy Department the ownership, the exclusive ownership, of all wireless communication for commercial purposes." Daniels explained that radio was "the only method of communication which must be dominated by one power to prevent interference. . . . The question of interference does not come in at all in the matter of cables or telegraphs but only in wireless." Some members of the House Committee to which Daniels was giving evidence asked whether it would not be sufficient to regulate the hours of operation and the wave lengths used by radio stations, while leaving them in private hands. But Daniels was not to be moved from his position:

> My judgment is that in this particular method of communication the government ought to have a monopoly, just like it has with the mails—and even more so because other people could carry the mails on trains without interference, but they cannot use the air without interference.

Later Daniels explained: "There are only two methods of operating the wireless: either by the government or for it to license one corporation—there is no other safe or possible method of operating the wireless." That led one of the Committee to ask: "That is because of the interference in the ether, is it?" Daniels replied: "There is a certain amount of ether, and you cannot divide it up among the people as they choose to use it; one hand must control it." Later, Commander Hooper, one of Daniels' advisers, told the Committee:

> . . . radio, by virtue of the interferences, is a natural monopoly; either the government must exercise that monopoly by owning the stations, or it must place the ownership of these stations in the hands of one concern and let the government keep out of it.[3]

The Navy in 1918 was in a much stronger position to press its claim than in the period before the 1912 Act. It had controlled the radio industry during the war and, as a result of building stations and the acquisition by purchase of certain private stations, owned 111 of the 127 existing American commercial shore stations. Nevertheless, the House Committee does not appear to have been convinced by the Navy Department's argument, and no further action was taken on this bill. Nor was this proposal ever to be raised again. The emergence of the broadcasting industry was to make it impossible in the future to think of the radio

3. From: hearings on H.R. 13159, A Bill to Further Regulate Radio Communication, before the House Committee on the Merchant Marine and Fisheries, 65th Cong., 3d Sess. (1918).

industry solely in terms of point-to-point communication and as a matter largely of concern to the Department of the Navy.

The broadcasting industry came into being in the early 1920s. Some broadcasting stations were operating in 1920 and 1921, but a big increase in the number of stations occurred in 1922. On March 1, 1922, there were sixty broadcasting stations in the United States. By November 1, the number was 564.[4] Herbert Hoover, as Secretary of Commerce, was responsible for the administration of the 1912 Act, and he faced the task of preventing the signals of these new stations from interfering with each other and with those of existing stations. In February 1922, Hoover invited representatives of various government departments and of the radio industry to the first Radio Conference. The Conference recommended that the powers of the Secretary of Commerce to control the establishment of radio stations should be strengthened and proposed an allocation of wave bands for the various classes of service. Other conferences followed in 1923, 1924, and 1925.[5] Bills were introduced in Congress embodying the recommendations of these conferences, but none passed into law. The Secretary of Commerce attempted to carry out their recommendations by inserting detailed conditions into the licenses. However, his power to regulate radio stations in this way was destroyed by court decisions interpreting the 1912 Act.

In 1921, Hoover declined to renew the license of a telegraph company, the Intercity Radio Company, on the ground that its use of any available wave length would interfere with the signals of other stations. The company took legal action, and in February 1923, a court decision held that the Secretary of Commerce had no discretion to refuse a license (*Hoover* v. *Intercity Radio Co.*, 286 Fed. 1003 [App. D.C., 1923]). This meant, of course, that the Secretary had no control over the number of stations that could be established. However, the wording of the court decision seemed to imply that the Secretary had power to choose the wave length which a licensee could use. A later decision was to deny him even this power. In 1925 the Zenith Radio Corporation was assigned the wave length of 332.4 meters, with hours of operation limited from 10:00 to 12:00 p.m. on Thursday and then only when this period was not wanted by the General Electric Company's Denver station. These terms indicate the highly restrictive conditions which Hoover felt himself obliged to impose at this time. Not unnaturally, the Zenith Company was not happy with what was proposed and, in fact, broadcast on wave lengths and at times not allowed by the license. Criminal proceedings were then taken against the Zenith Company for violation of the 1912 Act. But in a decision rendered in April 1926, it was held that the Act did not give the Secretary of Commerce power to make regulations and that he was required to issue a license subject only to the regulations in the Act itself (*United States* v. *Zenith Radio Corp.*, 12 F.2d 614 [N.D. Ill., 1926]). As we have seen, these merely required that the wave length used should be less than 600 or more than 1,600

---

4. See Schmeckebier (1932, p. 4).
5. For details of these conferences, see Schmeckebier (1932, pp. 6–12).

meters. The decision in the Zenith case appeared in certain respects to be in conflict with that in the Intercity Radio Company case, and the Secretary of Commerce asked the Attorney General for an opinion. His opinion upheld the decision in the Zenith case.[6] This meant that the Secretary of Commerce was compelled to issue licenses to anyone who applied, and the licensees were then free to decide on the power of their station, its hours of operation, and the wave length they would use (outside the limits mentioned in the Act). The period which followed has often been described as one of "chaos in broadcasting." More than 200 stations were established in the next nine months. These stations used whatever power or wave length they wished, while many of the existing stations ceased to observe the conditions which the Secretary of Commerce had inserted in their licenses.

For a number of years Congress had been studying various proposals for regulating radio communication. The Zenith decision added very considerably to the pressure for new legislation. In July 1926, as a stop-gap measure designed to prevent licensees establishing property rights in frequencies, the two houses of Congress passed a joint resolution providing that no license should be granted for more than ninety days for a broadcasting station or for more than two years for any other type of station. Furthermore, no one was to be granted a license unless he executed "a waiver of any right or of any claim to any right, as against the United States, to any wave length or to the use of the ether in radio transmission. . . ." This echoed an earlier Senate resolution (passed in 1925), in which the ether and the use thereof had been declared to be "the inalienable possession of the people of the United States. . . ." When Congress reconvened in December 1926, the House and Senate quickly agreed on a comprehensive measure for the regulation of the radio industry, which became law in February 1927.

This Act brought into existence the Federal Radio Commission. The Commission, among other things, was required to classify radio stations, prescribe the nature of the service, assign wave lengths, determine the power and location of the transmitters, regulate the kind of apparatus used, and make regulations to prevent interference. It was provided that those wanting licenses to operate radio stations had to make a written application which was to include such facts as the Commission

> may prescribe as to the citizenship, character, and financial, technical, and other qualifications of the applicant to operate the station; the ownership and location of the proposed station and of the stations, if any, with which it is proposed to communicate; the frequencies or wave lengths and the power desired to be used; the hours of the day or other periods of time during which it is proposed to operate the station; the purposes for which the station is to be used, and such other information as it may require.

6. 35 Ops. Att'y Gen. 126 (1926). The question was submitted on June 4, 1926, and the opinion rendered on July 8, 1926.

The Commission was authorized to issue a license if the "public interest, necessity or convenience would be served" by so doing. Once the license was granted, it could not be transferred to anyone else without the approval of the Commission. And, incorporating the sense of the 1926 joint resolution, licensees were required to sign a waiver of any claim to the use of a wave length or the ether.

The Commission was thus provided with massive powers to regulate the radio industry. But it was prohibited from censoring programs:

> Nothing in this Act shall be understood or construed to give the licensing authority the power of censorship over the radio communications or signals transmitted by any radio station, and no regulation or condition shall be promulgated or fixed by the licensing authority which shall interfere with the right of free speech by means of radio communications.

Nonetheless, the Act did impose some restrictions on a station's programing. Obscene, indecent, or profane language was prohibited. A station was not allowed to rebroadcast programs without the permission of the originating station. The names of people paying for our furnishing programs had to be announced. Finally it was provided that if a licensee permitted a legally qualified candidate for public office to broadcast, equal opportunities had to be offered to all other candidates.

The regulatory powers of the Federal Radio Commission did not extend to radio stations operated by the federal government, except when the signals transmitted did not relate to government business. These government stations were subject to the authority of the President. In fact, the allocation of frequencies for government use was carried out under the auspices of the Interdepartment Radio Advisory Committee, which had originally been formed in 1922 but which continued in existence after the establishment of the Federal Radio Commission.

In 1934 the powers exercised by the Federal Radio Commission were transferred to the Federal Communications Commission, which was also made responsible for the regulation of the telephone and telegraph industries. This change in the administrative machinery made little difference to the relations between the regulatory authority and the radio industry. Indeed, the sections of the 1934 Act dealing with the radio industry very largely reproduced the 1927 Act.[7] Amendments have been made to the 1934 Act from time to time, but these have related mainly to procedural matters, and the main structure has been unaffected.[8] In all essentials, the system as it exists today is that established in 1927.

7. The main difference between these two acts was the insertion in the 1934 Act of two new provisions. One was a prohibition against the advertisement or conduct of lotteries (Section 316, presently Title 18, U.S.C. § 1304). The other required anyone maintaining studios to supply programs (whether by wire or otherwise) for foreign stations which could be heard in the United States to obtain a permit from the Commission (Section 325(b)).

8. The Davis Amendment of 1928 which directed the Commission to make an equal allocation of broadcasting facilities among five zones of the United States and an equitable distribution, according to population, among the states in each zone was incorporated in the 1934 Act. But in 1936 the original working of the 1927 Act, which merely required the Commission to make "a fair, efficient and equitable distribution," was reinstated.

## THE CLASH WITH THE DOCTRINE OF
## FREEDOM OF THE PRESS

The situation in the American broadcasting industry is not essentially different
in character from that which would be found if a commission appointed by the
federal government had the task of selecting those who were to be allowed to publish newspapers and periodicals in each city, town, and village of the United
States. A proposal to do this would, of course, be rejected out of hand as inconsistent with the doctrine of freedom of the press. But the broadcasting industry
is a source of news and opinion of comparable importance with newspapers or
books and, in fact, nowadays is commonly included with the press, so far as the
doctrine of freedom of the press is concerned. The Commission on Freedom of
the Press, under the chairmanship of Robert M. Hutchins, used the term "press"
to include "all means of communicating to the public news and opinions, emotions and beliefs, whether by newspapers, magazines, or books, by radio broad-
casts, by television, or by films"(Commission on Freedom of the Press [1947,
p. 109] ). Zechariah Chafee had little doubt that the broadcasting industry came
within the protection of the First Amendment (Chafee, 1947). A dictum in the
Supreme Court expressed a similar view: "We have no doubt that moving pictures, like newspapers and radio, are included in the press whose freedom is guaranteed by the First Amendment" (*United States* v. *Paramount Pictures, Inc.,* 334
U.S. 131, 166 [1948] ). Yet, as Louis G. Caldwell has pointed out, a

> broadcasting station can be put out of existence and its owner de-
> prived of his investment and means of livelihood, for the oral dis-
> semination of language which, if printed in a newspaper, is protected
> by the First Amendment to the Constitution against exactly the same
> sort of repression. (1935, p. 203)

In the discussions preceding the formation of the Federal Radio Commission, Hoover distinguished between two problems—the prevention of interference and the choice of those who would operate the stations:

> . . . the ideal situation, as I view it, would be traffic regulation by
> Federal Government to the extent of the allotment of wave lengths
> and control of power and the policing of interference, leaving to each
> community a large voice in determining who are to occupy the wave
> lengths assigned to that community. (1925)

But, as we have seen, both of these tasks were given to the Federal Radio Commission. Some interpreted the fact that the Commission was denied the power of
censorship as meaning that it would not concern itself with programing but
would simply act as "the traffic policeman of the ether." But the Commission
maintained—and in this it has been sustained by the courts—that, to decide wheth-

er the "public interest, convenience or necessity" would be served by granting or renewing a license, it had to take into account proposed or past programing. One commentator remarked that by 1949, the "Commission had travelled far from its original role of airwaves traffic policeman. Control over radio had become more than regulation based on technological necessity; it had become regulation of conduct, and the basis was but emerging" ("Old Standards in New Context: A Comparative Analysis of FCC Regulation"[1950]).

The Commission is instructed to grant or renew a license if this would serve the "public interest, convenience or necessity." This phrase, taken from public utility legislation, lacks any definite meaning. It "means about as little as any phrase that the drafters of the Act could have used and still comply with the constitutional requirement that there be some standard to guide the administrative wisdom of the licensing authority" (Caldwell 1930). Furthermore, the many inconsistencies in Commission decisions have made it impossible for the phrase to acquire a definite meaning in the process of regulation. The character of the program proposals of an applicant for a frequency or channel is, of course, one of the factors taken into account by the Commission, and any applicant with a good lawyer will find that his proposals include live programs with local performers and programs in which public issues are discussed (these being program types which appear to be favored by the Commission). And when the time comes for renewal of the license, which at the present time is every three years, the past programing of the station is reviewed.[9]

A good illustration of the difference between the position of the owner of a broadcasting station and the publisher of a newspaper is provided by the case of Baker, who operated a radio station in Iowa and was denied a renewal of his license in 1931 because he broadcast bitter personal attacks on persons and institutions he did not like. The Commission said:

> This Commission holds no brief for the Medical Associations and other parties whom Mr. Baker does not like. Their alleged sins may be at times of public importance, to be called to the attention of the public over the air in the right way. But this record discloses that Mr. Baker does not do so in any high-minded way. It shows that he continually and erratically over the air rides a personal hobby, his cancer cure ideas and his likes and dislikes of certain persons and things. Surely his infliction of all this on the listeners is not the proper use of a broadcasting license. Many of his utterances are vulgar, if not indeed indecent. Assuredly they are not uplifting or entertaining.

9. It is unnecessary for my purpose to review the policies of the Federal Radio Commission and the Federal Communications Commission in choosing among applicants and passing on the renewal of licenses. For discussions of such questions, the reader is referred to Warner (1948), Edelman (1950), Federal Communications Commission (1957, particularly ch. 3).

Though we may not censor, it is our duty to see that broadcasting licenses do not afford mere personal organs, and also to see that a standard of refinement fitting our day and generation is maintained.[10]

It is hardly surprising that this decision has been described as "in spirit pure censorship"(Ibid.).

The Commission's attempts to influence programing have met with little opposition, except on two occasions, when the broadcasting industry made vigorous protests. The first arose out of the so-called *Mayflower* decision of 1940. A Boston station had broadcast editorials urging the election of certain candidates for public office and expressing views on controversial questions. The Commission criticized the station for doing this and renewed its license only after receiving assurances that the station would no longer broadcast editorals. In 1948 the Commission re-examined the question and issued a report which, while not explicitly repudiating the *Mayflower* doctrine, nevertheless expressed approval of editorializing subject to the criterion of "overall fairness." The Commission agreed that its ruling involved an abridgment of freedom but that this was necessary:

> Any regulation of radio, especially a system of limited licensees, is in a real sense an abridgment of the inherent freedom of persons to express themselves by means of radio communications. It is however, a necessary and constitutional abridgment in order to prevent chaotic interference from destroying the great potential of this medium for public enlightment [*sic*] and entertainment.

The Commission then went on:

> The most significant meaning of freedom of the radio is the right of the American people to listen to this great medium of communications free from any governmental dictation as to what they can or cannot hear and free alike from similar restraints by private licensees.

It is not clear to me what the Commission meant by this. It could hardly have been the intention of the Commission to pay a tribute to the "invisible hand."[11]

The second controversy arose out of the publication of the so-called Blue Book by the Federal Communications Commission in 1946, entitled *Public Service Responsibility of Broadcast Licensees*. In this report the Commission indicated that it was going to pay closer attention to questions of programing and that those stations which carried sustaining programs, local live programs, and programs devoted to the discussion of public issues and which avoided "advertis-

10. Decisions of the FCC, Docket No. 967, June 5, 1931. Quoted from Caldwell (1931).
11. Editorializing by Broadcast Licensees, 13 F.C.C. 1246, 1257 (1949). Cf. *Mayflower Broadcasting Corp.*, 8 F.C.C. 333 (1940).

ing excesses" would be more likely to have their licenses renewed. In the case of sustaining programs, it was suggested that they should be used with a view to

> (*a*) maintaining an overall program balance, (*b*) providing time for programs inappropriate for sponsorship, (*c*) providing time for programs serving particular minority tastes and interests, (*d*) providing time for non-profit organizations—religious, civic, agricultural, labor, educational, etc., and (*e*) providing time for experiment and for unfettered artistic self-expression. (Federal Communications Commission 1946, p. 55)

It was argued (by Justin Miller, of the National Association of Broadcasters, among others) that the publication of the Blue Book was unconstitutional, as being contrary to the First Amendment, but on this the courts have not given an opinion.

The examination by the Commission of the past activities of applicants has at times posed a threat to other freedoms. One example is furnished by the proceedings in the *Daily News* case. The publishers of the New York *Daily News* applied for permission to construct an FM station. The American Jewish Congress intervened, arguing that the application should be denied because the *Daily News* had

> evidenced bias against minority groups, particularly Jews and Negroes, and has published irresponsible and defamatory news items and editorials concerning such minorities . . . the *News* had thus demonstrated . . . that it is unqualified to be the licensee of a radio station because it could not be relied upon to operate its station with fairness to all groups and points of view in the community.

The admissibility of such evidence was questioned, but the Commission held that it could be received, although pronouncing it inconclusive in this case. The application of the owners of the *Daily News* was finally rejected on other grounds, although it has been suggested that the evidence of the American Jewish Congress in fact played a part in bringing about the decision. What seems clear is that a newspaper which has an editorial policy approved of by the Commission is more likely to obtain a radio or television license than one that does not. The threat to freedom of the press in its strictest sense is evident.[12] Another case involved the political activities of an owner of a radio station, Edward Lamb. In earlier hearings, Lamb had denied having Communist associations. When the license of his station came up for renewal in 1954, the Commission charged that his previous statements were false. According to Ralph S. Brown, the Broadcast Bureau of the

---

12. See *WBNX Broadcasting Co.*, 12 F.C.C. 805 (1948). For the view that this evidence may have had some effect on the Commission's decision, see "Radio Program Controls: A Network of Inadequacy" (1947).

Commission "produced in support of its charge as sorry a collection of unreliable and mendacious witnesses as have appeared in any recent political case." Finally, after lengthy proceedings, the license was renewed, but the Commission in its decision rejected the view that it "had no right to inquire into past associations, activities, and beliefs. . ." (1958, pp. 371–372).[13]

If we ask why it is that the Commission's policies have met with so little opposition, the answer, without any doubt, is that the Commission has been extremely hesitant about imposing its views on the broadcasting industry. Sometimes licenses have been renewed on condition that the programs to which the Commission objected were not broadcast in the future. Some operators have not had their licenses renewed largely or wholly because of objections to the programs transmitted. But the number of such cases is not large, and the programs to which objection was taken were devoted to such topics as fortune-telling, horse-racing results, or medical advice or involved attacks on public officials, medical associations, or religious organizations.[14]

It is difficult for someone outside the broadcasting industry to assess the extent to which programing has been affected by the views and actions of the Commission. On the face of it, it would seem improbable that the Commission's cautious approach would intimidate many station operators. However, the complete compliance of the industry to the *Mayflower* decision may be cited as evidence of the power of the Commission. Furthermore, the Commission has many favors to give, and few people with any substantial interests in the broadcasting industry would want to flout too flagrantly the wishes of the Commission.

## THE RATIONALE OF THE PRESENT SYSTEM

Chafee has pointed out that the newer media of communication have been subjected to a stricter control than the old:

> Newspapers, books, pamphlets, and large meetings were for many centuries the only means of public discussion, so that the need for their protection has long been generally realized. On the other hand, when additional methods for spreading facts and ideas were introduced or greatly improved by modern inventions, writers and judges had not got into the habit of being solicitous about guarding their freedom. And so we have tolerated censorship of the mails, the importation of foreign books, the stage, the motion picture, and the radio. (1942, p. 381)

13. For further details of this case and the questions it raises, see an article by the same author (1957).

14. See Federal Communications Commission (1957, pp. 150–151). The exact number of cases in which the failure to renew a license was due to past programing (that is, in which the renewal would have been made had the programing been different) is uncertain. See Smead (1959).

It is no doubt true that the difference between the position occupied by the press and the broadcasting industry is in part due to the fact that the printing press was invented in the fifteenth and broadcasting in the twentieth century. But this is by no means the whole story. Many of those who have acquiesced in this abridgment of freedom of the press in broadcasting have done so reluctantly, the situation being accepted as a necessary, if unfortunate, consequence of the peculiar technology of the industry.

Justice Frankfurter, in delivering the opinion of the Supreme Court in one of the leading cases on radio law, gave an account of the rationale of the present system:

> The plight into which radio fell prior to 1927 was attributable to certain basic facts about radio as a means of communication—its facilities are limited; they are not available to all who may wish to use them; the radio spectrum simply is not large enough to accommodate everybody. There is a fixed natural limitation upon the number of stations that can operate without interfering with one another. Regulation of radio was therefore as vital to its development as traffic control was to the development of the automobile. In enacting the Radio Act of 1927, the first comprehensive scheme of control over radio communication, Congress acted upon the knowledge that if the potentialities of radio were not to be wasted, regulation was essential.

To those who argued that we should "regard the Commission as a kind of traffic officer, policing the wave lengths to prevent stations from interfering with each other," Justice Frankfurter answered:

> But the Act does not restrict the Commission merely to supervision of traffic. It puts upon the Commission the burden of determining the composition of that traffic. The facilities of radio are not large enough to accommodate all who wish to use them. Methods must be devised for choosing from among the many who apply. And since Congress itself could not do this, it committed the task to the Commission.
>
> The Commission was, however, not left at large in performing this duty. The touchstone provided by Congress was the "public interest, convenience or necessity."
>
> . . . The facilities of radio are limited and therefore precious; they cannot be left to wasteful use without detriment to the public interest. . . . The Commission's licensing function cannot be discharged, therefore, merely by finding that there are no technological objections to the granting of a license. If the criterion of "public interest" were limited to such matters, how could the Commission choose between two applicants for the same facilities, each of whom is financially and technically qualified to operate a station? Since the very

inception of federal regulation of radio, comparative considerations as to the services to be rendered have governed the application of the standard of "public interest, convenience or necessity." *National Broadcasting Co.* v. *United States*, 319 U.S. 190, 213, 215–17 [1943])

The events which preceded government regulation have been described very vividly by Charles A. Siepmann:

> The chaos that developed as more and more enthusiastic pioneers entered the field of radio was indescribable. Amateurs crossed signals with professional broadcasters. Many of the professionals broadcast on the same wave length and either came to a gentleman's agreement to divide the hours of broadcasting or blithely set about cutting one another's throats by broadcasting simultaneously. Listeners thus experienced the annoyance of trying to hear one program against the raucous background of another. Ship-to-shore communication in Morse code added its pulsing dots and dashes to the silly symphony of sound. (1950, pp. 5–6)

Siepmann sums up the situation in the following words: "Private enterprise, over seven long years, failed to set its own house in order. Cutthroat competition at once retarded radio's orderly development and subjected listeners to intolerable strain and inconvenience" (Ibid.).

Notwithstanding the general acceptance of these arguments and the eminence of the authorities who expound them, the views which have just been quoted are based on a misunderstanding of the nature of the problem. Justice Frankfurter seems to believe that federal regulation is needed because radio frequencies are limited in number and people want to use more of them than are available. But it is a commonplace of economics that almost all resources used in the economic system (and not simply radio and television frequencies) are limited in amount and scarce, in that people would like to use more than exists. Land, labor, and capital are all scarce, but this, of itself, does not call for government regulation. It is true that some mechanism has to be employed to decide who, out of the many claimants, should be allowed to use the scarce resource. But the way this is usually done in the American economic system is to employ the price mechanism, and this allocates resources to users without the need for government regulation.

Siepmann seems to ascribe the confusion that existed before government regulation to a failure of private enterprise and the competitive system. But the real cause of the trouble was that no property rights were created in these scarce frequencies. We know from our ordinary experience that land can be allocated to land users without the need for government regulation by using the price mechanism. But if no property rights were created in land, so that everyone could use a tract of land, it is clear that there would be considerable confusion and that the price mechanism could not work because there would not be any property rights that could be acquired. If one person could use a piece of land for growing a crop, and then another person could come along and build a house on the land used for the crop, and then another could come along, tear down the house, and use the space as a parking lot, it would no doubt be accurate to describe the resulting situation as chaos. But it would be wrong to blame this on private enterprise and the competitive system. A private-enterprise system cannot function properly unless property rights are created in resources, and, when this is done, someone wishing to use a resource has to pay the owner to obtain it. Chaos disappears; and so does the government except that a legal system to define property rights and to arbitrate disputes is, of course, necessary. But there is certainly no need for the kind of regulation which we now find in the American radio and television industry.

In 1951, in the course of a comment dealing with the problem of standards in color television, Leo Herzel proposed that the price mechanism should be used to allocate frequencies. He said:

> The most important function of radio regulation is the allocation of a scarce factor of production—frequency channels. The FCC has to determine who will get the limited number of channels available at any one time. This is essentially an economic decision, not a policing decision. (1951, p. 802)

And, later, Herzel suggested that channels should be leased to the highest bidder. This article brought a reply from Dallas W. Smythe of the Institute of Communications Research of the University of Illinois and formerly chief economist of the Federal Communications Commission. In his article, Smythe presented the case against the use of the price mechanism in broadcasting.[15]

First of all, Smythe pointed out that commercial broadcasting was not a "dominant user of spectrum space" but "a minor claimant on it." He explained that "the radio spectrum up to at least 1,000,000 Kc is susceptible of commercial exploitation, technologically. On this basis, the exclusive use of frequencies by broadcasters represents 2.3 per cent of the total and the shared use, 7.2 per cent." But, according to Smythe, even these percentages may overstate the importance of broadcasting. "The FCC has allocated the spectrum to different users as far as 30,000,000 Kc. And on this basis commercial broadcasters use exclusively less than one tenth of one per cent, and, on a shared basis, two tenths of one per cent."[16]

Smythe then went on to explain who it was that used most of the radio spectrum. First, there were the military, the law-enforcement agencies, the

15. Smythe (1952) and a rejoinder by the student author, Leo Herzel, which appeared in a subsequent issue of the same journal.

16. Of course not all these frequencies would be equally desirable for use in the broadcasting industry.

fire-fighting agencies, the Weather Bureau, the Forestry Service, and the radio amateurs, "the last of which by definition could hardly be expected to pay for frequency use." (This is, of course, in accordance with the modern view that an amateur is someone who does not pay for the things he uses.) Then there were many commercial users other than broadcasters. There were the common carriers, radiotelegraph and radiotelephone; transportation agencies, vessels on the high seas, railroads, street railways, busses, trucks, harbor craft, and taxis. There were also various specialized users, such as electric power, gas and water concerns, the oil industry (which used radio waves for communication and also for geophysical exploration), the motion-picture industry (for work on location), and so on. Smythe commented:

> Surely it is not seriously intended that the non-commercial radio us- ers (such as police), the non-broadcast common carriers (such as radio- telegraph) and the non-broadcast commercial users (such as the oil industry) should compete with dollar bids against the broadcast users for channel allocations.

To this Herzel replied:

> It certainly is seriously suggested. Such users compete for all other kinds of equipment or else they don't get it. I should think the more interesting question is, why is it seriously suggested that they shouldn't compete for radio frequencies?

Certainly, it is not clear why we should have to rely on the Federal Communications Commission rather than the ordinary pricing mechanism to decide whether a particular frequency should be used by the police, or for a radiotelephone, or for a taxi service, or for an oil company for geophysical exploration, or by a motion-picture company to keep in touch with its film stars, or for a broadcasting station. Indeed, the multiplicity of these varied uses would suggest that the ad- vantages to be derived from relying on the pricing mechanism would be especially great in this case.

Smythe also argued that the use of market controls depends on "the economic assumption that there is substantially perfect competition in the elec- tronics field." This is a somewhat extreme view. An allocation scheme costs some- thing to administer, will itself lead to a malallocation of resources, and may en- courage some monopolistic tendencies—all of which might well make us willing to tolerate a considerable amount of imperfect competition before substituting an allocation scheme for market controls. Nonetheless, the problem of monopoly is clearly one to be taken seriously. But this does not mean that frequencies should not be allocated by means of the market or that we should employ a special or- ganization, the Federal Communications Commission, for monopoly control in the broadcasting industry rather than the normal procedure. In fact, the antitrust laws do apply to broadcasting, and recently we have seen the Department of Justice taking action in a case in which the Federal Communications Commission had not thought it necessary to act.[17] The situation is not simply one in which there are two organizations to carry out one law. There are, in effect, two laws. The Federal Communications Commission is not bound by the antitrust laws and may refuse an application for a license because of the monopolistic practices of the applicant, even though these may not have been illegal under the antitrust laws. Thus, the broadcasting industry, while subject to the antitrust laws, is also subject to another not on the statute book but one invented by the Commission.[18]

It may be wondered whether such an involved system is required for the broadcasting industry, but this is not the question with which I am mainly concerned. To increase the competitiveness of the system, it may be that certain firms should not be allowed to operate broadcasting stations (or more than a certain number) and that certain practices should be prohibited; but this does not mean that those regarded as eligible to operate broadcasting stations ought not to pay for the frequencies they use. It is no doubt desirable to regulate monopolistic practices in the oil industry, but to do this it is not necessary that oil companies be presented with oil fields for nothing. Control of monopoly is a separate problem.

## THE PRICING SYSTEM AND THE ALLOCATION
## OF FREQUENCIES

There can be little doubt that the idea of using private property and the pricing system in the allocation of frequencies is one which is completely unfamiliar to most of those concerned with broadcasting policy. Consider, for example, the comment on the articles by Herzel and Smythe (discussed in the previous section) which appeared in the *Journal of the Federal Communications Bar Association* and which was therefore addressed to the group with the greatest knowledge of the problems of broadcasting regulation in the United States: "The whole discussion will be over the heads of most readers" (Recent Articles, 13 Fed. Com. B.J. 89 [1953]). Or consider the answers given by Frank Stanton, president of Columbia Broadcasting System and one of the most experienced and able men in the broadcasting industry, when Representative Rogers in a congressional inquiry

17. See *United States* v. *Radio Corp. of America*, 358 U.S. 334 (1959).
18. Compare the statement of the court in *Mansfield Journal Co.* v. *FCC,* 180 F.2d 28, 33 (App.D.C., 1950): "Whether Mansfield's activities do or do not amount to a positive violation of law, and neither this court nor the Federal Communications Commission is determining that question, they still may impair Mansfield's ability to serve the public. Thus, whether Mansfield's competitive practices were legal or illegal, in the strict sense, is not conclusive here. Monopoly in the mass communication of news and advertising is contrary to the public interest, even if not in terms proscribed by the antitrust laws."

raised the possibility of disposing of television channels by putting them up for the highest bids:

> ROGERS. Doctor, what would you think about a proposition of the Government taking all of these channels and opening them to competitive bidding and let the highest bidder take them at the best price the taxpayers could get out of it?
>
> STANTON. This is a novel theory and one to which I have not addressed myself during my operating career. This is certainly entirely contrary to what the Communication Act was in 1927 and as it was later amended.
>
> ROGERS. I know, but if the Government owns a tract of land on which you raise cattle, they charge a man for the use of the land.
>
> Why would it not be just as reasonable to charge a man to use the avenues of the air as it would be to use that pasture? Why should the people be giving one group something free and charging another group for something that is comparable?
>
> STANTON. This is a new and novel concept. I think it would have to be applied broadly to all uses of the spectrum and not just confined to television, if you will.
>
> ROGERS. I understand that. Do you not think that would really be free enterprise where the taxpayer would be getting the proceeds?
>
> STANTON. You have obviously given some thought to this and you are hitting me for the first time with it. (Hearings on Subscription Television before the House Committee on Interstate and Foreign Commerce, 85th Cong., 2d Sess. 434 [1958]).

This "novel theory" (novel with Adam Smith) is, of course, that the allocation of resources should be determined by the forces of the market rather than as a result of government decisions. Quite apart from the malallocations which are the result of political pressures, an administrative agency which attempts to perform the function normally carried out by the pricing mechanism operates under two handicaps. First of all, it lacks the precise monetary measure of benefit and cost provided by the market. Second, it cannot, by the nature of things, be in possession of all the relevant information possessed by the managers of every business which uses or might use radio frequencies, to say nothing of the preferences of consumers for the various goods and services in the production of which radio frequencies could be used. In fact, lengthy investigations are required to uncover part of this information, and decisions of the Federal Communications Commission emerge only after long delays, often extending to years.[19]

19. A former chairman of the Federal Communications Commission argued that it could not be intelligent in its regulation "if . . . [the Commission's] information lags behind the latest developments and policies of the industry—if the industry knows more than the government does" (Edelman [1950, p. 20]). But it is inevitable that the industry will know more than the Commission.

To simplify the task, the Federal Communications Commission adopts arbitrary rules. For example, it allocates certain ranges of frequencies (and only these) for certain specified uses. The situation in which the Commission finds itself was described in a recent speech by Commissioner Robert E. Lee. He explained that the question of undertaking a study of assignments below 890 mc was being considered, but whether this would be done was uncertain.

> There is considerable discussion of such a move within and without the Commission. . . . The examination of the more crowded spectrum below 890 mc presents an extremely difficult administrative problem. While this should be no excuse, I hope that all will appreciate the limitations of our overburdened staff, which, as a practical matter, must be given great weight.

And, after referring to a possible change in procedure, he added:

> I am finding it increasingly difficult to explain why a steel company in a large community, desperate for additional frequency space cannot use a frequency assigned, let us say, to the forest service in an area where there are no trees. (*Broadcasting*, February 4, 1957, p. 96)

This discussion should not be taken to imply that an administrative allocation of resources is inevitably worse than an allocation by means of the price mechanism. The operation of a market is not itself costless, and, if the costs of operating the market exceeded the costs of running the agency by a sufficiently large amount, we might be willing to acquiesce in the malallocation of resources resulting from the agency's lack of knowledge, inflexibility, and exposure to political pressure. But in the United States few people think that this would be so in most industries, and there is nothing about the broadcasting industry which would lead us to believe that the allocation of frequencies constitutes an exceptional case.

An example of how the nature of the pricing system is misunderstood in current discussions of broadcasting policy in the United States is furnished by a recent comment which appeared in the trade journal *Broadcasting*:

> In the TV field, lip service is given to a proposal that television "franchises" be awarded to the highest bidder among those who may be qualified. This is ridiculous on its face, since it would mean that choice outlets in prime markets would go to those with the most money. (February 24, 1958, p. 200)

First of all, it must be observed that resources do not go, in the American economic system, to those with the most money but to those who are willing to pay the most for them. The result is that, in the struggle for particular resources, men who earn $5,000 per annum are every day outbidding those who earn $50,000 per annum. To be convinced that this is so, we need only imagine a situation occurring in which all those who earned $50,000 or more per annum arrived at the stores one morning and, at the prices quoted, were able to buy everything in stock, with nothing left over for those with lower incomes. Next day we may be sure that the prices quoted would be higher and that those with higher incomes would be forced to reduce their purchases—a process which would continue as long as those with lower incomes were unable to spend all they wanted. The same system which enables a man with $1 million to obtain $1 million's worth of resources enables a man with $1,000 to obtain a $1,000's worth of resources. Of course, the existence of a pricing system does not insure that the distribution of money between persons (or families) is satisfactory. But this is not a question we need to consider in dealing with broadcasting policy. Insofar as the ability to pay for frequencies or channels depends on the distribution of funds, it is the distribution not between persons but between firms that is relevant. And here the ethical problem does not arise. All that matters is whether the distribution of funds contributes to efficiency, and there is every reason to suppose that, broadly speaking, it does. Those firms which use funds profitably find it easy to get more; those which do not, find it difficult. The capital market does not work perfectly, but the general tendency is clear. In any case, it is doubtful whether the Federal Communications Commission has, in general, awarded frequencies to firms which are in a relatively unfavorable position from the point of view of raising capital. The inquiries which the Commission conducts into the financial qualifications of applicants must, in fact, tend in the opposite direction.[20] And if we take as examples of "choice outlets in prime markets" network-affiliated television stations in the six largest metropolitan areas in the United States on the basis of population (New York, Chicago, Los Angeles, Philadelphia, Detroit, and San Francisco), we find that five stations are owned by American Broadcasting—Paramount Theatres, Inc., four by the National Broadcasting Company (a subsidiary of the Radio Corporation of America), four by the Columbia Broadcasting System, Inc., and one each by the Westinghouse Broadcasting Company (a subsidiary of the Westinghouse Electric Corporation), the Storer Broadcasting Company, and three newspaper publishing concerns.[21] It would be difficult to argue that these are firms which have been unduly handicapped in their growth by their inability to raise capital.

20. On the Commission's policies with regard to financial qualifications, consult Edelman (1950, pp. 62–64), and Warner (1948, p. 22a).

21. The first four firms are so well known as not to require any notation. The Storer Broadcasting Company owns television stations in Toledo, Cleveland, Detroit, Atlanta, and Wilmington and radio stations in Toledo, Cleveland, Detroit, Philadelphia, Wheeling, Atlanta, and Miami. Of the three stations owned by newspaper publishing concerns, one in Philadelphia is owned by Triangle Publications (which publishes the Philadelphia Inquirer and other papers, owns four other television stations and some radio stations), one in Detroit is owned by the publisher of the *Detroit News*, and one in San Francisco is owned by the publisher of the *San Francisco Chronicle*.

The Supreme Court appears to have assumed that it was impossible to use the pricing mechanism when dealing with a resource which was in limited supply. This is not true. Despite all the efforts of art dealers, the number of Rembrandts existing at a given time is limited; yet such paintings are commonly disposed of by auction. But the works of dead painters are not unique in being in fixed supply. If we take a broad enough view, the supply of all factors of production is seen to be fixed (the amount of land, the size of the population, etc.). Of course, this is not the way we think of the supply of land or labor. Since we are usually concerned with a particular problem, we think not in terms of the total supply but rather of the supply available for a particular use. Such a procedure is not only practically more useful; it also tells us more about the processes of adjustment at work in the market. Although the quantity of a resource may be limited in total, the quantity that can be made available to a particular use is variable. Producers in a particular industry can obtain more of any resource they require by buying it on the market, although they are unlikely to be able to obtain considerable additional quantities unless they bid up the price, thereby inducing firms in other industries to curtail their use of the resource. This is the mechanism which governs the allocation of factors of production in almost all industries. Notwithstanding the almost unanimous contrary view, there is nothing in the technology of the broadcasting industry which prevents the use of the same mechanism. Indeed, use of the pricing system is made particularly easy by a circumstance to which Smythe draws our special attention, namely, that the broadcasting industry uses but a small proportion of "spectrum space." A broadcasting industry, forced to bid for frequencies, could draw them away from other industries by raising the price it was willing to pay. It is impossible to say whether the result of introducing the pricing system would be that the broadcasting industry would obtain more frequencies than are allocated to it by the Federal Communications Commission. Not having had, in the past, a market for frequencies, we do not know what these various industries would pay for them. Similarly, we do not know for what frequencies the broadcasting industry would be willing to outbid these other industries. All we can say is that the broadcasting industry would be able to obtain all the existing frequencies it now uses (and more) if it were willing to pay a price equal to the contribution which they could make to production elsewhere. This is saying nothing more than that the broadcasting industry would be able to obtain frequencies on the same basis as it now obtains its labor, buildings, land, and equipment.

A thoroughgoing employment of the pricing mechanism for the allocation of radio frequencies would, of course, mean that the various governmental authorities, which are at present such heavy users of these frequencies, would also be required to pay for them. This may appear to be unnecessary, since payment would have to be made to some other government agency appointed to act as custodian of frequencies. What was paid out of one government pocket would simply go into another. It may also seem inappropriate that the allocation of resources for such purposes as national defense or the preservation of human life should be subjected to a monetary test. While it would be entirely possible to exclude from the pricing process all frequencies which government departments consider they need and to confine pricing to frequencies available for the private sector, there would seem to be compelling reasons for not doing so. A government department, in making up its mind whether or not to undertake a particular activity, should weigh against the benefits this would confer, the costs which are also involved: that is, the value of the production elsewhere which would otherwise be enjoyed. In the case of a government activity which is regarded as so essential as to justify any sacrifice, it is still desirable to minimize the cost of any particular project. If the use of a frequency which if used industrially would contribute goods worth $1 million could be avoided by the construction of a wire system or the purchase of reserve vehicles costing $100,000, it is better that the frequency should not be used, however essential the project. It is the merit of the pricing system that, in these circumstances, a government department (unless very badly managed) would not use the frequency if made to pay for it. Some hesitation in accepting this argument may come from the thought that, though it might be better to provide government departments with the funds necessary to purchase the resources they need, it by no means follows that Congress will do this. Consequently, it might be better to accept the waste inherent in the present system rather than suffer the disadvantages which would come from government departments having inadequate funds to pay for frequencies. This, of course, assumes that government departments are, in general, denied adequate funds by Congress, but it is not clear that this is true, above all for the defense departments, which, at present, use the bulk of the frequencies. Furthermore, it has to be remembered that a pricing scheme for frequencies would not involve any budgetary strain, since all government payments would be exactly balanced by the receipts of the agency responsible for disposing of frequencies, and there would be a net gain from the payments by private firms. In any case, such considerations do not apply to the introduction of pricing in the private sector and, in particular, for the broadcasting industry.

The desire to preserve government ownership of radio frequencies coupled with an unwillingness to require any payment for the use of these frequencies has had one consequence which has caused some uneasiness. A station operator who is granted a license to use a particular frequency in a particular place may, in fact, be granted a very valuable right, one for which he would be willing to pay a large sum of money and which he would be forced to pay if others could bid for the frequency. This provision of a valuable resource without charge naturally raises the income of station operators above what it would have been in competitive conditions. It would require a very detailed investigation to determine the extent to which private operators of radio and television stations have been enriched as a result of this policy. But part of the extremely high return on the capital invested in certain radio and television stations has undoubtedly been due to this failure to charge for the use of the frequency. Occasionally, when a station is sold, it is possible to glimpse what is involved. Strictly, of course, all that can be sold is the station and its organization; the frequency is public property, and the grant of a license gives no rights of any sort in that frequency. Furthermore, transfers of the ownership of radio and television stations have to be approved by the Federal Communications Commission. However, the Commission almost always approves such negotiated transfers, and, when these take place, there can be little doubt that often a great part of the purchase price is in fact payment for obtaining the use of the frequency. Thus when WNEW in New York City was sold in 1957 for $5 million or WDTV in Pittsburgh in 1955 for $10 million of WCAV (AM, FM, and TV) in Philadelphia in 1958 for $20 million, it is possible to doubt that it would cost $5 million or $10 million or $20 million to duplicate the transmitter, studio equipment, furniture, and the organization, which nominally is what is being purchased.[22] The result of sales at such prices is, of course, to reduce the return earned by the new owners to (or at any rate nearer to) the competitive level. When, as happened in the early days of radio regulation but less often since the Commission refused to sanction transfers at a price much more than the value of the physical assets and the organization being acquired, the effect was simply to distribute the benefits derived from this free use of public property more widely among the business community:  to enable the new as well as the old owners to share in it. I do not wish to discuss whether such a redistribution of the gain is socially desirable. My point is different:  there is no reason why there should be any gain to redistribute.

The extraordinary gain accruing to radio and television station operators as a result of the present system of allocating frequencies becomes apparent when stations are sold.[23] Even before the 1927 Act was passed, it was recognized that stations were transferred from one owner to another at prices which implied that the right to a license was being sold.[24] Occasionally, references to this problem are found in the literature, but the subject has not been discussed extensively. In part, I think this derives from the fact that the only solution to the problem of excessive profits was thought to be rate regulation or profit control.[25] Such solutions were unlikely to gain support for a number of reasons. Although in the early days of the broadcasting industry it was commonly thought that it would be treated as another public utility, this view was later largely abandoned. An attempt to make broadcasters common carriers failed. And broadcasting has come to be thought of, so far as its business operations are concerned, as an unregulated

22. See the Annual Report of the Federal Communications Commission for 1957, p. 123, and for 1958, p. 121.
23. See "Radio and Television Station Transfers:  Adequacy of Supervision under the Federal Communications Act" (1955) and Warner (1948, ch. 5). Compare Dill (1938, pp. 208–209).
24. See Hearings on S. 1 and S. 1754, Radio Control, before the Senate Committee on Interstate Commerce, 69th Cong., 1st Sess. 38–47 (1926).
25. Consult Stewart (1937), Hettinger (1939), Salsbury (1940), and Lissner (1946).

industry. As the Supreme Court has said: ". . . the field of broadcasting is one of free competition." (*FCC* v. *Sanders Bros. Radio Station*, 309 U.S. 470, 474 [1940] ). In any case, the determination of the rates to be charged or the level of profits to be allowed would not seem an easy matter, although it has been claimed that "it should be possible for resource and tax economists to develop norms for levying such special franchise taxes" (Lissner 1946). Furthermore, rate or profit regulation with the concomitant need for control of the quality of the programs is hardly an attractive prospect.

It is an odd fact that the obvious way out of these difficulties, which is to make those wishing to use frequencies bid for them (allowing the profits earned to be determined not by a regulatory commission but by the forces of competition), received no attention in the literature, so far as I know, until comparatively recently. Herzel's article contains the first reference I have found. More recently, the suggestion has been mentioned on a number of occasions. In 1958 the proposal for bidding made its appearance in a bill introduced by Representative Henry S. Reuss. This bill would have established an order of priority for the various categories of applicants for radio and television licenses but contained the provision that, where there was more than one applicant falling into the highest category, the Federal Communications Commission would then grant the license to the highest bidder in that category, with the money to be "deposited in the Treasury of the United States to the credit of miscellaneous receipts." The same procedure would be applied when a license was transferred. Reuss explained: "The airwaves are the public domain, and under such circumstances a decision should be made in favor of the taxpayers, just as it is when the government takes bids for the logging franchise on public timberland."[26]

It is to be expected that even so modest a suggestion for bidding as that of Reuss would not be welcomed. From the earliest days of radio regulation suggestions have been made that those holding radio licenses should pay a fee to the regulating authority, but this has never been incorporated in the law. When, a few years ago, the Federal Communications Commission announced that it was considering a proposal that radio and television licenses should pay a fee to cover the costs of the licensing process (that is, the cost of the Federal Communications Commission), the Senate Committee on Interstate and Foreign Commerce quickly adopted a resolution suggesting that the Commission should suspend consideration of this proposal for the time being, since "the proposal for license fees for broadcasting stations raises basic questions with regard to the fundamental philosophy of regulation under the Communications Act. . ." (100 Cong. Rec. 3783 [1954] ).

It is not easy to understand the feeling of hostility to the idea that people should pay for the facilities they use. It is true that this attitude has been supported by the argument that it was technologically impossible to charge for

26. Press release dated April 14, 1958, from the office of Congressman Henry S. Reuss. See H.R. 11893, 85th Cong., 2d Sess. (1958).

the use of frequencies, but this is clearly wrong. It is difficult to avoid the conclusion that the widespread opposition to the use of the pricing system for the allocation of frequencies can be explained only by the fact that the possibility of using it has never been seriously faced.

## PRIVATE PROPERTY AND THE ALLOCATION OF FREQUENCIES

If the right to use a frequency is to be sold, the nature of that right would have to be precisely defined. A simple answer would be to leave the situation essentially as it is now: the broadcaster would buy the right to use, for a certain period, an assigned frequency to transmit signals at a given power for certain hours from a transmitter located in a particular place. This would simply superimpose a payment on to the present system. It would certainly make it possible for the person or firm who is to use a frequency to be determined in the market. But the enforcement of such detailed regulations for the operation of stations as are now imposed by the Federal Communications Commission would severely limit the extent to which the way the frequency was used could be determined by the forces of the market.

It might be argued that this is by no means an unusual situation, since the rights acquired when one buys, say, a piece of land, are determined not by the forces of supply and demand but by the law of property in land. But this is by no means the whole truth. Whether a newly discovered cave belongs to the man who discovered it, the man on whose land the entrance to the cave is located, or the man who owns the surface under which the cave is situated is no doubt dependent on the law of property. But the law merely determines the person with whom it is necessary to make a contract to obtain the use of the cave. Whether the cave is used for storing bank records, as a natural gas reservoir, or for growing mushrooms depends not on the law of property, but on whether the bank, the natural gas corporation, or the mushroom concern will pay the most in order to be able to use the cave. One of the purposes of the legal system is to establish that clear delimitation of rights on the basis of which the transfer and recombination of rights can take place through the market. In the case of radio, it should be possible for someone who is granted the use of a frequency to arrange to share it with someone else, with whatever adjustments to hours of operation, power, location and kind of transmitter, etc., as may be mutually agreed upon; or when the right initially acquired is the shared use of a frequency (and in certain cases the FCC has permitted only shared usage), it should not be made impossible for one user to buy out the rights of the other users so as to obtain an exclusive usage.

The main reason for government regulation of the radio industry was to prevent interference. It is clear that if signals are transmitted simultaneously on a given frequency by several people, the signals would interfere with each other and would make reception of the messages transmitted by any one person difficult, if not impossible. The use of a piece of land simultaneously for growing wheat and as a parking lot would produce similar results. As we have seen in an earlier section, the way this situation is avoided is to create property rights (rights, that is, to exclusive use) in land. The creation of similar rights in the use of frequencies would enable the problem to be solved in the same way in the radio industry.

The advantage of establishing exclusive rights to use a resource when that use does not harm others (apart from the fact that they are excluded from using it) is easily understood. However, the case appears to be different when it concerns an action which harms others directly. For example, a radio operator may use a frequency in such a way as to cause interference to those using adjacent frequencies.

Let us start our analysis of this situation by considering the case of *Sturges* v. *Bridgman* (11 Ch. D. 852 [1879]), which illustrates the basic issues. A confectioner had used certain premises for his business for a great many years. When a doctor came and occupied a neighboring property, the working of the confectioner's machinery caused the doctor no harm until, some eight years later, he built a consulting room at the end of his garden, right against the confectioner's premises. Then it was found that noise and vibrations caused by the machinery disturbed the doctor in his work. The doctor then brought an action and succeeded in securing an injunction preventing the confectioner from using his machinery. What the courts had, in fact, to decide was whether the doctor had the right to impose additional costs on the confectioner through compelling him to install new machinery, or move to a new location, or whether the confectioner had the right to impose additional costs on the doctor through compelling him to do his consulting somewhere else on his premises or at another location.[27] What this example shows is that there is no analytical difference between the right to use a resource without direct harm to others and the right to conduct operations in such a way as to produce direct harm to others. In each case something is denied to others: in one case, use of a resource; in the other, use of a mode of operation.[28] This example also brings out the reciprocal nature of the relationship which tends to be ignored by economists who, following Pigou, approach the problem in terms of a difference between private and social products but fail to make clear that the suppression of the harm which A inflicts on B inevitably inflicts harm on A. The problem is to avoid the more serious harm. This aspect is

27. Another possibility is that the doctor or confectioner might abandon his activity altogether.

28. In the case of *Sturges* v. *Bridgman*, the situation would not have been analytically different had the dispute concerned the ownership of a piece of land lying between the two premises on which either the doctor could have installed his laboratory or the confectioner could have installed his machinery.

clearly brought out in *Sturges* v. *Bridgman*, and the case would not have been different in essentials if the doctor's complaint had been about smoke pollution rather than noise and vibrations.

Once the legal rights of the parties are established, negotiation is possible to modify the arrangements envisaged in the legal ruling, if the likelihood of being able to do so makes it worthwhile to incur the costs involved in negotiation. The doctor would be willing to waive his right if the confectioner would pay him a sum of money greater than the additional costs he would have incurred in carrying out his consulting at another location (which we will assume to be $200). The confectioner would be willing to pay up to an amount slightly less than the additional costs imposed on him by the decision of the court in order to induce the doctor to waive his rights (which we will assume to be $100). With the figures given, the doctor would not accept less than $200, and the confectioner would not pay more than $100, and the doctor would not waive his right. But consider the situation if the confectioner had won the case (as well he might). In these circumstances the confectioner would be willing to waive his right if he could obtain more than $100, and the doctor would be willing to pay slightly less than $200 to induce the confectioner to do so. Thus it should be possible to strike a bargain which would result in the confectioner's waiving his right. This hypothetical example shows that the delimitation of rights is an essential prelude to market transactions; but the ultimate result (which maximizes the value of production) is independent of the legal decision.[29]

What this analysis demonstrates, so far as the radio industry is concerned, is that there is no analytical difference between the problem of interference between operators on a single frequency and that of interference between operators on adjacent frequencies. The latter problem, like the former, can be solved by delimiting the rights of operators to transmit signals which interfere, or might potentially interfere, with those of others. Once this is done, it can be left to market transactions to bring an optimum utilization of rights. It is sometimes implied that the aim of regulation in the radio industry should be to minimize interference. But this would be wrong. The aim should be to maximize output. All property rights interfere with the ability of people to use resources. What

---

29. It is, of course, true that the distribution of wealth as between the doctor and the confectioner was affected by the decision, which is why questions of equity bulk so largely in such cases. Indeed, if the efficiency with which the economic system worked was completely independent of the legal position, this would be all that mattered. But this is not so. First of all, the law may be such as to make certain desirable market transactions impossible. This is, indeed, my chief criticism of the present American law of radio communication. Second, it may impose costly and time-consuming procedures. Third, the legal delimitation of rights provides the starting point for the rearrangement of rights through market transactions. Such transactions are not costless, with a result that the initial delimitation of rights may be maintained even though some other would be more efficient. Or, even if the original position is modified, the most efficient delimitation of rights may not be attained. Finally, a waste of resources may occur when the criteria used by the courts to delimit rights result in resources being employed solely to establish a claim.

has to be insured is that the gain from interference more than offsets the harm it produces. There is no reason to suppose that the optimum situation is one in which there is no interference. In general, as the distance from a radio station increases, it becomes more and more difficult to receive its signals. At some point, people will decide that it is not worthwhile to incur costs involved in receiving the station's signals. A local station operating on the same frequency might be easily received by these same people. But if this station operated simultaneously with the first one, people living in some region intermediate between the stations may be unable to receive signals from either station. These people would be better off if either station stopped operating and there was no interference; but then those living in the neighborhood of one of these other stations would suffer. It is not clear that the solution in which there is no interference is necessarily preferable.

In some circumstances it has been suggested that cost considerations may lead to a minimizing of interference. Thus it has been said of mobile radio:

> Dollar discipline is a very effective force which prevents unwarranted overdesign of land mobile communications system. Vehicular communication is a business tool and like any other tool, the return on investment suffers if excessive overcapacity is provided. Experience has shown that land mobile station licensees are not willing to pay for equipment to provide coverage significantly in excess of their requirements. This attitude serves to effectively reduce adjacent area, co-channel interference to a minimum.[30]

But cost considerations alone cannot always be relied upon to bring about such happy results. The reduction of interference on adjacent frequencies may require costly improvements in equipment, and operators on one frequency could hardly be expected to incur such costs for the benefit of others if the rights of those operating on adjacent frequencies have not been determined. The institution of private property plus the pricing system would resolve these conflicts. The operator whose signals were interfered with, if he had the right to stop such interference, would be willing to forego this right if he were paid more than the amount by which the value of his service was decreased by this interference or the costs which he would have to incur to offset it. The other operator would be willing to pay, in order to be allowed to interfere, an amount up to the costs of suppressing the interference or the decrease in the value of the service he could provide if unable to use his transmitter in a way which resulted in interference. Or, alternatively, if this operator had the right to cause interference, he would be willing to desist if he were paid more than the costs of suppressing the interference or the decrease in the value of the service he could provide if inter-

30. Testimony of Motorola Inc., Statutory Inquiry into the Allocation of Frequencies to the Various Non-Government Services in the Radio Spectrum between 25 mc and 890 mc, FCC Docket No. 11997, March 30, 1959, p. 29.

ference were barred. And the operator whose signals were interfered with would be willing to pay to stop this interference an amount up to the decrease in the value of his service which it causes or the costs he has to incur to offset the interference. Either way, the result would be the same. It is the problem of the confectioner's noise and vibrations all over again.

The fact that actions might have harmful effects on others has been shown to be no obstacle to the introduction of property rights. But it was possible to reach this unequivocal result because the conflicts of interest were between individuals. When large numbers of people are involved, the argument for the institution of property rights is weakened and that for general regulations becomes stronger. The example commonly given by economists, again following Pigou, of a situation which calls for such regulation is that created by smoke pollution. Of course, if there were only one source of smoke and only one person were harmed, no new complication would be involved; it would not differ from the vibration case discussed earlier. But if many people are harmed and there are several sources of pollution, it is more difficult to reach a satisfactory solution through the market. When the transfer of rights has to come about as a result of market transactions carried out between large numbers of people or organizations acting jointly, the process of negotiation may be so difficult and time-consuming as to make such transfers a practical impossibility. Even the enforcement of rights through the courts may not be easy. It may be costly to discover who it is that is causing the trouble. And, when it is not in the interest of any single person or organization to bring suit, the problems involved in arranging joint actions represent a further obstacle. As a practical matter, the market may become too costly to operate.

In these circumstances it may be preferable to impose special regulations (whether embodied in a statute or brought about as a result of the rulings of an administrative agency). Such regulations state what people must or must not do. When this is done, the law directly determines the location of economic activities, methods of production, and so on. Thus the problem of smoke pollution may be dealt with by regulations which specify the kind of heating and power equipment which can be used in houses and factories or which confine manufacturing establishments to certain districts by zoning arrangements. The aim of such regulation should not, of course, be to eliminate smoke pollution but to bring about the optimum amount of smoke pollution. The gains from reducing it have to be matched with the loss in production due to the restrictions in choice of methods of production, etc. The conditions which make such regulation desirable do not change the nature of the problem. And, in principle, the solution to be sought is that which would have been achieved if the institution of private property and the pricing mechanism were working well. Of course, as the making of such special regulations is dependent on the political organization, the regulatory process will suffer from the disadvantages mentioned in the previous section. But this merely means that, before turning to special regulations, one should tolerate a worse functioning market than would otherwise be the case. It does not mean that there should be no such regulation. Nor should it be thought that, because some rights are determined by regulation, there cannot be others which can be modified by contract. That zoning and other regulations apply to houses does not mean that there should not be private property in houses. Businessmen usually find themselves both subject to regulation and possessed of rights which may be transferred or modified by contracts with others.

There is no reason why users of radio frequencies should not be in the same position as other businessmen. There would not appear, for example, to be any need to regulate the relations between users of the same frequency. Once the rights of potential users have been determined initially, the rearrangement of rights could be left to the market. The simplest way of doing this would undoubtedly be to dispose of the use of a frequency to the highest bidder, thus leaving the subdivision of the use of the frequency to subsequent market transactions. Nor is it clear that the relations between users of adjacent frequencies will necessarily call for special regulation. It may well be that several people would normally be involved in a single transaction if conflicts of interests between users of adjacent frequencies are to be settled through the market. But, though an increase in the number of people involved increases the cost of carrying out a transaction, we know from experience that it is quite practicable to have market transactions which involve a multiplicity of parties. Whether the number of parties normally involved in transactions involving users of adjacent frequencies would be unduly large and call for special regulation, only experience could show. *Some* special regulation would certainly be required. For example, some types of medical equipment can apparently be operated in such a way as to cause interference on many frequencies and over long distances. In such a case, a regulation limiting the power of the equipment and requiring shielding would probably be desirable. It is also true that the need for wide bands of frequencies for certain purposes may require the exercise of the power of eminent domain; but this does not raise a problem different from that encountered in other fields. It is easy to embrace the idea that the interconnection between the ways in which frequencies are used raise special problems not found elsewhere or, at least, not to the same degree. But this view is not likely to survive the study of a book on the law of torts or on the law of property in which will be found set out the many (and often extraordinary) ways in which one person's actions can affect the use which others can make of their property.

If the problems faced in the broadcasting industry are not out of the ordinary, it may be asked why was not the usual solution (a mixture of transferable rights plus regulation) adopted for this industry? There can be little doubt that, left to themselves, the courts would have solved the problems of the radio industry in much the same whay as they had solved similar problems in other industries. In the early discussions of radio law an attempt was made to bring the problems within the main corpus of existing law. The problem of radio interference was examined by analogy with electric-wire interference, water rights, trade marks, noise nuisances, the problem of acquiring title to ice from public ponds, and so on. It was, for example, pointed out that a "receiving set is merely a device for decoying to the human ear signals which otherwise would not reach it," and an analogy was drawn with a case in which one man had maintained a decoy for wild ducks but another on neighboring land had frightened the ducks away by shooting, so that they avoided the decoy. Some of the analogies were no doubt fanciful, but most of them presented essentially the same problem as that posed by radio interference. And when the problem came before the courts, there seems to have been little difficulty in reaching a decision.[31] No doubt, in time, statutes prescribing some special regulation would also have been required. But this line of development was stopped by the passage of the 1927 Act, which established a complete regulatory system.[32]

Support for the 1927 Act came, in part, from a belief that no other solution was possible, and, as we have seen, the rationale which has developed since certainly largely reflects this view. But some of those who favored government regulation in the early 1920s did so in order to prevent the establishment of property rights in frequencies. Their reasons for wanting government regulation were vividly expressed by Walter S. Rogers:

> There is no question that certain private radio companies believe that by something analogous to what we call "Squatters' Rights" they can secure an actual out-and-out ownership of the right to use wave lengths, and they do not want to get the right to use wave lengths through a license from any government or as a result of any international agreement. They want to hold completely the right to the use of wave lengths which they employ in their services. In a certain sense the development of radio has opened up a new domain comparable to the discovery of a hitherto unknown continent. No one can foresee with certitude the possible development of the transmission of energy through space. Really great stakes are being gambled for. And private interests are trying to obtain control of wave lengths and establish private property claims to them precisely as though a new continent were opened up to them and they were securing great tracts of land in outright ownership. (Rogers 1924, p. 254)[33]

31. See Davis (1927, particularly ch. 7). Articles dealing with this question are: Rowley (1927), Taugher (1928), Dyer (1932). In the case of *Tribune Co.* v. *Oak Leaves Broadcasting Station* (Cir. Ct., Cook County, Illinois, 1926), reproduced in 68 Cong. Rec. 216 (1926), it was held that the operator of an existing station had a sufficient property right, acquired by priority, to enjoin a newcomer from using a frequency so as to cause any material interference.

32. Although attempts were made to assert property rights in frequencies after the establishment of the Federal Radio Commission, such claims were not sustained. See Warner (1948, p. 543).

33. Rogers was adviser to the American Delegation to the Peace Conference in Paris, 1919. Compare Childs (1924).

Similar views were held in Congress. Harry P. Warner has explained that during the period before the 1927 Act,

> the gravest fears were expressed by legislators, and those generally charged with the administration of communications . . . that government regulation of an effective sort might be permanently prevented through the accrual of property rights in licenses or means of access, and that thus franchises of the value of millions of dollars might be established for all time. (1948, p. 540)

It may be that in some cases these views reflected a dislike of the institution of private property as such, but in the main what seems to have been feared is that private persons and organizations might establish property rights in frequencies without making any payment for appropriating what was called "the last of the public domain." The view that property rights in frequencies should be acquired in an orderly fashion and that those acquiring these rights should be required to pay for them is clearly one which commands respect. But this is not what happened as a result of the 1927 Act. In fact, government regulation brought about the very results which some of its supporters had sought to avoid. Because no charge has been made for the use of frequencies, franchises worth millions of dollars have been created, have been bought and sold, and have served to enrich those to whom they were first granted. Intertwined with the dislike of property rights acquired by priority of use was the fear that monopolies might be established. But, as we have seen (although in discussions of broadcasting policy it is often overlooked), it is not necessary to abolish the institution of private property in order to control the growth of monopolies.

When we contemplate the simple misunderstandings which are rife in discussions of government policy toward the radio industry, it is difficult to resist the conclusion that one factor that has helped to bring this about is terminological in character.[34] I have spoken, following the normal usage, of the allocation of frequencies (or the use of frequencies) and of the establishment of property rights in frequencies (or the use of frequencies). But this way of speaking is liable to mislead. Every regular wave motion may be described as a frequency. The various musical notes correspond to frequencies in sound waves; the various colors correspond to frequencies in light waves. But it has not been thought necessary to allocate to different persons or to create property rights in the notes of the musical scale or the colors of the rainbow. To handle the problem arising because one person's use of a sound or light wave may have effects on others, we establish the rights which people have to make sounds which others may hear or to do things which others may see.

Clarity of thought is even more difficult to achieve when we speak not of ownership of frequencies but of ownership of the ether, the medium

34. In the development of my ideas on this subject, I was greatly helped by an article by Segal and Warner (1947).

through which the wave travels. James G. McCain has argued that the "radio wave [should] be clearly distinguished from the medium through which it is transmitted. Metaphorically, it is the difference between a train and a tunnel." His reason for making this distinction is that it affords the "most satisfactory" basis for holding radio communication to be interstate commerce. His argument, briefly, is that the ether by reason of its omnipresence and the use to which it is devoted constitutes a natural channel for interstate commerce, thus making federal regulation of radio communication constitutional under the commerce clause (McCain 1940).[35] The Senate once declared the ether or its use to be "the inalienable possession" of the United States, and today all those to whom radio or television licenses are granted have to sign a waiver of any right not only to the use of a frequency but also to the use of the ether. This attempt to nationalize the ether has not been without its critics. There is some doubt whether the ether exists. Certainly, its properties correspond exactly to those of something which does not exist, a tunnel without any edges. And Stephen Davis has remarked: "Whoever claims ownership of a thing or substance may very properly be required to prove existence before discussing title" (1927, p. 15).[36]

What does not seem to have been understood is that what is being allocated by the Federal Communications Commission, or, if there were a market, what would be sold, is the right to use a piece of equipment to transmit signals in a particular way. Once the question is looked at in this way, it is unnecessary to think in terms of ownership of frequencies or the ether. Earlier we discussed a case in which it had to be decided whether a confectioner had the right to use machinery which caused noise and vibrations in a neighboring house. It would not have facilitated our analysis of the case if it had been discussed in terms of who owned sound waves or vibrations or the medium (whatever it is) through which sound waves or vibrations travel. Yet this is essentially what is done in the radio industry. The reason why this way of thinking has become so dominant in discussions of radio law is that it seems to have developed by using the analogy of the law of airspace. In fact, the law of radio and television has commonly been treated as part of the law of the air.[37] It is not suggested that this approach need lead to the wrong answers, but it tends to obscure the question that is being decided. Thus, whether we have the right to shoot over another man's land has been thought of as depending on who owns the airspace over the land.[38] It would

35. The grounds on which radio communication has been held to be interstate commerce are not those advanced by McCain. As he explains, the reasons given by the courts for holding radio communication to be interstate commerce are that radio waves cross state lines (even though the communication is intrastate) and potentially interfere with interstate communication. The advantage of McCain's approach would appear to be that it would allow federal regulation of intrastate communication which interferes with no one. Other articles dealing with this question are: Fletcher (1940) and Kennedy (1932).

36. See also the article by Segal and Warner (1947, pp. 112–114).

37. See, for example, Jome (1928). The *Air Law Review* dealt with radio law and aviation law. And lawbooks, for example, Manion (1950), are often organized in the same way.

38. See Ball (1928), Niles (1934), and Prosser (1941).

be simpler to discuss what we should be allowed to do with a gun. As we saw earlier, we cannot shoot a gun even on our own land when the effect is to frighten ducks that a neighbor is engaged in decoying. And we all know that there are many other restrictions on the uses of a gun. The problem confronting the radio industry is that signals transmitted by one person may interfere with those transmitted by another. It can be solved by delimiting the rights which various persons possess. How far this delimitation of rights should come about as a result of a strict regulation and how far as a result of transactions on the market is a question that can be answered only on the basis of practical experience. But there is good reason to believe that the present system, which relies exclusively on regulation and in which private property and the pricing system play no part, is not the best solution.

In defining property rights, it would be necessary to take into account the existence of international agreements on the use of radio frequencies.[39] Such agreements do not, of course, prevent bidding by individuals and firms for the facilities which have been allocated to the United States. But, to the extent that the ways in which frequencies can be used are specified in the agreements, the transfer and recombination of rights through the market are restricted. However, the reservation contained in the present agreements by which frequencies can be used "in derogation of the table of frequency allocations" when this does not cause harmful interference to stations in foreign countries operating in conformity with the table would seem to permit considerable flexibility in the way frequencies are used. (There is no legal restriction on military use of radio frequencies.)[40] The aim of the United States government should be to secure the maximum freedom for countries to use radio frequencies as they wish. To read the intentions of a government from the proceedings of an international conference is obviously hazardous. But on the surface it is not clear that the United States government wished to secure this maximum of freedom. In the conference of 1947, the group of countries led by the United States "wanted to take the frequency requirements of all the countries of the world and fit them 'by engineering principles' into the available frequency spectrum." The group led by the Soviet Union "wanted to use the old international frequency list as a point of departure, assigning frequencies on the basis of dates of notification" (Codding 1955, p. 94). In effect, the Soviet Union seemed to want the establishment of international property rights based on priority. Since the Soviet Union had registered notifications of claim to large parts of the radio spectrum, it is probably true that the acceptance of their proposals would have given the Soviet Union advantages. But it also seems clear from the conference proceedings that the Soviet Union was unwilling to give the details required for an assessment of its needs and did not wish to be bound in its internal arrangements by the decisions of an international conference.[41] In the National

---

39. For a detailed discussion of international agreements on the use of radio frequencies, see Codding (1952) and an article by the same author (1955).
   40. See Codding (1955).
   41. See Codding (1952).

Missile Conference held in Washington in May, 1959, two scientists (British and American) called for "the creation of an international communications commission to administer and police future myriad uses of the electronics spectrum in space communications, overseas space television, weather reports and other activities" (*Broadcasting*, June 1, 1959, p. 79). If this international body is to be patterned after the Federal Communications Commission, there are obvious dangers in this proposal. It would not be wise for the United States to press (possibly against Russian opposition) for the establishment of an international planning system which would make it difficult or impossible to operate a free-enterprise system in the United States.

## THE PRESENT POSITION

The Federal Communications Commission has recently come into public prominence as a result of disclosures before the House Subcommittee on Legislative Oversight, concerning the extent to which pressure is brought to bear on the Commission by politicians and businessmen (who often use methods of dubious propriety) with a view to influencing its decisions.[42] That this should be happening is hardly surprising. When rights, worth millions of dollars, are awarded to one businessman and denied to others, it is no wonder if some applicants become overanxious and attempt to use whatever influence they have (political and otherwise), particularly as they can never be sure what pressure the other applicants may be exerting. Some of the suggestions for improving the situation—for example, the enactment of a statutory code of ethics—may have merit in themselves. Others, such as the creation of administrative courts, may secure greater honesty at the expense of efficiency. But what needs to be emphasized is that the problem, so far as the Federal Communications Commission is concerned, largely arises because of a failure to charge for the rights granted. If these rights were disposed of to the highest bidder, the main reason for these improper activities would disappear. In the panel discussion on the Administrative Process and Ethical Questions held by the Subcommittee, a similar point of view was expressed by Clark Byse of the Harvard Law School:

> A TV license in some areas often is worth millions of dollars. The Administrative agency dispensing this bonanza operates under the broadest type of congressional direction. The agency is told to grant

42. See Hearings on Investigation of Regulatory Commissions and Agencies before the Special Subcommittee and Agencies before the Special Subcommittee on Legislative Oversight of the House Committee on Interstate and Foreign Commerce, 85th Cong., 2d Sess. (1958). The Subcommittee was not simply concerned with the Federal Communications Commission but with the operations of all the independent regulatory commissions. The publicity received and the emphasis on improper personal conduct in the hearings was due to the activities of Dr. Bernard Schwartz, chief counsel of the Subcommittee, who exerted himself with a zeal which went beyond the call of duty and whose services with the Subcommittee were finally terminated. See Schwartz (1959).

an application if public convenience, interest, or necessity will be served. It is true that the Commission has developed a number of criteria to govern its exercise of this broad grant of power. But the criteria are so general and numerous that it is often difficult to determine whether Commission action is the product of reasoned deliberation or of caprice. Would it not have been better if Congress had established some basic criteria concerning competence, diversification of mass communication media, and monopoly, and then had provided that the licenses should go to the highest bidder? There may be drawbacks to this suggestion in the TV area, and the device of automatic criteria perhaps cannot be widely adopted. But certainly the goal should be to limit discretion to the narrowest legitimate limits, particularly when the legislation authorizes distribution of a bonanza or contemplates the substitution of an administrative decision for a decision which would otherwise be determined by the forces of competition.[43]

At the present time the idea of using the pricing mechanism in the radio industry is coldly received, and it is not surprising that Byse's suggestion was not taken up in the report of the Subcommittee. In part, this hostile attitude is a reflection of the misunderstandings which have been discussed in previous sections;[44] but there is more to it than that. When Smythe had completed his economic case against using the pricing system (in the article discussed earlier), he introduced an argument of a quite different character. He said that a

> second broad postulate which seems to underlie proposals such as that advanced [by Herzel] is politico-economic in nature: that the public weal will be served if broadcasting, like grocery stores, uses the conventional business organization, subject only to general legal restraints on its profit-seeking activity. This postulate carries with it, usually, the parallel assumption that the educational and cultural responsibilities of broadcast station operators ought to be no more substantial at the most than those of the operators of the newspapers and magazines. . . .
> . . . [D]espite the extensive use made of these two assumptions by business organizations for propaganda purposes, there is a powerful tradition in the United States that the economic, educational and cultural rights and responsibilities of broadcasting are unique. (1952, p. 104)[45]

43. See the panel discussion by representatives of law schools, of the government, and of the bar, in Hearings cited in note 42, pp. 166–167. A similar point was raised by Arthur S. Miller of Emory University Law School (*Ibid.*, p. 172).

44. During the Hearings Representative Moulder asked Byse whether his proposal would not lead the Commission to "award the license not to the most competent, but to the one who has the most money?" (*Ibid.*, p. 186).

45. See note 15.

Smythe's position would seem to be that broadcasting plays (or should play) a more important role, educationally and culturally, than newspapers and magazines (and, I assume he would add, books) and that therefore there ought to be stricter governmental regulation of what is broadcast than of what is printed. It is possible to dispute both parts of this argument. But Smythe is right to claim that this view (or something like it) has been long and firmly held by most of those concerned with broadcasting policy in the United States. Thus Hoover in 1924 said:

> Radio communication is not to be considered as merely a business carried on for private gain, for private advertisement, or for entertainment of the curious. It is a public concern impressed with the public trust and to be considered primarily from the standpoint of public interest in the same extent and upon the basis of the same general principles as our other public utilities. (Hearings on H.R. 7357, To Regulate Radio Communication, before the House Committee on the Merchant Marine and Fisheries, 68th Cong., 1st Sess. 10 [1924])

And the present chairman of the Federal Communications Commission, John C. Doerfer, in 1959, said that regulation of programing

> stems from the potential power inherent in broadcasting to influence the minds of men and the concomitant scarcity of the available frequencies. . . . The conjunction . . . of potentially great persuasive powers and the insufficiency of desirable spectrum space, has been the mainspring of all actions: legislative, administrative or court, which has qualified those freedoms generally enjoyed by the journalist, the artist and the minister. (Doerfer 1959)

If the aim of government regulation of broadcasting is to influence programing, it is irrelevant to discuss whether regulation is necessitated by the technology of the industry. The question does, of course, arise as to whether such regulation is compatible with the doctrine of freedom of speech and of the press. In general, this is not a question which has disturbed those who wished to see the Federal Communications Commission control programing, largely because they thought a clear distinction could be drawn between broadcasting and the publication of newspapers, periodicals, and books (for which few would advocate similar regulation).[46] Thus, in a comment on the *Mayflower* doctrine, we read:

> . . . radio is unique. It involves a medium which, while quantitatively limited, has almost infinite capacities as a means for mass communi-

---

46. There have been some who interpret the doctrine of freedom of speech and of the press not as an absolute prohibition of certain types of government action but as being "permissive and . . . subject (under due process of law) to forfeiture," if it results in "serious damage to some aspect of the public interest" (Siepmann, op. cit. supra note 30, at 231). The establishment of a Federal Press Commission with powers similar to those of the Federal Communications Commission would presumably be compatible with this interpretation of the meaning of freedom of speech and of the press.

cation of ideas, and which is essentially unthinkable as a subject of
any but public ownership. To draw an analogy to freedom of the individual or of the press is fruitless in this area. (Radio Editorials and
the *Mayflower* Doctrine, 48 Col. L. Rev. 785, 788 [1948])

The Supreme Court made the distinction between broadcasting and the publication of newspapers rest on the fact that a resource used in broadcasting is limited
in amount and scarce. But, as we have seen, this argument is invalid. Another
common argument is that, since broadcasters are making use of public property,
the government has a right to see that such public resources are used "in the public interest." "Radio is a public domain to which licensees have only conditional
and temporary access. Its 'landlord' is the public. Licensees are 'tenant farmers.'
The public's 'factor' is the FCC" (Siepmann 1950, p. 222). This would seem to
give the government the right to influence what is printed in newspapers, periodicals, and books if one of the resources used were public property or subject to
government allocation. Justin Miller, the president of the National Association of
Broadcasters, in evidence to a Senate subcommittee in 1947, pointed out that
government regulation of what a newspaper could print would be held unconstitutional. But broadcasting also came within the protection of the First Amendment, and therefore, he argued, regulation designed to influence the programing
of broadcasting stations was unconstitutional. The senators seem to have been
completely unconvinced by Miller's arguments. Senator McFarland said:

> . . . there is a difference between the press and the radio. You can com-
> pare them but you cannot assume they are alike. You are granting
> frequencies in the radio field. Once a license is granted, it is worth a
> lot of money. That is not true with the press at all. That is where you
> people get off base, in my opinion.

And Senator White said:

> I just do not get at all the idea that there is a complete analogy be-
> tween a broadcast license, which comes from the Government and is
> an exercise of power by Government, and the right of anybody to
> start a newspaper, anybody who wants to, without any let or per-
> mission or hindrance from the Government. . . . [I]t is pretty diffi-
> cult for me to see how a regulatory body can say that a licensee is or
> is not rendering a public service if it may not take a look and take
> into account the character of the program being broadcast by that
> licensee.[47]

47. From: Hearings on S. 1333, to Amend the Communications Act of 1934,
before the Senate Committee on Interstate and Foreign Commerce, 80th Cong., 1st Sess.
120, 123 (1947). Miller's statement will also be found in National Association of Broadcasters, Broadcasting and the Bill of Rights 1–35 (1947). This interchange between Miller and
the Senators is discussed in *Regulation of Broadcasting: Half a Century of Government
Regulation of Broadcasting and the Need for Further Legislative Action*, a study by Robert
S. McMahon, for the House Subcommittee on Legislative Oversight, 85th Cong., 2d Sess.
(1958).

These comments point clearly to the misunderstanding involved in this defense of
the present system. The argument moves from the existence of public property in
frequencies to the assertion of the right which this gives to influence programing.
But, as we have seen, there is no reason why there should not be private property
in frequencies.[48] If regulation of programing is desirable, it has to be advocated
on its own merits; it cannot be justified simply as a by-product of particular
economic arrangements. To say that resources should be used in the public interest does not settle the issue. Since it is generally agreed that the use of private
property and the pricing system is in the public interest in other fields, why
should it not also be in broadcasting?

William Howard Taft, who was Chief Justice of the Supreme Court
during the critical formative period of the broadcasting industry, is reported to
have said: "I have always dodged this radio question. I have refused to grant writs
and have told the other justices that I hope to avoid passing on this subject as long
as possible." Pressed to explain why, he answered:

> . . . interpreting the law on this subject is something like trying to
> interpret the law of the occult. It seems like dealing with something
> supernatural. I want to put it off as long as possible in the hope that
> it becomes more understandable before the court passes on the ques-
> tions involved. (C.C. Dill, Radio Law 1–2 1938)[49]

It was indeed in the shadows cast by a mysterious technology that
our views on broadcasting policy were formed. It has been the burden of this
article to show that the problems posed by the broadcasting industry do not call
for any fundamental changes in the legal and economic arrangements that serve
other industries. But the belief that broadcasting industry is unique and requires
regulation of a kind which would be unthinkable in the other media of communication is now so firmly held as perhaps to be beyond the reach of critical examination. The history of regulation in the broadcasting industry demonstrates the
crucial importance of events in the early days of a new development in determin-

---

48. It was a weakness of Miller's presentation that he accepted the need for
government allocation of frequencies and apparently was unaware of the possibility of disposing of frequencies by using the pricing mechanism. Miller attempted to bring the Senators
to see the validity of his analogy between broadcasting and the publication of newspapers, so
far as the First Amendment was concerned, by citing a hypothetical example. He said that
there was a shortage of newsprint and that "some of these days we may have a government
agency authorized to make allotments of newsprint. . . . Would it be proper, under such circumstances, for such a government body to impose the sort of abridgments upon freedom of
the press that are now imposed on radio broadcasting? The question would seem to answer
itself." But if the government allocated newsprint to users without charge, there can be little
doubt that it would take into account what the newsprint was being used to produce. The
obvious way to avoid the government's doing this would be to sell the newsprint at a price
which equated demand to supply.

49. Taft was Chief Justice of the Supreme Court from 1921 to 1930. So far as
I can discover, the Supreme Court did not consider any radio case while Taft was Chief Justice.

ing long-run governmental policy. It also suggests that lawyers and economists should not be so overwhelmed by the emergence of new technologies as to change the existing legal and economic system without first making quite certain that this is required.

## Chapter Eight

# Managerial Discretion and Business Behavior

## O. Williamson

Reprinted from the *American Economic Review* 53 (December 1963): 1032–1057, by permission of publisher and author.

The importance of managerial discretion in the operations of the large corporation has been widely recognized. Carl Kaysen has recently characterized the large corporation as one "in which the constraints imposed by market forces are loose, and the scope for managerial choice is considerable" (1960, p. 90), and R.A. Gordon holds that the development of the large corporation has led "to a greater emphasis on the nonprofit goals of interest groups other than the stockholders. Almost certainly, the personal and group goals of . . . executives are a part of the total value system—the desires for security, power, prestige, advancement within the organization, and so on. . . . Profits are viewed as the basic constraint subject to which other goals can be followed" (1961, p. xii).

Although there is substantial support for these views, it is by no means universal,[1] and before general acceptance can be attained a number of questions need to be answered. Can operational significance be provided to these managerial goals? Can such a translation of managerial objectives be integrated into a theory of the firm from which meaningful theorems can be derived? What is the evidence that discretion has an important and systematic impact on business behavior? Specifically, what influence does competition in the product market, managerial tastes, and the diffusion of stockholder control have on the allocation of resources in the business firm? How do regulatory or other constraints influence nonprofit behavior?

My purpose in this article is to show that the first two of these questions can be answered in the affirmative, that the preliminary evidence tends to support the proposition that the opportunity for discretion does have a systematic effect on resource-allocation decisions, and that regulatory constraints are apt to produce particularly strong manifestations of nonprofit behavior. The first section introduces the notion of "expense preference" for translating managerial

1. For an argument that monopoly distortions are not great, see Harberger (1954) and Schwartzman (1959).

goals to an operational form, develops the implications of a model constructed around these objectives, and contrasts these with those obtained from the profits-maximization hypothesis. The second section examines some of the preliminary evidence on discretionary behavior. The effects of regulatory constraints are considered in the final section.

## SOME MODELS OF BUSINESS BEHAVIOR[2]

My purpose in this section will be to show how managerial objectives can be introduced into a theory of the firm, to develop the implications of a model responsive to what appears to be the salient motives of managers, and to contrast these with those obtained from short-period and multiperiod versions of the profits-maximization hypothesis.

### A Managerial Discretion Model

**Managerial Objectives.**  The following list represents a (largely overlapping) composite of the managerial motives identified as the result of the experiences and insights of the organization theorists, Chester I. Barnard (1962) and Herbert A. Simon (1961), and the study of business leadership of R.A. Gordon (1961): salary, security, power, status, prestige, professional excellence.[3] That they are neither equally significant nor entirely independent should be obvious. Rather than attempt a finer discrimination, however, it seems more fruitful to inquire into the behavior such motives produce.

The usual objection to introducing nonpecuniary elements into the theory of the firm is that such considerations, if not unimportant, are analytically evasive. Since their importance is an empirical question, it can hardly be dis-

---

2. The material appearing in this and the subsequent sections is developed in more detail in my unpublished doctoral dissertation, "The Economics of Discretionary Behavior: Managerial Objectives in a Theory of the Firm" (Carnegie Institute of Technology, 1963). The initial version of the model, which has since been modified, appears in Williamson (1963a).

3. In addition to the factors listed, Barnard and Simon also include expansion as one of the firm's objectives. Indeed, William J. Baumol has recently suggested that the firm is operated so as to maximize the rate of growth of sales (1962, pp. 1085–87), which is the dynamic counterpart of his static sales-maximization hypothesis (1959) and preserves the main theorems of his earlier model (1962, p. 1087). Although "expansion" objectives also enter into the model that we propose, it is a somewhat selective variety of expansion that will occur—namely, expansion of those types of activities that most contribute to the satisfaction of the management—rather than a generalized expansion of the entire scale of the firm. Whether this leads to a more fruitful construction is an empirical question and can scarcely be determined on a priori grounds. The preliminary evidence that is examined in the second part of this article appears to support the proposition that preferences towards specific varieties of expenses exist (rather than a generalized preference for expansion per se), but this is essentially an open question.

missed so easily. In order, however, to assess their influence, an analytical basis for examining them must be devised. Shifting attention from the motives to the *means* by which the motives are realized provides the necessary connection. That is, rather than attempt to introduce security, power, prestige, and so forth into the theory directly, we ask instead: to what activities do these motives give rise? These activities, rather than the motives, are then made a part of the model.

The essential notion that we propose in order to connect motives with behavior is that of *expense preference*. That is, the management does not have a neutral attitude towards costs. Directly or indirectly, certain classes of expenditure have positive values associated with them. In particular, staff expense, expenditures for emoluments, and funds available for discretionary investment have value additional to that which derives from their productivity.

Expansion of staff is an activity that offers positive rewards, the benefits of which can be enjoyed quite generally (Marshall 1932, pp. 321-22). Indeed, since promotional opportunities within a fixed-size firm are limited, while increased jurisdiction has the same general effect as promotion but simultaneously produces the chance of advance for all, the incentive to expand staff may be difficult to resist. Not only is it an indirect means to the attainment of salary (Simon 1957) but it is a source of security, power, status, prestige, and professional achievement as well.[4]

We use the term "emoluments" in a somewhat special sense. They refer to that fraction of managerial salaries and perquisites that are discretionary. That is, emoluments represent rewards which, if removed, would not cause the managers to seek other employment. They are economic rents and have associated with them zero productivities. Thus they are not a return to entrepreneurial

4. As has been observed among organization theorists, "the modern organization is a prolific generator of anxiety and insecurity," (Thompson 1961, p. 24). This insecurity is partly due to uncertainty with respect to the survival of the organization as a whole and, more important (and more immediately relevant to its individual members), of the parts with which the individuals identify. Attempts to reduce this condition can be expected; indeed, the direction these efforts will take can be anticipated. If the surest guarantee of the survival of the individual parts appears to be size, efforts to expand the separate staff functions can safely be predicted.

That staff contributes to power, status, and prestige should be self-evident. This is true within the organization as well as in the manager's business and social relationships outside the firm. The vast influence that executives in large industrial organizations enjoy arises much more from the perceived control over resources that they possess than from the personal wealth which they have attained.

The "professional" inducement to expand staff arises from the typical view that a progressive staff is one that is continuously providing more and better service. An aggressive staff will therefore be looking for ways to expand. Although in choosing directions for expansion the relative contribution to productivity will be considered, the absolute effect on profits may be neglected. As long as the organization is able to satisfy its performance requirements, there is a predisposition to extend programs beyond the point where marginal costs equal marginal benefits. The incentive to increase staff, having both natural and legitimate elements, is exceptionally difficult to resist.

capacity but rather result from the strategic advantage that the management possesses in the distribution of the returns to monopoly power. Being a source of material satisfaction and an indirect source of status and prestige, they are desirable as a means for satisfying goals in each of these respects.

The management would normally prefer to take these emoluments as salary rather than as perquisites of office since, taken as salary, there are no restrictions on the way in which they are spent, while, if withdrawn as corporate personal consumption (such as expense accounts, executive services, office suites, etc.), there are specific limitations on the ways these can be enjoyed. However, there are two considerations that make perquisites attractive. First, for tax purposes it may be advantageous to withdraw some part of discretionary funds as perquisites rather than salary. Second, perquisites are much less visible rewards to the management than salary and hence are less likely to provoke stockholder or labor dissatisfaction.[5] Hence a division of emoluments between salary and perquisites is to be expected.

Although it is difficult to specify what fraction of salary and perquisites is discretionary in the sense defined, it is possible, as we show in the second part, to test for the relation of these rewards to competition in the product market and managerial tastes. Thus, they can be identified ex post even if not ex ante.

The existence of satisfactory profits is necessary to assure the interference-free operation of the firm to the management. Precisely what this level will be involves a complicated interaction of the relative performance of rivals, the historical performance of the firm, and special current conditions that affect the firm's performance. Management, however, will find it desirable to earn profits that exceed the acceptable level. For one thing, managers derive satisfaction from self-fulfillment and organizational achievement, and profits are one measure of this success. In addition, profits are a source of discretion (indeed, we define "discretionary profits" as the difference between actual profits and minimum profits demanded). Discretionary profits represent a source of funds whose allocation may be importantly determined by managerial, in addition to economic, considerations. As with the expansion of staff, the expansion of physical plant and equipment provides general opportunities for managerial satisfaction and for much the same reasons.

**The Model.**   Since these notions will be introduced explicitly into a mathematical model, it will be useful to define them more precisely. The relationships that we shall use are:

---

5. Historically, whenever stockholder discontent has been rampant, management compensation has been a favorite target (Jordon 1961, p. 164). Likewise in wage negotiations, unions often make a point of executive salary levels. Emoluments, being much less visible, are less readily attacked.

$R$ = revenue = $P \cdot X$; $\partial^2 R/\partial X \partial S \geqslant 0$

$P$ = price = $P(X, S; \epsilon)$; $\partial P/\partial X < 0$; $\partial P/\partial S \geqslant 0$; $\partial P/\partial \epsilon > 0$

$X$ = output

$S$ = staff (in money terms) or (approximately) general administrative and selling expense

$\epsilon$ = the condition of the environment (a demand-shift parameter)

$C$ = production cost = $C(X)$

$M$ = managerial emoluments

$\pi$ = actual profits = $R - C - S$

$\pi_R$ = reported profits = $\pi - M$

$\pi_O$ = minimum (after tax) profits demanded

$T$ = taxes where $t$ = tax rate and $\bar{T}$ = lump-sum tax

$\pi_R - \pi_O - T$ = discretionary profits

$U$ = the utility function

From our statement of the firm's objectives, the firm is operated so as to

maximize: $U = U[S, M, \pi_R - \pi_O - T]$

subject to: $\pi_R \geqslant \pi_O + T$.

As formulated, the constraint is of the same form as the last term in the utility function. Hence, assuming that second order conditions are satisfied and disallowing corner solutions, the constraint becomes redundant so that we can treat the problem as one of straightforward maximization.[6] Substituting the functional relationships for profits into the expression we have:

maximize: $U = U[S, M, (1 - t)(R - C - S - M) - \pi_0]$.

The following first-order results are obtained by setting the partial derivatives of $U$ with respect to $X$, $S$, and $M$ equal to zero:[7]

$$\frac{\partial R}{\partial X} = \frac{\partial C}{\partial X} \tag{1}$$

$$\frac{\partial R}{\partial S} = \frac{-U_1 + (1 - t)U_3}{(1 - t)U_3} \tag{2}$$

$$U_2 = (1 - t)U_3. \tag{3}$$

6. Although this is a convenience, it is by no means a necessity. An inequality-constrained maximization could be handled by making use of the Kuhn-Tucker theorem (1951).

7. In these expressions, $U_1$, is the first partial of the utility function with respect to $S$, $U_2$ is the first partial with respect to $M$, and $U_3$ is the first partial with respect to $\pi_R - \pi_O - T$.

From equation (1) we observe that the firm makes its production decision in the conventional fashion by equating marginal gross revenue to the marginal costs of production. However, equation (2) reveals that the firm will employ staff in the region where the marginal value product of staff is less than its marginal cost. This equation can be rewritten as:

$$\frac{\partial R}{\partial S} = 1 - \frac{1}{(1-t)} \frac{U_1}{U_3}, \text{ where } \frac{U_1}{U_3}$$

is the marginal rate of substitution between profits and staff. In the profit-maximizing organization, staff has no value other than that associated with its productivity, so that this exchange rate is zero, and the equality of marginal costs and value products obtains. Equation (3) discloses that the firm will absorb some amount of actual profits as emoluments—the amount being dependent on the tax rate.

Having established the equilibrium conditions, the comparative statics properties of the model remain to be developed.[8] That is, we want to find how the system adjusts to a change in the condition of the environment (the demand-shift parameter $\epsilon$), a change in the profit tax rate ($t$), and a lump-sum tax ($\bar{T}$).

The results for a displacement by each of the parameters are shown in Table 8-1. The direction of adjustment of any particular decision variable to a displacement from its equilibrium value by an increase in a particular parameter is found by referring to the row and column entry corresponding to this pair.

**Table 8-1.   Responses to Displacements from Equilibrium for the Managerial Model**

| Variable | Parameter | | |
|---|---|---|---|
| | $\epsilon$ | $t$ | $\bar{T}$ |
| $X^0$ | + | + | – |
| $S^0$ | + | + | – |
| $M^0$ | + | + | – |

Actually the response to a change in the profits tax rate is not unambiguous. It can be shown that this response is separable into a net substitution effect and the equivalent of an income effect, where the net substitution effect is always positive and the income effect is always negative. The gross substitution effect is the combination of these two separate effects and hence depends on their relative magnitudes. Under reasonable assumptions, the gross substitution effect will be positive as shown in the table.[9]

8. The procedure we use for obtaining the comparative statics responses is described in Samuelson (1958, pp. 12–14).

9. Only when the firm is pressed very hard to satisfy its minimum-profits constraint is a reversal apt to occur.

### Entrepreneurial Models

The significance of these responses can best be discussed by comparing them to the corresponding results obtained from profit-maximizing models. Consider first the usual or single-period profit-maximizing model. As is well known, the equilibrium relations for this model require that the firm be operated so as to equate marginal gross revenue with the marginal costs of production and the marginal value product of staff with its marginal cost. The comparative statics responses are shown in Table 8-2.

**Table 8-2. Responses to Displacements from Equilibrium for the Short-Run Profits-Maximizing Model**

| *Variable* | *Parameter* | | |
|---|---|---|---|
| | $\epsilon$ | $t$ | $\overline{T}$ |
| $X^0$ | + | 0 | 0 |
| $S^0$ | + | 0 | 0 |

The differences between the models are more numerous than their similarities. Indeed, it is only with respect to the demand-shift parameter ($\epsilon$) that the two return the same results, and even here the result is not identical. In addition to the increases in staff and output that the profit-maximization model shows, the managerial model also indicates that spending for emoluments will increase as $\epsilon$ increases. Moreover, while the qualitative differences with respect to $\epsilon$ are not great, quantitative differences may produce sharper discriminations. In general; a profits-maximizing firm will adjust to changes in business conditions within narrower bounds than the utility-maximizing firm. The absence of slack in its operations, as contrasted with the calculated accumulation (and decumulation) of slack by the utility-maximizing firm, is responsible for these quantitative differences.

A more general entrepreneurial model can be obtained by devising a multiperiod or discounted version of the profits-maximization hypothesis. The variables are subscripted by time periods by $i$, where $i = 1, 2, \ldots n$, and $n$ is the planning horizon. Letting $r$ be the discount rate, profits in year $i$ will be discounted by $1/(1 + r)^{i-1}$. Let this be represented by $\alpha^{i-1}$. We make the assumption that production decisions in period $k$ affect costs in no other period or, if there are effects, that these are offsetting. However, staff expenditures in period $k$ are assumed to have a positive influence on future-period revenues over the entire planning horizon. Indeed, the length of the "period" can be defined as the interval beyond which current production decisions have no effect and the length of the planning horizon as the number of such periods for which current staff expenditures have a positive effect.

Table 8-3.   Comparative Statics Responses for the Discounted
Profits-Maximizing Model

| Variable | Parameter | | | |
|---|---|---|---|---|
| | $\epsilon$ | $t'$ | $t''$ | $\bar{T}$ |
| $X_1^0$ | + | + | 0 | 0 |
| $S_1^0$ | + | + | 0 | 0 |

Letting $\pi$ represent the discounted value of profits, the objective is to maximize:

$$\pi = \sum_{i=1}^{n} (1 - t)(R_i - C_i - S_i - T_i)\alpha^{i-1}.$$

First-order conditions for a maximum are obtained by setting the partial derivatives of $\pi$ with respect to $X_1$ and $S_1$ equal to zero. Thus we have:

$$\frac{\partial R_1}{\partial X_1} = \frac{\partial C_1}{\partial X_1} \tag{4}$$

$$\frac{\partial R_1}{\partial S_1} = 1 - \sum_{i=2}^{n} \frac{\partial R_i}{\partial S_1}\alpha^{i-1}. \tag{5}$$

Inspection of equation (4) reveals that the firm chooses that value of output for which the marginal gross revenue is equal to the marginal costs of production. Equation (5), however, shows that the current marginal value product of staff is less than its current marginal cost.[10] These equilibrium conditions are thus similar to those obtained from the managerial model.

Since the effects when the tax is levied for a period less than the planning horizon are different from those when the tax covers the entire horizon, the tax-rate effect is split into "temporary" (designated tax rate $t'$) and "permanent" (designated tax rate $t''$) types. The comparative statics responses for this model are displayed in Table 8-3.

Whereas the qualitative responses to a "temporary" change in the profits tax rate are identical to those obtained from the managerial model, a change in the "permanent" profits tax or the levy of a lump-sum tax (or bounty) produces no effect in the profits-maximizing organization. A response to both is

10. Over the entire horizon, however, the marginal value product of staff equals its marginal cost.

predicted by the managerial model. Hence a discrimination between the hypotheses on the basis of comparative statics properties is potentially achievable.

## SOME EVIDENCE

Changes in either the profits tax or a lump-sum tax provide the most direct basis for distinguishing between the utility and profits-maximization theories. Testing the effects of a profits tax, however, requires that a rather advanced type of simultaneous-equations model be devised, while lump-sum taxes are hard to come by. The first of these carries us beyond the range of the present analysis, and only preliminary evidence on the effects of the lump-sum tax is available. (See the section entitled "The Evidence from the Field Studies.")

Fortunately other tests of a less direct but nonetheless meaningful sort can be devised. For one thing, the comparative statics implications are limited to qualitative responses; quantitative differences are neglected. If, therefore, significant quantitative differences between the two theories can be shown to exist, these can be used for making a discrimination where qualitative properties are identical.

Secondly, tests of particular behavior are available. Thus, the utility-maximizing theory is based on the proposition that opportunities for discretion and managerial tastes will have a decided impact on the expenditures of the firm. More precisely, those expenditures that promote managerial satisfactions should show a positive correlation with opportunities for discretion and tastes. The profit-maximizing theory is somewhat ambiguous on this question. Interpreted as a theory which attends entirely to the stockholders' best interests, it clearly implies that expenditures which, under the utility-maximizing hypothesis, will be positively correlated with measures of discretion and tastes, will instead be uncorrelated with these relationships. Interpreted somewhat more loosely, closer agreement with the utility-maximizing hypothesis can be obtained. Thus, it is possible that the management first selects that physical combination of factors that maximizes profits and then absorbs some amount of actual profits as cost. These absorptions may be correlated with the same measures of discretion and taste as would be expected under the utility-maximizing theory. Hence, evidence that managers respond to opportunities for discretion is not inconsistent with the profit-maximizing theory, but neither is evidence to the contrary; the theory is simply silent on this question. However, the failure of firms to respond to opportunities for discretion constitutes a contradiction of the utility-maximizing hypothesis, while observations that firms do display expense-preference behavior supports it.

The executive compensation and retained-earnings analyses reported in the section on "Principal-Firm Analysis" are designed to test for the effects of discretion and taste in management expenditure decisions. The summary of the field studies in the following section is concerned with the question of physical magnitudes of adjustment to adversity and provides some indication of what criteria are involved in making expense adjustments as well as what effects a lump-sum tax has on business behavior.

### Principal-Firm Analysis

If the firm is operated so as to attend to managerial interests, then the classes of expenditures for which expense preference was indicated should be expanded beyond the levels called for by strictly profit considerations. The amount by which such expansions occur should be positively related to the opportunity for discretion and the tastes of the management. More precisely, if $X$ is an expenditure for which a positive expense preference exists, $I_1$ is an index of the absence of competition, $I_2$ is an index of management taste, $I_3$ is an index of stockholder diffusion, and $f(\pi)$ is the level of $X$ which would be supported solely by profit considerations, then under the utility-maximization hypothesis:

$$X = f(\pi)g(I_1, I_2, I_3)$$

where

$$\frac{\partial X}{\partial I_i} > 0.$$

Under the stockholder version of the profits-maximization hypothesis, the partial derivative of $X$ with respect to each of the $I_i$ will be zero.

Since it is in the large corporation that manifestations of discretionary behavior are alleged to be important, and as complete data are most readily available among larger industrial firms than their smaller counterparts, the tests are restricted to those firms that clearly qualified as "principal firms." Among the twenty-six industries included in the analysis, selection was limited to the two largest firms, ranked according to sales, in each.[11] The tests performed are cross-section tests for the years 1953, 1957, and 1961.

**Executive Compensation.** George Stigler has observed that the estimation of the effect of monopoly on profit may be complicated by the absorption of some fraction of "true" monopoly profit as cost. In particular, "the magnitude of monopoly elements in wages, executive compensation, royalties, and rents is possibly quite large" (1956, p. 35). Our interest here is limited to

---

11. Although the sample is a purposive rather than a random sample, the results probably generalize to a somewhat larger population. Based on the *1962 Moody's* listing of major industries (p. a-16 and a-17) twenty-four additional industries would be added to our list of twenty-six for a total of fifty major industries and, with two principal firms in each, one hundred principal firms.

testing only a part of this hypothesis. Specifically, we examine the effects of discretion on compensating the top executive.

Focusing on a single representative of management might appear to restrict severely the relevance of our results. If the compensation of the rest of the management group were determined independently of that of the chief executive, this would certainly be the case. However, payments between executive levels are carefully scaled (Baker 1938, p. 181; Koontz and O'Donnell 1955, p. 320; Simon 1957). Hence, the factors that influence compensation to the top executive can be presumed to affect the level of staff compensation generally.

Under the utility-maximizing hypothesis, a positive expense preference towards emoluments exists. In particular, executive salaries should be correlated with the opportunities for discretion. Letting $W_a$ be the actual salary of the management and $W_c$ be the competitive salary, we have: $W_a = W_c + (W_a - W_c)$, where $W_a - W_c$ is a measure of the monopoly returns withdrawn by the management (by virtue of its advantageous position) as economic rent.

As indicated above, the hypothesis that discretion influences expenses takes the form $X = f(\pi)g(I_1, I_2, I_3)$ where $f(\pi)$ is the expense incurred strictly on a profit-maximizing basis, and $I_1$, $I_2$, and $I_3$ are indices of the absence of competition, the tastes of the management, and the diffusion of the stockholders, respectively. Specifying $f(\pi)$ for purposes of studying executive compensation is somewhat difficult. A measure of hierarchical activity over which the executive in question has responsibility, together with the special abilities required for the position, probably measures this approximately. For the top executive, the level of hierarchical activity is effectively the entire staff structure. Thus let $f(\pi) = f'(S, Z)$ where $S$ is the level of staff (general administrative and selling expenses)[12] and $Z$ is an index of special ability.

We assume that the index of competitive pressure $(I_1)$ is reflected by the concentration ratio and the entry barrier in each industry. The concentration ratio reflects the influence of realized interdependencies between rivals. Where

12. Previous studies of executive compensation have used the total revenue of the firm for this purpose (McGuire, Chiu, and Elbing 1962; Roberts 1959). This has the advantage of minimizing errors of measurement that arise from differences in accounting practice but is probably not as good a proxy for "staff" as is general administrative and selling expense. Sales are defective for two reasons. For one thing, they reflect activity at levels below the management hierarchy whereas the size effect would be expected to act largely within the hierarchy (Simon 1957). Secondly, interfirm comparisons are complicated by differences in vertical integration policies. As a matter of curiosity, regressions replacing general administrative and selling expense by sales were run—with uniformly adverse results. The objections to using general administrative and selling expense as a proxy for hierarchical expense are largely related to differences in accounting practice among firms. However, the components of general administrative and selling expense very nearly give us a measure of the level of staff activity in the firm (for a list of the functions usually included see Vance [1952, chs. 17 and 18] ). Amounts charged to these accounts are, for the most part, current costs, and hence ambiguities arising from the use of historical costs are reduced.

concentration ratios are high, interdependencies will generally be intimate, and behavior between rivals will at least be circumspect and may involve explicit agreements. In either case, the influence of competition will be consciously controlled. Hence, an increase in the concentration ratio will tend to widen the opportunities for managerial discretion. Obviously, this measure is defective, and there will be exceptions. However we are content merely to account for average rather than exceptional behavior.

The barrier to entry measure, as developed by Bain (1962), is explicitly designed to estimate the extent to which firms are insulated from the effects of competition. Although concentration and entry conditions are correlated, they are by no means identical. In combination they provide a particularly good measure of the opportunities for discretion. High concentration together with a high barrier to entry will tend to produce substantial discretion, for not only is potential competition limited, but existing rivals are few enough to appreciate their conditions of interdependence. Low values for each of these measures will tend to produce the reverse effect, while mixed values, presumably, give rise to mixed effects.

To allay any suspicion that the concentration ratio and entry barriers are merely another measure of size, it might be noted that the product moment correlations between the logarithm of sales and the logarithms of "staff," concentration, and barriers (for the firms included in the sample) are about .75, -.13, and -.14, respectively. Quite clearly these latter two correlations are small enough that if concentration and barriers have an effect on compensation, it is not primarily due to their relationship to size.

A sharp measure of managerial tastes $(I_2)$ is not available. However, the composition of the board may act as a proxy measure of the extent to which management desires to operate the firm free from outside interference. Although low proportional representation of the management on the board of directors need not reflect a "taste" for active outside participation in the affairs of the firm, clearly a high internal representation does reflect the intent of the management to conduct the affairs of the firm free from such outside influence. We hypothesize that, as the management representation on the board increases, there tends to be a subordination of stockholder for managerial interests. In this sense, the composition of the board reflects management's attitude toward discretionary resource allocations and a voluntary change in comparison reflects a change in these "tastes."

An estimate of stockholder diffusion $(I_3)$ was not obtained. Such a measure would probably be correlated with the composition of the board variable. However the association may not be great. Where substantial concentration of ownership exists, there is frequently a tendency towards nepotism. This in turn may produce high internal representation rather than the high outside representation that would otherwise be predicted. If in fact the correlation were zero (and there were no other neglected variable to consider), our estimate of the composition effect would be unbiased. As it is, some bias may result from the lack of a diffusion measure.[13]

The effects of each of the independent variables on executive compensation should be positive. In addition, they are assumed to be multiplicative. Thus we assume that:

$$X_i = \alpha_0 S_i^{\alpha_2} C_i^{\alpha_2} H_i^{\alpha_3} B_i^{\alpha_4} U_i \tag{6}$$

where

$X_i$ = compensation of the top executive
$S_i$ = administrative, general, and selling expense (i.e., "staff")
$C_i$ = concentration ratio in the industry
$H_i$ = height of the barrier to entry in the industry
$B_i$ = composition of the board
$U_i$ = a random error term[14]
and the subscript $i$ refers to the $i^{\text{th}}$ firm in the sample.[15]

13. Alternatively, the composition of the board variable might be interpreted as reflecting the *joint* effects of management tastes and stockholder diffusion. What is really needed, however, are sharper measures that reflect each of these effects separately.

14. $U_i$ includes the effects of special abilities (the $Z$ variable mentioned above), the omitted stockholder-diffusion variable, numbers of years the top executive has held that position, and other neglected factors.

15. The number of observations for each of the years was twenty-six in 1953, thirty in 1957, and twenty-five in 1961. Inability to use all fifty-two of the firms studied (as in the second set of tests reported here) was largely due to the lack of estimates on the condition of entry for many of the industries. The sources of the data were as follows:

Executive compensation: as a matter of law, publicly held corporations are required to report executive compensation to the Securities and Exchange Commission. Although these data are a matter of public record, they are not readily available. *Business Week*, however, annually publishes executive compensation figures for a group of principal firms. It was from this source that the data on compensation were obtained.

General administrative and selling expense and composition of the board: both were obtained from *Moody's Industrials* (supplemented occasionally by other sources when the listing of officers in *Moody's* was incomplete).

Concentration ratios: data on concentration for 1953 were developed from the 1954 concentration ratios for the four largest firms reported in *Concentration in American Industry* (Washington, D.C., 1957). Concentration data for 1957 and 1961 were developed from the 1958 concentration ratios for the four largest firms reported in *Concentration Ratios in Manufacturing Industry 1958,* Pt. I (Washington, D.C. 1962). A weighted average of several of the SIC industry groups was sometimes used to arrive at a concentration ratio for the industries in question. Although such weighting procedures can produce distortions, this is probably not too serious in reasonably narrowly defined industry groups.

Barrier to entry: Bain's study (1962) provided the estimates of the height of the barrier to entry. In addition, I took the liberty of classifying textiles as an industry with a low entry barrier since Bain did not include textiles in his analysis, but there is general agreement that the industry has a low entry barrier. A dummy variable which took on the value 1 (ln 1 = 0) when the barrier to entry was low and $e$ (ln $e$ = 1) when the barrier was high

Taking logarithms of both sides of the equation and using these data to obtain least-squares estimates of the net regression coefficients, we obtain the results shown in Table 8-4.

The signs for each of the parameters in all three years are as predicted by the expense-preference hypothesis. Moreover, with the exception of the composition of the board coefficient, which is significant at the 10 percent level only in 1957, all of the regression coefficients are highly significant—two-thirds being significant at the 2.5 percent level.[16] Whereas the relation of executive compensation to general administrative and selling expense (i.e., "staff") is almost certain to be positive and significant, there is no reason to believe that the measures of taste and discretion that we introduce should have the effects shown (unless one endorses the view that management responds to opportunities for discretion in the ways indicated). Since the compensation of the chief executive generalizes to the entire staff structure, these results have broad significance for the resource-allocation process within the business firm. Furthermore, we would expect that these same measures of discretion would produce similar effects over the entire range of expenditures on emoluments.

Of course it could be argued that the concentration ratio and entry-barrier variables have positive regression coefficients because they are correlated with the profit rate—that this profitability effect is responsible for the results obtained. But obviously the causality runs from concentration and entry barriers to profits rather than the reverse. Thus, by focusing on the market structure, the model directs attention to the ultimate determinants of discretionary behavior (competition in the product market) rather than the apparent determinant (the profit rate). Although these market variables might not perform as well as the profit rate among the smaller firms in the industry, it does not seem inappropriate to use them for studying the behavior of the two largest firms where the relationship between market structure and behavior is probably reasonably direct. Indeed, it is of interest to note that: (a) if the profit rate on the stockholders

---

or substantial was used in the regressions. Two dummy variables to represent the substantial and high entry conditions separately were also tried. Although one might suppose that the parameter for the high-barrier dummy would exceed that of the substantial-barrier dummy, the results were somewhat mixed. As I have suggested elsewhere, however, the principal difference between a substantial and high barrier may be that in the former case the firm expands selling expense beyond its optimal level in order to discourage entry, with the result that the effective condition of entry is the same in substantial- and high-barrier industries (Williamson, 1963c). The question requires additional empirical investigation.

A list of the firms and industries included in the executive compensation and retained earnings analyses can be obtained from the author upon request.

16. The tests are one-tailed tests, which are appropriate since the hypothesis specifies that the signs should be positive (which they are). The standard errors shown are corrected for the finite population correction $[(N-n)/N]^{1/2}$, where $N$ is 100 in all years and $n$ is 26, 30, and 25 for 1953, 1957, and 1961, respectively.

Whether the results apply to a larger group than these 100 principal firms remains a subject for subsequent investigation.

Table 8-4.   Regression of Executive Compensation on "Staff,"
Concentration Ratio, Composition of the Board, and Barriers to
Entry

| | Year | | |
|---|---|---|---|
| | *1953* | *1957* | *1961* |
| "Staff" | | | |
| Coeff. | .228[a] | .240[a] | .218[a] |
| S.E. | .061 | .052 | .054 |
| Partial | (.564) | (.610) | (.614) |
| Concentration | | | |
| Coeff. | .503[a] | .513[a] | .422[b] |
| S.E. | .157 | .143 | .152 |
| Partial | (.517) | (.517) | (.470) |
| Composition | | | |
| Coeff. | .137 | .139 | .053 |
| S.E. | .118 | .101 | .120 |
| Partial | (.213) | (.224) | (.084) |
| Entry Barriers | | | |
| Coeff. | .446[a] | .221[b] | .200 |
| S.E. | .110 | .114 | .126 |
| Partial | (.606) | (.307) | (.290) |
| Coeff. of Correl. | | | |
| (adjusted) | .786 | .724 | .687 |

[a]Significant at the 0.1 percent level.
[a]Significant at the 2.5 percent level.

equity is substituted for the concentration ratio and entry-barrier variables, the coefficient of determination $(R^2)$ falls to two-thirds of the value obtained using these market variables in 1953 and 1961, and yields less than a 10 percent increase in $R^2$ in 1957; (b) if the profit rate, concentration ratio, and entry-barrier variables are all included, the profit rate is significant only in 1957 and has the wrong sign in 1961, while the concentration ratio and entry-barrier variables remain significant at the 10 percent level or better in every year.

Although the profit rate might perform better if a weighted average were used instead of current values, the argument offered above that this is an apparent rather than the ultimate determinant of behavior still applies. Moreover, the appropriate estimate of the profit rate is the actual rather than the reported rate. But the actual rate is unknown if, as the evidence above suggests, some fraction of actual profits is absorbed as salary and perquisites.

Some feeling for the responsiveness of salary to the independent variables in the regression equation can be obtained by taking the median of the estimates for each parameter and finding the effect on salary of increasing each individual independent variable by a factor of two. In some gross sense we can expect that executive salaries will possibly increase on the order of 17 percent if the level of staff activity were to double, on the order of 41 percent if the concentration ratio in the industry were to double, on the order of 10 percent if the internal representation on the board were to double, and on the order of 25 percent if the industry of which the firm was a part had a substantial or high barrier to entry rather than a low one. Thus, not only are the signs as predicted by the theory, but the magnitudes are sufficiently large to render somewhat doubtful the contention that discretionary effects are unimportant.

**Earnings Retention.** The composition of the board variable was used in the executive compensation model to reflect the tastes of the management for discretion. Internal representation on the board acts as a proxy for the attitude of the management toward outside influence. As the proportional representation of management on the board increases, it is assumed that stockholder interests tend to be subordinated to managerial objectives. This was manifested in the executive compensation regression by the positive regression coefficient associated with the composition of board variable.

A second test for this effect is to examine the relationship between composition of the board and earnings-retention policy. Consistency with our model requires that the earnings-retention ratio be directly related to the composition of the board. This follows since retained earnings are a source of discretion and a high internal representation provides the opportunity for management to shift the dividend policy to its advantage.

Alternative theories of the firm that regard managerial objectives as unimportant implicitly predict that there will be no association between the composition of the board and retention policy. Thus, our hypothesis of a direct association is tested against the null hypothesis of no association.

Earnings retention will, of course, be responsive to a number of considerations other than that of the composition of the board. Most important, investment opportunities will differ between industries and these could easily be overriding. If it can be assumed that the firms in the same industry have identical opportunities, however, these effects can be neutralized.

A paired-comparison technique was used to neutralize the industry effects. That is, between the two principal firms in each of the twenty-six industries we compare the composition of the board and earnings-retention ratio. The random variable can take on either of two values: 1 if the higher internal representation is paired with the higher earnings-retention ratio, and 0 otherwise. Hence it is distributed as a binomial. Under the hypothesis that no association exists, the expected number of times the positive association will occur, divided by the total number of observations, is one-half. Thus the null hypothesis is that the binomial parameter $p$ is .50. Our model, however, predicts that the positive association will occur more than one-half of the time—i.e., that $p$ exceeds .50.

The results for each of the three years as well as the pooled results for all three years are shown in Table 8-5. The proposition that internal representa-

**Table 8–5. Binomial Test for Association Between Composition of Board and Earnings-Retention Policy**

|  | *1953* | *1957* | *1961* | *All Years* |
|---|---|---|---|---|
| Number of observations | 25 | 26 | 26 | 77 |
| Expected number of positive occurrences under the null hypothesis | 12.5 ($p = .50$) | 13 ($p = .50$) | 13 ($p = .50$) | 38.5 ($p = .50$) |
| Actual number of positive occurrences | 13.5 ($\hat{p} = .54$) | 16 ($\hat{p} = .62$) | 18 ($\hat{p} = .69$) | 47.5 ($\hat{p} = .62$) |
| Probability that a value as high as observed would occur if the null hypothesis were true[a] | .34 | .13 | .02 | .02 |

[a]Normal approximation to the binomial was used to obtain the probabilities that the null hypothesis would produce the results observed.

tion has no effect on the earnings-retention policy between pairs of firms in the same industry is unsupported by the data. In every year the proportion of positive observations exceeds .50. In 1953 and 1957 the probability that a value as high as that observed if the null hypothesis were true is .34 and .13, respectively, and in 1961 this drops to .02. Clearly we are inclined to reject the hypothesis in favor of the alternative suggested. That is, due to the discretion associated with the retention of earnings and the opportunity to influence the retention policy which arises from representation on the board, the relation that we suggested (namely, that between pairs of firms in the same industry, the higher the internal representation, the higher the earnings retention rate) is supported by the data. Although it is possible that the composition of the board is acting only as an intervening variable and that the real explanation for this association lies elsewhere, no simple connection suggests itself.

The strongest evidence in favor of our hypothesis is provided by the pooled results for all three years. Here the observed number of positive occurrences would appear by chance under the null hypothesis with a probability of only two times in a hundred. Before the pooling of the observations can be justified, however, it is first necessary to establish that the observations are independent and that the association observed in one period is simply not carried over to the following period. Since the composition of the board and earnings-retention decisions reflect policy considerations that exhibit continuation in consecutive years, lack of independence between consecutive years would be expected. On the other hand, our observations are separated by a period of four years. The association between consecutive years may well be eliminated over this interval. Since the issue can scarcely be resolved on a priori grounds, we submit the hypothesis that the observations are independent to test.

A chi-square test for association was used. A low value of $\chi^2$ is consistent with the hypothesis that the observations between successive four-year intervals are independent. The value of $\chi^2$ between 1953 and 1957 is .0065, and between 1957 and 1961 is .62. Sampling randomly from independent populations, values as high or higher than this would occur 95 percent and 45 percent of the time, respectively. Hence the hypothesis of independence is supported, the pooling of the observations is justified, and the best test for the composition of the board effect is that of all three years combined. Here the possibility that the positive association observed has occurred by chance is only .02. Indeed, among pairs of principal firms we can expect that the firm with the higher internal representation on the board of directors will have a higher earnings-retention ratio about three-fifths of the time.

The above results are limited to directional effects only and say nothing about the magnitudes involved. This is probably all that the data justify. However, a crude estimate of the quantitative effect is available by an application of the general model suggested above for studying discretionary expenditures. Thus let

$R_{ik}$ = the retained-earnings ratio
$\rho_k$ = the rate of return on investment available to principal
 firms
$C_k$ = the concentration ratio
$H_k$ = the entry barrier
$B_{ik}$ = the composition of the board of directors
$V_{ik}$ = a random-error term[17]

The subscript $i$ refers to the firm, and the subscript $k$ refers to the industry of which the firm is a part. Then, assuming the relation is multiplicative, we have:

$$R_{ik} = \beta_0 \left[ f(\rho_k) \right]^{\beta_1} C_k^{\beta_2} H_k^{\beta_3} B_{ik}^{\beta_4} V_{ik}. \tag{7}$$

Taking the ratio of retained earnings between the $i$th and $j$th principal firms in the same industry yields:

$$\frac{R_{ik}}{R_{jk}} = \left( \frac{B_{ik}}{B_{jk}} \right)^{\beta_4} V'. \tag{8}$$

Taking logarithms of both sides of the equation, the value of $\beta_4$ can be estimated by least squares. The resulting estimates for 1953, 1957, and 1961 are .17, .17, and .16, respectively, but only the 1957 estimate is significant at the 10 percent

17. Neglected variables that may influence the retained-earnings policy include liquidity measures (such as the current ratio) times interest earned and other financial variables. Among principal firms in the same industry, such measures tend to display substantial stability.

level.[18] These estimates suggest that the retained-earnings ratio would increase by about 12 percent if the internal representation on the board of directors were to double.

A tenuous connection between the composition of the board and the investment policy of the firm can be obtained by noting the results obtained by Myron Gordon and M. Fg. Scott in their recent studies of investment financing. Gordon remarks that "the really surprising result is produced by return on investment. . . . In both industries there is a statistically significant tendency for the retention rate to fall as the corporation's rate of return increases. We must conclude that either [our estimate] is a poor measure of rate of return on investment or that corporations are not primarily influenced by the price of their stock in setting dividend rates" (Gordon 1962, pp. 231–32). And Scott, in a somewhat more broadly based study of dividend policy, observes that the "negative correlation of –.30 between undistributed profits . . . and the subsequent growth of earnings . . . is somewhat surprising. It suggests that stockholders . . . might benefit from more generous dividend distributions" (Scott 1962, p. 244). For a theory that makes the firm's objectives identical with those of the stockholders, such a result is somewhat disquieting. For an approach such as ours, however, which allows for the subordination of stockholder to managerial objectives, a possible explanation for these results based on the composition of the board analysis can be easily provided.

As was suggested above, high internal representation on the board of directors favors attention to managerial objectives, and this is manifested in a high earnings-retention rate. The funds thus provided are available to the management for the pursuit of expansionary objectives, and the resulting investment, being based on a combination of profit and expansionary goals, will exceed the amount dictated by profit considerations alone. As a result, the average rate of return in firms whose management is inclined to subordinate stockholder objectives can be expected to fall below that in firms where management interests are more nearly those of the stockholders.[19] Thus the tastes of the management, as

18. Since the estimates are sensitive to extreme values of retained earnings (values of $R_{ik}$ greater than .95 or less than .05), and since such extreme values ordinarily represent a transitory condition, these extreme values were removed in making the estimates. Thus the estimated values of $\beta_4$ apply to the range of retained earnings between 5 and 95 percent.

Actually, there is little theoretical reason for including the product market variables in the retained-earnings regression. They are included primarily for the purpose of indicating how variables common to both firms can be eliminated by using the ratio device. It is of some interest to note, however, that the estimate of $\beta_4$ obtained using only those industries with a high concentration ratio (>50), exceeds that obtained from industries with a low concentration ratio (≤50) in all three years.

19. In addition to the quantity of funds invested and diminishing-rate-of-return effect, there may also be political influences to consider (Cyert and March 1963). As the amount of available resources increases, the importance of political relative to economic cri-

revealed originally in the composition of the board, make their influence felt through the earnings-retention policy and thence on the return on investment. Where these tastes favor expansion, there is an adverse effect on the rate of return on investment. This indirect implication of our theory is precisely the result that Gordon and Scott report. Although conjectural, it suggests the value of including a taste variable, of which the composition of the board is a somewhat imperfect proxy, in future studies of the investment decision.

### The Evidence from the Field Studies

Simon has pointed out that "neither the classical theory of the firm nor any of the amendments to it or substitutes for it . . . have had any substantial amount of empirical testing" (1962, p. 8). To remedy this, he offers several proposals, one of which is the intensive interview. This has the advantage of permitting detailed observations that are unavailable in the ordinary survey, and these may provide insights into the ways in which the firm perceives its problems and the processes it employs in responding to them.

Unfortunately, field study observations are difficult to summarize. Their relevance derives largely from their detail, and, since the observations are few in number, statistical tests are often inappropriate. The field studies reported here are precisely of this kind. They nonetheless produce insights that would be difficult to obtain by other means. Of principal interest from our studies of the response of firms to adversity are the following:

1. In the face of a sharp drop in profitability, hierarchical expenses typically undergo extensive curtailment. One firm, after a long period of operating in a seller's market, responded to a sharp fall in profits with the following adjustments (Williamson 1962, pp. 5-11): (a) salaried employment over the entire organization was reduced by 32 percent; (b) headquarters employment was reduced by 41 percent; (c) the research and development staff was reduced from 165 personnel to 52, and much of its work was redirected to commercial R & D organizations; (d) the personnel and public relations staff was streamlined from 57 to 7; (e) a general reduction in emoluments of all kinds was realized. All this occurred with production unchanged. Return on investment over the interval was increased from the 4 percent level to which it had fallen to 9 percent. Further cutbacks in some areas are expected; additions are contingent on changes in volume and are tied to a new set of long-range plans.

Both the type and magnitude of these reductions suggest that the managers were operating the firm so as to attend to other than merely profitability goals in the period preceding the earnings decline. Invoking the notions of expense preference and discretionary spending makes it possible to provide an uncomplicated explanation for the adjustments observed.

---

teria will tend to increase. Any such a shift toward political considerations naturally has an adverse effect on the rate of return on investment.

2. The philosophy of management in instituting cutbacks is of particular interest. The chief budgeting officer in one organization made this observation (Williamson 1962, p. 13):

> In any large organization, certain plants or departments will have found ways to habitually operate more efficiently than others. This may be due to *competitive pressure* which has historically been felt in some products to a greater extent than others. It may be due to differences in *individual management philosophy*. . . . It follows . . . that any approach toward an arbitrary management dictate for an across-the-board slash in all cost areas will inevitably damage necessary functions in some areas, and leave remaining inefficiencies in others.

As a result, cost reductions were tailored to the individual divisions —taking their competitive history and management philosophies into account. Whereas such behavior is consistent with the managerial model, it is less clear that it should occur in a profit-maximizing organization.

Related observations of interest were the way in which headquarters overhead was allocated to achieve the effects of a lump-sum tax (*Ibid*., pp. 53–58) and the discretion that the division management was permitted in the allocation of any earnings in excess of the assigned profit goal (*Ibid*., pp. 26–28). In both respects, the behavior observed is readily accommodated by the managerial model but is not easily explained by the profit-maximizing hypothesis. In addition, the business literature abounds with descriptions of behavior that generally conform to those just cited.[20]

The detail revealed by the field studies, like the relationships found from the principal-firm analyses, suggests that, in order to explain and predict what appears to be a nontrivial range of business behavior, it may be necessary to make managerial objectives an integral part of the analysis. To treat them otherwise is to require ad hoc explanations for behavior which, broadly conceived, may be entirely rational and hence subject to systematic analysis and routine explanation.

## APPLICATION TO REGULATED INDUSTRIES

Armen Alchian and Ruben Kessel have recently argued that the presence of a regulatory constraint in the form of a maximum allowable rate of return tends to encourage expenditures on emoluments and other items that yield managerial satisfactions (1962). That is, if above-normal profits cannot be long continued

---

20. For recent surveys on such behavior, see Friedman (1971), Thompson (1958), and "White Collar Cutback" (1963).

and if supernormal profits will almost certainly invite the early attention of the regulatory commissions, the management of a regulated firm has an incentive to hold profits at or below some "safe" level by absorbing profits through expanding satisfaction-producing expenses. Alchian and Kessel argue that the behavior of these firms is best analyzed by substituting a general preference function for profits.

Although they do not formalize their argument, the effects they describe appear to be largely in accord with those obtained from the model that we have proposed. Thus, if the utility-maximization model is augmented to include a maximum-profit constraint, it is easily shown that when the firm encounters the region bounded by the constraint, the profit component in the utility function becomes fixed at this allowable maximum value, and expenditures on staff and emoluments will be increased to assure that this condition is not violated (Williamson 1963a). This is precisely the behavior they describe. Rather than generalize their argument, however, they restrict the application of their analysis to regulated industries (or others similarly confronted by a maximum-profit constraint—such as firms facing potential antitrust action). In all other circumstances, they claim, competition in the product market or competition in the capital market will remove any opportunities for such nonprofit behavior (Alchian and Kessel 1962, p. 160).

The position that competition in the product market will render impotent any tendencies to promote nonprofit expenditures is quite unassailable. The mechanism of natural selection enforces conformance to the profit-maximizing norm. However, their belief that in the absence of competition in the product market, the capital market will assign monopoly powers "to those who can use them most profitably" (Alchian and Kessel 1962, p. 160) lacks an equally efficacious enforcement mechanism. It requires that effective control of monopoly power reside with the stockholders and that this be transferable through financial (capital market) rather than by political (managerial) processes. It has been widely recognized, however, and it has been the force of our argument and evidence above, that the management, and not the stockholders, is in effective control of the monopoly power in the business firm,[21] and the transference mechanism is one of executive ascension rather than financial exchange. Subject to loose performance constraints imposed by the capital market (both the stockholders and the firm's creditors), the management is largely free to exercise the monopoly power that the firm possesses at its own discretion. Thus, while we fully agree with the Alchian-Kessel discussion on nonpecuniary motives and their suggestion

21. Edward S. Mason, for example, takes the position that "almost everyone now agrees that in the large corporation the owner is, in general, a passive recipient; that typically control is in the hands of management; and the management normally selects its own replacements" (1960, p. 4). See also Gordon (1961, pp. vi–x) and Rostow (1960).

that profits be replaced by a general preference function, we would suggest that regulated industries are merely a special case of the general case where competition in the product market—for reasons of concentration, conglomerate bigness, or barriers to entry—is weak.

## CONCLUSIONS

Based on the twin assumptions of self-interest and rational behavior, a general approach for introducing managerial objectives into a theory of the firm has been suggested. The notion of expense preference constitutes a critical part of the argument. It provides the essential connection for relating managerial objectives to operating behavior.

In addition to the comparative statics properties that were investigated, the managerial model also provides identical qualitative responses to those of the profits-maximizing model with respect to a sales tax (of either the specific or ad valorem variety). Thus the utility-maximization hypothesis preserves the main theorems of the profits-maximization hypothesis with respect to shifts in demand and application of a sales tax. Indeed, since there is little dispute concerning the general validity of these implications of the classical theory, it would be distressing to have the managerial model predict differently. However, when it comes to matters where the qualitative implications of the profits-maximizing model have been somewhat suspect, namely the effects of a profits tax and a lump-sum tax, the managerial model registers responses that contradict the classical theory.

The evidence presented is clearly suggestive rather than definitive. Such as it is, it generally supports the implications of the utility-maximization approach. Although it is not strong enough to provide a discrimination between the utility- and profits-maximizing theories, it does suggest that either firms are operated as indicated by the managerial model or, if "actual" profits are maximized, that reported profits are reduced by absorbing some fraction of actual profits in executive salaries and possibly in perquisites of a variety of sorts. This raises a serious question whether studies of monopoly power based on reported profits provide an accurate estimate of the effects of monopoly. It is possible that a nonnegligible part of true monopoly profits is absorbed internally.[22]

If subsequent results confirm the present findings concerning the effects of internal representation on the board of directors on executive compensation and dividend policy, the case for an independent board becomes much more compelling. Although Gordon has already argued this position persuasively (1961, pp. 343–51), the reasoning has lacked empirical support and there is little indication that his views have been heeded.

22. The results obtained by Gary S. Becker in his study of the effects of monopoly on discrimination (1957) also support this proposition.

A continuing investigation of the effects of discretion on managerial behavior would appear to be warranted. Indeed, we could not agree more with Becker's view that the economist *can* provide nonpecuniary motives with economic content and that "progress in this field has been hindered not so much by an intractable concept as by the economists' reluctance to take the concept seriously" (1962a, p. 179).

**Chapter Nine**

# Corporate Management and Property Rights

A. Alchian

Reprinted from *Economic Policy and the Regulation of Corporate Securities*, (H. Manne, ed.), American Enterprise Institute, Washington D.C., 1969, pp. 337–360, by permission of publisher and author.

Though we know securities regulation is what securities regulators do, we may not know why. Why should exchange of corporate property rights be permitted only under restricted conditions, whereas exchanges of noncorporate rights—such as rights in nonprofit corporations, or to proprietorships in houses and lands—are not equally regulated? What is there about corporate rights that calls for distinctive treatment?

Varied answers can be offered by economists. For example, securities in a corporation are homogeneous and purchased by many people; each potential stockholder in a corporation would bear a cost of independently discovering essentially the same information about the firm—a cost repeated for each potential buyer in some degree. If this information is required from each firm and made public, information search costs are reduced. For houses or privately owned, noncorporate enterprises, the turnover of identical rights is sufficiently small that potential costs savings are insufficient to justify the costs of compulsory revelation of all material and relevant data.

But one may still wonder why we insist that all public, corporate firms reveal information. Why not let those that choose to do so file full-disclosure reports; potential buyers could then ignore those which do not. Stockholders could then decide whether the change in stock values consequent to reduced information costs about the corporation is worth the cost of general disclosure. This would permit buyers to act on less information if they wish. It is hard to see how one can argue against such optional behavior unless he takes a paternalistic attitude—a position not without its advocates.

Another argument for compulsory disclosure is the reduction in fluctuation in security prices (as distinct from later or earlier fluctuation), but strong theory or evidence to support that proposition—or indeed even to deny it—is lacking.

Probably the most popular basis for regulation of the conditions under which corporate securities may be sold rests in the ingenious phrase "separation of ownership and control." Writers who have tried to put content into that phrase have elaborated by saying "no group of stockholders would be able under ordinary circumstances to muster enough votes to challenge the rule of management" (Larner 1966, p. 779). Or "barring blatant incompetence, management can count on remaining in office. . . . [S] o long as management possesses the confidence of the board [of directors], that body will usually not actively intervene to dictate specific policies" (Samuelson 1966, pp. 89–90). "Control lies in the individual or group who have the actual power to select the board of directors" and these presumably are some group other than the stockholders (Berle and Means 1933, p. 69).

Competition is said to be so restricted by the market power of large corporations as to change the role of competition; behavior by managers and employers is so insulated from the wealth-increasing interests of the owners that the conventional view of managers operating to increase owners' wealth is no longer germane (Kaysen 1965, p. 43).

Though these pronouncements lack empirically refutable content, their emotional impact rivals that of a national anthem.

The empirical evidence for the separation theme, if we judge by the data brought to bear, is the dispersion of stockholdings in our largest corporations, combined with management advantages in a proxy fight. Recent data suggest the dispersion of stock holdings over holders with small proportional amounts has increased (Larner 1966). Yet surely the music about separation of ownership and control requires more lyrics than that stockholding is dispersed among many stockholders with no holders having, say, 10 or more percent of the holdings. If that were all there were to the theme, it would mean merely that the expression "separation of ownership from control" had replaced the expression "dispersion of stockholdings." I would have thought that anyone propounding or testing a phenomenon to be called the separation of ownership from control would identify it with more than a measure of degree of stock ownership dispersion.

The expression probably suggests some behavioral implications. What are they? Is it that more dispersed holdings give less certainty to any one holder that his preferred use of the corporate resources will be the actual one? Or that the agent he prefers as the manager is not the one who is? Or that the probability that a *private* proprietor of $10,000 of goods can determine the use of those resources is higher than the probability that the preferred decision of an individual with a $10,000 interest in a million dollar enterprise will be the one executed. (But note that though his power of decision-making on $10,000 is reduced, it is increased over the remaining $990,000.) Any of these might denote the behavioral phenomenon implicit in the expression "separation of ownership from control." But I suspect it is not what is meant.

For clues to the meaning, we can note that a necessary attribute of ownership is the bearing of the value consequences of resources. We can interpret control to mean the authority to control decisions that will affect the value of resources. What must be meant by those who speak of separation of control from ownership is a reduced ability of the owners to revoke and reassign delegations of decision-making authority that will affect value.

In other words, it is assumed that the probability that any majority can be formed to reassign authority is lower the greater the dispersion of stock ownership. This may rest on two factors: (a) knowledge of negligence or inefficiency by an agent will be more expensive to disperse over a majority; (b) the knowledge of harmful managerial decisions will be less influential on each stockholder, as the proportionate interest of the largest stockholders is smaller and the number of stockholders is greater. In this sense, a manager's deviations from stockholders' interests are less likely to be policed. This is one empirically meaningful interpretation of the expression "greater separation of control from ownership."[1]

But some features of group ownership cut against this argument. A greater number of owners implies a greater variety of owners, some with more knowledge of the particular business. We can not assume legitimately that when there is one stockholder, he is the person most able to detect deviant behavior. Specialization of knowledge is not to be ignored; the corporate form enables a greater utilization of specialization of expert business knowledge. Despite the difficulty in reconciling several points of view, the variety of talents and the special knowledge may more than compensate. Committees are not entirely vehicles for blocking action.

Corporate voting mechanisms are frequently alluded to as both a principal cause and as evidence of a separation of stockholders from control. Management, with its accessibility to proxies at corporate expense, is alleged to dominate the voting (Berle and Means 1933). No minority group can be formed to fight the management. The picture is completed with an etching of a monolithic management group with common interests, no interpersonal conflicts of interest, and capable of perpetuating itself in office. (One is reminded of the naive cartel theory in which a group of erstwhile competitors agree to share a market, apparently with no conflicts of interests to be resolved or suppressed.)

But, in fact, if a management group is exploiting stockholders by operating an enterprise in a diversionary manner, opportunities will arise within the group for some to gain personally by eliminating that inefficient behavior. Management cannot be adequately analyzed if it is regarded as a single person; there is competition within management; managers can move to new jobs; and they compete for jobs by superior performance on present jobs. For example, few of us at the University of California strive to produce superior products in research and teaching because the taxpayers of California are uppermost in our interests. It is the appeal we offer to other potential employers that induces us to

---

1. Notice that one of the premises underlying this was *not* that in a group decision process one subgroup can exploit another, such as occurs in political voting for say a tariff or licensing restriction on entry to a profession.

act as if we were trying to satisfy our present employer's interests. Only if my future were irrevocably tied, like a slave, to my present employer would my behavior match that of the folklore indolent manager.

While we can leap from a monolithic view of management to the idea of effective separation of management from stockholder interest and control, we cannot do so if we recognize other significant management constraints. If that leap were valid, then I conjecture the tenure of office of managers in management-controlled corporations, as they are called, should be greater than in other corporations. Is the management more able to stay in office at unaffected salaries? Are stockholder profits in such corporations smaller? Is management compensation greater? Is the transition probability matrix of larger dispersed corporations different from others? I know of no empirical tests of these possible implications. Is what I have called the superficial analysis of the separation thesis incorrect, or is the alternative which does not dismiss so readily the competitive forces valid? Absent any empirical evidence in favor of the former, I shall not reject the latter.

In sum, demonstration of greater dispersion of stockholdings, along with our proxy system, does not establish that bearing-of-value consequences have been separated from the effective control of the decision-maker, nor that the wealth of the stockholder is less well guarded.

There seems to have been an embarrassing delay or unwillingness to formulate the thesis in such a way as to make it refutable or testable. One would have expected the advocates to have presented evidence. But in thirty years, we remain with almost no empirical evidence. *So, presumed implications still remain to be validated by empirical study*, and I know of none. There is one test, the survival test, but that is given almost no attention.

Since we observe an increased dispersion in corporate ownership, we should wonder why stockholders whose interests are less heeded by the top management would purchase stock in such corporations. Perhaps other advantages of the corporate form more than offset losses to stockholders imposed by the increased divergence of managers from stockholders' interests. This *could* be correct, and the fact that the dispersed ownership has increased certainly does not lend *support* to the implications of the general thesis that managerial activity in these situations will be less consistent with the shareholders' interests. Absence of a theory does not prove the phenomena are absent, but the concomitance of unspecified implications, little evidence, and inadequate logic is certainly not conducive to confidence.

## WEAKNESSES IN THEORY OF NEW CORPORATE ECONOMY

Some analytical and conceptual mistakes have been committed in attempts to deduce a distortion in managerial behavior. It has been said that profits accrue to

those who bear risks and make innovative decisions. Indeed, you can find economists who have referred to profits as rewards for innovative activity, with the
value effects serving to induce such innovation by rewarding the risk-takers. But
it is something else to say that managers who select the innovative uses are those
who bear or should bear consequent value effects. Whether or not they do depends upon prearranged contractual relationships with respect to property rights.

 The economic concept of profits refers to a particular value phenomenon—unpredicted value changes. Whoever has the title to goods is the person
who bears the profits and losses. "Owner" is the name given to that person. It
does not advance rigorous analysis to talk about profits as the "reward" to both
the owners *and* to managers who exercise delegated decision authority in determining uses of resources. This careless conjunction, common in the lay literature, leads to sentences like "if the courts, following the traditional logic of
property, seek to insure that all profits reach or be held for the security owners,
they prevent profits from reaching the very group of men (managers) whose action is most important to the efficient conduct of enterprise. Only as profits are
diverted into the pockets of control do they, in a measure, perform their second
function" (i.e., inducing innovation) (*Ibid*., p. 350).

 To believe that employed managers, with delegated authority to determine uses of someone else's resources, are the bearers of resultant profit or
loss is to lose sight of the essential attributes of the ownership-agency relation.
Managers do *not* bear those realized profit gains or losses. Owners do. The manager does not acquire those realized profits any more than does the designer or
builder of a profitable apartment house acquire or share in the realized profits—
all of which go to the apartment owner. Profits (or losses) from the construction
of an apartment house are borne by the owner, not the architect or builder. The
profits they initiated are not theirs and are not distributed to them unless they
initially had a contract to share in them—i.e., unless they initially had become co-
owners in the assets. Yet, although that is true, it does not follow that the wealth
or income of the architect or builder is unaffected or that he is left unrewarded.
A profitable apartment brings more demand for its architect or builder. Increased
demand leads to higher incomes for the architects and builders—or managers.

 It is one thing for agents with delegated authority to be rewarded for
creating profits for owners; it is a far different thing for delegated agents to share
*in those* profits. Profit receivers do not give up any of their accrued profits when
their agents are subsequently paid higher incomes for future services. The *past,
realized* profits are not redirected to or redivided among the managers in the form
of new subsequent contractual terms. Rather, the initial realized profits of the
resource owners were smaller because people anticipated that the wages of the
superior manager would be bid up in efforts to obtain his services. No *prior* contractual provision explicitly arranged between the parties is necessary for the
superior manager to realize a gain for superior services. His revealed superiority
is reflected in his higher market value.

I conjecture that confusion has arisen from the impression that a person gets what he produces—a manifestly false, if not empty, proposition. Instead he may get, via a contract, in the context of competition for his services, an amount commensurate with the most optimistic employer's belief of what he is *expected* to produce. If he prefers a different kind of contractual reward, viz., one in which his reward is contingent upon realized results, then he can become a co-owner of the resources whose values are to be affected and part of which value is to be his.

In sum, the fact that delegated agents are paid to produce value changes in goods by the way they use them does not in any sense imply that the agents deserve or will obtain part of *that* value change. This stands even though their subsequent contracts reflect their earlier performance in successfully producing past profits.

Belief that earlier realized profits must be shared among the owners and the so-called responsible superior managers or innovators results from a failure to recognize anticipatory capitalization in the market's valuation of resources. If the manager had to be rewarded by a payment out of the initial profits realized by the initial employer, then those who worry about separation of ownership and management functions would indeed have pointed out a problem.[2] But that is not the way a market values resources.

Neither is that the logic of economic theory nor the logic of conventional profit theory, despite some assertions to the contrary (Berle and Means 1933). The conventional and still valid wisdom presumes competitive market capitalization of foreseeable future events and assumes that once a manager displays evidence of a superior activity, the market (i.e., other people) will not ignore the implications about the future demand and costs for his services. Ignoring or denying the forces of open competitive market capitalization is, in my opinion, a fundamental error in the writing about ownership and control and about the modern corporate economy. Neither the role of competition in the markets for capital goods and services, nor its logic, is upset by the presence of large corporations with dispersed ownership.

Not only is market valuation ignored in the misinterpretation of the role of profits but it is ignored also in the contention that the modern stockholder's wealth is less well protected in the dispersed than in the concentrated ownership corporation. We have only to ask if anyone would pay as much for a share of stock in a corporation with dispersed ownership if he knew his wealth would be given less diligent interest by corporate managers. He would pay less in the knowledge he was to get less. The lower bid prices for stock would protect investor-owners from the foreseeable losses anticipated from less diligent concern for their wealth. Yet, corporations have thrived, and they would not have if the dispersed ownership corporation suffered from this value discounting.

2. Note that I refer to a separation of *functions*, not a separation of interests or a loss of control.

Resolution of these two conflicting interpretations lies in the possibility that either (a) the alleged greater diversionary activity is a myth, or (b) the dispersed large corporation is so advantageous in other respects that the diversionary tactics of the managers are financed out of those advantages while the stockholders get as much as they would in less dispersed corporations. If the former were true, the whole issue would collapse. If the latter were true, it would imply that the *forms* (but not value) of managerial behavior and of rewards in the dispersed ownership corporation are different and more costly (inefficient), but the managers would reap no extra gain. The consumer of products of those corporations would be paying a higher price than he otherwise would (but still, a price lower than if there were *no* dispersed ownership corporations). But could it not still be argued that the stockholders could have received a larger return? It would seem not, for if they could have, the number of dispersed corporations would have increased, thus lowering returns to the equivalent of what is being obtained in less dispersed ownership corporations. Let me elaborate on these points.

Managers do not reap some special or additional gain or economic rent from their ability to engage in diversionary tactics. Awareness of greater diversionary capability by managers or employees results in lower pecuniary salaries as managers and employees compete for the jobs permitting diversionary tactics.[3] Competition among managers and employers in seeking attractive, easy, or secure jobs implies a lower pecuniary reward in those jobs. A job with more leisure yields a lower wage; one with greater security yields a lower wage; one with more leisure and a given wage will have its security competed down. Substitution among the various facets of jobs occurs so that, on net of all considerations, the advantage of one job over another is competed away. All the various facets constitute forms of payment to the employee, whether the facets be leisure, wages, types of colleagues, working hours, vacation provisions, extent of surveillance by the employer, or what have you. Pecuniary salary will be lower for the same reasons that salaries of people working in factories or shops in more pleasant surroundings will be lower than they would have been with less attractive working conditions. Stockholders need not be activists in bringing this about.

This argues that the dispersed ownership corporation implies a difference in the vector or form of payments to managers and employees. But not all forms of compensation to employees are equally costly. The form of compensation in a dispersed corporation may indeed represent a higher cost vector to the corporation, but if the corporation can earn enough because of its advantages, it can in equilibrium bear this higher cost vector of a managerial salary. This does not mean the employees or managers are getting a more valuable or

---

3. Unless you believe, with Kaysen (1965), that executive compensation is not within control of the stockholders. If I knew what that really meant, I might test it. If it means what I suspect it was intended to mean, I think it is wrong. But then, ask yourself, "Does an owner have 'control' of the wages he pays in any kind of firm?"

preferable return than in less dispersed corporations. Instead they are being paid with a different, higher cost (i.e., less efficient), vector of rewards—one that costs more to provide but is no more preferable on net than those used in other corporations or businesses. It is different simply because the costs of controlling the various facets of the vector and changing it to a different one (say, one with higher wages and less leisure) is greater than the saving. The higher costs of such vectors (of given attractiveness to employees) can be financed out of the advantages of this type of corporation. If the costs of these forms of rewards to managers had not been higher, one might think there would have been larger earnings for the owners. But this would not be an entirely correct conclusion, for the number and scope of such corporations would have been greater, with consequent lower prices to consumers. The higher cost salary vectors, if indeed they are most costly, simply mean a sacrificed output potential for consumers—evidenced by higher prices than would have been paid for the larger output if the dispersed ownership corporation could police and control its managers' and employees' behavior as efficiently as is alleged for a smaller, less dispersed corporation.

To repeat, all this argues that the dispersed corporation changes the *forms* (and efficiency) of payment to employees and managers. It does *not* imply lower wealth for the stockholders nor higher earnings for employees and managers than in less dispersed corporations. If employees tend to be thieves, and if employers or employees are aware of this tendency, contractual money salaries will be adjusted so that part of the total salary is taken as legitimatized theft. The employers do not necessarily lose. The higher policing costs are borne by (i.e., discounted by lower wage offers to) the employees whose past conduct determines their present reputation and beliefs about future behavior. Similarly, if dispersed corporate ownership permits managers greater scope for anti-stockholder activity and if the stockholders or the employees are aware of this tendency, the terms of employment compensation will be adjusted.

The resultant implication is that in large, dispersed-ownership, for-profit corporations, we should expect different types of managerial and employee behavior and rewards than in small and closely held corporations. The large corporate pattern should reflect the greater costs of policing and revising delegated authority, but *without* necessarily resulting in lower wealth for the stockholder than in less dispersed corporations. These effects, insofar as they are foreseen or predictable, on the average will be reflected in anticipatory behavior and therefore in the valuation of initial capital investments or in stock prices on subsequent stock transfers. The stockholders are not any the poorer or their wealth less well secured.

How valid is this competitive, market equalization process in reality? We do not know. But that does not mean that we can gratuitously assume it is absent or weak as does most of the writing on the ownership-and-control-separation theme. Nor can we cavalierly assume the opposite.

Do dispersed ownership firms have historically lower rates of growth of stockholders' wealth (allowing for dividends and capital value growth) than less dispersed ownership firms? I have yet to see a test of this, though this appears to be a feasible evaluation. With attention to the regression phenomenon and with controls for types of industry, this should make a fine project for several doctoral dissertations—several, because of the value of replication and competitive testing of results.

Let us consider the presumed monolithic structure of management in the business firm. In reality, the firm is a surrogate of the marketplace, but differs in that longer-term general service contracts exist without continuous re-negotiations at every change of type of service. To analyze the firm as a single-operator institution within which it is assumed there is not the competition that exists in markets is to miss a significant portion of the competitive processes. Though a firm may continue with unchanged name and possibly even the same stockholders, the internal shifting of personnel within, as well as among, firms is market competition. The many people within a firm competing with each other and with people in other firms should suggest that the unit of analysis for competitive activity is the individual rather than an institution, which serves as an internalized market. Top management of a firm engages in screening employees, techniques, and proposals for new products which, if performed externally by separate firms, would be clearly evident as market functions. But when these functions are performed within the firm, the competitive market forces are hidden from obvious view and mistakenly ignored by careless analysts.

More significant than the rise and fall of firms, for purposes of behavioral analysis, is the rise and fall of individuals within firms. For many purposes (though not all) we can think of a firm (call it General Electric) as a marketplace, as if it were a city, within which individuals engage in atomistic competition. Competition among cities takes the form of individuals moving among cities and exporting ideas that have passed the test of profitability. While it is not correct to carry this analogy too far—and just how far "too far" is, I do not yet know—the analogy is very good in some respects. The long survival of some firm or of a few firms cannot be interpreted as evidence of a lack of market competition either within or between firms.

If it be argued that corporations with dispersed ownership or with so-called management control have separated the interests of stockholders from those of managers, we should expect differences in the rates of transition of individual employees within and between firms. We should perhaps expect a lower turnover of management in the dispersed corporation. Do we have any evidence of it? I have been unable to find it. However, I shall cite some evidence later for implying different types of behavior. For example, to continue to speak of a mythical firm called General Electric, the directors and president are quick to fire or demote a division chief whose profit record shows inferiority to some other potential division head. Replacement of an inefficient division head *may* be quicker within General Electric than if the division manager owned the division. The internal capital and personnel market may be more efficient than the external open market. I could go on and assert that there is greater mobility of managers and technical personnel within General Electric than among firms in an atomistic market economy, that new ideas are internally evaluated more quickly, cheaply, accurately, and on a broader scale than in a society made up of several firms aggregating the same size. I could assert that the labor market within General Electric is superior to the atomistic, so-called pure competitive market and is superior because there are specialists within General Electric who are rewarded more fully for collecting and evaluating information about people. Thus the usual outside employment agencies that specialize in providing personnel information would be less efficient than the personnel employment agencies operating within General Electric. But what the truth is, I do not know.

Further, the investment funds (capital) market *within* General Electric is fiercely competitive and operates with greater speed to clear the market and to make information more available to both lenders and borrowers than in the external "normal" markets. In fact I conjecture that the wealth growth of General Electric derives precisely from the superiority of its internal markets for exchange and reallocation of resources—a superiority arising from the greater (cheaper) information about people and proposals. Many "knowledge effects" that would be externalistic in an ordinary market are converted into beneficial internalities within the firm as incentives and rewards to those producing them.

The foregoing is intended to suggest that the traditional theory of profits, of private property, markets, and competition is not obsolete, and also that the separation-of-ownership-from-control theme still lacks validity deduced and established implications about exploitation of stockowners' wealth. Long prior to the wide dispersal of stockholdings in a corporation, potential conflicts of interest among stockholders were recognized. Political theory if not legal history tells us much about the probability of subgroups exploiting the remainder by the group decision process. Furthermore, the conflict of interest between principals and their agents has long been recognized, though I presume that it is not that idea which the separation of ownership and control is supposed to designate.

If I appear to be defending the old theory as adequate, let me beg off. Inadequacies in the old theory exist, but they derive from its use of a wealth instead of a utility maximizing postulate. The wealth maximizing postulate is usually appropriate (or less inappropriate) when applied to the firm as a unit of analysis. But in seeking to explain individual behavior *within* the firm, utility maximizing criteria are more general and powerful than wealth maximizing criteria. And I believe this would be equally true for the old-fashioned small firm.

Instead of a change in the modern society, it is the change in the objectives of economic theory that points up inadequacies in the old theory. We want now to interpret individual behavior, not merely firm survival as an entity. Although I say this is a change in objectives, I should be the first to assert that good old Adam Smith did exactly that in his *Wealth of Nations*. The adherents of the theme of a new modern corporate economy are saying what Smith said about corporations. Yet they are denying that the old competition theory is applicable; a somewhat strange twist, indeed.

There have been changes in our economy. But I do not believe that the idea of a replacement of a competitive era by an era of marketpower large firms will enrich our theory or understanding of behavior.

My own impression is that moves toward an economy with less open-market competition reflect a diversion of competition to the political processes, as resort is made to greater governmental control over economic access to markets and terms of exchange. Much of what passes for the new corporate economy should more accurately be called the new mercantilist, or the new political or politically regulated, economy, since it involves more political competition and the greater use of political rewards and penalties. And this move to political influence has occurred in both small and large firm industries. The solution offered (if such a political economy is a problem) usually is more political controls and political competition. This is beneficial to those most adept at political competition, for they would benefit from increased demand for their services as political competition displaces market competition in controlling economic activity. And this is what the obsolete economic theory implies.

## SUGGESTED AND TESTED BASES FOR ANALYSIS: HIERARCHICAL CONTROL AND TYPES OF PROPERTY RIGHTS

Advances in economic theory could be obtained by more explicit recognition of the political rewards-penalties structure in our economy. Advance could also be made with recognition and analysis of two other features—the hierarchical control task within a firm and the types of property rights prevailing in the firm. The hierarchical control structure has been analyzed in the context of a utility maximizing criterion by O. Williamson (1963b). For fear of flattering him, justifiably though unnecessarily, I shall merely note that the problem of inducing workers at the various hierarchical levels to gear their work to a specified common goal, as against individual interests, becomes more severe as the number of hierarchical layers or number of co-workers increases. The problem of surveillance, information-handling, and filtering is a difficult one even when there is perfect consonance of goals among the workers. Since large enterprises are usually of a corporate form with more dispersed ownership, it is easy to confound the effects of dispersed ownership with the problem of hierarchical control, and I conjecture that this has occurred.

## PROPERTY RIGHTS

But even if the confusion between stockholder dispersion and hierarchical controls is avoided, hierarchical control objectives are different in nonprofit or publicly owned enterprises (e.g., government agencies) from those in privately owned corporations. One objective—profitability—or effects on wealth of the owners will be given less weight in the former group. Profitability, combined with rights to profits, provides a clearer and stronger criterion for behavior of subordinates in for-profit corporations than in government agencies or not-for-profit enterprises. Absent that criterion and absent the "property" right to capture profits, resort is made to more detailed operating procedures and internal regulations.

The theme of separation of ownership and control in large dispersed corporations has been illustrated with public utilities and transportation companies, as well as with unregulated firms. The corporate manager's behavior has been characterized as resembling that of administrators of universities, philanthropic foundations, nonprofit corporations, unions, and government agencies. This suggests, and economic theory does indeed imply, that in corporations which are *not* profit-seeking or are *not* privately owned (at least in the sense of having saleable, marketable shares of ownership) behavior will deviate from that in a profit-seeking corporation. It deviates because stockholders in nonprofit or public utility corporations have less incentive (costs of doing so aside) for responding to market, competitive pressures for "efficient" or profit-making types of behavior. I shall try to elucidate this relatively neglected *basis for analysis* of the *kinds* of property rights and their relationship to economic and cultural behavior, because I believe something can be deduced and verified about the relationship between behavior and the types of property rights.

Crudely and broadly, let me identify one attribute of property rights in goods as being the probability of the effectiveness of my decisions about the use of those goods. That is, the greater the uses for a given good *and* the greater the probability that my decision about uses will be effective, the greater are my property rights in that good. Rights will be weaker if they have not been specified or explicitly recognized or if they have a small probability of being enforced by society.

Specification and identification of property rights is not costless. For example, water is a good to which property rights are very loosely specified, in part, because of the high costs of specification. But costs are high or low only *relative* to the value of the rights which could be specified. If the value of some right to a good rises, as that of rights to fresher water has during recent decades, the costs of specification, identification, and assignment of rights becomes more worth incurring. In general, the higher the value of potential rights to a good relative to costs of specifying those property rights, the greater will be the clarity of specification, identification, and assignment of rights in that good.

This proposition, that the increase in value of potential rights to goods leads to a stronger specification of rights, does not indicate what form the specification and identification will take nor to whom the rights will be assigned initially, nor whether they will be transferable. It does not say whether title will be taken by the state or will be assigned to individuals as private property; it does not say whether the rights will be transferable among people or whether the goods are transferable among alternative uses.

You will rightly regard the proposition as obvious insofar as it is precise enough to have meaning. Anyone knows it doesn't pay to keep track of worthless things, while for more valuable goods greater safeguarding costs are more worth incurring. But the influence of this proposition on our legal evaluation or development of property rights structures is by no means obvious and direct. The development of water law in the several states well illustrates the tortuous and hesitant progress toward more explicit specification and clear assignments of rights over water. The hold of precedent is rightly strong; adaptation to the changed values of rights and changed costs of specification is often inordinately delayed—or so it would seem from an examination of individual cases. Let me cite an example. In California, billions of dollars of wealth are being wasted simply because of the slowness in the adaptation of water law to changes in values of potential rights over water. A multi-billion dollar aqueduct, northern to southern California, is being built *now*, ostensibly to bring water to southern California. But in fact, the aqueduct is being built now not to bring more water to southern California but to establish or identify now who is to have rights over northern California water in the distant future. Building the aqueduct now to capture the present flow of water is justifiable only as a means of *presently* establishing one's *right* to the *future* flow of water. All that cost could be deferred if rights to water use were legally established and made transferable by paper records rather than by concrete and steel devices.

With but slight imagination we can perceive what would have happened had rights to future lumber, oil, gas, iron ore, and coal been assigned and controlled in that way. No imagination is required to know what has happened to our radio frequency spectrum, where a government board controls the use. Private rights which had begun to arise in common law and which evoked judicial protection for exclusive use and exchange were thwarted by government agents who denied this policing activity and the legality of exchangeability. Small wonder that the resultant mess occurred. Federal allocative authority over assignment and use was established instead of property rights enforcement via market competition. The alternative of exclusive, exchangeable, private rights (facilitated by state enforcement) to portions of that scarce valuable property—radio frequency spectrum—were not allowed to be established.

As you may know, lumber rights once were acquired not by title to standing trees, but by cutting the trees into lumber. If trees were not cut, the landowner could not count on clear title to the lumber. In some agricultural areas, land title could be established only after the claimant had stripped the trees from the land in order to manifest land *use* for agricultural purposes. Small wonder we stripped some of our midwestern forest lands.

Yet these results have been interpreted by famous historians as failures in the private property, capitalistic, competitive system. In fact, these results occurred where we did *not* have private property, capitalist market, or competitive controls over those resources. The law did not permit the title acquisition and exchange rights that would enable economic competition to induce economic use of resources. As I view that history, the symptoms were not those of a private-property, capitalist, competitive system, but of a different legal system of distributing and identifying rights which granted rights that induced undesirable behavior. Use values (of water or lumber) for future times or for different people simply could not be realized; current possessors or competitors seeking rights in the resources were told they could not retain or capture rights to those future, higher valued uses.

This suggests that while we endeavor to regulate people's activities by imposing more regulation, with consequent enhancement of the role of political competition, it would be wise to examine the behavioral effects of the legal system of establishing, identifying, and transferring various types of property rights. For example, in a not-for-profit organization, the so-called owners or trustees do not have the right to decide to use or divide the wealth of the organization for their personal use—a right which *is* held by stockholders of a for-profit private-property corporation. And in mutuals or cooperatives, while the members can vote to dissolve the enterprise and divide the proceeds among the members, they often cannot sell their rights. They can only abandon their interests in return for the initial investment, in contrast to private, for-profit corporate stockholders who can sell rights at open market prices. Whereas the present capital value—or wealth effect—is thrust on a stockholder as the value of his saleable stock changes, in a nonprofit or mutual or cooperative enterprise, a member without transferable capital value rights bears the future consequences of current decisions only if he remains a member until the time of the future consequence.

In a for-profit, private-property corporation, current stockholders gain or lose wealth when the future consequence is anticipated and reflected in stock values. If members consume capital or are less diligent in preserving the future earning power, they bear more of the cost immediately. These problems are present also in mutual associations and nonprofit organizations, since their managers do not have to answer to anyone whose capitalizable wealth is at stake. Absent property rights that permit capitalization of future events into present market values, stockholders have less incentive to be concerned with potential capital value effects, and so the manager is less responsive to implicit capital value effects.

To avoid misunderstanding, let me emphasize that the proposition is that the capitalization of future effects into present values, combined with the ability to *capture* that market wealth by selling to a second party, provides an effective stimulus to the control of actions that affect present capital values.

There is a difference in incentive effects between a capitalizable, saleable wealth right and a right to a stream of future receipts which will be obtainable only if one retains the claim into the future. For example, a mutual shareholder in a savings and loan association, or an owning managing director of a nonprofit institution, can legally reap the future rewards for present action only by remaining with the enterprise, whereas a stockholder could immediately capitalize and reap the gain by selling his interests. Market capitalization and sale provides a different reward or punishment for present actions than is true in the absence of capitalization possibilities. In sum the wealth-effects are more immediate to the stockholder than to the mutual shareholder or owner of an enterprise without capitalizable, saleable, property rights.

Before discussing noncapitalizable rights, let us consider a situation in which stockholders' rights to capture profits are restricted. The profits of a public utility are usually controlled by the state and limited to some maximum set by a regulatory agency. The *managers* will have incentives to strive for profits above the legal limit if the managers can conceal them from the regulators and capture them. And they can, to some extent. Higher earnings might be absorbed into cost-enhancing activities easing the life of the managers. Better offices, more congenial colleagues, and more relaxed business operation with shorter hours are means of "converting" potential profits into "higher cost" activities. Or, also, the managers can engage in discriminatory hiring practices, by heeding more the race, creed, and color of potential colleagues (Alchian and Kessel 1962).

This higher cost activity in a public utility is a form of profit conversion and would reduce survival prospects for firms with less restricted property rights. We should expect to see greater clusterings of employees according to race, creed, and religion, for example, in not-for-profit enterprises than in for-profit private enterprises. Empirical studies provide corroborative evidence. In sum, legal limitations on profits or on access to markets harm the interests of the relatively unpopular, unorthodox, or individualistic members of society. Given this fact, there is an inconsistency in the view of those who argue that market competition brings out the worst in people, if they also believe that discrimination in terms of race, creed, and color is undesirable.

The reason is simple. Any open-market competitors who were to discriminate in this high-cost way would be outcompeted by others who did not engage in such discrimination. But if the explicit net earnings are already at the upper legal limit in a public utility, there is less to gain by avoiding discrimination in favor of less productive but more popular colleagues. Remove the prospect for stockholders capturing greater capitalizable profit and the incentive to use lower cost, less discriminatory production techniques is reduced. No escape from this same *implication* is obtained by reliance on a regulatory body, for its members also lack the possibility of capturing capitalized wealth increments.

All this, though obvious, bears exposition because some of the separation-of-ownership-from-control discussion seems to be drawn from observations on behavior in public utilities. Here it is not the widely dispersed ownership, but a legally imposed profit restriction which induces stockholders to permit more management behavior deviating from the wealth interests of the stockholder.

If, with restrictions on capturable profits, we combine restricted or licensed *entry* to the market, as is typically the case for public utilities, then monopoly rent appears as a supplement to competitive economic profits. Monopoly rent, which regulatory folklore says belongs to the consumer, will be captured in the form of taxes or as an easier, more convenient, and better life for employees, managers, and regulators, or even possibly with higher than competitive wages. Unions, for example, find these public utilities relatively easy pickings insofar as the union can share in the monopoly rent. It follows also that public utilities will display more discrimination by race, creed, color, and age; they will display greater tenure of job, fewer firings, and other attributes at the cost of the consumers who could otherwise have had lower prices. And for this there is corroborative empirical evidence.

In addition to profit-limited firms, with or without market entry restrictions, there is another class of property arrangements that manifests similar behavior. These are the non-owned firms without stockholders, known as nonprofit institutions, mutual associations, cooperatives, union-type associations, or governmental enterprises. All lack private ownership rights in the enterprise; there are no capitalizable, alienable shares or rights. There are people who make decisions as to how certain resources shall be used *in the enterprise* and within the scope of activities of the enterprise, but no one nor any group has the right to divert the wealth of the organization to his or its personal benefit by taking it out of the enterprise. And furthermore, although rights to manage that enterprise can be bestowed on other parties, they are not saleable. The implications are profound.

A nonprofit (i.e., not-for-profit) enterprise may be successfully originated by some organizer-managing director. But increases in his wealth can not be extracted from the enterprise for use outside the enterprise, nor can he sell his management rights. His only way to convert profits to his personal benefit is to appropriately use the enhanced wealth *in* the enterprise. Again, fancier offices, better looking secretaries, more on-the-job fringe benefits, very liberal expense accounts policies, and higher salaries all have served as conversion tactics. If he were the owner, he would have capitalized that net earnings stream into a presently capturable wealth. Since he can not, he dissipates the potential profit-ability via business-connected expenditure to obtain more nonpecuniary, non-take-home sources of utility. He substitutes on-the-job advantages for personal, at-home consumption.

Nonprofit, or not-for-profit, enterprises differ from profit-restricted enterprises in two respects. First, in the former, profits are not legally restricted;

these enterprises just happen to make profits, according to the legal fiction of the situation. Second, there is no restriction on entry. The nonprofit enterprise is entitled to retain any available economic profits in the face of open-market competition. But neither the organizer nor anyone else can capitalize the profits into personal take-home wealth. However, the self-perpetuating, organizing-director, trustees, or board of directors can take higher salaries or, if profits accrue more rapidly than the director-manager can ethically divert them to personal benefit, put them in some sort of endowment. Had it been a for-profit enterprise, with saleable stock, the present *and future anticipated* earnings could have been distributed or, if retained, captured by the initial stockholders via the higher market value of saleable stock. We would expect nonprofit enterprises, insofar as they are profitable, to manifest and distribute their net earnings via business connected costs. Their costs may appear to be higher, but in fact those costs may be distributions of profits; the higher costs are not necessarily signs of inefficiency or higher real costs.

Mutual associations, of the sort that exist in the savings and loan business and in insurance provide evidence of the effects of an absence of private property rights. The legal fiction is that depositors or insurees are mutual owners. The mutual shareholders acquire shares that often cannot be liquidated by redemption, and there is no possibility of marketing them at a value reflecting the profitability of the mutual organization. Mutual shareholders are limited in their voting power to a maximum number of votes, usually a very small percentage of all votes. Proxies can be solicited, but no one can start with a large or significant base of his own votes. There is less gain in raiding a mutual association or waging a proxy battle to put in new management as a means of improving profitability, because if such an attempt were successful, the potential gains would not be reflected in capitalized market values of saleable shares. The winner of a proxy battle would have to take on some managerial position and reward himself by a salary collected during his tenure of office. Not only is his salary subjected to a higher tax rate than capitalized value but, more fundamentally, a series of future net earnings is a less powerful incentive than the choice between that course and capturing the currently capitalized present value.

However, the organizing manager-directors of mutual associations do have some means, even if roundabout, by which some of the profits can be capitalized. One way is for the operator-organizer to own private, for-profit accessory companies selling insurance and other complementary services to the mutual. The mutual's purchases of such services can be made from these side companies which charge higher than competitive rates, thereby siphoning off the net earnings and enabling their conversion into capitalizable stock values of the service companies.

Market competition by other potential managers for the mutual manager's job will be ignored because the director, to whom an appeal must be made, is the manager himself. And any potential savings from the more efficient potential manager would be given little weight, since the present director cannot capitalize the value of the potential savings. I am not claiming that mutual shareholders are incapable of controlling the managers, just that their costs of doing so are greater and the gains are smaller than for privately owned corporate institutions.

Evidence for these higher cost or aberrant activities of mutuals (not necessarily indicative of less able, efficient, or alert management) has been obtained by Alfred Nicols in a study of mutual and private-stock savings and loan associations (1967). Reported costs per dollar of new loans, turnover of management, nepotism, and responsiveness of interest rates to changed market conditions show that the mutuals had higher costs, higher nepotism, smaller management turnover, and slower response via interest rate changes.

This does not mean that the managers are less alert or informed of the possibilities. They exploit those possibilities in ways that yield benefits they can capture; the wealth potential is being exploited in ways other than take-home, capitalizable wealth for nonexistent stockholders.[4]

4. A study of this is provided by B. Weisbrod in his investigation of nonprofit hospitals (1965). He identifies what he regards as nonprofit maximizing behavior, and the analysis is rather suggestive. A stronger test could be provided if one were to make a similar study of proprietary hospitals.

## Chapter Ten

# The Not-for-Profit Hospital as a Physician's Cooperative

M. Pauly
M. Redisch

Reprinted from the *American Economic Review* 63 (March 1973): 87–99, by permission of publisher and authors.

The private, nonprofit hospital has usually been regarded by economists as an organizational anomaly. In particular, it has been alleged that the predominance of the not-for-profit structure within the American hospital system is associated with a weakening of the usual market constraints of competition and profit orientation. As a result, this critical element in any analysis of the medical care system in the United States has usually been modeled with a mixture of anecdote and ad hoc assumption. It is typically assumed that "all objectives of nonprofit organizations can be described in terms of some type(s) of output (broadly defined) or capital stock."[1] William Baumol and Howard Bowen describe these goals as "bottomless receptables into which limitless funds can be poured" (1965, p. 497).

Model variation occurs as investigators place combinations of key variables in either the objective function or the constraint set of the hospital. Joseph Newhouse (1970) and Martin Feldstein (1971) studied the implications of the maximization of quantity-quality subject to a budget constraint. Millard Long's (1964) model is one of quantity maximization subject to both a budget and a quality constraint. Paul Ginsburg (1970) assumed maximization of weighted output subject to a budget and an availability of capital constraint. Maw Lin Lee (1971) included types of physical capital in the hospital objective function. And Melvin Reder (1965) talked of hospitals trying to maximize "the weighted number of patients treated (per time period), the 'weights' being the professional prestige to the doctors attending them" (p. 480).

This last model is the only one to (even) hint at a nonpassive role for the physician in a model of hospital behavior.[2] In this paper we propose an alternative model in which the physician emerges as a traditional income maximizing

---

1. See Ginsburg (1970, p. 42).
2. Paul Feldstein (1966) and Carl Stevens (1970) have discussed the role of the physician in the hospital, but have not provided an explicit model.

economic agent who is "discovered" in a decision-making role within this not-for-profit enterprise. Our model is similar to the model of the firm customarily used by economists, in that it is based on the assumption of net income maximization. Only a somewhat unusual definition of net income is needed to enable us to apply in our short-run analysis many of the conclusions of the orthodox model of the firm. In the longer run, however, our model, while still based on net-income maximization, yields different predictions about the institution's response to changes in demand and supply parameters. Furthermore, it may be possible to generalize parts of our model to other private, nonprofit service firms such as universities and symphony orchestras, which produce and sell services to individual consumers, many of whom are not poor.

Specifically, we assume that the group of attending physicians on the hospital's staff enjoys de facto control of the hospital at any point in time. Given this assumption, we develop a model in which the hospital operates in such a way as to maximize the net income per member of the physician staff. Results are obtained which are similar to those derived from models of producers' cooperatives in Yugoslavia and collective farms in the USSR. The physician plays a role analogous to that of the Yugoslav worker and the Russian peasant. Our results are also similar to those obtained from the "theory of clubs," developed by James Buchanan (1966) and others.

## THE MODEL

We simplify the problem initially by assuming that patients pay the full market price for care and that the decision-making group in the hospital is able to impose its collective will on individual members. The implications of weakening these assumptions to allow for customary forms of health insurance and for imperfect cooperation among controlling individuals will be discussed in later sections.

The product produced in the hospital is hospitalization services. We shall assume that this output can be represented by a single variable $Q$.[3] To produce this output, physical capital $(K)$, nonphysician labor $(L)$, and physician or medical staff labor $(M)$ are used. The production process can be summarized by the production function

$$Q = F(K, L, M) \tag{1}$$

In European countries in which physicians who treat patients in the hospital are employed by and paid by the hospital, this three-input production

3. Derivatives of two quite different surrogates for hospital output have been used most often by economists doing empirical research. One is based on the number of inpatient days and outpatient visits at the hospital while the other is concerned with the number of cases treated in the hospital. The "case treated" corresponds most closely with the measure of output implied by our model.

function is the obvious one.[4] But in the United States, the hospital patient is subject to two separate billings. The hospital charges him only for the use of capital and nonphysician labor. The physician presents a separate bill for the use of his "personal" physician's services. This dual billing system has led to a conceptually false dichotomy in much of the health economics literature. The physician and hospital are often viewed as independent economic entities selling services in functionally segmented health markets. This view appears to provide the rationale for the hospital-administrator-oriented, output-maximization theories of hospital behavior discussed earlier.

We propose an alternative view. It seems obvious that the patient's demand is primarily for the service produced by the physician and hospital acting in combination, not for the separate components, even though there probably is a separate demand for some attributes, such as amenities or additional patient days for recuperating, that the hospital alone produces.

The critical assumption of our model is that the physician staff members enjoy de facto control of hospital operations and see to it that hospitalization services are produced in such a way as to maximize their net incomes. The appearance of physician control is not hard to establish. The staff physicians have direct control over the number and types of patients admitted and over the types of services they receive; they control output. The staff physicians can determine, within rather broad limits, what use of the hospital will be made in treating a patient; they control many of the production decisions. They have indirect control over many other aspects of the hospital's operation, such as capital investment and the level of nursing care, in the sense that no administrator can afford to incur the displeasure of the medical staff, interfere with medical staff prerogatives, or make decisions which will deter large numbers of physicians from remaining on the hospital's staff or using that hospital for their patients. The trustees, who have nominal control over the hospital's operation, usually look to the medical staff when making decisions on operations or capital investment.

We first assume that the physicians on the staff of a hospital at any point in time act in such a way as to maximize the sum of the money incomes of all staff members. Such as assumption implies a process of group decision-making resulting in a kind of perfect cooperation not likely to be observed in practice. It also ignores nonmonetary components of a physician's income, such as leisure time and prestige, which are likely to be of some importance. Nevertheless, this model is useful as a benchmark from which to consider the effects of alternative assumptions.

We postulate an economic short-run period as one in which the number of physicians on the hospital staff, $M$, remains constant. Each physician is presumed to supply a constant, homogeneous amount of medical input.

4. This was the form used by M. Feldstein (1967) in his study of hospitals in the United Kingdom.

The patient's demand is primarily for the service produced by the physician and hospital acting in combination, not for the separate components. This can be formalized by postulating a demand function for "hospitalization services" faced by the physician staff that takes the form

$$Q = Q(P_T), \qquad \frac{\partial Q}{\partial P_T} < 0 \tag{2}$$

where $P_T$ is the combined price paid by the patient for the physician and hospital components.[5,6]

We also assume that the hospital component of $P_T$ is set so as to allow the hospital to just break even, with no gain or loss.[7] That is, we assume that the hospital price $P_h$ is set to produce the equality:

$$P_h Q = wL + cK \tag{3}$$

where $P_h$ is the unit price the hospital charges for use of nonphysician labor and capital, $w$ is the wage rate for nonphysician labor, and $c$ is the user cost of capital.[8]

5. Some empirical justification of this assumption may be found in Donald Yett et al. (1971), where it was estimated that the elasticity of demand for *hospital* output with respect to *surgeon's* fees is 0.7.

6. If the market for output is perfectly competitive, $|\partial Q /\partial P_T|$ will be infinite; otherwise, the individual hospital demand curve for output will have a negative slope.

7. If the hospital received contributions, it may set a target loss equal to the contributions, but this will not alter our analysis. Moreover, after the fact the hospital may have a profit or loss, but this is assumed to result wholly from stochastic factors.

8. The interpretation of the user cost of capital $c$ is worth comment. When capital is provided through borrowed funds, the interpretation is clear; $c$ is equal to $(r + d)P_K$, where $r$ is the interest rate at which the funds were borrowed, $d$ is the depreciation rate, and $P_K$ is the price of capital goods. When unrestricted donations are used to pay for the marginal unit of capital, the user cost is $(r' + d)P_K$, where $r'$ is the opportunity cost of using contributed funds for hospital physical capital, i.e., the rate which could have been earned on those funds if they had been invested elsewhere (say, in government bonds). When donations are made with the restriction that they be used for physical capital investment, they will affect the marginal user cost of capital only if the hospital receives so much in donations that it does not have to turn to any other source for funds for capital investment (unless, of course, the conditions for contribution of restricted funds specify a certain amount of the hospital's own funds as matching payments). If restricted donations fall short of the amount which, given the interest rate $r$, the hospital wishes to invest so that the hospital borrows, the relevant *marginal* user cost of capital must involve the interest and depreciation rates. Except for the case in which restricted donations are so large that the amount of capital that is bought with them exceeds the amount which would be indicated by the marginal conditions, donations, whether unrestricted or restricted, are really equivalent to lump sum subsidies. Only if the hospital's price and output policies affect contributions (and within wide margins, they do not seem to) should contributions be treated as other than lump sum grants. In a world of uncertainty, however, the total of donations past and present may affect a lender's willingness to lend, since they provide collateral. Even in this case, current donations are likely to be important only if they are large relative to total nonborrowed capital.

The hospital is to be run so as to maximize the net incomes of the physicians on the staff at any point in time. If the number of physicians in the short-run analysis is taken as given at $\overline{M}$, the problem is to maximize $P_T Q - P_h Q$ (which is equal to $P_T Q - wL - cK$) subject to the production function (1), with the level of $M$ set at $\overline{M}$, and the demand curve (2). This problem is obviously identical to that facing an orthodox profit-making firm with one input held constant. The marginal conditions for optimal employment of labor and capital are the same, namely, that marginal factor costs equal their respective marginal revenue or value products.[9]

It may be useful at this stage to contrast the model of the nonprofit hospital just developed with the orthodox model of the profit-maximizing firm. In the latter case, all labor inputs and capital services financed by debt are paid their competitive costs. Nondebt capital then obtains the residual income, which is usually assumed to consist of payment of the opportunity cost of that capital (normal profits) and economic profit. The only difference between this model and the physician-profit maximization model of the hospital is that in the latter it is the physician input, rather than the nondebt capital input, which obtains economic profits, the residual income. If a profit-maximizing firm submitted two bills for its services—one just covering the cost of labor and debt-financed capital, produced in a nonprofit firm, and the other from a separate legal institution covering the services of equity capital, the analogy would be complete.

## LONG-RUN INDIVIDUAL HOSPITAL EQUILIBRIUM

The number of physicians on the staff of any hospital obviously is not fixed but is variable over time. What determines the size of the hospital's staff? The answer to this question depends critically on the assumption made about the hospital's staffing policy. We shall outline the results of three alternative policies—closed staff, open staff, and a policy in which new physicians can be hired by the hospital.

9. The model implies cost minimization in the sense that, given the physician input, quantities of labor and capital are chosen which, given their marginal supply prices, minimize costs. Cost minimization is also a characteristics of output-maximization models. However, normative conclusions that have been derived from empirical cost function studies regarding socially optimal scale of hospital facilities are considerably weakened when it is realized that there is no reason to suppose that, in comparisons across hospitals or over time, the physician input actually is constant, or even variable in a random way. The physician input has been left out of cost and production function studies of U.S. hospitals. Unless the physician input is specified or is known to be a constant ratio to $K$ and $L$, there is no way of knowing the true social costs of all the inputs associated with any scale of output, and hence no way of determining the cost-minimizing scale. Observed decreasing hospital costs, for instance, may only represent a systematic increase in physician input with size. Furthermore, when we allow imperfect cooperation of the physician staff in our model in a later section, we will find that minimization of even nonphysician costs in the technical sense by the hospital is a very unlikely conclusion.

### Closed Staff

Many hospitals in the United States restrict staffing privileges; they do not permit any physician to join the hospital's staff just because he wishes to do so, even if he is licensed to practice medicine and surgery. The decision on whether or not to admit a new member to the staff (or whether to replace a member who has left) is made by the existing members of the hospital's staff of physicians. If we assume that once a physician is admitted to the staff, he has privileges identical to those of the existing members, the appropriate maximand for the hospital appears to be the maximization of net income per physician, $Y_M$. Physicians will be willing to add members to the staff as long as it causes each member's net income to rise.

This implies that the objective function to be maximized is

$$Y_M = (P_T Q - cK - wL)/M \tag{4}$$

subject to the production function (1) and the demand curve (2). The necessary first-order conditions for an extremum become

$$w = P_T \frac{\partial Q}{\partial L} + \frac{\partial P_T}{\partial Q} \frac{\partial Q}{\partial L} Q \tag{5a}$$

$$c = P_T \frac{\partial Q}{\partial K} + \frac{\partial P_T}{\partial Q} \frac{\partial Q}{\partial K} Q \tag{5b}$$

$$Y_M = P_T \frac{\partial Q}{\partial M} + \frac{\partial P_T}{\partial Q} \frac{\partial Q}{\partial M} Q \tag{5c}$$

In long- or short-run equilibrium, the physician-hospital conglomerate firm that we have postulated will equate the marginal supply price of all non-physician inputs to their respective marginal revenue or value products. However, in our model, physicians all share equally in the residual income of this health enterprise, the shares depending on their assumed equal shares of a total output. Condition (5c) states that physician staff size is determined in long-run equilibrium by equating the marginal revenue product of physicians to the net average revenue product of the physician staff. This makes intuitive sense. The hospital "pays" for new physicians by allowing them a proportionate share of total output and, hence, of net revenues. Staff physicians will want to welcome warmly a new member as long as his contribution to total revenues of all staff physicians is greater than the average current income per physician which he receives.

Of course, condition (5c) cannot be satisfied unless there are physicians willing to work at the hospital for the earnings available. That is, the equilibrium value of $Y_M$ must be at least as large as the income stream available to a physician in his next best opportunity. There will be a supply curve of physicians to any hospital. The shape of this curve will depend in part on the income a

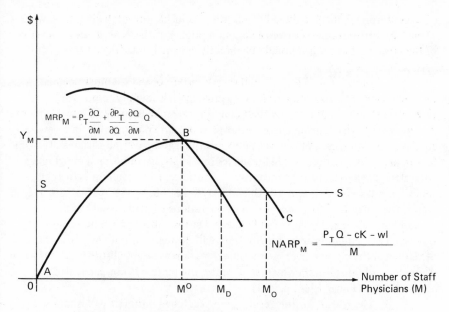

**Figure 10-1.** The Long-Run Equilibrium Position of a Hospital Operating in an Urban, Physician-Intensive Environment

physician could get in other hospitals, and his valuation of other uses of his time, both as leisure and as office practice.

Figure 10-1 depicts the long-run equilibrium position of a hospital operating in an urban, physician-intensive environment. The physician supply curve, *SS*, may therefore be assumed to be approximately infinitely elastic, and we also assume that it is at a low level relative to income possibilities in this particular hospital. Within the hospital, capital and nonphysician labor take on short-run optimal values as physician staff size, $M$, varies along the horizontal axis. *ABC* thus represents the maximum attainable income per physician for each specific value of $M$. Returns to scale and elastic demand lead initially to the upward sloping segment of *ABC*, but eventually decreasing returns and diminishing marginal revenue cause the curve to turn down. The maximum maximorum, $Y_M^*$, of this set of short-run maximums is reached at the intersection of the marginal revenue product and net average revenue product curve, when physician staff size reaches its long-run equilibrium value of $M^*$.

This model is very similar to those developed by Benjamin Ward (1958, 1970), Evsey Domar (1966), Walter Oi and Elizabeth Clayton (1968), Jaroslav Vanek (1970), and others who explain the economic behavior of the Soviet collective farm or the Yugoslav producers' cooperative. The physician plays a role analogous to that of the Russian peasant and the Yugoslav worker. Institutionally, the arrangements differ because the physician receives his "share" of the enterprise's income directly from the sale of his output, whereas the worker on a collective receives it from a common pool. But this is because, in the case of the hospital, output can usually be directly assigned to particular staff members.

Our model of the hospital shares certain of the seemingly paradoxical conclusions of these cooperative-collective models. Supply response to changes in product and factor market conditions can be in perverse directions. An upward shift in the demand curve for hospital output could result[10] in a new equilibrium with higher price levels, *lower* output, and *fewer* physician staff members to share the greater total net revenues of the physician-hospital conglomerate enterprise. "Members have an incentive to contract membership to hoard the spoils" of a demand increase (see Oi and Clayton 1968, p. 43). An increase in a factor price may lead to an expansion of operations to help spread the misery around among a larger group of individuals. On the other hand, a lump sum subsidy, such as a philanthropic contribution, will decrease output and staff size. "Even when the co-op moves in the same direction as a capitalist firm, its response is usually more sluggish. For market stability, the picture is not particularly reassuring" (see Domar 1966, p. 739).

The reason for this result can be sketched out briefly:[11] suppose a hospital faces a given price for output, and price increases by some amount. This will produce a proportionate increase in the marginal revenue product of physicians, assuming that $K$ and $L$ are held constant, but the income per physician $(Y_M)$ will increase more than proportionately. The maximum average income would be attained at a smaller value of $M$.

The values of $K$ and $L$ will not, of course, remain constant. They will increase in response to increases in their marginal products. But $M^*$ will still decline unless increases in $K$ and $L$ increase the marginal revenue product of physicians and do so by a large enough amount to offset the increase in average income. This need not happen; $Q$ and $M^*$ may decrease, or not increase much, whereas in a profit-seeking firm the use of an input and the amount of output would almost certainly increase with a rise in the price of output.

### Discriminatory Sharing or Hiring Model

To consider the consequences of altering the "equal sharing" assumption, we suppose that the hospital depicted in Figure 10–1 is allowed to hire physicians at the supply price, $OS$. The hospital will then organize production in the same way as would a profit-maximizing firm. The physician input will be increased until the marginal revenue product and the marginal supply price of physicians' services are equal to each other. Staff physicians will be able to cap-

10. Unambiguous results concerning the direction of supply response cannot be determined unless specific restrictions are placed on the nature of the demand shift and the form of the production function.

11. For a more extensive development, see the references cited in the preceding paragraph.

ture, in their own incomes, the excess of the marginal products of the infra-marginal hired physicians over their supply price. Equilibrium will be at $M_D$. But note that there is explicit discrimination in returns to homogeneous labor in this situation; the ability to sustain a stable equilibrium under these circumstances is highly suspect. As Pauly (1970) has shown, a system of clubs in which some identical persons receive less than others is not likely to be stable. It may well be that the internship-residency programs so prevalent in the United States may be an institutionalized method of getting around the inherent instability in the discriminatory hiring model by creating artificial, functionally viable distinctions among homogeneous physicians.[12] Determination of the ratio of "partner" physicians to "hired" physicians is likely to be arbitrary. The economic well-being of those physicians left with full staff privileges varies inversely with this ratio.

### Open Staff Model

Alternatively, we can retain the equal-shares assumption, and examine the economic behavior of hospitals that do not restrict entry to their physician staff. Any licensed physician who chooses to do so may become a full partner in the firm. Equilibrium at $M_o$ in Figure 10-1 is characterized by equality of average income per member of the physician staff and the marginal supply price of physicians services.

Of course, for a hospital in a rural area with few physicians, or in an area where many physicians have attractive alternatives to membership on that hospital's staff, the situation might be somewhat different. Faced with a sharply rising supply curve for physicians' services, $S'S'$ in Figure 10-2, the physician staff will be in equilibrium at $M_{oo}$. The hospital might as well call its policy open staffing, since it would be willing to add new members in order to move up the rising part of the net average product curve and increase income per staff member. Such a "frustrated closed staff" hospital only needs to adopt a closed staff policy when the number of staff members reaches $M^*$.

Note that the discriminatory-hiring and open-staff hospitals, either the "true" open-staff hospital or the frustrated closed-staff one, do not exhibit the potentially perverse supply responses that were uncovered in the closed staff model. Increases in demand will lead to increases in physician staff and output.

## LONG-RUN INDUSTRY EQUILIBRIUM

The closed-staff hospital in the long run tries to adjust its physician staff size to achieve maximum income per physician. But if physicians in a hospital achieve

12. Interns and residents serving in U.S. hospitals currently comprise about 15 percent of all MD's and, of course, provide a considerably higher percentage of hospital based physicians' services. In several of the cost function studies, there have been attempts to estimate the effect these physician trainees have on hospital costs and revenues. Our model would suggest that it might prove more fruitful to analyze the ways in which trainees can increase the incomes of those physicians with regular staff privileges.

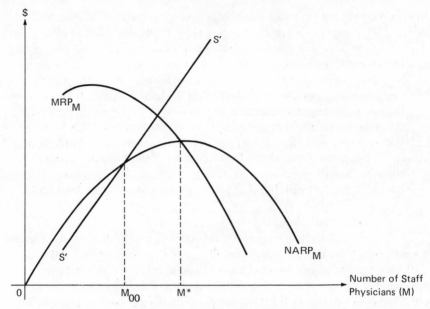

**Figure 10-2.**  Supply Curve for Physicians' Services

incomes below those of other identical physicians on the staffs of other hospitals in that area or in other areas, the low-income physicians may wish to join the staffs of high physician-income hospitals. If they are prevented from joining the staffs of existing hospitals, as would occur if those hospitals were large enough so that average income was maximized, it will be worthwhile for $M^*$ of those rejected physicians to join a new hospital, a duplicate in size of the old one. Indeed, the formation of new hospitals will continue as long as higher incomes can be earned, bidding up the supply price of physicians and bidding down the price of final output (and hence the curve of average income) until a position of long-run equilibrium is attained at which average income, marginal income, and marginal supply price are equal to each other and equal across hospitals. In the open-staff model, long-run equilibrium is also reached by the formation of new hospitals, but here the new hospitals draw off excess members from existing hospitals, raising average incomes since average size shrinks. This process will continue until formation of a new hospital does not raise average income. Finally, in the discriminatory-hiring model, physicians who are paid less than staff physicians (i.e., hired) will find it advantageous to try to join a hospital of their own in which they are all staff members and receive incomes equal to those of physicians in existing hospitals.

Thus these models have identical long-run industry equilibria (when the number of firms is variable), but the closed-staff model has a radically different long-run firm equilibrium and may move in a perverse direction from that of the discriminatory-hiring firm. The open-staff model, on the other hand, responds in the same way as would the discriminatory-hiring (or profit-maximizing) hospital, but is likely to have a quantitatively different response. Although the final industry outcomes under these institutional arrangements are the same, the adjustment process by which that outcome is reached is very different in each case.

## IMPERFECT COOPERATION ON THE HOSPITAL STAFF

In this section we wish to relax the assumption of perfect cooperation by the hospital's staff of physicians. The *individual* physician may in fact have direct control over the process of producing output. He is able to order use of nursing and other inputs for his patients, in his character of professional expert. At best, the hospital can determine only a stock of inputs; the physician controls the flow of services from them. This is in contrast to a producers' cooperative (or even a nonprofit university) in which, presumably, a central management is somewhat more able to prevent individualistic behavior. Moreover, each physician's income from the hospital-connected services depends entirely on his own output, in contrast to the producers' cooperative model in which an individual worker's income partly depends on his own output but also depends on his share of total profits or surplus income. The physician shares group income insofar as he shares group output.

     We assume, as before, that the hospital price is set at a level which permits the hospital to break even. It is now easier to see why this assumption is itself a consequence of the physician profit-maximization hypothesis. Other things being equal, hospital profits mean higher hospital prices, which reduce physician incomes. To be sure, hospital profits could be used for capital investment which may enhance future physician incomes, but (a) physicians may not want to invest in the hospital and (b), as Eirik Furubotn and Svetozar Pejovich (1970) have noted, the fact that property rights are not vested in investment from profits makes it even less desirable than owned investment.

     Since prices for services are not (yet) set at marginal cost,[13] and since the physician does have the power to direct the application of labor and capital services in producing his output, noncooperative behavior can occur. Suppose the hospital follows the policy of charging an all-inclusive daily rate. Suppose ordering the use of more labor in the production of some output will permit the phy-

---

13. In fact, it does not appear that hospitals do price at marginal cost. They have moved away from the use of an all-inclusive daily rate, the same for all patients, toward itemized bills, but they are still far from charging marginal cost as a price. And in theory, it is unlikely that prices could be set equal to marginal cost. Unless marginal cost just equals average cost, marginal cost-pricing by the hospital of its services would violate the no-profit, no-loss constraint assumed above. Moreover, the use of different prices for different qualities of outputs involves transactions and information costs, which may be substantial.

sician to charge more for that unit of output, because the "quality" of the output is enhanced. If the application of more nonphysician labor raises the price $P_T^i$ that can be charged by the $i$th physician but if the same price $P_H$ is charged for all units of hospital output, regardless of whether or not extra labor is ordered, the physician will want to use labor for his $Q_i$ patients up to the point at which the following equality is satisfied:

$$\frac{\partial P_T^i}{\partial L} Q_i = \frac{Q_i}{Q} w \tag{6}$$

That is, the individual physician only considers a fraction $Q_i/Q$ of the cost of the labor he orders to be employed, whereas group profit maximization would require him to take account of the costs his action imposes on other physicians' patients. Consequently, imperfect cooperation leads to the use of too much labor relative to the amount that would be used if group incomes were maximized with perfect cooperation.

How great these departures from perfectly cooperative usage will be depends upon how well the staff as a group can control the actions of its individual members. It seems reasonable to suppose that the magnitude of the departure from cooperative behavior should get larger as the size of the staff gets larger.[14] There are at least three reasons for making this assumption.

1. When the staff size is small, each physician bears a larger share of the cost of his own actions.
2. When the staff size is small, departures from cooperative behavior on the parts of others are more noticeable to any single member.
3. When the staff size is small, mutually agreeable group decisions are more likely to be arrived at, since the cost of decision-making is less.

In terms of the geometric analysis, introduction of imperfect cooperation in this way shifts the curve of net revenue per member down and to the left. The conclusion is obvious; lack of perfect cooperation makes the (second best) optimal size of the staff and hospital smaller than it would otherwise be.

## THE EFFECT OF INSURANCE

To this point we have assumed that patients confronted the full market price for care. Insurance coverage of medical costs may weaken the applicability of this assumption. The hospital is typically paid on the basis of costs incurred. If there

14. A similar analysis of the effect of size is provided by Olson (1962). Other applications to medical care can be found in the work of Newhouse (1972) and Lindsay (1968).

are no copayments or deductibles at all, this arrangement effectively eliminates market control over the hospital component of the price of hospitalization, since higher hospital costs and prices have no effect on the cost actually paid by the patient (except through the premium, which only matters if the premium rises so high that the person drops coverage). Moreover, the allocation of costs within the hospital to insured patients, especially Blue Cross members, is often done on average cost basis. The only restraint on the physician's prescribing the use of hospital capital and labor for his fully insured patient is the upward pressure his behavior would exert on the prices paid by his noninsured patients. Conversely, under average cost allocation some of the market discipline is lost for the non-insured by the transfer of some costs to the insured.

If every patient had full coverage, cost-based hospital insurance, there would be no constraint on the amount of capital and labor that physicians combine with their services. Capital and labor would therefore be employed up to the point at which the marginal contribution of each to the physician's revenue was zero. This produces Cadillac-quality medicine. The only constraint on the use of these inputs would be offered by the upper limit on the number of things a hospital can do for a patient which might have some justification. Over time, technological change might be expected to relax even this constraint.

When insurance covers part of each patients' hospital bill, the factor prices of hospital inputs $K$ and $L$ are effectively reduced as far as the group of physicians is concerned. One would expect an increase in the usage of hospital inputs relative to physician inputs for producing a given output. Hospital unit costs would rise. Thus our model provides an explanation of the positive relationship between hospital insurance coverage and hospital unit prices and costs found by M. Feldstein (1971). In addition, our model yields the important result that, *ceteris paribus*, increased hospitalization insurance should increase physician prices and physician incomes.

## TOWARD A THEORY OF THE NOT-FOR-PROFIT ENTERPRISE

To this point we have taken the not-for-profit nature of the typical American hospital as given. In this section we offer an explanation of why this organizational form has arisen.

There are two ways in which the hospital might operate if it were on a profit-maximizing basis. It might combine the services of nonphysician labor and physical capital, and sell them to or through the physician, who combines them with his own input to produce the output of hospitalization services. Alternatively, the hospital might perform the job of combination itself, hiring the physician input and selling the final output. In either case the direct control over the use of nonphysician labor and capital would not be held by the physician. In the first case, he would have to use the market for control, which is not always efficient in the sense of minimizing all costs, including transactions costs, as direct control. In the second case, he himself would be under the direction of the supplier of equity capital. It is surely possible that there are some products which are not produced efficiently when a representative of the owners of equity capital directs their production, or when the market is used to organize the production process instead of the use of direct controls within a single organization. The most efficient method might be for the supplier of an important component of the labor input to direct the production process.

This would tend to happen when human capital is important in the production of some output and when the flow of services of that human capital cannot well be directed from outside but is controlled by the person in whom the capital is embodied. As Alchian and Demsetz (1972) have noted, the wage system tends to break down when marginal products cannot be monitored closely. This may be a reasonable conjecture in the case of the production of hospital services. Many of the decisions the physician has to make are decisions which cannot be supervised directly and which have contingent outcomes. There probably needs to be some incentives for the physician. Financial interest in the outcome of his actions is one such incentive, and that incentive is at its greatest when the physician bears the full residual income, when the consequences of his actions are not spread over suppliers of physical capital.[15]

The production process requires some physical capital. In a labor-managed firm in which most of the assets of labor are embodied in nontransferable human capital, not all of the physical capital can be borrowed, since collateral cannot be provided. Another necessary condition therefore for the emergence of the not-for-profit form would seem to be the willingness of individuals to contribute for its equity capital. In principle, contributions could either be voluntary or provided through government. Where voluntary contributions are sufficient, government contributions would not be expected to emerge. On the other hand, voluntary contributions may arise in precisely those cases in which the government fails to act. They may also arise in cases in which the government through tax deductibility subsidizes private contributions. The source of contributions, whether unsubsidized voluntary, subsidized voluntary, or governmental, is not critical to the argument, except to the extent that one form (for example, government) implies more external control over physicians' actions than another.

These contributions could be motivated by a desire on the part of contributors to make output available to themselves or to those whom they

15. To see this, think of each physician as a firm. The socially most efficient institutional arrangement is the one which maximizes the net present value of this firm. The present value is a contingency, depending on the state of nature (for example, what's really wrong with his patients, whether an epidemic occurs, etc.) and the amount of effort that the physician makes. The amount of effort, in turn, depends upon the share of profits the physician receives. The appropriate share for the physician, even given the greater risk he bears, may be approximately equal to one.

would like to see consume it. That is, the motivation could either be based on the potential receipt of private benefits or of external benefits. Contributions are a logical way for potential purchasers of the outputs of labor-managed firms to make possible production of the output, which they or those about whom they are concerned will use. If there are barriers to entry by profit-seeking firms (as there are in higher education and, to some extent, in the hospital industry as well), potential consumers may be willing to contribute if that is the only way that output, which yields them consumers' surplus, can be made available. It is not surprising that private not-for-profit firms which sell output—hospitals, universities, symphony orchestras—tend to provide output which is used *not* by the poor but partly by the contributors themselves.[16]

## CONCLUSION

The main thrust of the model we have suggested here, and the one which differentiates it from models of the not-for-profit hospital that have been suggested by others, is the use of the maximization of physicians' income as the characteristic function. The potential absence of perfect cooperation distinguishes it from similar models of producers' cooperatives. In a methodological sense, our model seems to be more attractive than those which simply assume that the not-for-profit organization maximizes a variable such as "quantity of output," because it explains what the organization does in terms of the economic motivation of those who control it.

More importantly, it appears to provide an appealing explanation of some peculiar characteristics of not-for-profit hospitals. The supposed quality consciousness of such hospitals, for example, is easily explained; "quality" is a synonym for application of nonphysician labor and capital in physician-income-enhancing ways, and noncooperative behavior could easily lead to "too high" quality. "Duplication of facilities" probably owes its existence to closed staffing and lack of perfect cooperation. Other aspects of hospital behavior could also be explained by considering their effect on physicians' income; the pattern of investment, for example, might be best explained by changes in the ability of capital to enhance physicians' incomes. The inelastic supply response of hospitals to Medicare and Medicaid is also consistent with our model.

Even the average size of hospitals, which seems, by most accounts, to be below the optimal or cost-minimizing level, can easily be explained. In the first place, empirically observed cost curves may be misleading if we add the physician

---

16. This last point is an important consideration. It is sometimes alleged that these firms have attained a nonprofit status so that they may better provide services to the poor. However, the recent experience in this country is for the poor to receive health services from government-operated hospitals, to receive education in government-operated institutions, and not to partake at all of the output of symphony orchestras, theater groups, or private universities.

input. But more importantly, in a period of rising prices our model shows that hospitals will tend to be small, and for two reasons. First, smallness tends to permit maximization of net income per physician. Second, smallness is necessary to permit coordination of the medical staff.

A narrower range of possible observations is consistent with our model than with the general utility-maximization model. Appropriate choice of the variables to enter the utility function can make almost any observed behavior consistent with utility maximization. In particular, the definition of quality is not clear. Our model specifies the variable in the objective function. In principle it will also predict quantitative as well as qualitative responses, in the sense that physician income can be measured while utility cannot. Unfortunately, at present hospital-specific data on physicians' incomes or prices do not exist which would permit us to provide a conclusive test of the model. Nevertheless, we hope that more data can be made available to test this model.

# Part III

# The State and Property Rights Assignments

## Chapter Eleven

# The Importance of Incentives

Attentuation of property rights is said to take place as restrictions are imposed
on the uses to which an asset can be put and on the freedom of the owner
to transfer rights in the asset to others. It should be emphasized, however, that
most of the restrictions discussed here are those established by the state. To
argue for a change in the content of the right of ownership, therefore, is to
argue for a change in the allocation of resources to which legal support is
given. In other words, as Samuels (1971) has noted:

> . . . opportunities for gain, whether pecuniary profit or other ad-
> vantage, accure to those who can use government. . . . If income
> distribution and risk allocation is a partial function of law (of
> property) then the law is an object of control for economic or other
> gain . . . whether the instances be tariff protection, oil subsidies,
> real estate agents' attempts to ban "for sale" signs on private homes
> or any other type of property rights. (P. 444)

It follows, of course, that a theory of property rights cannot be
truly complete without a theory of the state. And, unfortunately, no such
theory exists at present. The ongoing studies of Buchanan, McKean, Niskanen,
North, Tullock and other scholars are increasing understanding of the general
area, but these investigations must still be regarded as preliminary. Of special
interest here is the fact that some comprehension of the behavior of bureaucracy and the state can be developed from consideration of individual utility
maximizing behavior. Indeed, it can be argued that changes in the content of
property rights depend on the relationship between an ex ante estimate of benefits to the ruling class from reorganizing the existing property rights assignments
and the ex ante or even ex post estimates of the costs to be incurred in policing and enforcing the changed structure of rights. If this reasoning is valid, the
"efficient" size of the political organization should be affected, inter alia, by

the size of markets and the state's military endowment. While systematic discussion of these themes cannot be attempted here, it may be observed that the hypothesis linking changes in property rights to man's search for greater utility is both interesting in itself and consistent with the basic individualist bias of the property rights approach.

Another problem connected with the existence of the state concerns the functioning of government bureaucracies. Despite the large and growing magnitude of bureaucratic activity in capitalist countries, economists have given relatively little attention to the analysis of bureaucratic operation. Thus, until recently, not much was known about the distinctive characteristics of bureaucracies, and no satisfactory theory of their behavior or welfare implications had been framed. This lack is being made good, and the elements of the bureaucratic optimization problem have now been suggested. On the assumption that individuals functioning in bureaucracies have the same general motivations as other men, understanding of the reactions of bureaucrats requires knowledge of property rights structures and the opportunities decision-makers have for appropriating rewards.

Unfortunately, there is good reason to believe that existing institutions are often constituted so that rewards are not forthcoming for efficient and socially useful behavior on the part of government employees or other bureaucrats. The situation is not hopeless, however. If the pattern of economic incentives influences action, it follows that incentives can be changed so as to induce more desirable behavior. Current property rights research considers possible reforms within the constrained utility maximization framework and is able to offer some plausible suggestions for the improvement of bureaucratic efficiency. The articles by Professors McKean and Niskanen, reprinted as Chapters 12 and 13, indicate the general direction of thinking in this area. Normally, perhaps, the problems of bureaucracy are associated with advanced industrial economies; but as Sanchez and Waters show in their study of corruption, bureaucratic activity yields some special and very significant difficulties in less developed economies. Again, the focus of the analysis is on incentives.

The literature discussed so far has been concerned, fundamentally, with economic systems in which private ownership of capital is possible. The property rights approach, however, has also proved to be useful in interpreting the observed behavior of the firm operating within a socialist environment.[1] For example, there exists a significant degree of similarity in the content of the bundle of property rights defining ownership of the Soviet firm and the content of the bundle defining ownership of the modern capitalist corporation. In the latter organization, we know that hired managers have some freedom to pursue their own independent interests. Given the high detection, policing, and enforcement costs, the manager of a dispersed ownership capitalist firm finds the

---

1. In the pioneering work of Ward (1957) and Domar (1966), the property rights approach is not developed in detail but is implicit.

"prices" of various types of utility producing behaviors to be relatively low, and he "purchases" certain of these behaviors at the expense of stockholders' interests. Indeed, knowledge of the institutional structure makes it possible to predict such specific practices as managerial consumption of nonpecuniary income, maintenance of a ratio of retained earning to profits in excess of the stockholders' time preference, etc. But when the manager's position in the capitalist firm is viewed in these terms, it is but a short step to the recognition that the Soviet manager occupies an essentially similar position in his firm. That is, the relationship between the Soviet manager and the state is analogous to that between the capitalist manager and the stockholders.[2] The costs to the state of detecting, policing, and enforcing a desired pattern of behavior in the manager are obviously greater than zero and, in fact, can be substantial. Therefore, the Soviet manager is able, within his own estimate of these costs, to attenuate the state's ownership in the firm; or, what amounts to the same thing, use some of the firm's resources to increase his personal satisfaction (utility) at the expense of the government objectives.

Observers of the Soviet economy have often called attention to the tendency of managers to violate Soviet regulations in order to protect their own interests and gain some room for independent policy-making. These so-called informal activities, however, are easily incorporated into the standard theory of production and exchange through the use of the property rights approach. Thus, the Soviet manager's desire for larger allocations of productive inputs (including labor), his interest in maintaining unreported stocks of inputs and outputs, and his tendency to understate the productive efficiency of his plant can all be rationalized as strategies to improve his personal position.

Still another area of application for the property rights approach is found in the labor-managed firm of Yugoslavia. Since the economic reform of 1965, the institutional structure has been such that the employees of the Yugoslav firm *own the residual*.[3] Further, the workers, through a democratically elected Workers' Council, are empowered to *revise* or *terminate* contractual stipulations. Nevertheless, the content of the employees bundle of property rights in the firm differs from that of stockholders in the West. Significantly, Yugoslav workers can neither sell their rights to others nor take them away when they leave the employ of the firm. For, under Yugoslav law, an individual has no ownership rights in the firm's capital stock, merely the *right of use* of

2. It should be pointed out, however, that because of the absence of a capital market in the Soviet system, the manager's performance cannot be evaluated on the basis of the profits realized by the firm. By contrast, profits serve as an important signal of managerial success in the capitalist world, and stockholders can use this objective signal in forming their investment plans.

3. In the spring of 1972, the Yugoslav government introduced regulations based on so-called social contracts, that reduced the firm's freedom to determine the allocation of its net product. This new policy, of course, implies some attenuation of the collective's ownership rights in the residual.

that capital. Thus, a person acquires the right to a share in the residual by joining the firm and loses all his rights when he leaves it. Moreover, the firm has a
legal obligation to maintain the value of its capital stock indefinitely (via
depreciation and other allocations from the residual).

Given the special institutional structure of the labor-managed system,
the employees of the Yugoslav firm face two fundamentally different wealth-
increasing alternatives: (a) the option to leave a part of the residual with the
firm to purchase additional capital goods, or (b) the option to take the entire
residual out as wages and, then, to invest individually in savings accounts, jewe'
ry, or in anything else the law allows. It is important to reemphasize, however,
that there is a significant difference in the conditions of ownership under (a)
and (b), and this difference affects the comparison of returns in the respective
areas. Since the return from the joint investment in capital goods via retained
earnings is received in the form of *incremental wages* and for only as long as the
employee remains with the firm, the required internal rate of return on such
investment must be substantially higher than the rate of return on fully owned
assets to make category (a) investment preferable to category (b). The "equal-
izing" differential between the two rates can be estimated and is attributable, as
noted, to differences in the content of property rights.

It does not seem unreasonable to say that many phenomena observed in the Yugoslav economy can be given plausible explanation if the implications of the special property rights structure are traced through systematically.
Our theory tells us that the content of the bundle of property rights that defines
ownership in the Yugoslav firm, together with the absence of a system of capital markets, will affect the workers' time preference and their choice of investment alternatives. These conditions suggest, in turn, that the banking system
will tend to take on a crucial role in freeing the rate of investment from the limitations imposed by the rate of voluntary savings. Thus, it is possible to predict
such events as the growing inflationary pressure, the serious liquidity crisis
faced by firms, and the high rate of unemployment that have characterized
recent Yugoslav history.

The preoccupation of traditional welfare theory with static optimization problems and the abstract conditions for Pareto optimality has tended
to divert attention from institutional considerations.[4] But the form of economic
organization a system adopts and, in particular, the property rights structure it
sanctions, must be understood to exert a critical influence on the results the
system produces. Thus, socialism and capitalism cannot be regarded as alternative "technical means" for achieving efficient resource allocation. Nutter considers one important aspect of this question in his article; and Bajt, Furubotn,
and Pejovich provide further arguments to show that different property rights
arrangements can be expected to lead to quite different patterns of economic
behavior.

4. For example, see Bator (1957).

# The Modern Capitalist Economy

## Chapter Twelve

# Property Rights Within Government, and Devices To Increase Governmental Efficiency

## R. McKean

Reprinted from the *Southern Economic Journal* 39 (October 1972): 177–186, by permission of publisher and author.

Numerous devices to increase governmental efficiency have been tried or advocated. Examples include cost-benefit analysis, program budgeting, the tax-expenditure budget, reorganizations, stock and industrial funds, contracts with private firms instead of in-house government production, and the volunteer army. All of these devices can have desirable effects, and I wish to emphasize that I am not opposing their use. The *magnitude* of their impacts, however, depends crucially on the issue: What do these devices do to the property rights or appropriability of rewards—and therefore to the "incentives"—of individual officials in government? In order to appraise the significance of these devices, one should look critically at the capturability of rewards confronting voters, legislators, top officials, and other government personnel. If a device has little impact on appropriability, one should not expect dramatic impacts on behavior and decisions. Few economists believe that mere exhortation will greatly influence private firms, yet many persons seem to have a curious faith in exhortation when they turn to government agencies.

In this article I wish to summarize the significance of property rights and appropriability, review the connection between appropriability and efficiency, and then reassess the probable impacts of several efficiency-promoting devices.

## PROPERTY RIGHTS AND APPROPRIABILITY

I use the term "property rights" in a broad sense that includes one's effective rights to do things and his effective claims to rewards (positive or negative) as a result of his actions. These rights help shape his set of opportunities and therefore the tradeoffs that confront him. Explicit contracts, tacitly understood contracts, ethical precepts, behavioral rules or customs, and tradition, as well as legislation, affect each person's effective rights. Other variables, too, such as one's physical and mental abilities or the law of gravity, play roles in determining opportunity sets, but for present purposes the effect of rights structures on appropriability is my main interest.

Exclusion costs and other transaction costs, of course, help determine "effective" claims. For instance, difficulties in excluding the nonpayer (e.g., the ship that doesn't pay for the use of the lighthouse's beams) attenuate one's ability to sell a product and reap any rewards. High transaction costs—the costs of negotiating, acquiring information about products or markets, contracting, and enforcing contracts—reduce the appropriability of rewards from producing outputs. To repeat, *effective* rights to take various actions, such as selling land or just holding it idle, and *effective* rights to take home proceeds (or obligations to pay liabilities if one damages someone else's interest) help determine what rewards can be captured from what actions.

Enforcement is crucial in shaping appropriability. If the law forbids me to pollute the river, but the law is rarely enforced, the only cost to me from polluting the river may be a twinge of conscience. If people are not punished for stealing my apple crop, or if they do not incur liabilities for carelessly damaging it, they will engage in more of these activities, and my ability to capture gains by maintaining an apple orchard is attenuated. High enforcement costs, or lax enforcement, may erode the ability of anyone to appropriate rewards from deals that might be mutually advantageous.

Property rights and opportunity sets exist in the public sector and with public ownership. Some official may have the right to lease but not to sell municipal lands. Some have rights to sell assets if they go through the proper procedure but do not have claims to the proceeds. If an official is responsible only for constructing roads, he may be able to collect rewards (e.g., promotion) from that activity but not from the creation or preservation of recreational possibilities. The rights of officials to do or not to do various things and their effective claims to various payoffs help determine what net rewards officials can capture from what actions. And in government, too, exclusion costs, transaction costs, and enforcement costs have much to do with *effective* appropriability.

How does this affect behavior? As noted before, the claims structure helps shape individuals' opportunity sets. An individual's opportunity set shows the tradeoffs confronting him: the rewards he can expect, and the rewards he must forego, if he undertakes action A; the liabilities he can anticipate if he disposes of acid on someone's land or in the nearby river. The more rewarding some course of action, the more of it he will take (other things remaining the same); the more costly to him some course of action, the less of it he will take. This does not imply that people are terribly selfish. Many persons may be concerned about other persons' well-being and comparatively conscientious about disposing of litter. If *in addition* they can capture other gains from not littering (e.g., avoid fines), some persons will do still less littering. Avoiding a penalty, incidentally, is "rewarding," and throughout the discussion the opportunities to appropriate gain will include the opportunities to reduce penalty or disutility.

## APPROPRIABILITY AND ECONOMIC EFFICIENCY

Lack of appropriability is widely accepted as one way to explain why inefficiencies exist (Arrow 1962; Head 1965). If each individual had "full" appropriability, it would mean that he could capture the full marginal gains resulting from his actions (and therefore be reimbursed if someone took anything from him). As a consequence, each person would also have to pay the full marginal costs inflicted on others, since the others, too, would be able to keep gains, i.e., be reimbursed if someone made use of their resources or inflicted costs on them. Thus, each individual could appropriate net marginal gains *only* from actions that were efficient in either production or consumption—actions that moved toward either the production-possibility boundary and/or the utility-possibility frontier. Note that "full" appropriability means this kind of appropriability by *all* individuals—not unlimited ability on the part of some to take things away from others. One could define efficiency and appropriability in terms of various social welfare functions, and analogous propositions would hold. Here, however, I will trace out the arguments with Pareto optimality in the background as the criterion.

With zero transaction costs—which implies clear assignment of rights, zero coercion, and full appropriability—people would trade various claims so that there would be no inefficiencies (Coase 1960; Demsetz 1964). With positive transaction costs, all individuals do not have complete appropriability; there will be inefficiencies in comparison with a zero-transaction-cost world, and there *may* be inefficiencies in comparison with attainable situations (Coase 1960; Demsetz 1964). If firms cannot appropriate the full marginal benefit from engaging in basic research or air-pollution abatement, the basic research and pollution-abatement that they produce may be too little; a better situation may be attainable. If households cannot capture the full marginal benefit of being friendly or of reducing garbage output, they may produce too little friendliness and too much garbage.

This may sound as though imperfect appropriability yields only one kind of inefficiency: the kind resulting from externalities. But note that using the customary definitions, *any* inefficiency reflects an externality. Precise definitions of externalities imply that gains from further trade are available (Buchanan and Stubblebine 1962) or, what amounts to the same thing, that someone's utility or output depends on an unpriced or improperly priced resource (Mishan 1965; Buchanan 1967).[1] *Any* falling short of either the production-possibility boundary or the utility-possibility boundary means that gains from trade are available—or, in Mishan's terms, that some resource is improperly priced. If with zero transac-

---

1. For precise algebraic expressions of these definitions, see the original articles by Mishan (1965) and Buchanan and Stubblebine (1962).

tion costs there is an inefficiency due to monopoly, some "gravy" is available, and the prospective gainers (consumers) could hire the monopolist to produce the correct output. There is an interdependency: like the beekeeper in the nectar-pollen example, or the man who doesn't keep his garden sufficiently pretty to suit his neighbors, the monopolist is failing to produce extra units of an output that people would be willing to pay the cost of. The wrongly priced resources include both the monopolist's product and something that might be called "the abandonment of the monopolist's output restriction" (for which a market fails to exist). If counting phenomena like monopoly as an externality is repugnant—and it does seem foolish to have "inefficiencies" and "externalities" mean the same thing—then it seems to me that we must redefine externalities.

In the real world, where there are positive transaction costs, the concept that we have in mind most of the time is the Buchanan-Stubblebine "potentially Pareto-relevant externality." This is an interdependency generating "desire on the part of the externally benefited (damaged) party (A) to modify the behavior of the party empowered to take action (B) through trade, persuasion, compromise, agreement, convention, collective action, etc." (Buchanan and Stubblebine 1962, pp. 373-374). It may seem that "desire to modify behavior" should be translated to read "willingness to pay marginal cost (exclusive of transaction costs) of modified behavior." Otherwise every producer leaves an endless trail of externalities: many of us desire that General Motors modify its behavior by producing a Chevrolet and selling it to us for ten dollars. Unfortunately, however, amounts below marginal cost are usually not so obvious; I might be willing to pay fifty cents per month to induce my next-office colleague to make less noise, but unless we bargained about it, how could one tell whether or not that amount was below the marginal cost to him? Furthermore, in practically all cases, what one is concerned about is the aggregate amount that a group of persons would pay; and it is unclear whether or not that aggregate would amount to marginal cost. Hence, we have to fall back on the Buchanan-Stubblebine definition even though its coverage is uncomfortably large. With positive transaction costs, all the familiar examples fall into this "potentially relevant" category, e.g., nectar and pollen, pollution, noise, immunization, and congestion. There *may* be net gains from trade, and we keep groping for better arrangements, but we don't know for sure that a better outcome is attainable. In the monopoly case, transaction costs prevent consumers from bargaining with the monopolist, and they are left with a desire to modify his behavior. And, it might be noted, governments, as well as private firms and households, do things that leave individuals with a desire to modify those actions.

The main propositions are correct whether we speak of the zero-transaction-cost boundaries or the attainable boundaries, and whether we speak of the private or public sector: any unambiguous inefficiency reflects an externality, and any alleged inefficiency is an alleged, i.e., potentially relevant, externality (though not all potentially relevant externalities are inefficiencies). Finally—

the point that is directly pertinent to this article—attenuated appropriability means that one should expect inefficiencies and alleged inefficiencies in the public (as well as in the private) sector, because many individuals' abilities to capture and retain gains attributable to their actions are impaired. Lack of appropriability can be said to result in *all* departures from the production-possibility and utility-possibility frontiers.

## APPROPRIABILITY IN THE PUBLIC SECTOR

The nature of right assignments in the public sector, together with transaction costs, seem certain to limit appropriability there severely. Transferability[2] of ownership with retention of proceeds is absent. Voters cannot buy and sell shares of common stock in government. Neither can legislators or officials. Thus no one has a well-defined claim to a share of increases in present values. Furthermore, voters and individuals in government rarely have bonus arrangements linked to "profits" or exclusive claims to shares of residual income.[2] If there were zero transaction costs, claims of various sorts would be assigned and traded. In such circumstances, for example, mutually advantageous deals would surely modify or eliminate the price support program. But negotiation and enforcement costs pertaining to deals among millions of voters, urban workers, farmers, and Congressmen would be prohibitive.

As a result of this rights structure, almost no one can count on rewards for increased efficiency *per se* or need fear penalties for inefficiency (within a fairly wide range of behavior). Consider voters, since they are similar to stockholders and influence considerably what actions politicians and thence officials will find rewarding. The amount of benefit or tax reduction that individual voters could receive from *incremental efficiency*[3] is small, while the cost to each of acquiring information, forming pressure groups, and monitoring government officials is large. As a result, voters rarely press for increased efficiency, e.g., programs to benefit them *only* if the gains exceed the costs to others. Beyond some point, of course, flagrant inefficiency (i.e., big clearly perceived opportunities for increased efficiency) will bring forth pressure groups or retaliation at the voting booth; but over a wide range voters cannot capture significant net rewards from worrying about economic efficiency.[4]

They can appropriate rewards, of course, by joining pressure groups urging measures from which *they* would receive monetary or psychic benefits. Such measures—welfare programs, irrigation projects, stopping the war or extend-

2. For the significance of "transferability" and "exclusivity," see Alchian (1961).

3. Remember that incremental efficiency means an excess of gains (as perceived by the individual gainers) over costs (as seen by those bearing these costs).

4. There are always a few, of course, who can capture some inner satisfaction from advocating greater efficiency, because they happen to attach great value to efficiency as a matter of principle.

ing the war—are from their standpoint "redistribution" measures; advocates
would be concerned about the extra satisfaction *they* would get from these policies, not about the costs, i.e., the decreases in satisfaction that others would get.
If the costs are concentrated on small numbers of voters, some cost-bearers may
find it economical to oppose the measures, and the bargaining process may cause
these costs to be taken into account, alleviating the inefficiency that would
otherwise occur. If either costs or gains are spread thinly over millions of voters,
though, many individuals will not find it worthwhile to make their objections or
advocacy felt.

The results of such bargaining in government are admittedly hard to
evaluate (McKean 1965). In both sectors implicit or tacit bargaining—without a
true market or overt contract—sometimes enhances the ability of individuals to
fend off confiscation of their resources (i.e., forcible imposition of costs) or to
capture gains resulting from their actions. In other words, such bargaining can
put crude shadow prices on some apparently unpriced goods and take us closer
to full appropriability. Generally, however, it seems safe to assume that in government, negotiations between those particular groups that have strong bargaining power will result in imprecise and improper shadow prices that do not reflect
the bids and offers of voter-minorities and less influential groups. If so, the bar-
gains do no more than alleviate the lack of appropriability.

As a consequence of attenuated voter appropriability, individual
Senators and Congressmen are not rewarded for Pareto-optimal moves per se or
penalized for inefficient moves, though the bargaining *among* these legislators
may reflect many of the cons as well as the pros in designing legislation. In effect,
because each Senator must bargain with the others, he can sometimes capture rewards for weighing *part* of the gains against *part* of the costs (as individual voters
see them). Note, though, that by its very nature, majority rule rewards officials
for seeking majority support, not for taking into account *all* gains or *all* dissent
(which "full" appropriability would force each participant to do). Thus, while
the process may avoid flagrant disregard of gains and costs in formulating legislative patterns,[5] it is crude and imprecise compared to markets or models portray-
ing the conditions for reaching the production-possibility or utility-possibility
frontiers.

In carrying out programs the appropriability of gains from avoiding
inefficiencies is even more attenuated. Since neither Congressmen nor the President can capture much reward from (feel voter pressures for) efficiency per se,
they will not, over a wide range, put the heat on officials to seek economic efficiency. They will apply pressure for particular achievements or "redistributions"
that look like vote getters, and perhaps press for technical efficiency in carrying

---

5. Also, needless to say, one may well regard majority rule as the best attainable
rule and government as the best attainable arrangement for handling many activities. But this
does not justify "overestimating" or distorting the kind of performance to be expected from
these institutions.

out clearcut tasks like issuing driver's licenses, but will seldom press for economic efficiency—i.e., a weighing of *all* costs against *all* gains (as seen by *recipients*) in carrying out these activities. As a consequence of this and the rest of the institutional arrangement, government officials can rarely capture many rewards (*extra* take-home proceeds, probabilities of promotion, prestige, appreciation, etc.) from Pareto-optimal steps.

At the same time, while they can take home few rewards, officials will have to make sacrifices, since they do have rival sources of utility, if they pursue overall economic efficiency. In the public sector government officials are not driven toward profit maximization, but they find that particular accomplishments are rewarding, e.g., fulfilling quotas in doing whatever superiors do want done. They will have to sacrifice chances of promotion, approval, and so on if they do *other* things, such as using resources to reduce their contribution to pollution. Even where they will incur no such sacrifice, government personnel must forego other rewards, such as convenience or alternative specific achievements for which they have a taste, if they seek Pareto efficiency. Thus government personnel find it costly to themselves—they forego pecuniary or non-pecuniary benefits—if they sacrifice assigned outputs or use their discretion to reduce inefficiency.[6] Government employees frequently face internal regulations, of course, intended to reduce their discretion; voters and higher officials have decided that such rules are often better than pervasive discretionary authority, since other means of monitoring employee behavior in the public sector are even more expensive. But these internal regulations, while perhaps better than the alternative, yield their own inflexibilities and inefficiencies—and still leave much scope for discretionary action.

All this may sound like an attempt to make a diatribe against government sound objective and dispassionate—like the wife who said of her husband that, on the one hand, he had some bad faults, but, on the other hand, he had some good faults. But, seriously, it isn't intended as a general condemnation of government. I'm not suggesting that I know of a better attainable arrangement; I'm simply urging that our expectations from the government as well as the private sector be realistic.

## EFFECTS OF DEVICES INTENDED TO INCREASE GOVERNMENT EFFICIENCY

With this highly attenuated appropriability in mind, let us examine some of the devices that are intended to increase governmental efficiency. Most of these de-

6. In the private sector, managers are driven toward profit maximization but have some discretion, because of the information and enforcement costs that stockholders face (see Alchian 1965). In exercising this discretion, managers must sacrifice pecuniary or nonpecuniary benefits to themselves if they seek certain Pareto optimal moves, e.g., reduce their use of "free" rivers as sewers. Managers cannot be expected, in either sector, to ignore whatever pecuniary and nonpecuniary benefits are available to them.

vices probably offer some gains, and a few, like the volunteer army, are extremely important, but except where they affect opportunity sets significantly, one should not expect major shifts in decisions and behavior.

For example, cost-benefit analysis *by itself* merely provides extra information. If made public, *good* analysis may make it a bit embarrassing to advocate flagrantly inefficient projects, *slightly* changing the lineup of pressures and therefore appropriability for certain legislators and officials. If voters are almost indifferent, legislators and bureaucrats may capture some inner satisfaction or convenience by being guided by the cost-benefit information. But typically (I assert) the existence of such information does not *greatly* alter anyone's ability to capture gains, and therefore does not greatly alter the costs or rewards to officials from reaching their decisions.[7] Similarly, program budgeting and the tax-expenditure budget[8]—by themselves—merely make information available. One should expect significant changes in appropriability only if some special factor (e.g., a particularly zealous and determined set of top officials who get satisfaction from seeing these devices employed)[9] penalizes personnel for not "using" the information. Otherwise, whatever actions were previously rewarding to individual voters, legislators, and agency personnel will continue to be rewarding to them.

Consider a more complicated example, the use of stock and industrial funds. These are government activities that are given working capital and are supposed to simulate private profit-seeking businesses (Breckner 1950). If it is a retail activity, such as the sale of uniforms to military personnel, it is usually called a stock fund. If it is a production activity, e.g., a laundry or printing operation, it is usually called an industrial fund. Customers, mainly government agencies, must pay for their purchases out of their budgets instead of merely requisitioning them, and the enterprises are supposed to maximize profits or minimize losses. (These operations are somewhat like Lange-Lerner firms that are *instructed* to operate according to some rule.)

What actually happens to appropriability? In the case of the clothing funds, personnel are given a fixed budget or clothing allowance, and can capture *take-home* gains by taking care of their uniforms more economically. One can therefore expect significant adjustments. Government agency buyers, however,

---

7. Appropriability has a good deal to do with the way one can expect cost-benefit analyses to be prepared as well as the way one can expect them to be interpreted and used. See De Alessi (1969, pp. 16–23). Incidentally, the criterion usually underlying cost-benefit analysis appears to be Pareto optimality (since observed or simulated market prices are used).

8. The tax-expenditure budget exhibits the "expenditures" we make by foregoing taxes—expenditures to achieve particular objectives, sometimes the same objectives that are simultaneously being pursued by ordinary expenditure programs. For example, we "buy" assistance for the aged both by having welfare programs and by giving people over sixty-five special tax breaks.

9. Even then, such zealous officials are unlikely to survive if other types of behavior can reap stronger voter and bureaucratic support.

while they end up with a budgetary constraint, cannot pick up much (if any) *take-home* gain from incremental efficiency. They can generally be expected to demand less of the goods they must now pay for, because even if choices are made at random, aggregate demand curves have negative slopes (Becker 1962b). But dramatically increased efficiency should not be anticipated, because the device by itself gives no agency official any new rewards for combining inputs efficiently. After all, many government agencies must pay for most of their inputs, yet officials seem to have little passion for least-cost combinations.

How about the managers of the funds themselves? Will they now be able to capture gains from being efficient? The answer, whatever the published directives or rules say, depends on whether their superiors really base salary increases and promotions on the managers' profit-and-loss reports and other indicators of efficiency. Remember, their superiors are not stockholders who collect dividends or who can buy and sell shares of present values. Their superiors are not higher executives beholden to stockholders. Instead their bosses (clear back to the voters) consist of persons who can collect few rewards for rewarding subordinates for efficiency. I doubt if there is any *consistent* pressure on these managers to achieve economic efficiency. I conjecture that Congressmen and other superiors find it relatively unrewarding to monitor them, relatively rewarding to let them charge "monopoly" prices or use certain inputs free of charge, and relatively rewarding to take care of deficits from time to time. (Even if such devices yielded no gains, this would not be at all inconsistent, it seems to me, with the fact that someone found it rewarding initially to sell people on the use of these devices and to set them up.)

As another example, consider the volunteer army.[10] If the Defense Department were compelled by law to rely on volunteers, those eligible for service would surely behave so as to increase economic efficiency, because the arrangement would procure those eligibles who were least unwilling to serve. Here the persons deciding whether or not to volunteer could appropriate take-home gains for making economical decisions. It is often alleged, however, that the Department, because it would have to pay opportunity cost to obtain personnel, would now procure the proper mix, or a more efficient mix, of manpower instead of having, say, too many cooks and not enough jet mechanics. It is further alleged that, for the same reason, officials would now choose a more efficient combination of land, labor, and capital.

The higher price for manpower, other things remaining the same, might well induce the Department to procure fewer soldiers, and relatively less of the higher-priced skills, than it would procure at lower prices.[11] (As just noted,

10. I do not wish to downgrade the real virtues of a volunteer army, the main one being that it would restore a most significant component of our freedom of choice. I am reassessing only some of the minor advantages sometimes claimed for this device.

11. Since Congress would surely change the budget, however, other things would not stay the same, and one cannot be *sure* that the two changes together would reduce the amount purchased.

demand curves are negatively sloped, even if decisions are random.) So the volunteer system would work in the right direction as far as input mixes are concerned. Note, however, that it would not give any official new rights to take home rewards for greater efficiency. Thus I would not expect to see the same scale and type of adjustments that a private profit-seeking firm would make if suddenly forced to pay more for an input. Congressmen and other officials would find it no more rewarding than before to plan differential pay schedules carefully to acquire the personnel mix that was desired. They do use differential pay to some extent now, but find it inconvenient and not very rewarding, from their standpoint, to keep making the hard painful decisions that extensive use of differentials would entail. I see no reason to believe that "a" volunteer army by itself would bring any more sophistication to the use of differential pay. After all, in most school districts we find unified salary schedules, though we have a volunteer teacher system. Hence I do not see that officials would be more careful in deciding upon the mix they desired, setting pay differentials, or procuring the most efficient mix.

With respect to the combination of land, labor, and capital, there is again little reason to expect dramatic adjustments. As before, no one would be able to capture much of the gain from increments in efficiency. In other government agencies we already have a volunteer system, but it is by no means clear that efficient combinations of land, labor, and capital are typically selected.

Another illustration of the point is the use of various contracts with private firms. The ways that cost-plus and other contracts affect *firms'* behavior have been discussed a good deal, but less attention has been given to the incentives of government contracting officials and the ways in which these incentives affect the outcomes. Again it seems to me that we have unconsciously assumed that the employees of private firms are utility maximizers but the employees of governments are something else. For example, fixed-price contracts with profit-seeking firms for clearly specified outputs, such as existing types of equipment, give those firms the ability to appropriate gains from extra efficiency in producing whatever quality of product they do produce, and the arrangement will usually consume a less valuable package of resources than would in-house production. Note, however, that fixed-price contracts do not significantly change the opportunity sets facing the government personnel involved. Contracting officials can usually take home no *extra* rewards for increments in tough bargaining and unpleasant conflict with the contractor's representatives; extra work in preparing or checking cost estimates; incremental care in comparing prices at which various government agencies are buying the items;[12] extra effort to weigh the gains and costs of procuring alternative qualities; additional attention to monitoring the quality actually produced by the firm; or extra care to see that future contracts are awarded accordingly to suitable indicators of past performance. As a result,

12. Indeed, with centralized procurement, there is less and less *opportunity* to compare prices for items purchased by government.

even this straightforward type of contract can yield highly variable outcomes: the fixed price may be unnecessarily high; the contracting and monitoring process may be surprisingly wasteful and expensive; firms may find it profitable to neglect quality control (the quality of such known objects is not expensive to monitor, but sometimes no one can capture rewards from careful monitoring); firms may find it advantageous to put "too many" resources into bargaining and "governmental relations." The point is simply that while fixed-price contracts are excellent devices wherever they can be used, even from this arrangement one should not expect too much in view of governmental employees' opportunity sets.

When one turns to incentive contracts, in which the firm is rewarded for keeping costs below a target and penalized for overruns above the target, the factors discussed above make it tempting to agree on too high a target and to repeat the other forms of behavior that were mentioned. Multi-dimensional incentive contracts reward the contractor for improving on target delivery dates and target performance (e.g., several dimensions of performance in the tenth missile produced). The phenomena noted in connection with fixed-price contracts are likely to be multiplied and to bring about an easy set of targets, or several kinds of "storming," or other undesired behavior by the contractors (McKean 1968, pp. 158–160). Again, when assessing the effectiveness of such devices, one should keep in mind the appropriability-structure confronting the governmental contracting and monitoring employees—and the effect that *their* behavior will have on the behavior of the contractor.

Finally,[13] we should recognize the influence of property rights and appropriability in assessing the use of experts and scientific advisors by governments. The network of advisory services drawn on by the federal authorities is large. The President's Science Advisory Committee (PSAC) is only one of many official advisory groups, and the Office of Science and Technology is only one of many government offices that provide scientific inputs. "Semipublic institutions also provide a great deal of advice to the executive branch. For example, the National Academy of Sciences and the National Academy of Engineering, through the National Research Council, supervise the work of about 500 committees. . . . Taken together, these public and semipublic advisory groups involve more than 15,000 or 20,000 individual scientists and engineers" (Perl 1971, p. 1212).

Some apparently find it surprising (as well as appalling) that this network often has little impact on policy decisions (Perl 1971, pp. 1211–1215). If one thinks in terms of appropriability, however, it is clear that unless the information affects numerous voters' views, the words of advisory groups cannot be expected to affect officials' property rights and their decisions greatly or persis-

---

13. I shall not attempt here to examine still other devices, such as reorganizations. The latter *re-shuffle* appropriability and sometimes, if carefully designed, may widen the distribution of individuals' abilities to capture and retain gains from actions that promote economic efficiency.

tently. If new scientific information does alter (or seems likely to alter) voters' feelings, legislators and hence government personnel can capture gains from modifying their behavior. At minimum certain officials can now appropriate rewards by setting up another committee or ordering a new study. If changes in the voters' positions persist, government personnel have claims to rewards (e.g., votes, support from colleagues, budget increments, promotions, approval, reduced criticism) from new policy choices that have truly been affected by the scientific information and advice. If voters never become aroused, however, or if the concern that resulted from the scientific advice dies down, persons in government will still find it rewarding to base their decisions on other considerations. Again, of course, if voters are indifferent, legislators and top officials have some discretion and an opportunity for statesmanship. They may be at least temporarily influenced by the information. Yet, if voters are really indifferent to this issue, the influence is unlikely to have survival power, because devoting one's efforts to some other activities (pertaining to issues on which voters are not indifferent) can pick up greater support. There is nothing mysterious about it; if we want scientific advice to play a greater role, institutional changes to enable individuals to reap rewards from such decision-making must be discovered and introduced.

The general conclusion is simply that in appraising special tools to increase efficiency, one should examine what happens to property rights and appropriability in order to form realistic expectations about the effects. Also, in trying to invent improved devices or institutional changes, or in launching new programs, we should keep the impacts on rights and opportunity sets in the forefront of our minds, and not just assume that good intentions pave the road to economic efficiency. Closely related conclusions have been stated or implied by numerous others,[14] but in my opinion one can appreciate the points more vividly and accurately by thinking in terms of appropriability and specific rights structures. As Adam Smith might have said, it is not from the benevolence of the balloter, bureaucrat, or branch chief that we should expect our public goods but from their regard to their own interest.[15]

14. See, for example Buchanan (1967); Downs (1967); Niskanen (1971); Tullock (1965). Niskanen and Tullock especially have contributed to the important task of inventing ways to compensate government personnel so as to approach an improved appropriability-structure.
15. Adam Smith's general views about government behavior, and even his analytical framework, were similar to those in this paper (see Rosenberg [1960] ).

## Chapter Thirteen

# The Peculiar Economics
# of Bureaucracy

W. Niskanen

Reprinted from the *American Economic Review* 58 (May 1968): 293–305, by permission of publisher and author.

Economics does not now provide a theory of the maximizing bureaucrat. The currently dominant approach to public administration is to provide the organizational structure, information system, and analysis to bureaucrats who, for whatever reason, want to be efficient. This approach, however, does not develop, or explicitly recognize as relevant, the conditions for which the personal objectives of the bureaucrat are consistent with the efficiency of the bureaucracy.

At present, with a large and increasing proportion of economic activity being conducted in bureaus, economists have made no substantial contribution to answering the following questions: What are the distinguishing characteristics of bureaucracies? What are the critical elements of a theory of bureaucracy? Specifically, what do bureaucrats maximize and under what external conditions? What are the consequences of maximizing behavior under these conditions? For example, what is the equilibrium output and budget of a bureau for given demand and cost conditions? What are the effects of changes in demand and cost conditions? What are the welfare consequences of bureaucratic organization of economic activity? What changes in organization and the structure of rewards would improve the efficiency of a bureaucracy? This article presents a simple model of the maximizing bureaucrat and, based on this model, a set of tentative qualitative answers to these questions.

## THE MODEL

The model outlined in this section is based on the following two critical characteristics of bureaus:

1.  Bureaucrats maximize the total budget of their bureau, given demand and cost conditions, subject to the constraint that the budget must be equal to or greater than the minimum total costs at the equilibrium output.
2.  Bureaus exchange a specific output (or combination of outputs) for a specific budget.

For this article, then, bureaus are defined by these two characteristics.

Among the several variables that may enter the bureaucrat's utility function are the following: salary, perquisites of the office, public reputation, power, patronage, ease of managing the bureau, and ease of making changes. All of these variables, I contend, are a positive monotonic function of the total budget of the bureau.[1] Budget maximization should be an adequate proxy even for those bureaucrats with a relatively low pecuniary motivation and a relatively high motivation for making changes in the public interest. It is an interesting observation that the most distinguished public servants of recent years have substantially increased the budgets of the bureaus for which they are responsible.

The second characteristic—bureaus exchange their output for a total budget rather than at a per unit rate—is generally recognized, but the implications of this characteristic for the behavior of a bureau are not. This characteristic gives the bureau the same type of "market" power as a monopoly that presents the market with an all-or-nothing choice.[2] A bureau, thus, can appropriate all of the consumer surplus. As is shown later, however, this characteristic leads to significantly different output, budget, and welfare conditions for a bureau than for a monopoly.[3]

The equilibrium conditions for a bureau, as defined by these two characteristics, are developed below by considering a bureau faced by linear demand and cost conditions. First, consider a bureau that buys factors in a competitive market and for which

$$V = a - bQ$$

and

$$C = c + 2dQ,\text{[4]}$$

where

$V \equiv$ marginal value to consumers
$C \equiv$ minimum marginal cost to bureau

---

1. This article develops only the static model of a bureau and does not explore the time dimension of budget maximization.

2. I am indebted to Gordon Tullock for this powerful insight.

3. This characteristic applies strictly to a "pure" bureau, such as the Department of Defense. Many economic institutions such as the Post Office, most colleges and universities, and most hospitals sell part of their output at a per unit rate and a substantial proportion of their output for a budget.

4. The marginal cost function for a bureau that is not a discriminating monopsonist includes the factor surplus. The average cost function to this bureau and the corresponding marginal cost functions for a monopoly or bureau which is a discriminating monopsonist would be $C = c + dQ$.

and

$Q \equiv$ output of bureau.

For these conditions, then,

$$B = aQ - \frac{b}{2} Q^2$$

and

$$TC = cQ + dQ^2,$$

where

$B \equiv$ total budget of bureau

and

$TC \equiv$ minimum total cost to bureau.

The equilibrium level of $Q$, for these conditions, is determined as follows: Maximization of $B$ leads to an upper level of $Q = a/b$. The constraint that $B$ must be equal to or greater than $TC$, under some conditions, leads to a lower level of $Q = 2(a - c)/b + 2d$. These two levels of $Q$ are equal where $a = 2bc/b - 2d$. For a bureau that buys factors in a competitive market, the equilibrium level of $Q$, thus, is where

$$Q \begin{cases} = \dfrac{2(a - c)}{b + 2d} & \text{for } a < \dfrac{2bc}{b - 2d}. \\[2ex] = \dfrac{a}{b} & \text{for } a \geqslant \dfrac{2bc}{b - 2d}. \end{cases}$$

Figure 13-1 illustrates these equilibrium levels of output for representative demand and cost conditions.

For the lower demand condition represented by $V_1$, the equilibrium output of a bureau will be in the budget-constrained region where the area of the polygon $ea_1hi$ is equal to the area of the rectangle $efgi$. At the equilibrium level of output, there is no "fat" in this bureau; the total budget just covers the minimum total costs, and no cost-effectiveness analysis will reveal any wasted resources. The output of this bureau, however, is higher than the Pareto-optimal level. The equilibrium level of output is in a region where the minimum achiev-

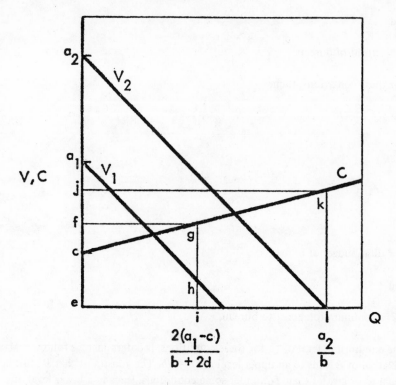

**Figure 13-1.** Equilibrium Output of Bureau

able marginal costs *ig* are substantially higher than the marginal value to consumers *ih*, offsetting all of the consumer surplus that would be generated by
efficient operation at lower budget levels. If minimum marginal costs increase
with output as a consequence of increasing per-unit factor costs (rather than
diminishing productivity), this bureau will generate a substantial factor surplus
equal to the triangle *cfg*—larger than would be generated at the lower, Pareto-
optimal output. Legislatures predominantly representing factor interests understandably prefer the provision of public services through bureaus.

For the higher demand conditions represented by $V_2$, the equilibrium
output of a bureau will be in the demand-constrained region where the marginal
value of output is zero. In this case the total budget will be equal to the triangle
$ea_2l$ and will be larger than the minimum total costs equal to the rectangle *ejkl*.
At the equilibrium level of output, there is "fat" in this bureau. A careful analysis
would indicate that the same output could be achieved at a lower budget, but
the analyst should expect no cooperation from the bureau since it has no incentive to either know or reveal its minimum cost function. In this region, the equilibrium level of output is dependent only on demand conditions. The output of

**Table 13-1. Equilibrium Conditions for Alternative Forms of Economic Organization Facing Same Demand and Cost Conditions**

| Product Market | Monopoly | | Competitive | Bureau | |
|---|---|---|---|---|---|
| Factor Market | Competitive | Monopsony | Competitive | Competitive | Monopsony |
| *Measures* | | | | | |
| Output | 50 | 55.6 | 100 | 166.7 | 200 |
| Revenue: | | | | | |
|   Total | 7,500 | 8,024.7 | 10,000 | 19,444.4 | 20,000 |
|   Average | 150 | 144.4 | 100 | 116.7 | 100.0 |
|   Marginal | 100 | 88.9 | 100 | 33.3 | 0 |
| Costs: | | | | | |
|   Total | 4,375 | 4,552.5 | 10,000 | 19,444.4 | 20,000 |
|   Average | 87.5 | 81.9 | 100 | 116.7 | 100.0 |
|   Marginal | 100.0 | 88.9 | 100 | 158.3 | 125.0 |
| Profits | 3,125 | 3,472.2 | 0 | 0 | 0 |
| Consumer | | | | | |
|   surplus | 1,250 | 1,543.3 | 5,000 | 0 | 0 |
| Factor | | | | | |
|   surplus | 312.5 | 0 | 1,250 | 3,472.2 | 0 |

this bureau is also higher than the Pareto-optimal level, operating at an output level where the minimum marginal costs are equal to *lk* and the marginal value to consumers is zero, again offsetting all of the consumer surplus. The factor surplus generated by this bureau, of course, is also substantially larger than would be generated by a lower, Pareto-optimal output level.

## COMPARISON OF ORGANIZATIONAL FORMS

A better understanding of the consequences of bureaucratic organization of economic activity can be gained by comparison with the consequences of other forms of economic organization facing the same demand and cost conditions. Table 13-1 presents the equilibrium levels of output and related variables for a private monopoly which buys factors on a competitive market, a private monopoly which discriminates among factor suppliers, a competitive industry, a bureau which buys factors on a competitive market, and a bureau that discriminates among factor suppliers. Each form of organization faces the same following demand and cost conditions:

$$V = 200 - 1.00\,Q$$

$$C = 75 + .25\,Q.[5]$$

5. This is the average cost function to a monopoly or bureau that is not a discriminating monopolist, the marginal cost function to a discriminating monopsonist, and the supply function to a competitive industry.

The traditional concern about private monopolies is that they produce too little output. Operating in an output region where marginal value is greater than marginal cost, they do not generate as much surplus value as would a competitive industry. For the demand and cost conditions shown in Table 13–1, a private monopoly would generate a sum of profit plus consumer and factor surplus around 75 percent that of a competitive industry.

For these demand and cost conditions, a bureau that buys factors on a competitive market will have an equilibrium output around two-thirds more than the competitive industry. This bureau will generate no profits or consumer surplus but will generate a factor surplus around 55 percent of the total surplus from a competitive industry. For these conditions, a bureau that discriminates among factor suppliers will have an equilibrium output twice that of a competitive industry and will generate no profits or surplus value.

A comparison of the supply and cost conditions is also helpful. A monopoly has no supply function; it will set an output such that marginal revenue equals marginal cost, with the output sold at a uniform price. A bureau also has no supply function; it will exchange increments of output at the demand price for each increment to an output level such that the budget equals the minimum achievable costs or the marginal value of the increment is zero. In a sense, a bureau also has no separate marginal cost function. The incremental resource withdrawal for a budget-maximizing bureau will be equal to the demand value, as the difference between this value and the minimum incremental cost will be financed from the consumer surplus appropriated at lower output levels. Only if a bureau is efficient at lower output levels, for whatever reason, would the incremental resource withdrawal be equal to the minimum incremental cost. One implication of this condition is that an analyst may not be able to identify a demand-constrained bureau's minimum cost function from budget and output behavior. All this may yield is the bureau's estimate of its demand function; in the static case, all bureaus will appear to have declining marginal costs and in a sense they do. An estimate of a demand-constrained bureau's minimum marginal cost function must be constructed from detailed estimates of the production function and factor costs—creating an extraordinary demand for analysis.

For different reasons, in summary, both private monopolies and bureaus operate in output regions that are inherently nonoptimal. The substitution of a bureau for a monopoly to provide some product or service, however, solves no problems; this substitution will reduce the aggregate surplus value and serve only the interests of the owners of specific factors.

## EFFECTS OF CHANGES IN DEMAND AND COST CONDITIONS

The model outlined in the second section may also be used to estimate a bureau's response to changes in demand and cost conditions.

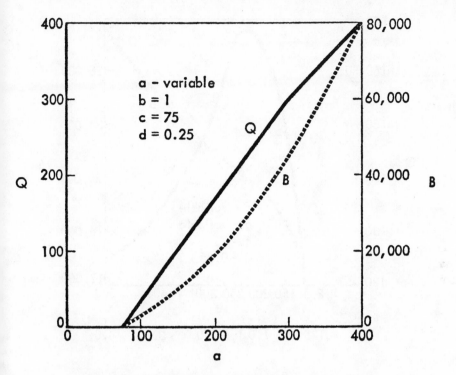

**Figure 13-2.** Effects of Demand Shift

### Demand Shifts

Figure 13-2 illustrates the changes in a bureau's equilibrium output and budget, for given cost conditions, in response to shifts in demand.

In the budget-constrained output region, the output of a bureau will grow by more than the amount of a demand shift, even when faced by increasing marginal costs. A bureau producing an output at constant marginal costs will grow at twice the rate of a competitive industry under the same conditions. In this region, the budget per unit output will increase only by the amount of the increase in the minimum unit costs.

In the demand-constrained output region, the output of a bureau will grow by the same amount as the demand shift, regardless of the slope of the minimum marginal cost function. The slower rate of growth of a bureau in this region is still higher than the rate of growth of a competitive industry facing increasing marginal costs. In this region, the budget per unit output increases rapidly, by an amount proportionate to the demand shift, regardless of the slope of the minimum marginal cost function.

A bureau, like a private monopoly, will often find it rewarding to try to shift its demand function. The incremental budget that would result from a

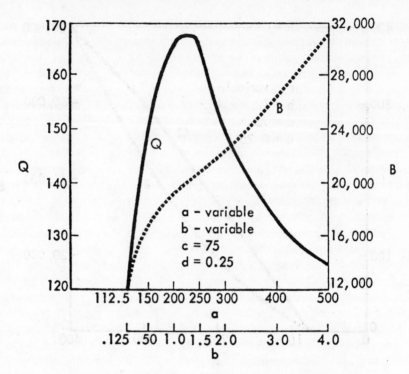

**Figure 13-3.** Effects of Changes in the Demand Slope

demand shift will be particularly high in the demand-constrained output region. One would expect, therefore, that bureaucrats would spend a significant part of their time on various promotional activities, supported by the owners of specific factors.

### Changes in the Demand Slope

Figure 13-3 illustrates the changes in a bureau's equilibrium output and budget, for given cost conditions, in response to changes in the slope of the demand function. The indicated changes in the intercept and slope are such that the output of a competitive industry, given the same cost conditions, would be constant at a level of 100 for each combination.

In the budget-constrained output region, the equilibrium output of a bureau will increase with increasing (negative) demand slopes; in the demand-constrained region, output will decline with increasing demand slopes. A bureau faced by a nearly horizontal demand function will produce an output at a budget per unit output only slightly higher than that of a competitive industry, but the total budget and the budget per unit output will increase monotonically with higher demand slopes. This suggests that a bureau may find it rewarding to try to increase the slope of the demand function for its output by promotional activities citing public "need" or military "requirement" to be fulfilled regardless of cost. A more important suggestion is that a bureau operating in a highly competitive output market would be relatively efficient. However, the present environment of bureaucracy—with severe constraints on the creation of new bureaus or new outputs by existing bureaus, and the passion of reformers to consolidate bureaus with similar output—seems diabolically designed to reduce the competition among bureaus and increase the inefficiency (and, not incidentally, the budget) of the bureaucracy.

### Cost Shifts

Figure 13-4 illustrates the changes in a bureau's equilibrium output and budget, for given demand conditions, in response to shifts in the minimum marginal cost function.

In the budget-constrained output region, a downward shift of the minimum marginal cost function will increase the equilibrium output of a bureau at a rapid rate. A bureau producing an output at constant minimum marginal cost will grow at twice the rate of a competitive industry for the same downward

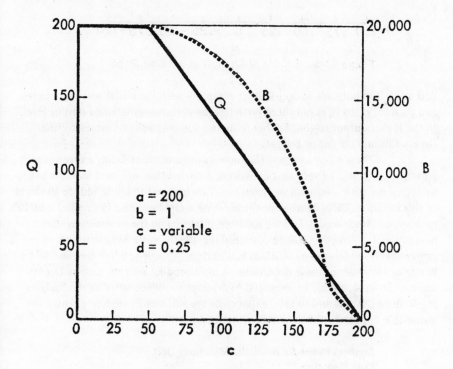

**Figure 13-4.** Effects of Cost Shifts

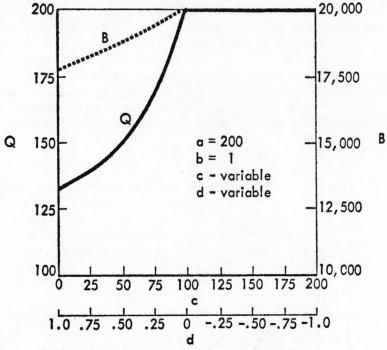

**Figure 13–5.** Effects of Changes in the Cost Slope

cost shift. The bureau's budget will grow rapidly with the initial cost reductions and then very slowly as output approaches the demand-constrained output level. In the higher output region, further reductions in cost will not increase either the equilibrium output or budget.

These effects suggest that new bureaus or those facing exogenous increases in costs will be very cost conscious. Such bureaus will have an incentive to determine their minimum marginal cost function and to try to reduce the level of this function. Older bureaus or those facing a rapid increase in demand couldn't care less on either count. Tullock has been intrigued by the observation that bureaus both attempt to reduce costs and manifestly waste huge amounts of resources. This model suggests that, in equilibrium, a single-product bureau will be in one or the other of these conditions. A multiproduct bureau, such as Department of Defense, should be expected to attempt to reduce costs on the budget-constrained outputs and to assure that costs are sufficiently high to exhaust the obtainable budget on the demand-constrained outputs.

### Changes in the Slope of the Minimum Unit
### Cost Function
Figure 13–5 illustrates the changes in a bureau's equilibrium output and budget, for given demand conditions, in response to changes in the slope of

the minimum marginal cost function. The indicated changes in the intercept and slope are such that the output of a competitive industry, given the same demand conditions, would be constant at a level of 100 for each combination.

In the budget constrained output region, the equilibrium output of a bureau that buys factors on a competitive market will increase with a reduction of the slope of the minimum unit cost function to a level, with constant unit costs, that is twice the output of a competitive industry. The bureau's budget will also increase with a reduction in the slope of this function, but relatively slowly. Both output and budget are invariant to changes in the slope of the cost function in the demand-constrained output region.

These effects suggest that bureaus may have an incentive to use production processes with a higher cost at low output levels and a lower cost at high output levels. In the static case, however, this incentive is not very strong and may be offset in part by pressure through the legislature from the owners of specific factors.

### Critical Tests of This Model

This model suggests an image of a bureau with a level and rate of growth of output that is up to twice that of a competitive industry facing the same conditions. Demand by consumers may be the basis for establishing a bureau, but the interests of this group in preserving the bureau will diminish or disappear as the bureau creates no consumer surplus, except by negligence. A bureau, however, creates a substantially larger factor surplus than would a competitive industry, and the primary interests in continuing the bureau (or a war) are likely to originate from the bureau itself and the owners of specific factors. In the demand-constrained output region, a bureau's only concern about costs is to assure that they exhaust the obtainable budget. A bureau should be expected to engage in considerable promotion, in cooperation with the owners of specific factors, to augment the demand for its output, and to reduce—through persuasion, restrictions on entry, and consolidation—the elasticity of this demand.

These are serious charges. A set of critical tests of these assertions are difficult to pose. The best tests that I can conceive are to compare the output and costs of a bureau with those of a private firm with the same type of product. A comparison of the Social Security Administration and insurance companies, public and private hospitals, public and private statistics gathering organizations, of public and private police and garbage disposal services may be sufficient. Such tests, however, will be difficult as the existence of potential competition may present the bureau with a highly elastic demand, and some of the private firms producing a similar product have some of the characteristics of bureaus. A test of these assertions about a bureau that is the sole producer of a set of products, such as the Department of Defense, is even more difficult and probably more important. For such bureaus, an internal comparison at different points of time or, possibly, with bureaus producing a similar product in another political jurisdiction could be made.

## FURTHER IMPLICATIONS FOR ANALYSIS
## AND POLICY

### Analytic Developments

The static model of a single-product bureau outlined in Section II should be extended in several dimensions. First, the consequences of the time-dimension of budget maximization should be developed. Louis DeAlessi's preliminary analysis suggests that a bureaucrat's concept of his property rights will lead to a preference for capital-intensive production processes. Second, the behavior of a multi-product bureau that receives a single budget (or several budgets not specific to product type) should be explored. And third, the behavior of "mixed" bureaus, such as the Post Office, educational institutions, and public hospitals should be explored.

### Policy Implications

This model of a bureau, if the suggested tests fail to disconfirm its assertions, has important implications for the organization for the production of the large and increasing proportion of our national output now produced by bureaus. What changes could be made to improve the efficiency of the production of these goods and services?

First, and probably most interesting, bureaucratic provision of these goods and services could be maintained, but each bureau would operate in a competitive environment and face a highly elastic demand function. The creation of new bureaus would be encouraged. Existing bureaus would be permitted and encouraged to produce products now provided by other bureaus. "Antitrust" restrictions would prevent collusive behavior to divide products or output among bureaus and to prevent the dominance of one bureau in a single product. The legislature would be willing to shift some part of the output of one agency to another, based on output and budget performance. The resulting bureaucracy would consist of many single and multiproduct bureaus without any obvious relation (in use) of the products offered by any single bureau. (As such, it would look a little like the corporate sector of our economy.)

Second, the incentives of bureaucrats could be changed to encourage them to minimize the budget for a given output or set of outputs. For example, the salaries of the top 5 percent of the personnel of a bureau could be a negative function of the budget of a bureau for a given set of outputs. This would still permit a political determination of the output level for the combination of bureaus providing the same product. Such a system would require more precise measurement of output than now, but would not require the monetary valuation of this output. Such a system may also attract better managers to the bureaucracy.

Third, the type of goods and services now provided by bureaus could be financed through government or foundations as is now the case, but the provision of these services would be contracted to private, profit-seeking economic institutions. The bureaucracy, as such, would disappear, except for the review and contracting agencies. This system would also require better measures of output than now, but better measures are necessary for improved efficiency under any organizational form.

# The Centralized Socialist Economy

Chapter Fourteen

# The Soviet Manager and Innovation: A Behavioral Model of the Soviet Firm

E. Furubotn
S. Pejovich

English translation of: "Le chef d'enterprise soviétique et l'innovation: un modèle comportment." Reprinted from *Revue de L'Est* 3 (January 1972): 29–45, by permission of the publisher.

In recent years, the traditional theory of the firm has been extended to consider cases where the firm's objective appears to be the maximization of some *utility index* rather than simple monetary profits. This shift in analytical focus is straightforward enough, but the change has led to improved understanding of the possible patterns of managerial behavior and has permitted greater insight into the operation of business firms in various socioeconomic environments (Alchian 1965, 1969; Furubotn 1964; Furubotn and Pejovich 1970a).

     The objective of the present work is to employ the utility approach and formulate an optimization model that is capable of explaining the *observed* behavior of the Soviet firm. The article begins with a description of the organizational framework within which the Soviet firm is presumed to operate.[1] Then, in section II, the nature of the Soviet manager's utility function is considered along with certain major constraints imposed on the manager by the state. The next section attempts to show how the manager's behavior is influenced by the prevailing institutional structure. It appears that, despite the constraints established by the central production plan, the manager can create some freedom of action for himself and thus can pursue policies designed to insure his survival. The actual extent of choice here depends on the manager's knowledge of institutional arrangements (both formal and informal) and on the level of risk he is willing to assume. The implications of the limited set of managerial choices for the functioning of the firm are discussed in section IV. Finally, section V summarizes the findings and assesses the general position of the firm in the Soviet system. Perhaps the most significant result yielded by the model is an explanation of why the Soviet manager may actively seek cost-saving improvements in an economic environment that seems, at first view, to be characterized by waste, inefficiencies and a total lack of incentives to innovate.

     1. Simplifying assumptions are made throughout in order to minimize the difficulties of exposition. Although this treatment does some violence to descriptive accuracy, the resulting image of Soviet institutions is not greatly distorted.

I

Let us assume that the firm in the Soviet Union operates subject to the following conditions:

1. The manager is the only link between the firm and the central authorities.[2]
2. The state establishes a production plan for each firm in the system. A plan specifies the firm's official output quota; it also indicates the quantities of most variable inputs (other than labor) to be received by the firm and designates the suppliers of the respective items.
3. The firm is also constrained by a financial plan that is the monetary equivalent of the firm's production plan. An authorized bank supervises the use of budgeted funds, extends short-term credit when approved expenditures precede planned receipts, and generally oversees the firm's operations. The firm is required to deposit the entire proceeds from sales at the bank each day; consequently, any outstanding debt to the bank is automatically liquidated as receipts come in.
4. The price at which the firm sells its output is set by the state and equals the average planned cost plus the average planned profit per unit (inclusive of turnover tax) for the industry as a whole. By assumption, the firm considered in the analysis is a "representative" firm. Thus, given the allocation of planned supplies, the approved wage fund and the administratively set product and input prices, production of any output in excess of the quota implies average costs lower than those planned and average profit higher than the planned level.[3]
5. The central authorities judge the firm's performance on the basis of two success indicators:[4]  (a) the achievement of the gross output target and (b) the realization of the average planned cost and profit.[5]
6. The state decides on the allocation of physical capital to the firm, transfers existing capital, and determines the use of depreciation funds. The firm, how-

2. Numbers of people are responsible for reporting to their respective administrative superiors about the firm's activities (Ames 1965, pp. 35–37). It follows that the government is likely to receive more accurate information about the firm than it would if the manager were the only person reporting to the state.

3. This is not quite true, but our assumption here simplifies the analysis without changing its results materially. To calculate profits, operating costs are compared to sales not to gross output. Thus, it is possible for a Soviet firm to fulfill its production plan and show profit loss. In effect, then, we assume that the firm's entire output is sold.

4. The number of indicators was in excess of thirty until 1965 when the government announced that the indicators would be reduced to nine. See Blackman (1968, pp. 264–5) and Nove (1958).

5. For example: ". . . in the oil industry in 1956 the director received a bonus of 40 percent of his salary for fulfilling the output plan, and 4 percent for each 1 percent overfulfillment" (Nove 1961, pp. 31–32). Moreover, a percentage of excess profit can be allocated as rewards to the manager and other employees.

ever, pays neither rent nor interest charges on its fixed assets.

7.  The firm is free to buy labor services in the open market but has important constraints on its activities. The production plan delimits the size of the firm's wage fund, and administratively set wage scales specify the relative rates of pay for different skills.

In the institutional setting described, a certain division of decision-making power is implied between the state and the firm. This structure, in turn, suggests a probable pattern of behavior for the firm's manager. Since the manager's tenure on the job, promotions, and monetary rewards depend on his ability to produce at least the planned production quota, the output variable must play a central role in his formulation of policy. The rigid output target makes the Soviet manager desirous of accumulating both fixed assets and variable inputs—for accumulation insures the manager of survival in case of severe production difficulties and increases the likelihood of his fulfilling the official output quota under more normal circumstances.[6] Significantly, the mechanics of accumulating fixed and variable inputs differ. The manager will tend to view capital goods as a free reserve[7] and concentrate on devising arguments to convince the state of his firm's urgent need for additional capital to achieve the given output quota, or arguments to justify a request for a lower output target. By contrast, the firm's accounting cost of production varies with the acquisition of supplies of variable inputs and, thus, the manager who wishes to accumulate variable inputs must convince the state that the firm's production function has *lesser* technical efficiency than it actually possesses. In the Soviet system, accumulation of productive inputs represents a rational policy objective and the means for its implementation exist.[8]

## II

Based on the discussion of the preceding section, the Soviet manager's utility function can be written as:

$$U_t = \phi(q_t, S_t; Q_t), \tag{1}$$

---

6. The manager might also find it expedient to accumulate stocks of the commodity being produced if the existence of such stocks could be kept from higher authorities. To follow this strategy, however, the manager would have to possess excess supplies of inputs in, at least, some periods so as to achieve outputs in excess of quotas.

7. Liberman (1962) made the same point.

8. The 1965 Soviet reform, if implemented, will introduce some changes in the pattern of behavior of the Soviet manager. In this article, the 1965 reform is ignored because there is strong evidence to suggest that no major changes have taken place, and also because the output quota approach has dominated the Soviet scene for so long that its vestiges are unlikely to be erased overnight. See: Blackman (1968); *New York Times* (6 November, 1969); Pejovich (1969b); Zaleski (1967).

where $q_t$ is the output of the firm in period $t$ and the parameter $Q_t$ represents the firm's planned output quota for period $t$ (as determined by the central authorities). Variable $S_t$ is a measure of the stock or inventory of the variable input[9] accumulated by the manager over time through informal means [Berliner, J. "The Informal Organization of the Soviet Firm." *Quarterly Journal of Economics* 66 (1952): 342–365] and held back from active production in period $t$.

The magnitude $Q_t$ is significant because, in general, the manager is likely to place a very high value on additional output as long as the firm's current output is below the planned level ($Q_t$). Depending on the precise shape of the incentive-penalty structure, however, the manager may choose to add to stocks (at the expense of current output) even though $Q_t$ has not been reached (Zaleski 1967). For example, 90 percent fulfillment of the plan may be preferred to 95 percent fulfillment in any period $t$ so that adequate stocks can be accumulated to deal with expected production difficulties in period $t + 1$. In other words, tradeoffs between $q_t$ and $S_t$ can be conceived both below and above the point of 100 percent fulfillment of the plan.

At any cross-section of time, output in excess of the quota implies greater material rewards and prestige for the manager. But the activities of the firm extend over time and the manager must also consider his ability to meet future quotas and to secure future rewards. Ultimately, the rationale for including the stock variable $S_t$ in the preference function rests on the existence of uncertainty in the Soviet economy. Since there is general understanding among Soviet managers—and outside observers (Levine [1966])—that input allocations are frequently delivered late or not at all, the firm's possession of *unplanned* reserve stocks serves to obviate production crises. While the manager who fails to fulfill his production plan may be able to justify his shortfall to the state, he will obviously be in a better position if he can produce the required output consistently on schedule.[10] Stocks contribute to the index $U$ by giving the manager added assurance that he will be able to meet future output targets even when planned resource allocations are not received. Certainly after output $Q_t$ has been achieved, there will be some tradeoff of current production ($q_t$) for stock accumulation ($S_t$) because of the security the latter yields.

Next, consider the constraints to which the Soviet firm is subject. At any period $t$ within the "short-run" interval,[11] the manager sees the conditions

9. To simplify discussion, the model assumes that only one variable input is involved in the productive process.

10. The Soviet manager may not be able to accumulate inventories of all desired inputs. Then, he will tend to use informal channels to trade surplus items with other managers. This is how something like a free market creeps into the Soviet system and, in the opinion of many observers, saves it from breakdown.

11. In the context of the Soviet organizational framework, we shall define the short-run as the interval of time during which the state does not change the quantity of capital ($K^0$) in the firm's possession. This treatment is consistent with the approach taken in conventional microeconomic theory where, normally, no attempt is made to discuss the reasons for capital fixity. Under capitalism, however, pure economic logic can account for the short-run phenomenon. See DeAlessi (1967) and Furubotn (1964).

of input supply and use in terms of certain technical relations. He knows from experience that the official input allocation $R_t$ will not necessarily be delivered in total or, if it is delivered, will not all arrive in time for use in producing the $t$-th period's output quota $(Q_t)$.[12] It seems reasonable to assume, then, that the manager calculates an expected input delivery for period $t$ $(V_t)$ on the basis of some subjectively determined probability distribution.[13] If the expected delivery is considered equivalent to the same number of input units possessed with certainty [Friedman, M., and Savage, L. "The Utility Analysis of Choices Involving Risk." In *Readings in Price Theory,* edited by George J. Stigler and Kenneth Boulding. Homewood, Ill.: Richard D. Irwin, 1952] the stock level at $t$ can be defined as:

$$S_t = V_t + S_{t-1} - v_t. \tag{2}$$

Expected delivery $(V_t)$ plus the previously accumulated stock of this input $(S_{t-1})$ minus the current use of the input $(v_t)$ equals the current stock held for operations in future periods $(S_t)$.

At this point, a question arises as to how the manager can accumulate units of the variable input when the flow of the input to the firm is legally controlled and the official allocation is based on the planned output. The answer lies in the pattern of behavior the Soviet manager adopts in reporting the firm's short-run production function. In practice, the manager is able to gain a certain amount of slack for his operations by convincing the state that his production function shows relatively low technical efficiency. Thus, the *reported* production function might be specified as:

$$q_t = F(v_t; K^0, m), \tag{3}$$

while the *true* relation, characterized by greater efficiency, is:

$$q_t = f(v_t; K^0, n). \tag{4}$$

In equations (3) and (4), the flow of output per period $(q_t)$ depends on the contemporaneous use of the variable input flow $(v_t)$ in conjunction with the capital stock or "plant" $(K^0)$ that has been placed at the disposal of the firm by the state. The stock-flow function (3) differs from (4) because of an assumed difference in the respective technological parameters $(m$ and $n)$. For simplicity, we conceive of the situation as analogous to the case of neutral technological change and say that $n$ implies greater overall efficiency than $m$.

12. The manager would have an incentive to report the consumption of the full input allocation even if some deliveries were late and he had to deplete his stocks. If such a report were not made, the state would infer that the firm needed less of the input to produce the output quota.

13. As a first approximation, we can assume that the distribution is normal, and centered such that the probabilities of securing amounts greater than the official input allocation are low.

In effect, the Soviet manager controls the magnitude of the gap between parameters $n$ and $m$ by his power to falsify, to a greater or lesser degree, the true production capabilities of his firm.[14] But there are, of course, definite limitations on the extent to which the manager can misinform the government authorities. In the first place, industry production norms are known, so that the state has at least an approximate idea of efficiency levels in the sector. If the manager's report shows great departure from relevant industry norms, the government's suspicion is likely to be aroused, and direct investigation of the firm by the state's experts can follow. The implication is that the manager assumes increasing personal risk the more he understates his firm's efficiency (i.e., makes $m$ smaller than $n$). Moreover, the possibility is always present that other functionaries at the firm will make reports to the state that contradict the manager's testimony. The Soviet manager, then, has to reach a decision about the reported production function (3) in light of his willingness to take risks, his knowledge of the true technological relations,[15] his estimate of the costs and difficulties that the state must face in order to make a detailed check on conditions at the firm, etc. While different managers will tend to reach different solutions for reported efficiency, the potential gains from falsification of the production relation make it unlikely that the true function (4) will be reported by anyone.

Assume that the reported production relation (3) is approved by the state. Then, existing accounting procedures lead to a particular input allocation for the firm. If $w$ is the fixed price per unit of the variable input, commodity price at any period $t$ equals the average planned variable cost plus the average planned profit $\pi$ (inclusive of turnover tax).[16] In other words, the "representative" firm's total planned receipts and outlays are:

$$Pq_t = wv_t + \pi q_t \tag{5}$$

With plausible assumptions concerning the shape of the production function, only one value of $v_t$ will be consistent with the requirements of accounting equation (5).

Since the firm claims that its output varies with the employment of the variable input according to the *reported* relation (3), it is possible to substi-

14. For example: "The manager who succeeds in convincing the planners that he needs more inputs to reach stated output figures protects himself against the accusation of having disobeyed the central command. . . .Every manager will desire to build up reserves of material and labor and he can do this by misinforming the planners" (Halm 1968, p. 250).

15. As a practical matter, the Soviet manager may well lack detailed technical knowledge of his "true" production function. The assumption of precise knowledge of (4) is a convenient simplification but, for purposes of the article, it is sufficient merely that the manager know his firm's production capabilities more accurately than the state.

16. The simplifying assumption here is that the firm must earn an absolute profit ($\pi$) per unit of output for each given rate of production. The basic results of the analysis would be the same, however, if the planned profit were calculated in some other way, such as a constant percentage over operating expenses.

tute (3) in (5) and solve for the required amount of the variable input in terms of the known parameters of the system (i.e., $m$, $P$, $w$, $\pi$, etc.). The magnitude of $v_t$ given by the solution is the input allocation that will, presumably, be approved by the government. Let $R_t$ be the symbol for this official allocation of the variable input in period $t$. Then, having $R_t$ and the reported function (3), the planned output for the firm in the $t$-th period follows immediately. Soviet reality is, of course, more complex than our analytical sketch suggests, but the preceding material seems to reflect the essential aspects of the firm's situation. If the firm has certain production capabilities (3) and is to meet the general remuneration and profit requirements stipulated by (5), the Soviet authorities understand that the firm's input allocation must be $R_t$ and its output quota $Q_t$.

## III

Contrary to the intention of central planning, the Soviet manager is able to create a set of opportunity choices for himself. The origin of this set lies in the difference between the firm's approved and true production functions. Alternatives appear when the manager knows the characteristics of the firm's true production function (4) and is able to convince the central authorities that the firm has lesser productivity.

      The range of managerial choice can be determined on the basis of the given allocation $R_t$ and quota $Q_t$. From knowledge of $R_t$, the manager is able to establish the value of the expected input delivery $V_t$. Then, various strategies can be formulated for the use of $V_t$. At one extreme, the manager may decide to commit all of the flow $V_t$ to current operations. Since $V_t$ is an expected magnitude, the output calculation must also appear in expected terms; the expected output corresponding to input $V_t$ is symbolized as $E_t$. The size of $E_t$ relative to $Q_t$ depends on the influence exercised by two opposing forces. First, since production will always be undertaken with the technically more efficient process (4), $E_t$ will be larger (ceteris paribus) the greater the gap between the reported and the true production functions. On the other hand, $E_t$ will be smaller (ceteris paribus) the smaller the value of $V_t$ relative to $R_t$. In what may be regarded as the normal case, the expected delivery $V_t$ will be somewhat less than the official allocation $R_t$, but the true production function is likely to be substantially more efficient than the reported function. Thus, on balance, the manager's decision to use all of $V_t$ in current production implies an output $E_t$ greater than the quota.

      Overfulfillment of quota ($E_t > Q_t$) puts the firm in a generally favorable position. The excess output is desirable in itself and has the effect of reducing the relative costs of the firm and increasing its profit per unit over the required level. But the production strategy $E_t > Q_t$ also carries an unfavorable consequence; specifically, the firm will exhaust the $t$-th period's input allocation and add nothing whatsoever to stocks. By contrast, the manager can choose to produce merely the planned output. If this strategy is followed, not all the expected input allocation need be earmarked for current production. Using the efficient process (4), a lesser input volume than $V_t$ (say $M_t$) is capable of producing $Q_t$. Then, the firm can plan on accumulating $V_t - M_t$ units of the variable input to add to stocks in period $t$. The "sacrifice" implied here is, of course, that the rewards for overfulfillment of the quota are foregone.

The set of opportunity choices open to the Soviet manager includes the two extreme output-employment policies: $(E_t, V_t), (Q_t, M_t)$ just described, and all intermediate points lying between these extremes. The manager can elect to accumulate stocks at any rate from $V_t - M_t$ to zero; or, in terms of output, produce nothing beyond the official quota or overfulfill the quota in varying amounts up to the limit $E_t - Q_t$. Strictly speaking, the manager's production choices are even wider than those noted if he is willing to pursue more venturesome policies. For example, when previously accumulated stocks exist, the manager can plan to produce the maximum output $A_t$ based on the use of $V_t + S_{t-1}$ units of the variable input in process (4). Alternately, the accumulation of stocks can proceed at a greater rate than $V_t - M_t$ provided that the firm deliberately fails to meet the quota in period $t$ and plans instead to produce some output less than $Q_t$ (say $Z_t$) with input $N_t$. In general, then, the firm is technically free to operate at any point along the segment of the total product curve (4) whose end points are $N_t$ and $V_t + S_{t-1}$.[17]

From what has been discussed, it is clear that the firm is not tied to the centrally planned operating point $(Q_t, R_t)$. Moreover, the Soviet manager's decisions relative to the *desired* employment level and output can be understood as the results of an optimization process in which the manager seeks to maximize his utility function (1) subject to the (true) production function (4) and the expected stock relation (2). The utility function at any time $t$ reflects, inter alia, a subjective forecast of the firm's supply situation over the next period or the next few periods. The greater the deficiency anticipated by the manager between official input allocations in future periods and actual deliveries, the more weight he is likely to place on the stock variable at $t$ ($S_t$), and conversely. In any event, given the system (1), (4), (2), substitutions can be made and the utility function written in terms of the employment variable $v_t$ and certain background parameters[18] $(K^0, n, V_t, S_{t-1}, Q_t)$. Then, following conventional procedures familiar from the theory of the consumer, it is possible to secure the first- and second-order conditions for a utility maximum.[19]

In the elementary model considered, the utility-maximizing solution yields values for the optimal employment level of the variable input ($v_t^*$), the

---

17. It should be re-emphasized that since $V_t$ is an expected magnitude, the alternatives considered here represent merely the basis on which the manager formulates his *plans*.

18. The limit to the facilities the firm has available for the storage of current inputs must also play a part in the manager's optimizing decision. See section IV.

19. The optimization problem takes the following form:

Max.         (1)      $U_t = \phi(q_t, S_t; Q_t)$,

optimal commodity output ($q_t^*$), and the optimal input stock ($S_t^*$). By assumption, these "ideal" policy choices for period $t$ result from the manager's attempt to reach the most satisfactory personal adjustment to the hazards and rewards of the Soviet system. Wrong judgments are quite conceivable, but the manager shapes policy in light of his own understanding of self-interest. Since the optimizing procedure described above must be repeated, period after period, with updated equations analogous to (1), (4), (2), a succession of solutions will emerge for the firm over time and the manager's capabilities as a decision-maker will be revealed. Success in the Soviet system can be said to depend on having the "right" preference function. If the manager's function is appropriate in the sense that it leads to an output stream considered desirable by the state, he will survive and prosper; if not, he will tend to be eliminated from the ranks of Soviet managers.

Yet even when the manager creates a large set of opportunity choices for himself and chooses wisely within this set, he may still find himself in difficulty. According to the model, optimization involves the use of an expected value: $V_t$. Thus, in any given period (trial), the actual delivery of variable input to the firm will tend to be *larger* or *smaller* than the calculated magnitude $V_t$. If the standard deviation of the distribution of actual input deliveries is small,[20] the firm should normally be able to meet its assigned output target $Q_t$—with an occasional assist from accumulated stocks ($S_{t-1}$). But, whatever the standard deviation, there is at least a finite chance that deliveries in some period will fall far short of both the approved flow $R_t$ and the expected value $V_t$. At the same time, the available stock $S_{t-1}$ may not be large enough to overcome the input

---

subject to:

$$(4) \quad q_t = f(v_t; K^0, n)$$

$$(2) \quad S_t = V_t + S_{t-1} - v_t.$$

Since the objective function (1) can be written in terms of the variable $v_t$ alone, the first-order condition for the maximum is found by setting the first derivative ($dU_t/dv_t$) equal to zero, or:

$$-\frac{dS_t}{dq_t} = \frac{1}{\partial q_t/\partial v_t}$$

This condition indicates that, at equilibrium, the manager's subjective rate of substitution of stock for output has to equal the ratio: one over the marginal product of the variable input. The interpretation here is straightforward; $1/\partial q_t/\partial v_t$ is, in effect, a ratio of the shadow price of output to the shadow price of stock. A unit of the variable input can generate satisfaction for the manager either by contributing to the production of output ($q_t$) or to the accumulation of the input inventory ($S_t$). Since these alternative uses of $v_t$ are mutually exclusive, the "cost" of diverting a unit of the input from output to stock is the marginal product ($\partial q_t/\partial v_t$) forgone. Similarly, the "cost" of shifting a unit of the input from stock to output is the loss of one unit of inventory.

20. The magnitude of the standard deviation as perceived by the manager will influence the latter's attitude toward the relative weight given the stock variable in the utility function.

deficit, and so the firm's output will be less than the quota. In the Soviet Union, as elsewhere, chance can influence managerial careers.[21]

## IV

Ceteris paribus, the manager's position is secure as long as the firm's actual production[22] in any period $(a_t)$ is equal to or greater than the target output for that period $(Q_t)$. There is need, however, to examine the longer term consequences of overfulfillment of quota. If $a_t > Q_t$, the manager will inform the state authorities that the entire allocation of the variable input $(R_t)$ was used to produce output $a_t$, and that the differential $(a_t - Q_t)$ resulted from good management. The manager can expect to be rewarded for his "efficiency," but the accounting relations may undergo reorganization. Insofar as the productive improvement is viewed as irreversible, the state will conclude that an input allocation equal to $R_t$ should be able to yield the output $a_t$ in the next period $(t + 1)$. Thus, the state is likely to approve a *revised* production function[23] for period $t + 1$.

$$q_{t+1} = G(v_{t+1}; K^0, M). \tag{6}$$

This relation reflects generally greater technical efficiency, i.e., parameter $M$ replaces $m$ of equation (3) and $M > m$. The revision of the firm's production function in response to its success is an often-mentioned and much-debated factor in the Soviet economic system. The rationale for revision is simple; the policy permits the state to assign reasonable quotas *while economizing on the high cost of acquiring information about the production abilities of business firms.* Any adjustment must, of course, be related to both the magnitude and frequency of the firm's overfulfillment of plan. From the manager's standpoint, then, the choice of an optimal production strategy may be further complicated by the need to estimate the limits of the "zone of tolerance" within which no changes in output targets will result from an overfulfillment of plan.

Assume that the new total product function (6) lies above the originally reported curve (3) at all points, but below the true curve (4) because $M < n$. If the product price $P$ and other background conditions remain the same, the (required) equality of total revenue and total cost $(Pq_{t+1} = wv_{t+1} + \pi q_{t+1})$ implies a new solution for the official input allocation and output quota. The state

---

21. Given time, the manager may be able to free himself from any charges of inefficiency by proving that the output shortfall was not his fault but due instead to the inadequacy of input deliveries.

22. Note that $a_t$ can be greater than, less than, or equal to the ideal output $(q_t^*)$ planned by the manager on the basis of the expected allocation $V_t$.

23. Just how the state redefines the firm's production function is an open question. To limit complications, we assume that the improvement in efficiency is regarded as something akin to neutral technological change and can be reflected by the variation of a general technical parameter $(M)$.

will allocate some greater amount of the variable input to the firm than $R_t$.[24]
and expect the firm to produce more output than $Q_t$. The revised values can be
designated as $R_{t+1}$ and $Q_{t+1}$, respectively.

    A significant result of the reorganization is that the Soviet manager's
range of opportunity choices becomes smaller in period $t + 1$. The same general
analysis of the choice set discussed in section III is relevant, but the boundaries
of choice are now different. Because we assume diminishing physical returns in
(4), the manager's output choices must be more restricted in period $t + 1$ than in
the original situation. But, as before, what the manager's decision will be with
respect to desired output and accumulation depends on his utility function. If his
equilibrium solution for period $t + 1$ is such that actual output exceeds the quota
$(a_{t+1} > Q_{t+1})$, the sequence of events sketched above will repeat itself in period
$t + 2$, and the manager's range of output choices will be restricted still further.
Indeed, as long as the firm's output for any period is greater than the officially
designated quota for that period, the state will eventually revise its efficiency
estimates for the firm and establish a new (and larger) production target for a
subsequent period. As the reported productivity curve rises and approaches the
true productivity curve more and more closely, the scope for independent output
policy grows progressively smaller. In principle, this dynamic process, or "ratchet
effect," can go on round after round until the approved production function *co-
incides* with the true function at some period $T$. At this stage, the Soviet manager
has no real options; he must plan to produce an output equal to the government
quota based on (4) and be prepared to draw down previously accumulated stocks
whenever the official allocation is not delivered.

    Disappearance of choice is important because it means that the firm
is left vulnerable to the behavior of external suppliers and may often find itself
unable to meet the planned output requirement. The question is, then, whether
the manager can devise any policy that will tend to preserve his effective control
over the firm's stock-output position. At first thought, it might seem that the
manager could stop the inexorable movement to the zero-choice limit merely by
deciding to produce no more than the planned output. For, when the quota is
not exceeded, the state has no compelling reason to revise production standards
upward. Under such conditions, the manager apparently retains some freedom of
action. While the potential gains from overfulfillment of quota are sacrificed by
the attempt to maintain actual output equal to $Q_t$ each period, the possibility of
continuing enlargement of stocks exists, and the firm therefore enjoys great protection against the failure to meet assigned output targets.

    The difficulty with this line of reasoning is, of course, that there must
be a *limit* to the amount of the variable input that can be stored by the firm, or
to the amount that can be laid away without arousing the attention of the state.

---

24. It can be shown that the new input allocation $(R_{t+1})$ must be greater than
the old $(R_t)$ by considering the accounting equation (5) and the respective production
functions (3) and (6).

Stocks will tend to accumulate as long as the firm's efficiency is greater than reported and actual output equals the quota; but such an accumulation process can go on indefinitely. Thus, stocks can, in theory, become indefinitely large. To stay within the storage limit, the manager must ultimately use some of the surplus input in active production.[25] Such action means, in turn, that the firm's quota will be overfulfilled in some period and that the official output target for the next period is likely to be raised. The existence of a storage constraint, then, has fundamental significance for the model. When all essential characteristics of the system are considered, there appears to be no strategy the Soviet manager can follow that will allow him to avoid revealing the firm's true production function. In the end, he must lose the advantage of unreported efficiency.

The most the manager can hope to accomplish in the conditions described is to *delay* the date at which his policy choices vanish and he is forced to operate in strict accordance with the input allocation and quota imposed by the state. From a purely formal standpoint, the use of a sophisticated decision-making technique like optimal control theory might permit the manager to determine the *ideal* long-term strategy to ameliorate his position[26] and, perhaps, put off for a time the inevitable day of reckoning. It should be clear, however, that the manager's best interest lies not in wringing the greatest advantage from given background conditions, but in *changing the data of the system periodically*. The welfare of the Soviet manager requires the continual renewal and extension of production choices beyond those given by the state. And a way to achieve such renewal exists. At any moment, the manager can enlarge his set of opportunity choices, and enjoy relative independence for some finite interval of time into the future, provided he is able to *raise* the firm's total product schedule and *conceal* the shift from the state.

The manager has two general lines of action open to him in the attempt to raise productivity. He may seek additional fixed assets from the state, or he may introduce cost-saving innovations into his productive organization. Naturally, he is also free to pursue both policies simultaneously, but this possibility does not require separate discussion. The significance of fixed assets is

25. It might be objected that an alert manager could arrange to trade surplus amounts of the current input for additional capital equipment that would enhance the firm's productivity. But, in fact, such behavior is expressly forbidden by Soviet law. The firm is strictly accountable for its assigned capital stock and, hence, is unable to trade fixed inputs for current inputs. As a logical possibility, it is conceivable that the manager could dispose of excess stock by using the variable input wastefully in production, or by destroying amounts in excess of the storage limit. Such behavior, however, would seem to be very risky and most unlikely.

26. The model presented, which assumes a myopic day-to-day approach to optimization, would seem to have greater credibility as a device for explaining behavior. The objective is not to secure a *normative* solution indicating how an omniscient Soviet manager ought to operate but rather to throw some light on the question of how an actual manager might be expected to react.

obvious. Under normal conditions, an increase in the firm's capital stock will make it possible for the manager to understate his firm's true production once again. But there is a problem here. Insofar as the firm has been meeting or over-fulfilling its quota with the existing capital stock, the manager must be able to offer some cogent arguments to explain his need for additional capital. His success in convincing the state authorities probably depends on his ability to cultivate and utilize personal relations and also on his capacity to persuade the authorities that special circumstances make his needs for additional fixed assets more urgent than those of other managers.

When the manager is genuinely efficient and capable of initiating innovations which enhance the firm's productivity, the total product curve is shifted upward and unit costs are reduced. But whether the manager benefits from such reorganization turns on the question of concealment. If knowledge of the effects of innovation can be withheld from the state, the manager will be free to re-establish a certain range of policy choices. The state will become aware of the firm's cost-saving innovation only to the extent the manager discloses it by producing more than planned output. In other words, contrary to the conclusions of most authors,[27] *the Soviet system has a built-in incentive for the manager to search for cost-saving improvements, provided that the manager can choose the rate at which the effects of these improvements are made known to the state.*[28] The analysis of the article emphasizes that efforts will always be made to stave off the convergence of the reported and the true production functions. Ultimately, it is the manager's ability to innovate and conceal the full effects of the innovation from the state that determines his capacity to survive.

## V

The main conclusions of the paper can be summarized as follows:

1. It is feasible to construct a model of the Soviet firm based on the optimizing behavior of the Soviet manager. Assuming that the manager is always concerned with promoting his own interests, he must find some utility-maximizing policy adjustment consistent with the special set of institutional constraints under which he is forced to operate. From the standpoint of the firm, the mana-

27. Most authors have missed this point because the Soviet system provides no incentives to the manager to innovate and *announce* his innovation. For example: ". . . it remains true that the structure of the Soviet economy does little effectively to encourage the search for the new at local level, and not a little to discourage it" (Nove 1961, pp. 167–71). And, ". . . Managers have, furthermore, shown only slight interest in reducing costs—since each cost reduction is integrated into the subsequent plan . . ." (Spulber 1962, p. 68).

28. By extension of this logic, it becomes apparent that the manager also has incentive to introduce new products or modify existing ones. Specifically, the manager can be expected to seek permission from the state to undertake changes because product innovation represents another means he can use to keep the authorities uncertain about the firm's true production function.

ger's attempt to advance his personal objectives reflects itself as a particular output program. In general, by analyzing the nature and implications of the manager's policy choices, it is possible to explain some characteristic features of the Soviet firm's operations such as: (a) false reporting to the state, (b) insatiable demand for fixed assets, and (c) persistent desire to accumulate stocks of raw materials and other current inputs.

2. Contrary to the intent of the state's planning procedure, the manager is able to secure a set of opportunity choices with respect to the firm's output-accumulation policy. If the manager is willing to take the risk of misinforming the state about the firm's true production capabilities, he can acquire sufficient resources to accumulate stocks, overfulfill quota, or both.

3. Under static conditions where the set of institutional and technical parameters is fixed, the range of the Soviet manager's policy options necessarily diminishes over time, and choice must ultimately disappear. But because this pattern holds, the utility-maximizing manager has strong incentive to undertake action that changes his economic environment. Ceteris paribus, the manager can preserve a range of opportunity choices by pursuing one or more of the following policies: (a) acquiring additional fixed assets, (b) implementing cost-saving innovations, (c) introducing new or modified products. The manager's success in gaining room for maneuver, however, depends on his ability to *conceal* from the state the true implications of any reorganization based on (a) through (c). While no single act of reorganization is sufficient, continual change in productive arrangements can sustain the manager's area of freedom and contribute to the viability of the Soviet system as a whole.

4. There are forces within the Soviet economy that can promote innovative behavior. Despite the apparent lack of incentives at the micro-level, the operation of managerial self-interest is sufficient to initiate change. The existence of this innovative potential is important, of course, because it helps to explain how the Soviet economy can experience some economic advances in an environment that is ridden with waste and inefficiencies.

## Chapter Fifteen

# Markets Without Property:
# A Grand Illusion

### G. Warren Nutter

Reprinted from *Money, the Market, and the State* (N. Beadles and L.
Drewry, Jr., eds.), Athens: University of Georgia Press, 1968, pp. 137–145,
by permission of publisher and author.

It is now thirty years since Oskar Lange wrote his famous essay on how a socialist
economy might rationally allocate resources without a capital market (1936,
1937). His objective was to refute the contention, which he attributed to Ludwig
von Mises, that economic calculation is impossible unless markets are organized
on the basis of private ownership of property. While granting the case for competitive pricing, Lange argued that it could be simulated within a regime of collectivized property by setting prices centrally and instructing productive units to
behave in accord with a simple set of rules. A socialist economy could, in his
view, thereby gain all the allocative benefits of competition without suffering the
distributive evils of capitalism.

Experience has cast many doubts on the feasibility of Lange's simulated market socialism, but his theoretical case would seem to remain entrenched
as economic orthodoxy. It is widely viewed in Eastern Europe today as pointing
the way toward economic efficiency in a collectivized society. The time has perhaps come to question the soundness of Lange's theoretical case.

I

Let us start with Lange's basic premise:

> The economic problem is a problem of *choice* between alternatives.
> To solve the problem three data are needed: (1) a preference scale
> which guides the acts of choice; (2) knowledge of the 'terms on which
> alternatives are offered'; and (3) knowledge of the amount of re-
> sources available. Those three data being given, the problem of choice
> is soluble.
>
> Now it is obvious that a socialist economy may regard the data
> under 1 and 3 as given, at least in as great a degree as they are given
> in a capitalist economy. The data under 1 may either be given by the

demand schedules of the individuals or be established by the judgment of the authorities administering the economic system. The question remains whether the data under 2 are accessible to the administrators of a socialist economy. Professor Mises denies this. However, a careful study of price theory and of the theory of production convinces us that, the data under 1 and under 3 being given, the 'terms on which alternatives are offered' are determined ultimately by the technical possibilities of transformation of one commodity into another, i.e., by the production functions. The administrators of a socialist economy will have exactly the same knowledge, or lack of knowledge, of the production functions as the capitalist entrepreneurs have. (*Ibid.*, pp. 604.)

Thus posed, the problem of economic organization becomes purely technical; it is merely one of coordinating given wants and resources through given technology. Lange would solve the problem essentially by instructing plant managers to minimize costs and to equate marginal cost with price, and officials in charge of whole industries to set prices so that markets are cleared and to determine investment so that marginal cost for the industry equals price. He would allow competitive selling of labor and competitive buying of consumer goods, both motivated by self-interest, but neither is required in his system.

Lange recognized that formal rules alone will not make a system work. His mechanism for establishing an equilibrium state is the process of trial and error, the *tâtonnement* of Walras. The central planning board is to set a pattern of prices and observe what happens as plant managers, consumers, and workers adjust to it. As surpluses arise here and shortages there, the board is to revise the pattern of prices and observe once again the effects. Through-successive repetition of this procedure, an equilibrium pattern of prices is ultimately to emerge. The resulting state of affairs will presumably be indistinguishable from competitive equilibrium:   costs will be everywhere minimized and output optimized.

There are many grounds on which Lange's theoretical apparatus can be attacked, but I want to take his basic premise as my point of departure. In what sense is it true that "the 'terms on which alternatives are offered' are determined ultimately by the technical possibilities of transformation of one commodity into another?" In what sense is technology a "given" in the economic system and in what sense a consequence? Is the employed technology independent of the process of *tâtonnement*?

Since an economy must always start from where it is, let us imagine one in being with an established system of prices, however it may have been determined. The question arises among the decision-makers, whomever they might be, whether it is desirable to set up a new productive unit in a particular industry. The engineers are called in to sketch out the production function based on the current state of the arts, and the accountants to detail the terms on which resources can be hired or purchased. This information will enable the decision-makers to chart out minimum costs for alternative scales of plant on the basis of present and anticipated costs of resources.

Even at this stage of decision, the choice of employable alternative technologies, narrowly defined, cannot be disentangled from the existing price structure. Many possible arrangements of resources are ruled out because, under prevailing prices, they are relatively uneconomical. For each significantly different price structure that might exist, the array of optimal employable technologies will differ. There is no such thing as "the best set of techniques" independent of economic valuations.

Hence the choice of technology becomes an economic problem even in the planning stage, before resources have been committed into specific forms, plants, and facilities. Commitment requires appraisal of still another economic variable: the anticipated price of the commodity to be produced. And once resources are committed—plants are built—the range of technological-economic alternatives is altered from what it was before commitment. What is done cannot be undone without cost.

Consider the case of a mistake that has been made by building too large a plant. Even in a completely stationary economy there would be no cost-less way of remedying this error. The cheapest way to disinvest would be to let the plant depreciate. If the resources released through depreciation were employed elsewhere to yield a normal return, those still embodied in the plant would be bound to yield less than they would have if the correct plant had been erected in the first place. The original production function would become relevant only after the plant had been fully depreciated, a process that might require a century or more of time.

Needless to say, correcting of errors and misjudgments in investment is much more costly in a changing and growing economy. Within any relevant economic environment, the rational policy to follow over some period of time is a mixture of depreciating and altering committed investments, and the best policy in any instance depends in a complex manner on a host of expectations about costs of resources, prices of products, and changes in technology.

These observations are commonplace in standard economic theory, and they have been thoroughly discussed in the literature.[1] The only point worth stressing is that every equilibrium state of an economy depends on the dynamic path through which it is reached. The economic outcome at any moment—or, to revive a neglected term, the economic conjuncture—may or may not represent an equilibrium state in a meaningful sense, but whether it does or not, it is the result of the process of adjustment as well as the so-called givens of the economy. For every significantly different dynamic path, there will be a different equilibrium state even if the basic givens were to start out the same in every case.

1. See, for instance, Stigler (1939).

In other words, the Walrasian principle of *tâtonnement* is valid only in the formal sense that a competitive economy can reach *some* equilibrium state through a process of trial and error. It is invalid in the strict sense that there is a unique equilibrium regardless of how it is reached, except possibly for the most primitive market economies.

We are surely led to conclude that economies must be judged at least as much on their mechanisms for adjusting to changed circumstances as on their formal apparatus of pricing. The important question to raise about a Lange-type socialist economy, from the point of view of "static efficiency," is whether its adjustment mechanism would be as sensitive and responsive as that of a private enterprise market, whether its process of trial and error would dampen to an equilibrium solution as quickly and effectively—whether, in fact, it would ever reach an outcome with characteristics of efficiency commonly attributed to a competitive market.

## II

We may approach this issue by observing how a private enterprise economy runs. Consider the classical firm cast in the role of an enterprise within a market economy and a regime of private property. The entrepreneur—the owner of the enterprise itself but not necessarily of the capital invested in it—is interested in earning as much as he can. This simple motive combined with the entrepreneur's skill determines the size of the firm, or how many activities are organized within it and how many through the market place. It also determines the methods of organization used and the costing and pricing policies followed. Whatever increases the entrepreneur's earnings for a given effort will be done; whatever decreases them will not be. Private property and freedom of enterprise fix simultaneously the firm's role in the economy, costs incurred, prices charged, and output produced.

There is nothing automatic about this process, of course. The firm must be managed in accord with the owner's interests, and this task grows geometrically with the size of the firm. Proper orders must be both given and obeyed, and hired managers and workers as such normally have no direct interest in either giving or obeying orders that benefit the entrepreneur alone. The entrepreneur must therefore link the manager's interests to his own through surveillance or partnership, in varying degrees and mixtures. Managers must do the same with respect to workers.

Badly supervised management must be expected to press forward its own advantages to the detriment of the entrepreneur. If salaries are fixed, other means will be found to raise incomes at company expense. Secretaries will be hired for beauty as well as and instead of efficiency; offices will be comfortably furnished with plush carpets and original paintings; richly appointed executive dining facilities will be arranged on the premises; a park of limousines and aircraft will be set up and staffed with courteous and personable chauffeurs and pilots; ample allowances for business entertainment will be provided; and so on. Ways will also be found to reduce the workload: banker's hours, lengthy business lunches, conferences on the golf links, and so on. Lesser workers and employees will have more limited opportunities for on-the-job leisure and perquisites, but they will not lack ingenuity in exploiting them.

Mismanagement may go undetected as long as it merely keeps the entrepreneur's earnings lower than they might otherwise be, but it is immediately brought to light when it results in actual losses. Private property sets a limit to divergence of interest between manager and owner. Lack of success in one or the other—management or entrepreneurship—will eventually be eliminated by the ultimate disciplinarian: bankruptcy.

Private property rights are, of course, never absolute, being always restricted by the political order of any society. Property rights in fact measure the degree of the holder's liberty; the amount of property together with the rights, the degree of his power. As Armen Alchian has so clearly argued in much of his recent work, the pricing behavior of a firm will depend directly on the nature of property rights held by its effective owner.

For example, let the owner's earnings be taxed at a flat percentage rate. It is now in his interest to consume some of his income in perquisites enjoyed through his business. Like the badly supervised manager, he will try to set up a well-appointed office staffed with attractive personnel and to add other well-known side benefits. Business affairs will be discussed at expensive restaurants and night clubs or in conferences scheduled at pleasing localities. In hiring managerial personnel, it will become worth while to pay less attention to managerial talents and more to conversational skills, golfing or bridge-playing abilities, and the charm of wives. Tax authorities will naturally frown on such practices, but they can control them only to a limited extent short of taking over actual management of the firm. And then similar practices would arise to the benefit of the tax office.

In other words, costs of doing business will rise as the entrepreneur takes advantage of his firm as a place for consuming services at a bargain rate in terms of net earnings forgone. The changed cost conditions will probably also lead to higher prices and lower output as well as smaller take-home earnings.

Let us take one further step and fix a progressive schedule of tax rates beginning with the flat rate already supposed. Presumably even more income will be consumed through the firm, raising costs and prices and lowering output and earnings further. If the tax rate becomes confiscatory at some point, the entrepreneur loses all personal incentive to realize higher earnings. He will try to gear his business so as never to generate more than that maximum net revenue before taxes, eating up any excess in perquisites if necessary, unless motivated by patriotism or concern for the public good as attended to by government out of tax revenues. As Alfred Marshall once suggested, such motives may be high, but they are not always strong or abundant.

## III

How do these situations differ from behavior of a state-owned enterprise? The first thing to do is to identify the effective owner. If an abstract entity such as the state is to be called the owner, then government must be the concrete agency charged with trusteeship. Government will be of some definite form, ultimately responsible to some group of persons for whom it is acting as agent, and it will presumably be responsive at least indirectly to their interests. Ultimately, then, the persons controlling government are the effective owners of state-owned enterprises, while government or some part of it serves as manager.

The interests of owner and manager will diverge here just as surely as within a regime of private property, and the means of bringing accord are the same: surveillance and partnership. But the political order raises new problems. In the first place, it is seldom easy or sensible to change a government because a single enterprise has been mismanaged. In the second place, mismanagement is not readily recognized by interested parties and communicated among them.

Government is, after all, a unified institution, capable of only a limited degree of divisibility. In the market for private property, on the other hand, ownership can be subdivided almost indefinitely, and each owner can divest himself of his property at any time and transfer it elsewhere. Hence management of a single enterprise can be turned over at any moment without materially affecting the rest of the economy, and awareness that something is wrong in an enterprise is quickly transmitted from owner to owner through transactions in capital markets.

An even graver drawback for state-owned enterprises is virtual absence of the ultimate discipline of bankruptcy. In principle, there may be no reason why each enterprise cannot be endowed with its own limited capital and be forced to make its own way on those fixed resources, being put into bankruptcy when it becomes insolvent. But in practice every government is reluctant to follow this course: an enterprise serves political as well as economic ends; bankruptcy reflects on the credit of the government itself; receivership for collective property can hardly be transferred from the political arena; the managers and workers in an enterprise, having no transferable property rights, have more to gain from preserving a losing venture than from dissolving it; and so on. It is generally more expedient to subsidize a floundering state-owned firm than to put it into receivership or out of business.

In the face of all these difficulties, how can those to whom government is responsible keep a close eye on the efficiency of governmental enterprise, in the first place, and remedy divergence of interest, in the second? Few examples of institutions successful in promoting these objectives come to mind.

The sheer technical problems of costing and pricing in state enterprises are minimized when they operate within a general environment of private enterprise, since the market place resolves most difficulties. An ocean of private enterprise will determine the level of a bay of governmental enterprise. It is only when the roles are reversed—when governmental enterprises become the ocean and private ones the bay—that the problem becomes serious. Are prices and activities to be set by some central political organ or by some kind of market or quasi-market?

One hardly needs to catalog the shortcomings of a centralized command economy. They are well known and acknowledged, perhaps most forcefully at the moment by commentators in the Soviet world itself. The virtues of decentralized decisions and mutual interaction are recognized throughout most of the civilized world today, and all Soviet economies except Communist China and its allies are seeking ways to decentralize economically while preserving an authoritarian political order.

These efforts are bound to be disappointed. Mutual interaction in an economy dominated by government enterprise can be accomplished only by subdivision of political authority, since collective ownership must be divisible into units subject to mutual competition if effective markets are to arise. The larger the economy, the more intensive the divisibility needed.

This is not to say that the extreme form of Stalinist economy cannot be improved upon without sacrificing an authoritarian political system. Yugoslavia is a case in point. Quasi-markets were created by establishing semi-autonomous collectivized enterprises with the right, although limited and controlled, of competing with each other. Obvious improvements in efficiency have been experienced without an immediate threat to the political system, but serious problems have also accumulated that may have no easy solution without political changes as well. The most pressing is the one already emphasized: how to deal with firms that are suffering persistent losses. So far, the system has provided no answer, no effective surrogate for bankruptcy proceedings.

## IV

If we now come full circle and return to Lange's model of socialism, we see how empty his theoretical apparatus is. Markets without divisible and transferable property rights are a sheer illusion. There can be no competitive behavior, real or simulated, without dispersed power and responsibility. And it will not do to disperse the one without the other. If all property is to be literally collectivized and all pricing literally centralized, there is no scope left for a mechanism that can reproduce in any significant respect the functioning of competitive private enterprise.

We could go further and dwell on the problems of generating innovation and progress in a Lange-type system, but something should be left for others to discuss. We may be content here with criticism cast in a static context.

Lange's error began with his basic premise. It is not true that administration of an economy is simply a technical problem devolving from the basic given conditions. Nor is it true that "the administrators of a socialist economy will have exactly the same knowledge, or lack of knowledge, of the production functions as the capitalist entrepreneurs have." Nor could simulated markets work in the same way as real ones if those administrators did have the same knowledge.

If capitalism has faults, so has socialism. At the top of the list is absence of competitive markets, simulated or otherwise.

# The Decentralized Socialist Economy

# Chapter Sixteen

# Property Rights and the Behavior of the Firm in a Socialist State: The Example of Yugoslavia

E. Furubotn
S. Pejovich

Reprinted from *Zeitschrift für Nationalökonomie*, Band 30 (Heft 3–4, 1970): 431–454, by permission of the publisher.

In recent years, increasing numbers of East European economists and governmental officials have become openly critical of the performance of socialist economic systems; their contention is that the respective governments have failed to solve the problem of devising an *incentive* and *control* system which is able to induce public administrators to direct production efficiently. Moreover, they seem quite eager to "rediscover" the very same set of market institutions which only a decade ago they used to decry as "transforming mankind into a horde of profit-seeking beasts."

Yet, the fact that economic reforms are easier to decree than to put into effect has somehow escaped attention. A number of papers have been written in the United States and elsewhere in the world on the content of proposed reforms in East European countries and on the results anticipated from their implementation. However, the profession has paid considerably less attention to the analysis of changes in property-rights structures that the effectuation of reforms would require.[1]

The real analytical issue in discussing economic reforms in Eastern Europe is not what their effects would be—those can be found in the *Wealth of Nations*. Instead it is a search for a set of institutions which yield efficient market solutions in a world where capital goods cannot be privately owned. Accordingly, the present article will endeavor to develop a theory of the socialist firm which takes into account the characteristic property-rights structure in a socialist state and explains the pattern of behavior imposed on decision-makers by this structure. Emphasis will be on the factors which determine (a) the firm's decision with respect to its short-run rate of output and net investment, and (b) the government policies toward the firm. The evaluation of government policies shows

1. See Pejovich (1969b).

the importance of relating the prevailing property-rights structures to the pattern of the firm's behavior.[2]

The analysis is based on the Yugoslav firm and the conditions under which it operates. There are two main reasons for this selection: (a) Yugoslavia is the first communist country that has *actually* decentralized its economic system without falling back on the institution of private property rights over the means of production; and (b) the Yugoslav "model" incorporates some of the ideas present in the currently debated reforms in Eastern Europe and forecasts their possible future.

The article begins with a brief outline of the institutional framework within which the Yugoslav firm operates, proceeds to the analysis of the firm's output and net investment decisions, and ends with a few remarks on the importance of relating market phenomena to the structure of property rights in the economy.

## THE FRAMEWORK

Since 1950–51, the right to manage the firm in Yugoslavia has been, within the limits determined by law, in the hands of its employees.[3] The collective, through its elected body, the Workers' Council, makes all major decisions, such as the rate and quality of output and investment, the level of employment, hiring and firing of workers, etc. Moreover, the collective has sufficient power to ask for the removal of the firm's director.

The director of a Yugoslav firm is selected in a public contest by a commission jointly appointed by the Workers' Council and local government. He implements the decisions made by the collective, controls and organizes production, and is responsible directly to the Workers' Council. It follows that the director of the Yugoslav firm can afford to be neither a dictator nor a paternalistic supervisor. He has to show some tangible evidence of successful management of the firm by generating acceptable wages and must be able, at all times, to persuade the collective concerning the wisdom of his ideas on policy.

As of 1965 the scheme of the distribution of total revenue of the Yugoslav firm is:[4]

---

2. The importance of relating property-rights structures to the behavior of the firm underlines A. Alchian's and W. Nutter's recent writings. See, for example, Alchian (1965) and Nutter (1968).

3. See the Law on Management of Enterprises by Workers' Collectives, Sluzbeni List, Belgrade, July 5, 1950.

4. Based on: *Nove Mere Za Sprovodjenje Privredne Reforme,* Belgrade: Knjizevne Novine, 1968, p. 71.

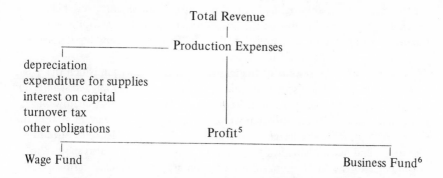

The unique feature of this scheme is the exclusion of the wage bill from the cost of production. It means that the actual take-home pay of the Yugoslav worker depends on and varies with (a) the realized profits of his firm; (b) the distribution of profit between the Wage and Business Funds; and (c) the criteria used to distribute the Wage Fund among the firm's employees. As of 1965 the Workers' Council has been given direct control over (b) and (c) and retained indirect control over (a) through its output decisions. It should be mentioned at this point that the majority of product prices in Yugoslavia are still determined administratively.

The Yugoslav firm does not and, in fact, cannot legally own capital goods. Yet, the emphasis on the relation between the firm's profit and the average earnings per unit of time for the labor input makes it imperative for the collective to control the quantity and quality of its capital, i.e., to enjoy some kind of well-defined property rights over its firm's assets. The law on the Management of Fixed Capital by Enterprises of December 1953 gave the Yugoslav collective the *right of use*[7] over its firm's capital. This law allowed the firm to produce, buy and/or sell capital goods subject to only two major constraints: (a) the firm must maintain the book value of its assets *via* depreciation allowances or otherwise (e.g., if the firm sold assets to another firm for less than their book value, the difference must be deducted from the firm's profit and earmarked for investment); and (b) the firm must pay interest on the value of its capital to the state (four percent as of 1965). The purpose of this obligation is, in addition to assert-

5. The term *profit* is not a direct translation from Serbo-Croatian. A more appropriate term would be *income*. Profit is used to avoid some possible confusions in the text between income of the firm and incomes of its employees.

6. The Business Fund consists of three different funds (Reserve Fund, Collective Consumption Fund, and Investment Fund). For simplicity we assume that all moneys allocated to the Business Fund are used for the investment purpose.

7. See the Law on the Management of Fixed Capital by Enterprises, Sluzbeni List, Belgrade, December 1953.

ing the state's ownership rights, to provide funds for administratively planned investment projects and to induce the profit-oriented firm to use capital goods efficiently. It should be noted, however, that the firm selling capital goods can transfer only the *right of use* to the buying firm.

This brief outline of the institutional setting within which the Yugoslav firm operates suggests two possible behavioral goals: (a) *wage maximization per worker* and (b) *wealth maximization per worker*. The analysis below will show that wealth maximization per worker is clearly a more relevant goal. It offers more comprehensive insight into the mutual interdependence of output, employment, and net investment decisions by the collective, and also shows the dependence of the equilibrium solution on the property-rights structure extant. Moreover, the action of the Yugoslav government in instituting the 1965 economic reform suggests that the state itself recognizes wealth maximization per worker as a fundamental behavioral goal.[8]

## THE WAGE MAXIMIZATION HYPOTHESIS

Let us consider a socialist firm operating subject to the production function:

$$x = f(L, K), \tag{1}$$

where $x$ is commodity output, $L$ is a homogeneous labor input, and $K$ represents the flow of capital services emerging per period from the capital equipment controlled by the firm. At any moment, the firm has the use of a definite volume of capital services; for the initial period, this flow can be designated as $K^0$.

Now, if we assume that any incremental capital acquired in the first period will not be integrated into the firm's productive organization until the next period, the available flow of capital services is fixed at $K^0$ until the beginning of period two. Assuming, further, that labor is effective immediately (i.e., without any lag), we have a type of short-run situation in the initial period, and at each cross-section of time thereafter. Under these "short-run" conditions, interest centers on variations in the labor input.

For example, the profit function for period one takes the following form:

$$\pi = P \cdot f(L, K^0) - Z(K^0). \tag{2}$$

Granting that the firm can sell any output it wishes at the official price ($P$), profit ($\pi$) equals price times output minus cost $Z$. The latter stands for the produc-

8. The *profit maximization per worker* goal can be ignored because it yields the same output and employment solutions as the wage maximization hypothesis; moreover, it provides no insight into the possible investment behavior of the firm. To simplify the analysis it is assumed that all monies allocated to the Business Fund are earmarked for investment, and that this Fund is the firm's sole source of investment funds.

tion expenses of the firm as enumerated in section II. For convenience, the magnitude of cost $Z$ can be taken as a function of the flow of capital services. Thus, as the relations are established, profit depends solely on the variable $L$, given the background data.

We know from the scheme of the distribution of total revenue that profit is distributed between the Wage and Business Funds in the proportions agreed upon by the Workers' Council. Thus:

$$\pi = W \cdot L + I, \tag{3}$$

where $W$ represents the wage rate per unit of labor and $I$ is the monetary value of the Business Fund. In principle, $I$ can take on any value from zero to some upper limit established by the need to maintain a minimally acceptable wage $(W^*)$; i.e., $0 \leqslant I \leqslant (\pi - W^*L)$. However, it is clear that if the workers are motivated strictly by the desire to maximize the average wage rate in any period, the Business Fund must be set at zero.

Of course, with $I = 0$, the expression for the wage rate reduces to:

$$W = \frac{P \cdot f(L, K^0) - Z}{L}. \tag{4}$$

Here, $W$ is a function of the variable $L$, and the first-order condition for the maximum is easily secured.[9]

$$\frac{dW}{dL} = -\frac{P \cdot x}{L^2} + \frac{P \cdot f_L}{L} + \frac{Z}{L^2} = 0. \tag{5}$$

Relation (5) can be rewritten in terms of more familiar economic concepts:

$$P \cdot AP_L - \frac{Z}{L} = P \cdot MP_L. \tag{6}$$

At the wage maximizing equilibrium, the value of labor's average physical product minus average fixed cost per unit of labor must be equal to the value of labor's marginal product. Note that if depreciation costs, interest charges, etc., are zero (i.e., $Z = 0$), the optimal operating position falls at the point where average and marginal products are equal (i.e., at $AP_{max}$). On the more reasonable assumption of a positive value for $Z$, the solution changes; the greater $Z$, the more the operating point is pushed in the direction of larger labor employment and $AP_L > MP_L$.

9. On the usual assumption of a declining marginal product for labor, the second-order conditions for the maximum will also hold.

The first-order condition (5) involves the variable $L$ and a number of parameters. Thus, knowing the form of the production function, equation (5) can be solved directly for the ideal employment level ($\bar{L}$):

$$\bar{L} = g(Z, P, K). \tag{7}$$

The direction of influence of each parameter is suggested by the sign of its partial derivative:

$$\frac{\partial \bar{L}}{\partial Z} > 0, \quad \frac{\partial \bar{L}}{\partial P} < 0, \quad \frac{\partial \bar{L}}{\partial K} \gtrless 0.$$

For example, a decrease in capital charges ($Z$) or an increase in the price of the commodity leads to a decrease in the equilibrium volume of employment. Further, as Ward (1958) has shown,[10] similar relations hold with respect to output; of special interest is the fact that output and price are inversely related over the relevant economic range of the production function.

Unfortunately, analysis of the role of capital is more difficult. A change in the flow of capital services can require an increase, decrease, or no change in employment.[10] The result hinges on the mathematical forms ascribed to: (a) the production function and (b) the cost function $Z = Z(K)$. Depending on the choice of the production function, the ideal labor solution may also be affected by the *magnitude* of the change in capital services. Thus, for small increases in $K$, a decrease in the level of employment might be indicated, while for large increases, an increase in employment could be required. Without precise stipulation of the formal system considered, no generalizations can be made.

The preceding discussion can be summarized with the aid of some simple geometric figures. Figure 16-1 shows the basic elements considered in equations (4)-(6). When fixed costs ($Z$) are zero, the greatest possible wage per worker is found at the point where ray $OA$ is tangent to the value of the total product curve $OJM$ (i.e., $\tan \Phi = P \cdot AP_L = P \cdot MP_L$). The associated labor input is $L_0$; this is the least labor that will be employed whatever the value of $Z$ (or $I$). Once $Z$ becomes positive, the maximum wage rate is determined by drawing a ray from origin $Z$ and discovering the point at which $ZB$ is tangent to curve $OJM$; in the diagram, the point is $F$ and the optimal labor input $L_1$. Since

$$\tan \Theta = \frac{P \cdot x - Z}{L} = W,$$

10. In Figure 16-1, the effect of a greater flow of capital services might be observed as a substantial leftward shift of curve $ORJM$ and a modest rise of cost line $ZZ$ to $Z'Z'$. Then, the point of tangency between a ray from $Z'$ and the new productivity curve would imply an equilibrium labor input less than $L_1$.

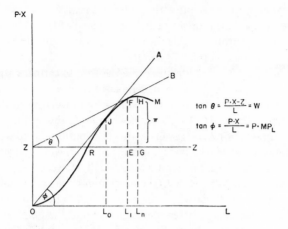

**Figure 16-1.** Worker Wages and Input

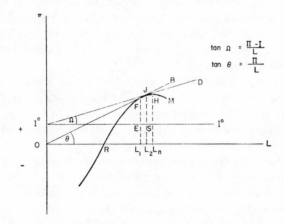

**Figure 16-2.** Profit Earned by Firm at Each Level

the slope of $ZB$ equals the average wage rate and it is obvious that a lower average wage is implied at any labor input less than or greater than $L_1$ (i.e., consider slope of $ZB$ over the range $RJFH$).

Figure 16-2, obtained by subtracting fixed costs $(Z)$ from the value of total product $(P \cdot x)$, represents the profit $(\pi)$ earned by the firm at each possible employment level $(L)$. We know that under the wage maximization per worker hypothesis, the equilibrium labor input will be $L_1$ (where $\pi/L = d\pi/dL$). Then, having $L_1$, the equilibrium output becomes determinate via equation (1). However, all this implies that the allocation to the Business Fund is nil; strict wage maximization is inconsistent with $I > 0$. And it may well have been the assumption of wage maximization as the behavioral goal of the collective which led the Yugoslav government to provide various complicated guidelines for the distribution of profits in the late 1950s and the early 1960s.[11]

If administrative guidelines cause the firm to earmark a particular sum $I^0$ for the Business Fund, the immediate consequences are seen as a reduction in the wage rate and an increase in the labor input (relative to the $I = 0$, case). For example, Figure 16-2 shows that when $I = 0$, the optimal employment level is $L_1$; the total profit $L_1 F$ is available for distribution to the workers. With the Business Fund set at $I^0$, the same operating position would leave only $EF$ for the Wage Fund and the wage rate would have to fall. However, adjustment of employment and output is indicated. The maximum wage compatible with $I^0$ is given by a labor input of $L_2$ or where the value of tan $\Omega$ [i.e., $(\pi - I)/L$] is a maximum. Geometrically, the latter condition is met at the point of tangency ($J$) between the ray $I^0 D$ and the profit curve $RFM$. As equation (3) suggests, the total profit generated here $(L_2 J)$ is divided into two portions, with $SJ$ going to the Wage Fund and $L_2 S$ to the Business Fund. In the hypothetical limiting case at point $H$, the Business Fund reaches its ultimate value; $I^0 = \pi$ and the wage rate ($W$) is zero (i.e., tan $\Omega = 0$). Since the marginal physical product of labor is zero at $H$, the solution implies that profits (and $I$) are being maximized while labor's return is ignored completely.

The range of feasible employment and output levels for the firm is now clear. Given the production function (1) and the values of fixed cost ($Z$) and commodity price ($P$), the labor input must be equal to $L_1$ or $L_n$ or any value between these limits. The amount of labor actually used will depend on the allocation made to the Business Fund ($I$). For, over the operating range $L_1 - L_n$, tradeoffs between $I$ and $W$ can proceed *continuously*. At input $L_1$, $I = 0$ and the wage rate is a maximum; at input $L_n$, $I$ is a maximum and the wage rate is zero; at intermediate positions, the inverse relationship holds but both $I$ and $W$ are positive. Figure 16-2 shows that a lesser input than $L_1$ leads to a lower wage and no increase in $I$, while an input greater than $L_n$ leads to lesser $I$ and no increase in $W$. Thus, values for $L$ other than the set $L_1 \leqslant L \leqslant L_n$ are of no interest; the effective arc of the profit function is $FJH$.

## THE ROLE OF THE FIRM DIRECTOR

The 1965 economic reform abolished the administrative guidelines for the distribution of profits. Yet, the firms have continued to channel some of their profits into the Business Fund. In fact, the share of self-financed investments rose 8 percent in 1966. Such evidence, of course, tends to refute the pure wage maximization hypothesis which requires that $I$ be equal to zero, and a question arises

11. See the Law on the Distribution of Profits by Enterprises, Sluzbeni List, Belgrade, April 18, 1962.

as how the Wage Fund–Business Fund proportions are reached. Various theories can, perhaps, be advanced to explain the willingness of workers to divert some fraction of the firm's profits to *I*. However, it would seem that any plausible theory must give consideration to the pivotal position of the manager in the Yugoslav firm.

As indicated earlier, the manager, or director, is responsible to the Workers' Council and must elicit cooperation from the firm's labor force if he is to function effectively in his job. Nevertheless, the director's interests and motivations are not identical with those of the workers, and it is a mistake to assume that he will always support a simple wage maximization program. On the one hand, the director recognizes that his own salary can be increased, along with the basic wage rate, as the Business Fund is reduced and made to approach zero. But the director is also concerned with investment policy and the economic growth achieved by his firm. Since he represents the central government,[12] he is particularly aware of national purposes and priorities; at the same time, he knows his long-term career is likely to be influenced by the degree to which his guidance of the firm contributes to the realization of national goals. On this logic, the maintenance of relatively high investment rates by the firm may seem essential to the director. In general, the director occupies a middle ground between the local workers and higher level government authorities. He must be sensitive to the desires of both groups and take actions which are broadly acceptable, if not pleasing, to both.

For analytical purposes, the conflicting motivations of the director can be reflected by a simple preference function:

$$U = \Phi(I, W). \tag{8}$$

Here, the director's relative satisfaction is assumed to depend on the magnitude of the firm's Business Fund ($I$) and the level of the wage rate ($W$). The former variable is best understood as a surrogate for prestige and the longer-term advantages which accrue to the manager of a vigorous, growing firm. Similarly, the wage rate is important to satisfaction because the value of $W$ is correlated with the director's current income, his popularity with the firm's workers, and his immediate job security. In the conventional manner, we can assume substitution is possible between $I$ and $W$, and thus derive a set of indifference curves from (8). As drawn in Figure 16-3, these curves are continuous and convex with respect to the origin. The general orientation of the curves is conditioned by the director's estimate of the minimum volume of retained earnings ($I^*$) and minimum wage ($W^*$) that will be acceptable to the central authorities and workers, respec-

12. For example, the Basic Law on Commercial Enterprises of April 1965 states that the director's duty is to control the Workers' Council decisions and to inform the state whenever he *feels* that the collective's action is contrary to the intent of the positive laws and regulations.

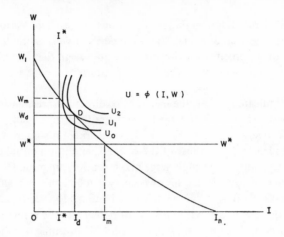

**Figure 16-3.**   Director's Preferences

tively.[13] Since any point in the $I$-$W$ space can be assigned a utility number ($U$) via the ordinal function (8), we have a complete representation of the director's preferences and can infer his behavior. Presumably, he will rank alternative wage-investment policies[14] and seek to implement that policy ($I^0$, $W^0$) which promises him maximum satisfaction.

Of course, any attempt on the part of the director to maximize utility is subject to certain constraints. In the first place, there are limits on the director's ability to persuade the Workers' Council to accept a wage rate much lower than the maximum wage $W_1$ (found where $I = 0$ and the labor input is $L_1$ in Figure 16-2). How far wage policy can depart from pure wage maximization is an open question, but it seems clear that there is some scope for reduction of $W$. The director is more than a mere member of the collective conferring with the Workers' Council. By virtue of his key position as organizer and controller of production, he tends to possess greater information and perspective on the alternatives confronting the firm. The workers must recognize the director's special knowledge of the firm just as they are aware of his special responsibility to interpret the legality of decisions reached by the Workers' Council. It follows that an individual having such power and endowed with strong leadership qualities

13. An operating point lying outside the quadrant formed by the lines $I^*I^*$ and $W^*W^*$ would imply strong dissatisfaction on the part of the workers, the government authorities or both groups. Since such dissatisfaction would tend to make the director's position tenuous and generally unpleasant, he could be expected to assign relatively low utility numbers to points where either one or both of the $I^*$, $W^*$ minima are violated.

14. Knowing $I^0$, we can find the value of $L$ which will yield the maximum wage consistent with the specified $I^0$. Then, with the equilibrium labor force determined, the equilibrium output can be established.

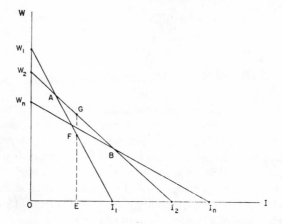

**Figure 16-4.** Variation of Wage Rate with Different Distributions of Profit to the Business Fund

should be able to influence group choice of the firm's wage-investment program.[15] Analytically, the extent of the director's capacity to shape policy (and reduce the wage rate from $W_1$) might be shown by the position of the straight line $W^*W^*$ in Figure 16-3; if the director assesses his persuasive abilities correctly, he can feel free to urge any wage in the range $W_1$ to $W^*$.

Another, more fundamental, constraint which limits the director's choice of operating positions in the $I$-$W$ plane is determined by the shape and position of the firm's profit function (curve $RJM$ in Figure 16-2). Earlier discussion has explained that the firm will maintain its labor input $(L)$ in the range: $L_1 \leqslant L \leqslant L_n$. Figure 16-2 illustrates three possible production points $(L_1, L_2, L_n)$, and we see the associated total profits are $L_1F$, $L_2J$, and $L_nH$. Now, if total profit is allocated exclusively to the Business Fund, the respective profit magnitudes just noted can be plotted as $I_1$, $I_2$ and $I_n$ on the horizontal axis of Figure 16-4; the wage rate will, of course, be zero in each case. By contrast, if total profit is allocated wholly to the Wage Fund, the wage rates $W_1$, $W_2$ and $W_n$ emerge and these can be plotted on the vertical axis of Figure 16-4.[16] Then, the straight lines $W_1I_1$, $W_2I_2$, and $W_nI_n$ are drawn to reveal the possible tradeoffs between $W$ and $I$ at each employment level. In other words, *with a given value for L*, profit $(\pi)$ is determinate and we obtain a linear equation in $I$ and $W$ show-

15. For example, the director could attempt to explain the importance of the collective's decisions and indicate how the firm's activities mesh with the general pattern of economic activity in the nation. By appealing to the patriotic motives of the workers, the propensity for high current wages might be reduced to some extent.

16. Note that the various wage rates are reflected in diagram 2 as tangents of the successive rays $OF$, $OJ$, and $OH$. Clearly, the wage rate diminishes as the labor input becomes greater than $L_1$.

ing how the wage rate varies with different distributions of profit to the Business Fund.

$$W = -\left(\frac{1}{L^0}\right)I + \left(\frac{\pi^0}{L^0}\right). \tag{9}$$

Figure 16-4 indicates that the wage rate must fall monotonically from $W_1$ as net investment $(I)$ is increased from zero. However, the rate of fall of $W$ can be lessened as $I$ is enlarged if the employment level is changed (see Figure 16-2). For example, when the Business Fund allocation is specified as $E$, the corresponding wage rate will be $EF$ if the original employment level $(L_1)$ is maintained. But if the labor input is increased to $L_2$, the wage rate consistent with $E$ becomes $EG$. In general, there is a unique and optimal volume of employment for each possible value of $I$. Assuming continuity of the functions, the maximum wage consistent with any stipulated magnitude of $I$ is given by a continuous curve[17] like $W_1 I_n$ in Figure 16-3. This optimal tradeoff curve is convex with respect to the origin and implies that employment and output increase steadily as $I$ increases over the range zero to $I_n$.

Theoretically, the director of the Yugoslav firm sees the curves $W_1 I_n$, $W^* W^*$, and $I^* I^*$ in Figure 16-3 as constraints on his freedom to determine wage-investment policy for the collective. Granting this interpretation, the determination of the firm's *one-period equilibrium* follows at once. The solution depends on the director's preference map; since he is assumed to be a utility maximizer, the optimal operating point must be at $D$ where an indifference curve $(U_1)$ is tangent to $W_1 I_n$ and lies within $I^* I^*$ and $W^* W^*$. The equilibrium wage rate $(W_d)$ and net investment $(I_d)$ are apparent from the diagram; but knowing these values, equilibrium employment $(L_d)$ and output $(x_d)$ are easily found with the help of equations (1), (2), (3).

When the director is viewed as a central figure in the formulation of policy, we can offer a plausible explanation of why the firm is unlikely to pursue a pure wage maximization program i.e., $I = 0$, $W = W_1$). In addition, the introduction of the utility approach (Figure 16-3) permits discussion of how the national government is able to use informal channels to exert influence on the collective's production, employment and investment plans. Nevertheless, it should not be concluded from the preceding analysis that there is necessary conflict between the desires of the workers for higher wages and the insistence of the director on greater retained earnings and investment. In shaping the opinions of the collective, the director can emphasize, quite logically, that high rates of

---

17. The equation for curve $W_1 I_n$ can be obtained if a specific mathematical expression is given for the production function. The problem is to find the maximum $W$ for any given value of $I$ in the range: $0 \leqslant I \leqslant [P \cdot f(L, K^0) - Z]$. Since $W = P \cdot f(L, K^0) - Z - I$ in the situation envisioned, we are able to determine the optimal labor input $(L)$ and, by way of substitution, obtain a relation in the variables $W$ and $I$.

net investment by the collective ($I > 0$) may be advantageous to the local workers as well as to the economy as a whole. The key to the reconciliation of interest is simple; once the workers recognize the implications of additional capital for physical productivity, they can understand that the best income stream *over time* may depend on the firm's investment in a growing capital stock. In short, a worker concerned with his wealth position, as opposed to his income level in a single period, is likely to vote for policies which require: $I > 0$, $W < W_1$.

## THE WEALTH MAXIMIZATION HYPOTHESIS

Now, if we assume that the employees' goal is to maximize the present value of their expected earnings subject to their time preferences and expected periods of association with the firm, the problem of choosing an operating point on the wage-investment tradeoff curve ($W_1 I_n$ in Figure 16-3) becomes the familiar one of balancing the attractions of current and future consumption. However, under socialism, where capital goods cannot be privately owned, the exchange of current for future consumption is influenced by an important limitation not found in a capitalist system. The situation is as follows. We find that the workers in Yugoslavia have two major wealth increasing alternatives:

1. *Investment in non-owned assets.* If the collective decides to allocate some of the firm's profits to the Investment Fund, current wages become lower, but additional capital goods can be purchased in which the employees have certain limited rights. Specifically, the workers can expect to benefit from the enhanced future revenues and profits which the added capital should make possible. As long as the workers remain employed by the firm, they are in a position to realize gain through greater wage payments. The behavioral implication of this quasi-ownership must clearly be a shortened time horizon of the collective (which depends on the average length of employment expected by the majority of employees) and a high time preference rate relative to that which would prevail if the workers were granted the right of ownership over the assets acquired by the firm during the period of their employment.

2. *Investment in owned assets.* In the Yugoslav economy, such assets are individual saving accounts. Theoretically, the collective might choose to place all of its profit into the Wage Fund and allow each worker to follow his own savings plan. Since saving accounts are *owned* by depositors, it would be advantageous for the collective to distribute the firm's entire profit to the Wage Fund *unless* some investment opportunities in non-owned assets are available which promise returns at least as attractive as the returns on saving accounts.

The institutional structure just described has intrinsic interest, but its main importance for the study of the socialist firm lies in the theoretical domain. We must be able to explain how the existence of these distinct types of investment alternatives influence the collective's decisions on employment, output, the wage rate, and the rate of net investment.

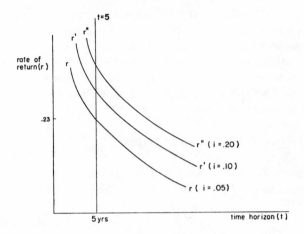

**Figure 16-5.** Time Horizon and Required Rate of Return on Non-Owned Assets

To begin the task of constructing such an extended theory, we can consider a highly simplified model of the Yugoslav firm. Assume all workers have identical preference functions and time horizons. Then, if each individual expects to quit the firm in one year, the following situation holds. One dollar invested in *owned* assets (i.e., saving accounts) at 5 percent would yield five cents in a year. Moreover, the investor is free to take his initial deposit back at the end of the year. Ceteris paribus, this means that the workers would choose to leave one dollar with the firm if the investment in *non-owned* assets were to promise a yield of at least $1.05 in a year (to be paid in the form of higher wages). The $1.05 payout is required, of course, because the workers cannot take back their initial investment in non-owned capital. Further, since the Yugoslav firm has a legal obligation to maintain the value of its assets indefinitely, the *rate* of return ($r$) which would make non-owned capital goods as desirable as saving deposits at 5 percent ($i = 0.05$) is 105 percent for a one-year time horizon. It can easily be shown that this rate would be 23 percent, 19 percent, 13 percent, 8 percent, and so on for time horizons of five, six, ten, and twenty years.

The relationship between the time horizon and the required rate of return on non-owned assets is established in Figure 16-5. The curve $rr$ shows the net rate of return which makes one dollar invested in non-owned assets (via allocations to the Business Fund) just as attractive as one dollar deposited in owned saving accounts at 5 percent for each given time horizon of the collective (i.e., expected length of employment). This type of curve provides a simple means for comparing the investment opportunities available to the employees of a socialist

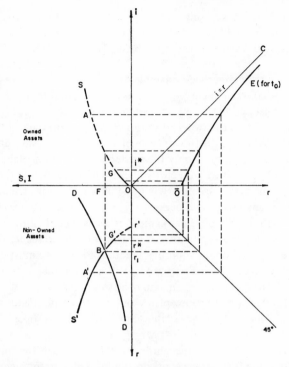

**Figure 16-6.** Curves for Each Conceivable Rate of Interest

firm.[18] When the time horizon ($t$) is short, a very great difference is required between the rate of return on physical capital ($r$) and the interest rate ($i$) to make an "investor" indifferent as to which type of asset he chooses; this condition suggests how the prevailing structure of property rights can affect economic decisions.

The curve $rr$ in Figure 16-5 has been constructed to show the $i$-$r$ equivalencies, for different $t$, on the assumption that the rate ($i$) paid on savings (owned assets) is 5 percent. But, obviously, a family of curves similar to $rr$ can be established for each conceivable rate of interest ($i$). Then, having these alternate curves (as $r'r'$, $r''r''$, etc.) and assuming a particular time horizon ($t_0$) for the collective, we are able to associate an $r$ value for any given rate of interest ($i^0$). The curve $\overline{O}E$ in the first quadrant of Figure 16-6 indicates the set of $i$-$r$ equivalents

---

18. Another investment alternative open to the collective is to lend funds to other firms. However, this possibility has a long way to go before it becomes a practical investment alternative. First, the maximum rate at which funds can be lent to other firms is currently set at 10 percent. This would require a time horizon of over fourteen years to make this alternative preferable to private savings at 5 percent. Second, the earnings from lending funds to other firms *must* legally be allocated to the Business Fund.

when the time horizon is $t_0$ —e.g., if $t_0$ represented a horizon of five years, one point on the curve would be: $r = .23$, $i = .05$. Note that in a capitalist system, where capital goods can be owned by individuals, the analogue of $\bar{O}E$ would be the 45° line $OC$; this is so because, risk and durability differences aside, rates of return like $i$ and $r$ are directly comparable.

The conversion curve $\bar{O}E$ is a useful analytical tool, but before employing it we must be clear about our assumptions concerning the Yugoslav firm. Earlier work has shown that when attention is confined to the *instantaneous*, or one-period, case, it is possible to conceive of a pure wage maximization policy as optimal for the workers; then, only the existence of governmental guidelines or the intervention of the firm's director will cause net investment ($I$) to rise above zero. However, the *dynamic* case offers quite different perspective. Even a simple extension of the analysis to two periods suggests that the wage maximization solution can be improved upon. For example, if we assume the firm has already adjusted its labor input, output and net investment so as to secure the maximum possible wage in period one, the problem reduces to this. We must demonstrate that the employees can reach a *preferred* position, given their time indifference curves,[19] by violating the original maximizing solution (say, $L_1$, $x_1$, $W_1$, $I = 0$ in Figure 16-2) and moving to a new plan where the labor input and commodity output are the same, but the wage rate is lower and net investment is positive $(L_1, x_1, W', I > 0)$.

The first step is to recognize that the individuals forming the collective's labor force are free to save some portion of their current incomes even if the firm chooses to retain no earnings in the Business Fund. Precisely how much workers decide to save at each possible rate of interest paid on savings accounts can be summarized in a saving's schedule for the collective. Ceteris paribus, the shape and position of the latter will be determined by the attitude of the workers toward present and future consumption[20] —i.e., by the preferences reflected in time indifference curves derived from functions like: $U = F(C_t, C_{t+1})$. In any event, we draw the curve $SS$ in the second quadrant of Figure 16-6 to represent the savings that will be forthcoming at various interest rates when a pure wage maximization policy ($W_1$, $I = 0$) is followed and the firm's Wage Fund is at a stipulated level $\pi_1$ (or $L_1 F$ in Figure 16-2). Of course, the portion of the curve which shows complete interest inelasticity is correlated with the limiting wage $W^*$ previously discussed in connection with Figure 16-3. It should also be recognized that when the official interest rate offered on savings accounts is rigidly fixed by the government at some level $i^*$, the (dashed) portion of the $SS$ curve lying above $i^*$ will not come into effective play.

19. Note that we have assumed that all workers have identical preference functions.

20. In the analysis that follows, we rule out the possibility of borrowing on future income to increase present consumption.

Given the information conveyed in the first and second quadrants, we can derive an alternative savings function $S'S'$ which specifies the volume of saving that the collective would be willing to make at each rate of return ($r$) on non-owned assets (owned savings accounts being zero). To accomplish this task, the curve $SS$ which appears in $S$–$i$ space must be mapped in $S$–$r$ space in quadrant three. Using the 45° line in quadrant four, the determination of $S'S'$ is easily made. We see that, consistent with our earlier findings, the rate $r$ has to be greater than the corresponding rate $i$ to elicit any given volume of savings from the collective. The latter fact carries an important implication. There will be no incentive for anyone to enter the "market" for non-owned assets unless the yield promised by such investment is equal to or greater than the criterial value $r^*$— where $r^*$ is the rate of return on *non-owned* assets that is equivalent to the official rate offered on savings accounts ($i^*$). As Figure 16-6 shows, the collective would be content to reduce the Wage Fund by as much as $OG'$ dollars when investment in physical capital for the firm yields the relatively high return $r^*$. However, if the rate expected (say $r'$) is less than $r^*$, rational behavior would demand that all the firm's profits be allocated to the Wage Fund. Under the latter strategy, the workers would be able to save out of higher current income (increased wages) and put $OG$ dollars into savings accounts at the rate $i^*$. Since $i^*$ is effectively larger than $r'$, advantage would be gained and the workers' wealth increased.

From what has been argued above, it follows that the collective's supply schedule of savings (retained earnings) is given by the curve $r^*G'A'S'$; at rates of return below $r^*$, the optimal Business Fund allocation ($I$) becomes zero. Clearly, the form in which the collective should invest its savings varies with the prevailing economic circumstances. As long as $i^*$ is superior to the return $r$, *owned assets* are preferable, and the collective is free to save according to the curve $OGi^*$ in quadrant two. On the other hand, when $r$ is effectively greater than $i^*$, *non-owned assets* are best and the Business Fund should be an increasing function of $r$ in conformity with the schedule $r^*G'A'S'$. Finally, when the rate of return on non-owned assets is just equivalent to the interest rate on savings, the form of investment is a matter of indifference.[21] Assuming conditions of risk and liquidity are comparable in the two sectors, the desired savings $OG = OG'$ can be channeled into either owned or non-owned assets with equal benefit.

21. The present analysis has been conducted on the assumption that owned and non-owned assets may show differences in effective return, but are alike in other essential respects—e.g., risk level, liquidity, etc. As long as this simplistic view is held, the only basis for preferring one alternative to another lies in the rate of return, and savings must tend to flow exclusively into the asset form promising the higher yield. However, if owned and non-owned assets differ in many important characteristics, as seems likely, workers may find it desirable to sacrifice monetary yield for other advantages. Then, savings can be allocated to both asset categories simultaneously even when a rate differential ($r \lessgtr i^*$) does exist. As Nutter has pointed out to the authors, the latter situation can be explored with the aid of indifference analysis.

The mechanism of asset choice is such that the equilibrium value of $r$ plays a central role in determining the distribution policy of the firm. Specifically, if we know: (a) the workers' preferences with respect to saving, (b) the firm's total profits $\pi_1$, (c) the time horizon $t_0$, and (d) the rate of interest $i^*$, the ideal allocation to the Business Fund ($I$) must depend on the magnitude of $r$ which, in turn, depends on the capital productivity function. In diagramatic terms, $r$ and $I$ are decided by the intersection of the supply curve $r^* G' A' S'$ with the productivity curve $DD$. As usual, net investment is desirable as long as the expected return is greater than or equal to the opportunity cost of finance capital. When the respective curves intersect at point $B$, the flow of funds to savings accounts is zero, the level of the Business Fund is $OF$ and the equilibrium rate of return on added capital is $r_1$. Of course, displacement of the $DD$ curve to the right or left of its existing position in Figure 16-6 would lead to a new equilibrium value for $r$ and different solutions for $I$ and the increment to savings deposits ($S$).

The importance of the investment demand schedule $DD$ makes clarification of its meaning essential. While the concept is analogous to the conventional marginal efficiency of investment function, $DD$ has some unique features which require discussion. In the first place, we are concerned only with the opportunities the given *firm* possesses for the use of additional capital. Thus, it is essential to define the position of the firm at the first period; for the present case, the situation is as follows:

$$\pi_1 = P \cdot f(L_1, K^0) - Z(K^0). \tag{10}$$

With input levels specified as $L_1, K^0$, definite values for output ($x_1$) and revenue emerge. Similarly, there is a definite value for current production expenses ($Z^0$) which is proportional to the magnitude of the capital stock controlled by the firm. Then, having these data, the profit level ($\pi_1$) becomes determinate.

If, as we assume, the firm is pursuing a pure wage maximization strategy, the labor input is optimally adjusted, and the ratio $\pi_1/L_1$ must yield the maximum wage rate ($W_1$) obtainable with the fixed service flow ($K^0$) supplied by the capital stock each period. Now, the workers can take their (high) wages and save in accordance with a schedule like $SS$ in quadrant two. However, the possibility of investing in non-owned assets might be posed. For example, the workers could be asked to accept reduction of the Wage Fund this period on the understanding that in the next period all profit would go to the Wage Fund. The critical question is this: What is the magnitude of the payoff in higher wages that can be expected next period when a present reduction of the Wage Fund equal to $I$ is made?

With an unchanging economic environment, we know that any increase in the firm's profits in the next period must be attributable to added physical capital ($\Delta M$) financed by the Business Fund ($I$). If the price of the relevant type of capital good ($p$) is constant, we have the relation:

$$I = p \cdot \Delta M. \tag{11}$$

Assuming each unit of physical equipment releases a fixed volume of productive services ($a$) per period, it is possible to translate from stock units to flow units:

$$\Delta K = a \cdot \Delta M, \tag{12}$$

and it is seen that:

$$\Delta K = \frac{I \cdot a}{p}. \tag{13}$$

Since workers in Yugoslavia cannot be dismissed from their jobs easily and since the hiring of additional employees in period two would tend to lower the prospective "wage payoff,"[22] the firm's labor force can be assumed to remain stable at the initial level $L_1$. Then, the (average) rate of return yielded by an increment of capital is given by the expression:

$$r = \frac{\left[ P \cdot f \left( L_1, K^0 + \frac{I \cdot a}{p} \right) - Z \left( K^0 + \frac{I \cdot a}{p} \right) \right] - [P \cdot f(L_1, K^0) - Z(K^0)]}{I} \tag{14}$$

or, in simpler terms, by:

$$r = \frac{\pi' - \pi_1}{I}. \tag{15}$$

The difference between the initial profit level ($\pi_1$) and the profit level generated in period two ($\pi'$) is the important consideration. In the elementary case examined here, change arises from an increase in the volume of capital services used in production (from $K^0$ to $K^0 + \Delta K$); thus, the rate $r$ is, effectively, a function of the variable $I$. Knowing the properties ascribed to production function (1) and the expenses function $Z(K)$, it is clear that $r$ must decline monotonically as $I$ (or $\Delta K$) increases. On the one hand, capital services must show diminishing marginal productivity relative to the fixed labor input $L_1$; on the

22. This assumes that the production function and $Z(K)$ are such that $\partial \bar{L}/\partial K \leqslant 0$.

other, capital charges and the various items contributing to production expenses ($Z$) tend to rise at least proportionally with a growing capital stock. The result is that curve $DD$ is assured of a negative slope.

Granting the fundamental validity of the preceding model, Figure 16-6 shows that wage maximization need not represent an optimal policy for the collective. When the productivity schedule $DD$ is in a favorable position and intersection with the savings' function occurs at a point like $B$, "investment" in *non-owned assets* can be attractive to the workers. Pure self-interest can dictate departure from the simple wage maximization policy suggested by Ward; hence, even without the pressure of government guidelines, some fraction of profits may be diverted to the Business Fund. In our scheme, equilibrium requires that $I = OF$. For the first period, the average wage rate desired by the workers[23] turns out to be:

$$W' = \frac{\pi_1 - OF}{L_1}, \tag{16}$$

rather than the theoretical maximum of $\pi_1/L_1$.

Apparently, the solution $(L_1, x_1, W', I = OF)$ is *preferable* to the wage-maximizing solution $(L_1, x_1, W_1, I = 0)$. But to say this is not to assert that the former constitutes the *optimum* operating position for the collective. So far, we have only permitted adjustment of the Wage Fund–Business Fund proportions while keeping the labor input and commodity output levels rigidly fixed at $L_1, x_1$. The analytical difficulty here can be understood in these terms. Presumably, the equilibrium values $L_1, x_1$ were set by the firm when its object was to make the wage rate a true maximum[24] (and the Business Fund zero). However, if the collective had known in advance that the Business Fund allocation was going to end up as $I = OF$, an employment level different from $L_1$ could have been chosen initially and a wage rate higher than $W'$ established.[25] Let us say the higher wage is $W_2$ and the corresponding labor input is $L_2$. Then, the following comparison is possible. In the *first period*, $W_2 > W'$, but because $L_2$ must be greater than $L_1$, $I^0/L_2 < I^0/L_1$, and the wage payoff ($w$) in the *second period* can be smaller for the $L_2$ organization than for the $L_1$ organization[26] (i.e., $w_2 < w_1$). The pattern of wages over time need not be a simple one.

23. In other words, economic rationality tends to push workers away from savings accounts bearing the fixed rate $i^*$ and toward non-owned assets yielding effectively higher rates. Not only do workers benefit from broader options but it seems that the opportunity is created for greater aggregate saving in the economy—e.g., contrast the savings rates $OG$ and $OF$ in Figure 16-6.

24. The labor input was adjusted to yield the wage $W_1$, but the subsequent decision to increase the Business Fund to $OF$ caused $W'$ to emerge as the actual wage.

25. As was pointed out earlier in connection with Figures 16-3 and 16-4, movement along the optimal tradeoff curve $W_1 I_n$ implies variation of $L$.

26. The following relations hold for the productive combinations based on labor inputs $L_1$ and $L_2$, respectively ($L_1 < L_2$).

Whether $L_2$ or $L_1$ proves to be the more efficient input magnitude depends on a complex set of conditions—including such things as the length of the time horizon, the characteristics of the production function, the shape of the savings' schedule, etc. Nevertheless, an unambiguous choice can always be made between alternative operating positions if the concept of present value is utilized. In the example just given, the different labor employments led to different income streams for the workers; the respective outcomes are suggested by the wage series: $W' + w_1$ and $W_2 + w_2$. No matter how disparate the individual components here, the present value of each stream can be found with the aid of the interest parameter $r*$.[27] By comparing the present values generated, rational choice between the input levels $L_1$ and $L_2$ becomes possible.

The foregoing discussion focuses on two sharply defined operating alternatives in order to explore the mechanics of the production-investment model. From what has been said, it may be inferred that determination of the optimal values for $L, x, I, W$ and $w$ involves the solution of a general equilibrium system. The problem can be approached most simply by means of Figure 16–7 showing saving-investment-employment interrelationships, and it is to this which we now turn.

Figure 16–7 is consistent with the earlier Figure 16–6 and is designed to amplify the information contained in the third quadrant of the latter figure. Instead of a single pair of savings and capital productivity curves $(S', D)$, Figure 16–7 establishes a family of such curves: $S_1', S_2', \ldots, S_n'; D_1, D_2, \ldots, D_n$. Each schedule, relating dollars saved or dollars invested to the return $(r)$ on non-owned assets, is based on a particular value of the labor input $(L)$. For reasons already explained (see Figure 16–2), the range of economic magnitudes for labor in the *first time period* (with capital services equal to $K^0$) is: $L_1 \leqslant L \leqslant L_n$.

$$r_1 = \frac{\pi_1' - \pi_1}{I^0}, \quad r_2 = \frac{\pi_2' - \pi_2}{I^0}, \quad \text{where } r_1 \leqslant r_2. \tag{i}$$

$$w_1 = \frac{\pi_1'}{L_1}, \quad w_2 = \frac{\pi_2'}{L_2}, \quad \text{or} \quad w_1 = r_1 \cdot \frac{I_0}{L_1} + \frac{\pi_1}{L_1}, \quad w_2 = r_2 \cdot \frac{I_0}{L_2} + \frac{\pi_2}{L_2}. \tag{ii}$$

Since we know:

$$\frac{I^0}{L_1} > \frac{I^0}{L_2} \text{ and } \frac{\pi_1}{L_1} > \frac{\pi_2}{L_2},$$

it follows that the second period wage rates can assume the relative magnitudes:

$$w_1 > w_2.$$

27. The choice of $r*$ as the rate to be used in discounting any income stream is not made without some trepidation. We know the present value calculation is sensitive to the discount rate employed but, at the same time, the Yugoslav economy provides no clear-cut market rate of interest which measures the general opportunity cost of capital. In these circumstances, the selection of $r*$, or the return on non-owned assets which is equivalent to the official rate $i*$, seems a reasonable compromise.

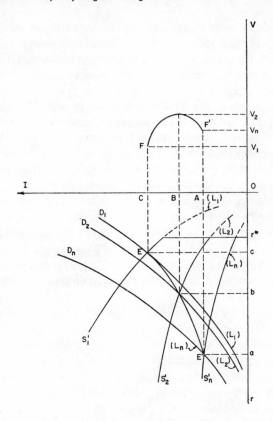

**Figure 16-7.**   Savings-Investment-Employment Interrelationships

Thus, we limit the diagram to representations of the $S_j'$, $D_j$ curves in this range ($j = 1, 2, \ldots, n$).

Equation (14) indicates that the rate of return $r$ is a function of $L$ and $I$ (or $\Delta K$). Assuming the production function possesses normal mathematical properties and is homogeneous of degree one, it is clear that $r$ will vary directly with $L$ and inversely with $I$. The respective curves $D_1, D_2, \ldots, D_n$ have negative slopes; and along any vertical line erected at $I^0$, a curve associated with a higher value of $L$ will show a higher value of $r$.

By contrast, the savings functions $S_1', S_2', \ldots, S_n'$ have positive slopes and are organized so that, at any return $r^0$, lesser volumes of saving are correlated with greater values of $L$. Each schedule $S_j'$ is supposed to reflect the savings that the collective would be willing to make, at different rates of return, if all of the firm's profits were paid out to the workers in period one[28] ($I = 0$).

---

28. Analytically, it is convenient to preserve the fiction that all profits ($\pi$) are paid out initially in the form of wages. Then, we assume the workers decide on equilibrium

Since the collective's membership is strictly proportional to $L$ and since total profit ($\pi$) increases at only a decreasing rate with $L$, the average wage ($\pi/L$) and the modal income must fall as $L$ is increased. This condition implies, in turn, that the savings generated by the collective will be less at higher levels of employment than at lower.

The positive slopes of the curves ($\partial S_j'/\partial r > 0$) are justified on the usual grounds; presumably, greater willingness to save is induced by the prospect of higher rates of return. Note, however, that no funds will be forthcoming for investment in *non-owned* assets at rates below $r^*$. When the reward falls below this level, the workers must prefer to invest their savings in state banks and obtain the official interest rate $i^*$. In Figure 16-7, the dashed portions of the $S_j'$ curves suggest the regions of the respective savings schedules where savings are withheld from the firm's Business Fund.

For any level of the labor input, as $L_1$, there is a capital productivity curve ($D_1$) and also a savings curve ($S_1'$). Under normal conditions, these curves will intersect at some point in the third quadrant; and, provided that the point of intersection implies a rate of return greater than $r^*$, a positive allocation ($I > 0$) will be indicated for the Business Fund.[29] The figure shows the intersection of $D_1$ and $S_1'$ at point $E$—with $I = C$, $r = c$. Analogous points can be found for the schedules associated with other labor input magnitudes (e.g., $D_2$, $S_2'$; $D_n$, $S_n'$). The locus of these intersections is then plotted as $EE'$. Each point on $EE'$ represents a *potential* equilibrium position for the "investment market" in period one; and from this it follows that the equilibrium value of the Business Fund lies in the range: $A \leqslant I \leqslant C$.

Clearly, the basis for choosing the ultimate equilibrium $I$ has to be established. However, it is important to recognize that the decision on the size of the Business Fund for the first time period is only one part of a broader problem. We must define what is meant by the optimum operating position of the firm at *each time period* and, then, go on to determine simultaneously the ideal values for the variables $L, x, W, I$ in period one and their counterparts in period two. Fortunately, the short time horizon of the model makes for some simplifications. Since we assume a maximum wage payout in the second period (with the workers reaping the benefits of their "investment" in the previous period), the Business Fund is zero at time two. Similarly, if the wage rate in period two is to be maximized, there is not likely to be any incentive to *increase* the labor input of

---

savings ($I$) and immediately make this sum available to the firm for investment in capital equipment. What remains of total profits (i.e., $\pi - I$) is spent by the collective exclusively on consumption goods. The results produced in the foregoing situation are equivalent to those which would appear if the magnitude $I$ were subtracted from profits at the outset and the wage $\pi - (I/L)$ paid to workers who save nothing from their incomes.

29. From a purely formal standpoint, we can conceive of intersections occurring on the $r$ axis above $r^*$. For example, if the collective displays great reluctance to save, it is possible that equilibrium will be reached where $I = 0$.

period two beyond the level of period one.[30] Thus, assuming that workers cannot be fired, the magnitude of the labor variable must be stable over time.

Discussion of optimal policy need not be difficult. When we accept the hypothesis that workers are concerned with their *wealth positions*,[31] the problem is merely to consider how the collective can maximize the present value of the income stream paid to the average employee over the two-period time horizon. The latter task involves the information supplied in Figure 16-7. By construction, the locus $EE'$ specifies all of the potential equilibrium values for $I$. If we take any arbitrary point on the locus, say point $E'$, two key values emerge— $I = A$, $L = L_n$. Knowing $L_n$ (and $K^0$), output and total profit ($\pi_n$) are determinable. With $I = A$, the corresponding wage rate is $W_n = (\pi_n - A)/L_n$. Further, equation (13) permits us to translate from the given $I$ magnitude to $\Delta K$. This means, in turn, that the capital flow in period two is now known. The latter, together with the second period's labor input (which is also equal to $L_n$) yield output and profit ($\pi'$) for the second period. Since $I$ has to be zero at time two, the wage rate is: $w_n = \pi'/L_n$. Altogether, we have found: $L_n, x_n, W_n, I = A$ for the first period and $L_n, x'_n, w_n, I = 0$ for the second period.

The wage rates $W_n$ and $w_n$ are the crucial elements here. For, with their aid, we can calculate the average worker's income stream and, hence, the present value ($V_n$) of that stream. Obviously, every point on the locus $EE'$ implies a pair of values $I, L$ and a present value $V$. Plotting of the respective levels of $V$ in the $I - V$ plane generates the curve $FF'$; and it is this curve which figures in the final solution of the model. To find the maximum point on curve $FF'$ is to determine the optimum operating position for the firm. In Figure 16-7, it appears that the members of the collective will secure the greatest advantage when investment in non-owned assets is equal to $OB$ and the labor input is $L_2$. The mechanics of the system are clear and so is its practical inference. As long as workers display rationality and have some insight into the technical relationships of production, we should expect to see the Yugoslav firm move in the general direction suggested by the model.[32]

---

30. As noted above, the ideal employment level ($\bar{L}$) can change in any direction when the flow of capital services available to the firm is increased (i.e., $\partial \bar{L} / \partial K \lessgtr 0$). We assume here that existing conditions are consistent with: $\partial \bar{L}/\partial K \leqslant 0$. Other assumptions could be used, but the preceding is plausible and makes for a simpler discussion of the model.

31. The director of the firm might well be the one to explain the advantages of wealth maximization to the workers. Insofar as the director's preference map is similar to that depicted in Figure 16-3, he serves his own interests by inducing the collective to accept a positive allocation to the Business Fund.

32. Obviously, the solution presented in the system of diagrams is merely suggestive. The basic model is adaptable to a wide variety of assumptions about the nature of the technical and behavioral relations influencing the operation of the Yugoslav firm.

## CONCLUSION

The analysis presented in this article suggests that no satisfactory theory of a socialist firm can be derived without explicit reference to property-rights structures. While the model developed here is rudimentary and rests on highly simplified assumptions, it does point the way to greater understanding of the socialist problem. We see that a major theoretical, as well as empirical, problem of economic decentralization in socialist countries is not their *willingness* to substitute economic for administrative criteria, but their *ability* to solve the problem of obtaining free market results in an environment in which means of production cannot be privately owned. More generally, the success of economic reforms in Eastern Europe will depend on how successful those states are in developing a set of institutions which yield market solutions in the production and distributions of goods and, at the same time, retain public ownership over the means of production.

## Chapter Seventeen

# Property in Capital and in the Means of Production in Socialist Economies

A. Bajt

Reprinted from the *Journal of Law and Economics* 11 (April 1968): 1–4, by permission of publisher and author.

I should like to discuss the problem of property in socialist economies. My main concern is with the efficiency of socialist economic systems, and it is from this point of view that I am engaging in this discussion. It is not my intention to deal with the problem *in extenso*. Instead, I prefer to sketch only my answer to two questions related to the problem of property. In my view, these two questions touch upon the very essence of the problem.

## I

The first question relates to the concept of relations of production and its relation to the property structure of the economy. In my discussion of this point I shall remain within Marx's theoretical framework and even use Marx's terminology. According to Marx's economic and social doctrine, there have to be distinguished, from the viewpoint of relations of production which form the social content of an economy, property in the *economic* and property in the *juridical*, or legal, sense of the word. Alternatively, one could speak of the economic structure of the society on the one hand and of its legal and ideological suprastructure on the other. It is the law which determines the legal structure of the economy. The question of property in the economic sense of the word, however, is a question of fact. In the economic sense of the word, the property structure of the economy is reflected in its distribution structure. In the economic sense of the word, the owner of a factor is the one to whom the income of this factor flows. While property in the legal sense of the word has something to do, and particularly historically had to do, with the property in the economic sense of the word, the legal structure of property does not reflect necessarily its economic counterpart. The legal owner, let us say, of a house, may be one person, and the economic owner quite another person. For instance, the tenant who, as a result of legal regulations, does not pay a rent which is higher than depreciation, does not pay, in other words, any price for services he enjoys. He is, in effect, the economic owner of the house.

Let me use these two concepts of property in order to analyze two national economies, one with private property rights in factors and the other with public, or social, property in factors in the juridical sense of the word. From Marx's point of view, the enormous institutional difference between the two economies does not necessarily mean that relations of production are as enormously different as well. By an elaborate tax system it is possible to create, within the private property economy, relations of production, that is, the distribution of income, that approaches rather closely that which can be labeled socialist. On the other hand, in an economy with constitutionally abolished private property rights and constitutionally established state or social ownership of the means of production, there can be created a system of distribution in which the real relations of production approach closely those found in an economy with private property. In other words, we may have, in the last instance at least, exactly the same real relations of production within quite different institutional frameworks, and, to express it differently, quite different real relations of production within the same institutional framework.

In analyzing different economies and in categorizing them as socialist and capitalist ones, we are usually inclined to be too much impressed by their institutional structure, that is, by their legal, or constitutional structure. If this were not the case, we could discover elements of socialism in capitalist countries and of private property relations in socialist countries, and we would be able not to classify countries into black and white categories but would have to measure the *degree of socialization* in these different countries. Speaking a priori, we might even discover that the degree of socialization, measured by some appropriate criteria, is higher in some capitalist than in some socialist countries.

## II

The second question that needs some clarification is the concept of capital. I find it useful to distinguish, in connection with nonlabor and nonnatural inputs or factors, two kinds of inputs or factors instead of only one. These are capital and entrepreneurship. Under capital I understand the undifferentiated income invested in all previous periods in order to increase the productive capacities of the economy. In this sense capital exists in any society and epoch, be it capitalist or not. The main function of the entrepreneur is to give to this undifferentiated capital a concrete form, to convert it into real capital goods in such a way as to get as high a positive present relative net capital value as possible. This converting and combining is done by buying and selling other factors of production, primarily of labor and capital equipment, by some sort or other of market activity.

I find the distinction between the two factors, capital and entrepreneurship, useful for the following reason. In my view, social or state ownership of the means of production, which is the main institutional cornerstone of
socialist economies, need not apply to means of production in the real sense of
the word, that is, in the sense of machines and other capital equipment. The social or state ownership of *capital* in the sense just explained seems to be quite sufficient. If one wants to expand and improve entrepreneurial activity, one cannot
avoid the flow of entrepreneurial product to entrepreneurs, whoever they may
be, individual persons or, as in my country, workers' collectives. In other words,
one cannot negate the economic necessity that entrepreneurs be proprietors of
their products.

Socialist economies realized very early that in order to get an adequate supply of labor you have to get rid of any idea of "uravnilovka" which
means, in terms of my discussion, the nationalizaton of the factor labor, primarily of skilled labor. The socialist principle, "to everybody according to his work"
has been interpreted therefore in such a way as to cover rather highly differentiated labor incomes. Once we separate capital goods from capital and find entrepreneurial activity to consist in converting capital into factors and inputs, we are
able to recognize that entrepreneurial activity does not have anything to do with
capitalist activity, which consists in supplying private capital to production, but
that it is merely a special kind of work which it is necessary to supply in adequate
quantities and quality to production, and that the principle "to everybody
according to his work" can be extended to it just as some decades ago it has been
extended to skilled labor.

I cannot go into a discussion of how entrepreneurial incomes can be
separated from capital incomes and labor incomes. It seems, however, pretty clear
that entrepreneurial incomes can never be regarded as state or society incomes
and that it is only capital in the sense just explained that can be state- or society-
owned if one wants to supply production with all the factors necessary to the
modern, highly differentiated process of production. The socialist character of
production can be fully guaranteed by a social or state property in *capital*, needless to say that in the economic and not in the legal sense of the word, which in
real life is secured by charging enterprises with adequate interest on capital with
the proceeds flowing into state or social funds.

If I understand the present Yugoslav development, it is along these
lines that it goes. In other words, we are realizing more and more that entrepreneurship cannot be avoided in a modern economy and that in order to get it,
you have to pay for it. While at first we merged both parts of the income of
enterprises, wages, and profits, into a homogeneous entity, the so-called income
of enterprise, there has been more and more tendency in recent times to search
for a way of distinguishing them and of using profits in measuring the efficiency
of entrepreneurial activity.

## III

At the beginning of this article I argued that from Marx's point of view it is the real relations of production as reflected in the structure of distribution and not the legal and the ideological suprastructure that decides whether or not, and in what degree, a particular national economy is a socialist economy. This does not mean, however, that legal forms are without any impact on the economic substructure. If one wants to develop entrepreneurial activity in socialist enterprises, one has to provide enterprises with adequate legal rights in order to exchange factors and products in as free a manner as possible. We avoid the term property rights in this connection and try to substitute some less embarrassing term, such as, for instance, "rights of utilization and administration," for it. However, once you take the independence of enterprises and their enterpreneurial activity, be they individual or collective, seriously, as we do in Yugoslavia, it always comes to the situation that enterprises do behave, and the legal structure has to enable them to behave, as if they were owners of the means of production which they use. I would not be surprised, therefore, if somewhere in the future this will find its expression in giving enterprises property rights in their means of production (property in the legal sense). If we distinguish the real economic relations as reflected in the structure of distribution from their legal or constitutional counterpart on the one hand, and capital from capital goods or factors which in their actual combination have to be viewed as a result of entrepreneurship on the other, as I have tried to do here, one would be inclined to agree that this would not do any harm to the socialist character of the economy but would very probably improve the quality of its decision-making and, in this way, its efficiency.

## Chapter Eighteen

# Bank Credit and the Labor-Managed Firm: The Yugoslav Case

## E. Furubotn

Reprinted from *Canadian-American Slavic Studies*, 1974 by permission of the publisher.

As a result of the reforms carried out over the period 1950–1965, economic decentralization took place in Yugoslavia, and many features of an idealized labor-managed system were incorporated into the country's legal and institutional structure.[1] Thus, by the mid-sixties, the economy operated with a virtual absence of planning from the center, and the Yugoslav firm had emerged with substantial freedom from administrative control. According to the regulations established, socialist workers held important legal rights. The employees at each firm were empowered to elect a Workers' Council, and the latter group, in conjunction with an appointed manager, was supposed to shape the firm's policies and decide on the disposition of resources.[2] This form of organization, of course, implies distinctive economic behavior. In contrast to the capitalist firm where activity is conducted so as to maximize profits for the firm's owners,[3] the labor-managed firm can be expected to have a quite different objective. The policies followed must tend to be those that conduce to the welfare of the workers comprising the collective. In other words, assuming that self-interest motivates behavior, the labor-managed firm is likely to pursue policies designed to maximize an index such as *wealth per worker*.[4] The difficulty with this arrangement, however, is

1. See: The Law on Management of Enterprises by Workers' Collectives, Sluzbeni List, Belgrade, July 1950; The Law on the Management of Fixed Capital by Enterprises, Sluzbeni List, Belgrade, December 1953; Spiljak (1961); *Nove Mere Za Sprovodjenje Privredne Reforme* (1968); Vojnich (1970); Horvat (1971). Horvat's work provides a valuable bibliography.

2. See *Kujigovodstvo* (1968, especially pp. 13–43 and 94–116).

3. Profit maximization is usually assumed to be the goal of the capitalist firm, but other objectives are conceivable, and in recent years alternative theories of the firm have been developed which do not presuppose simple profit maximization. For a summary of some of this work, see Furubotn and Pejovich (1972c).

4. Since the theory of the labor-managed firm is still being developed, opinions differ as to what constitutes the proper maximand. The range of formal models is suggested by the following examples: Ward (1953); Domar (1966); Vanek (1970); Furubotn and S. Pejovich (1970a); Furubotn (1971).

that the collective may find it advantageous to take actions that are inconsistent with efficient allocation of the nation's resources or with *community* welfare. And, in fact, the recent history of Yugoslavia suggests that disharmonies between the collective and society are very real.

To formulate an adequate model of the Yugoslav firm, it is essential to consider how the collective approaches the task of resource allocation. In particular, interest centers on the uses to which the firm's net product, or "profit," is put. Two basic questions exist: (a) What decision-making agencies and institutional constraints influence the allocation of the firm's net product between the share retained by the firm and the share going to external claimants?[5] (b) How is the decision made on the distribution of the firm's share between the *Wage Fund* (which establishes the income the collective can devote to current consumption) and the *Business Fund* (which indicates the amount retained for investment in the firm)?[6] These respective allocations are crucial because the decisions reached determine, either directly or indirectly, the magnitudes of key economic variables and the growth path of the firm over time. It follows from this interpretation that the pure theory of the labor-managed firm can be developed in terms of an optimization model that explains the basis of the collective's net product allocations, and theorizing along these lines has already taken place.

The objective of the present paper is to consider how the availability of long-term bank credit affects the collective's internal distribution of net product and, thereby, the consumption opportunities of the workers and the equilibrium position ultimately attained by the firm. Obviously, factors other than bank credit can influence the collective's allocation of funds; for example, such things as the formal and informal control measures introduced by government must change firm behavior. Nevertheless, it is convenient analytically to focus on bank credit as the sole external variable affecting the firm's decision process and to develop an idealized model of the labor-managed firm that can serve as a first approximation to reality.[7] There are several reasons for concentrating on bank credit. In the first place, banking operations are quantitatively important. Since the 1965 reform, there has been practically no administrative planning in the Yugoslav economy and this condition, coupled with the lack of developed capital markets, has permitted the banks to become major suppliers of

5. The share of net product (or dohodak) going to "other" claimants is determined in the immediate sense by the legal and contractual obligations of the firm. Ultimately, however, government policy and the firm's own decisions with respect to contractual obligations such as bank debts are the factors responsible for the size of the outpayments to others. See Vojnich (1970).

6. The internal funds of the Yugoslav firm include, besides the Wage Fund and the Business Fund, the Collective Consumption Fund and the Reserve Fund. For a discussion of the nature of these funds and an explanation of their significance for economic behavior, see Furubotn and Pejovich (1972a).

7. The model formulated in section I represents an extension of a simpler construction presented in Furubotn (1971).

investment funds to business firms.[8] Moreover, from a theoretical standpoint, it seems clear that the possibility of bank-borrowing must exert a very significant effect on the behavior of the labor-managed firm. Indeed, one can say that understanding of the firm's employment, output, and investment choices cannot be achieved without knowledge of the role of bank credit in the optimization model.

I

The first step in the analysis must be to set up a simplified representation of the Yugoslav firm. Thus, assume that the typical business unit operates subject to a stock-flow production function:

$$q_t = f(L_t, K_t) \tag{1}$$

where $q_t$ represents the flow of commodity output in any period $t$, $L_t$ is the input of labor services, and $K_t$ is the stock of capital equipment available for production in period $t$. The time intervals considered are finite and, by assumption, the physical capital acquired in one period cannot be used in active production until the next period.

If the firm is able to sell any output it produces at the fixed price $(P_t)$ set by the government, the profit function becomes:

$$\pi_t = P_t \cdot f(L_t, K_t) - M_t - Z(K_t). \tag{2}$$

That is, according to the accounting scheme effective in Yugoslavia after 1965, the firm's "profit" $(\pi_t)$, or share of the net product produced in period $t$, equals total revenue minus production expenses. These expenses include the total interest payments[9] $(M_t)$ owed at period $t$ on bank loans $(B_j, j = 0, 1, \ldots, t-1)$ received by the firm from some initial period zero to $t-1$. Production expenses also include depreciation charges, interest charges paid to the state for the use of capital goods, expenditures on raw materials and supplies, etc. For convenience, it is assumed that all production costs, with the exception of the interest on bank loans, can be represented by the single-valued function $Z(K_t)$.[10]

When the firm's employment level $(L_t)$, capital stock $(K_t)$, and interest obligations $(M_t)$ are known for period $t$, the corresponding profit level

8. See Statisticiki Bilten, November 1972, p. 74; Furubotn and Pejovich (1971).

9. Interest on credit is paid from net product *before* the share (or profit) of the firm is determined. The payments on principal, however, are paid from the firm's share of net product or, more specifically, from the portion of the firm's share of net product allocated to the Business Fund.

10. The raw material input and the other inputs implied by Z can be thought of as "factor shadows." See Danø (1966, pp. 100–102).

$(\pi_t)$ can be determined from equation (2). It is this profit that the Workers' Council must allocate. Under Yugoslav law, the Council has power to decide on the proportions in which the firm's profit is to be distributed among the Wage Fund $(W_t)$, the Business Fund, and other internal funds.[11] Theoretically, all of the profit could be allocated to the Wage Fund; then, current wages would be as high as possible, given the data of the system. There are, however, practical limits to such a policy. Insofar as the firm has borrowed from banks in the past, funds for the repayment of principal are necessary, and these funds have to be secured from the profit residual. If $B'_t$ represents the total of required principal repayments at time $t$, this sum must be subtracted from $\pi_t$ and diverted to the Business Fund; ceteris paribus, the Wage Fund suffers an equivalent reduction. Moreover, if the workers decide that it is advantageous to "invest" in the firm[12] and vote for earnings to be retained $(I_t)$, another portion of $\pi_t$ will go to the Business Fund. In other words, considering the possibilities of capital repayment and self-financed investment, the expression for the Wage Fund emerges as:

$$W_t = \pi_t - B'_t - I_t. \tag{3}$$

The collective receives $W_t$ dinars as its income for period $t$. Then, abstracting from the tax structure (Furubotn and Pejovich 1970b) and ruling out any other forms of saving and investment for the workers, it follows that $W_t$ is precisely the sum the collective can spend on consumption during period $t$—i.e., $W_t = C_t$.

The translation of wage payments into consumption aggregates is important because it permits consideration of the collective's consumption opportunities over time. With a $T$ period planning interval, the time stream of consumption the collective can attain will vary, ceteris paribus, with the net capital investment undertaken by the firm in each period through $T$ and with the schedule of loan repayments maintained over these $T$ periods. Since investment can be financed by the collective itself and/or through bank loans, the crucial variables are the time profiles: $I_1, I_2, \ldots, I_T; B_1, B_2, \ldots, B_T;$ and $B'_1, B'_2, \ldots, B'_T$.

Now, if certain simplifying assumptions are granted, it is possible to establish a multiperiod preference function for the collective:

$$U = \phi(C_1, C_2, \ldots, C_T). \tag{4}$$

11. In the spring of 1972, however, the central authorities introduced regulations, based on so-called social contracts, that reduced the firm's freedom to determine the allocation of its net product. These social contracts established the basic philosophy guiding distribution but also indicated the *specific* criteria for the allocation of the firm's earnings among the various funds and for the distribution of personal incomes. See: *Sluzbeni Glasnik*, SRS, July 17, 1971; Sluzbeni List Beograda, June 15, 1972; *Samoupravni Sporazum o Uska-Djivanju Raspodele Dohotka i Licnih Dohodaka Organizachija Udruzenog Rada Dela Trgovine u Beogradu*, Belgrade, June 25, 1972.

12. Workers have merely the right of use of the capital accumulated and no transferable rights in such "non-owned" assets. See Furubotn (1971, pp. 186-191).

This function is the aggregative counterpart of the utility function traditionally used in the theory of rational saving and possesses analagous formal properties.[13] In any case, given (4), the choice problem facing the collective can be conceived as one of constrained maximization. The workers must select, from among the feasible time streams of consumption, that stream which maximizes the group's multiperiod utility index.[14] Of course, each feasible consumption stream is associated with particular time profiles (or vectors) of self-financed investment, bank-borrowing, and loan repayment, and thus ideal values for the latter are determined by the choice process.

The details of the collective's choice problem are somewhat cumbersome to explain, but the essential features of the case can be brought out adequately in terms of an elementary two-period model ($T = 2$).[15] This approach has the added advantage of allowing diagrammatic treatment, and the equations considered below will be represented in Figure 18-1. In order to simplify the discussion still further, the following assumptions are made: (a) labor employment is fixed at the original level ($L_1$) for each period examined;[16] (b) no self-financed investment or bank-borrowing occurs during the last period ($I_2 = 0, B_2 = 0$); (c) the firm initiates any borrowing in period one ($B_0 = 0, B_1 \geqslant 0$) and the principal of the loan in question is paid back in period two ($B'_1 = 0, B'_2 = B_1$); (d) there is a fixed price per unit ($p$) for the capital equipment used by the firm, and thus an expenditure of $I_1 + B_1$ dinars translates into a certain number of units of physical capital ($I_1/p + B_1/p$) that the firm can add to the initial capital stock ($K_1$) and utilize in the next period; and (e) the bank rate is fixed at $i$. Given the assumptions ($i$) – ($v$), then, it is a straightforward matter to consider the implications of net capital accumulation ($I_1 > 0, B_1 = 0$; or $I_1 = 0, B_1 > 0$; or $I_1 > 0$, $B_1 > 0$) for the collective's consumption opportunities.

From equations (2) and (3), it is evident that the expression for the first period's consumption level is:

$$C_1 = P \cdot f(L_1, K_1) - Z(K_1) - I_1 \qquad (5)$$

To the extent the collective finances capital expansion by diverting profits to the Business Fund ($I_1$), current wages and consumption ($C_1$) must become smaller.

13. See Friedman (1957, pp. 7–14).

14. From a behavioral standpoint, the assumption is that the workers act as if they were capable of ranking alternative time streams of consumption in order of preference and choosing the best available. Such a presumption seems reasonable. Note, however, that the use of optimal control theory would require a less tenable behavioral position—viz., that the workers act as if they were able to secure numerical solutions to the control problem.

15. The procedure can, of course, be generalized and employed in situations where $T$ is large but finite.

16. Assuming that the production function is homogeneous of degree one and that the initial capital-labor ratio is low, there is no incentive for the firm to seek additional employees. If the labor input is held constant at $L_1$ while capital is accumulated, the system will move toward equilibrium factor proportions and the remuneration going to the collective will increase.

The positive effects of this sacrifice, however, do not appear until the next period when the increment to the capital stock $(I_1/p)$ permits greater output and total profit. Neither the costs nor the benefits of a bank loan taken out at the end of period one $(B_1)$ are observable in period one—or in equation (5). For the simple two-period system being explored, there is no loan repayment in the first period $(B'_1 = 0)$, and the interest charges $(iB_1)$ together with the principle sum $(B_1 = B'_2)$ are paid out of the second period's profits $(\pi_2)$. As in the case of $I_1$, the physical capital purchased with the loan $B_1$ comes into effective play in period two when the capital increment $B_1/p$ makes itself felt.

With this background established, the interpretation of the collective's position in period two follows immediately. The attainable level of consumption is:

$$C_2 = P \cdot f(L_1, K_1 + B_1/p + I_1/p) - iB_1 - Z(K_1 + B_1/p + I_1/p) - B'_2. \qquad (6)$$

According to the assumptions of the model, the firm is able to utilize additional real capital productively because its initial factor endowment $(L_1, K_1)$ was "labor-intensive"—with a high ratio of labor to capital. Thus, by maintaining the labor input at its original level $(L_1)$ and adding to the capital stock, the firm can increase both the average and marginal products of labor; total output increases at a decreasing rate as capital is expanded. In other words, the collective is able to achieve relatively greater future consumption $(C_2)$ by increasing the magnitude of $I_1$ and/or $B_1$. However, self-financed investment $(I_1)$ requires a reduction of $C_1$; essentially, consumption is shifted forward from one time period to another. By contrast, bank credit $(B_1)$ enables the collective to enjoy some net improvement of future consumption $(C_2)$ with no sacrifice of present consumption $(C_1)$.[17]

The information contained in equations (5) and (6) provides a basis for deriving the collective's *consumption opportunity locus*. That is, since (5) implies: $I_1 = P \cdot f(L_1, K_1) - Z(K_1) - C_1$, and $B'_2 = B_1$, appropriate substitution in (6) yields the locus equation:

$$C_2 = P \cdot f(L_1, K_1 + B_1/p + [P \cdot f(L_1, K_1) - Z(K_1) - C_1]/p) - iB_1 - Z(K_1 + B_1/p$$

$$+ [P \cdot f(L_1, K_1) - Z(K_1) - C_1]/p) - B_1. \qquad (7)$$

The initial input mix $(L_1, K_1)$ is known along with the price set $(P, p, i)$ and, therefore, equation (7) reduces effectively to a relation in the variables: $C_1, C_2$ and $B_1$.

17. According to Yugoslav law, the workers cannot elect to disinvest and convert past investments into money to finance greater current consumption. This is true, moreover, whether the previous investments in the firm were self-financed or financed by bank loans. See Boskovic (1966).

$$C_2 = F(C_1, B_1). \tag{8}$$

Equation (8) has a straightforward interpretation; the relation defines all the efficient time streams of consumption $(C_1, C_2)$ that are open to the collective,[18] given any value of $B_1$.

The properties of this general opportunity locus can be discussed more fully and systematically in terms of Figure 18-1. In the latter, the collective's aggregate consumption expenditures in period one and period two are indicated on axes $C_1$ and $C_2$, respectively. Each point in the quadrant shown can be interpreted as a particular consumption stream. Point $X$ is of special significance, however, because it represents what may be called the basic consumption opportunity of the collective. When both self-financed and bank-financed investment are ruled out, the position of the collective is decided by the data of the system—viz., the firm's initial input combination $(L_1, K_1)$, the price per unit of output $(P)$, and the characteristics of the production and expense functions $(f, Z)$. With all of the firm's profit $(\pi_1)$ allocated to the Wage Fund each period, a constant level of consumption can be maintained over time: $C_1 = C_2 = \pi_1$; this is the meaning of point $X$.

Of course, other alternatives are available to the collective. Assuming, first, that bank credit can be secured in *any amount demanded* as long as the costs of borrowing are met, the situation is as follows. The collective, facing diminishing returns with increases in the capital stock, will presumably set the value of $B_1$ so that $C_2$ is a maximum for any given value of $C_1$. Thus, when no self-financed investment is undertaken $(C_1 = \pi_1)$, the formal problem is to maximize the function:

$$C_2 = F(B_1; \pi_1^0) \tag{9}$$

derived from (7). Not surprisingly, we find that, at equilibrium, the value of the marginal product of capital (credit) must equal the marginal cost of borrowing and operating:

$$P \cdot f_K = (1 + i) + Z_K \tag{10}$$

This expression, involving the variable $B_1$ and known parameters, can be solved for the optimal value of bank credit $(B_1^*)$. Relative to the diagram, if the firm employs $B_1^*$, movement will be along the vertical line $W_1 X$ from point $X$ (where $B_1 = 0, I_1 = 0$) to the limit point $Y$ (where $B_1 = B_1^*, I_1 = 0$). In the case studied, the improvement of productive capacity achieved through the bank loan $B_1^*$ permits the firm to increase its revenue sufficiently to pay back the principal

18. An "efficient" time stream is efficient in the sense that, for any level of consumption in period one, consumption in period two is the maximum permitted by the physical system.

and interest on the loan in period two and still have something left over. Thus, *without sacrificing any current consumption* $(C_1 = \pi_1)$, the collective is able to attain a higher level of consumption in period two than would be the case in the absence of borrowing. In other words, point $Y$ represents an unambiguously superior consumption stream to that implied by point $X$, and this fact explains the attraction of bank credit to the collective.[19]

When self-financed investment is undertaken $(I_1 > 0)$, the consumption level in period two can be even higher than $W_1 Y$. By law, the collective is free to reduce the allocation to the Wage Fund in the first period $(W_1 = C_1 < \pi_1)$ and use the retained income to finance additional investment in the firm. The situation envisioned is one where the optimal amount of bank credit has already been obtained, but where the total investment fund is now being supplemented through the collective's self-finance efforts $(B_1 = B_1^*, I_1 > 0)$. From a formal standpoint, the effect of $I_1$ on $C_2$ can be described by the equation (see equation [7]):

$$C_2 = F(C_1; B_1^*). \tag{11}$$

The relation in question is shown as curve $YY'$ in Figure 18-1. As the firm's stock of physical capital is increased beyond $K_1 + B_1^*/p$ through self-financing activity, total product and profits rise. But because the labor input is fixed at $L_1$, diminishing marginal productivity of capital insures that the opportunity locus $YY'$ will display curvilinear form, with $C_2$ increasing at a decreasing rate as $C_1$ is made smaller.

For reference purposes, it will be convenient to establish a number of other loci that are analogous to $YY'$. Thus, assume the collective restricts the Wage Fund and ploughs profits back into the firm, but can secure no bank credit whatsoever $(B_1 = 0, I_1 > 0)$. Under these conditions, the relevant locus is $XA$. Capital increments are added to the initial stock $K_1$ and, again, diminishing marginal productivity produces a curve that increases at a diminishing rate. However, for any given level of $I_1$, the marginal rate of transformation $(dC_2/dC_1)$ on curve $XA$ will be greater than the corresponding marginal rate associated with curve $YY'$. This is so because the productive operations implied by $XA$ are conducted with lesser capital intensity than those on $YY'$. In the figure, curve $RR'$ appears between $XA$ and $YY'$. The interpretation of this new locus follows immediately from what has been said. $RR'$ is typical of the family of curves that becomes effective when the collective has *limited access* to bank credit $(0 < B_1 < B_1^*, I_1 > 0)$. For whatever reason, the situation here is such that credit availability ends before the firm reaches the limit to borrowing set by equation (10).

---

19. It is true, of course, that relatively high interest rates and/or low productivity of capital could make borrowing impossible.

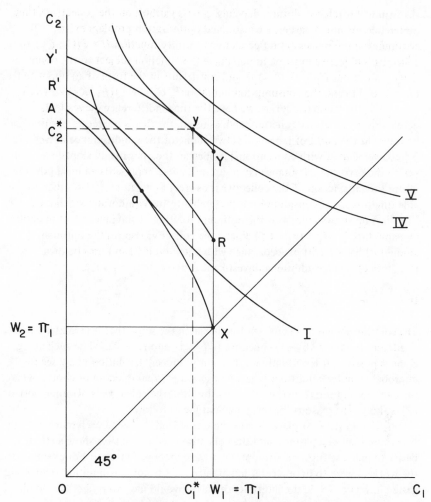

**Figure 18-1.** The Consumption Opportunities of the Collective

Thus, at point $R$, the firm's position must be characterized by the inequality:

$$P \cdot f_K > (1 + i) + Z_K. \tag{12}$$

Nevertheless, even though additional bank-financed investment is ruled out at $R$, the collective can still vote to reduce current consumption ($C_1$), continue capital accumulation, and move along the curve toward $R'$.

　　In the absence of any special constraints on bank credit, the Yugoslav firm can be expected to obtain the optimal volume of credit from the system ($B_1^*$) and operate somewhere along the opportunity locus $YY'$. Precisely where the firm will reach equilibrium depends, ceteris paribus, on the collective's time preference. As noted earlier, a constrained optimization problem exists.[20] If community preferences are reflected by the utility function $U = \phi(C_1, C_2)$, the collective's objective must be to maximize this function subject to the nonnegativity restrictions $C_1 \geqslant 0$, $C_2 \geqslant 0$, and constraints in the form of an opportunity locus like (11) and the consumption limitation[21] $C_1 \leqslant P \cdot f(L_1, K_1) - Z(K_1)$.

In geometric terms, we have the time-indifference curves I, II, . . . derived from the utility function, and, as usual, the firm's operating position can be found at the point of tangency between one of these indifference curves and $YY'$. Given curves with conventional properties (i.e., negatively sloped and convex to the origin), such a tangency point, of course, represents an ideal position where the satisfaction of the collective is as great as it can be.[22] No other attainable time stream of consumption is preferable to the equilibrium stream: $C_1^*$, $C_2^*$. The diagram shows point $y$ as the optimum solution. Total investment in period one amounts to: $B_1^* + (\pi_1 - C_1^*)$ dinars; the collective secures the optimum amount of bank credit in accordance with equation (10) and uses its own resources to finance additional investment to the extent: $\pi_1 - C_1^*$.

## II

The solution shown in Figure 18–1 is special in the sense that it indicates a positive level of "saving" by the collective ($C_1^* < \pi_1$ and $I_1 > 0$). While such an outcome is possible, it is certainly not necessary. Indeed, a solution like $y$ seems improbable under conditions where workers enjoy real freedom of choice, where the bank rate of interest ($i$) is relatively low, and the collective's planning horizon ($T$) is short. The reasons for this judgment are as follows:

In the first place, it must be recognized that time preference can fall into more than one pattern; and the collective need not always show a strong desire to increase future consumption at the expense of present. For example, if the workers were to have greater impatience for current consumption than is suggested in Figure 18-1, the indifference curves would have to reflect this condition and show relatively steeper slopes. Quite possibly, then, there would be no

20. This optimization problem is of the type encountered in nonlinear programming and can be approached by way of the Kuhn-Tucker conditions. See G. Hadley (1964, ch. 6) and Lancaster (1968, ch. 5).

21. This condition merely emphasizes the fact that the collective cannot borrow against its future income in order to increase the Wage Fund and present consumption.

22. At equilibrium the marginal utility of consumption in any period $t$ should be no greater than the marginal imputed cost of consumption in $t$. The "cost" in question arises from the fact that the greater the consumption in period $t$, the greater the implicit reduction in the consumption levels of all other periods coming before or after $t$. An optimal consumption plan is, of course, one that gives due weight to the subjective valuations attached to consumption at each period over the whole planning interval; and intertemporal tradeoffs must be considered in this light.

point of tangency between an indifference curve and locus $YY'$. Over the relevant range of values, the rate of time substitution of consumption $(dC_2/dC_1)$ would always be greater than the marginal rate of transformation on $YY'$; hence a corner solution would result and self-financed investment would be zero. In this general situation, the availability of bank credit permits the collective to operate at point $Y$ and attain a higher level of welfare than it would enjoy if credit were more restricted $(B_1 < B_1^*)$.

Another reason why the collective can be reluctant to participate in the financing of the firm's investment arises because the yield on such investment may not be high enough to prompt the action. In communist Yugoslavia, the property rights structure is different from that in the West and Yugoslav citizens have only the *right of use* of capital equipment. This arrangement means, inter alia, that workers who sacrifice current wages—equation (3)—in order to "invest" in the firm do not acquire claims on capital in the usual Western sense and, thus, have substantially weaker incentives to invest (Furubotn and Pejovich 1970a pp. 443-454; Furubotn 1971, pp. 186-191).

To the extent that increments of physical capital increase the productivity of the firm's fixed labor force $(L_1)$, profits rise and the workers can reasonably anticipate higher wages in future time periods. Reduction of the Wage Fund through diversion of profits to capital formation represents a type of "investment," then, that can yield "dividends" in the form of enhanced wages. While the workers have no claim whatsoever on the principal invested, they do have certain rights in the firm's earnings *for as long as they remain employees of the firm*. If workers should resign and leave, though, they lose all claims—even those on the earnings of the capital stock their earlier sacrifices have helped to finance. In short, the worker-investors have no transferable rights in the firm's accumulated capital; they hold what may be termed *non-owned* assets.

The fact that Yugoslav workers have attenuated ownership rights in capital has direct significance for investment decisions. The contrast in the conditions of yield for conventionally owned and non-owned assets makes this clear. In the case of owned assets, or savings deposits placed with the state banks at rate $s$,[23] a sacrifice of $S$ dinars in period one permits consumption of $S + sS$ dinars in period two. But the same sum "invested" in the firm leads to a different income term for period two. The principal is never returned as such; thus, assuming a rate of return $r$ on non-owned assets (Vojnich 1970), a sacrifice of $S$ dinars in period one makes possible a consumption level of $rS$ dinars in the second period. When longer time horizons are considered, the problem becomes more complicated because various reward streams are conceivable. That is, different patterns of wage improvements over time can be made on the basis of the greater productivity generated by self-financed investment. On the assumption that the entire increase in output each period is paid to the workers synchronously in the

23. Yugoslav law permits individuals to have full ownership rights in savings deposits—hence the term "owned" assets.

form of higher wages, the conversion formula for an alternative involving the investment outlay $(S_0)$ considered over a $T$ period planning horizon can be written as follows:

$$S_0 = \sum_{t=1}^{T} (rS_0)_t / (1+s)^t. \tag{13}$$

The present value of the reward stream from non-owned assets must just equal the initial investment outlay made by the collective $(S_0)$ if non-owned and owned assets are to be equivalent.

      Equation (13) implies that a non-owned asset must promise a *higher* rate of return than an owned asset in order for the two investment possibilities to be accepted as equally attractive. It is also apparent that the required differential between $r$ and $s$ has to become larger and larger as the period of investment $(T)$ is shortened. When definite values are specified for $T$ and the existing bank rate $s_0$, it is possible to calculate the corresponding critical yield on non-owned assets $(r^*)$ that must be reached or exceeded if the collective is to have any incentive to divert profits from the Wage Fund to the Business Fund. Assuming a relatively short planning horizon and a moderate level for the interest rate $s_0$, the prognosis for saving is poor. More concretely, it appears that unless additional capital can be employed very productively within the firm (i.e., the opportunity locus $YY'$ is pitched quite steeply), the free-choice solution voted by the collective will be one that avoids self-finance and favors, instead, consumption or other more remunerative forms of investment.[24]

      Finally, it should be noted that the willingness of the collective to save and reinvest its own funds in the firm may be retarded by the very availability of bank credit. Insofar as the collective is able to attain, or approach, the desired credit volume $B_1^*$, *its voluntary saving* $(\pi_1 - C_1^*)$ *tends to be reduced relatively*.[25] The reason for this effect becomes obvious when the implications of capital accumulation are considered. If the firm goes as far as possible with bank financing of investment *before* it allocates its own savings to capital expansion, the effect is to eliminate the more attractive investment opportunities and leave only those promising lower returns for self-finance.[26] Thus, unless the growing income of the collective occasioned by $B_1$ leads to substantially lesser

      24. For example, individuals are free to earn interest on savings at the state banks or to invest in their own education and training.

      25. The shrinkage of saving will tend to be greater the lower the interest rate on bank loans.

      26. By construction, we know that along any vertical line such as $C_1^* y$ associated with a given level of saving, the slopes of the respective opportunity curves become progressively greater as movement is made from $YY'$ to $XA$—i.e., $(dC_2/dC_1)_{YY'} < (dC_2/dC_1)_{RR'} < (dC_2/dC_1)_{XA}$.

impatience for present consumption,[27] the fall in the rate of return (marginal product of capital) acts to limit the collective's own savings.

The obvious question that arises, at this point, is why the collective should be committed to a definite sequence of financial operations—with bank credit being utilized before the collective's own savings. In effect, what has been proposed above is a two-stage procedure for finding the equilibrium values of bank credit ($B_1^*$) and self-financed investment ($I_1^*$). First, the optimal amount of credit is determined via condition (10) on the assumption that the collective's saving is nil. Then, the opportunity locus $YY'$ is plotted and used in conjunction with the collective's preference function to discover the optimal amount of self-investment ($I_1^*$). The justification for the rigid sequence is easily made provided certain assumptions are accepted. Specifically, we must assume that: (a) the marginal product of capital falls monotonically, (b) the supply of bank credit is infinitely elastic at the going interest rate $i$, (c) the rate of interest is low enough relative to the return on capital investment to permit some positive amount of bank borrowing, (d) the rate of time substitution of consumption ($dC_2/dC_1$) increases steadily as $C_1$ is diminished, and (e) the collective is concerned exclusively with the promotion of its own interests and seeks to maximize the utility function (4). Given (a) through (e), it follows that strong incentive exists for the collective to utilize bank credit to the fullest degree *before* employing any of the firm's own savings. This is so because only by such strategy can the collective attain the greatest possible level of capital accumulation and maximize welfare. In practice, various obstacles may prevent the firm from adhering to this optimization procedure,[28] but it remains true that the collective will reach relatively inferior positions by departing from the rule of "credit first."

Figure 18–2 clarifies the last point by establishing the alternatives open to the collective. The effective savings schedule is shown by curve $SABS$. Segment $SA$ indicates how much of the firm's current profit the workers would be willing to divert from current consumption to the accumulation of *owned* assets, given various interest rates. When the bank rate is fixed at $s_0$, the portion of the collective's savings schedule lying above $A$ has no direct relevance and, thus, is not drawn. If a greater volume of savings than $OA$ is to be secured, the rate of return must be above $s_0$; and, under the institutional conditions operative in Yugoslavia, a reward larger than $s_0$ is effectively possible only if favorable opportunities exist for investment in *non-owned* assets. Specifically, the yield

27. For example, the indifference curves could become flatter (show less impatience for present consumption) as movement was made to higher levels of real income. Then, the collective might save more as more bank credit was provided.

28. For example, in 1972 the government moved to limit the extent of bank participation in the financing of business investment. A law was enacted specifying that a bank could not make a loan to a business firm for investment in fixed assets unless the firm secured at least 20 percent of the total cost from its own funds (Sluzbeni List, Belgrade, December 1972).

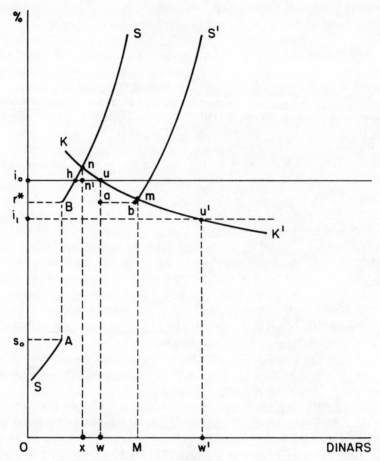

**Figure 18-2.**  Bank Credit and Investment

promised by additional capital investment in the firm must be above the critical value $r^*$ as calculated from equation (13). The return $r^*$ is the equivalent of $s_0$ but represents only one translation of a rate from the owned to the non-owned domain; in general, each value of $s$ implies a corresponding value for $r$ (given $T$). Thus, the curve segment $BS$ can be developed to show the collective's savings behavior at rates above $s_0$. Consistent with preference function (4), $BS$ represents the flow of retained earnings that will be forthcoming at different capital yields ($r$). Of course, when the actual return on non-owned assets is less than $r^*$, the allocation to the Business Fund will be zero, and all saving will be undertaken by members of the collective at the state banks.

Besides the savings schedule $SABS$, the other element of importance in Figure 18-2 is the marginal efficiency of investment curve $KK'$. The latter is shaped by the firm's initial position $(L_1, K_1)$ and the characteristics of the production function; its negative slope reflects the diminishing productive contribution capital makes to the firm when the labor force is fixed at $L_1$. Now, according to the diagram, if no bank credit whatsoever is available, $OX$ dinars will be saved and invested in non-owned assets. If self-financed investment is undertaken first, and bank credit used only after the point where no further savings are forthcoming, total investment will be $Ow$ dinars—assuming the interest rate is $i_0$. The greatest investment, however, occurs when bank credit is obtained first and the total investment fund is composed of $Ou$ dinars of credit plus $wM$ dinars of savings contributed by the collective. It is possible for bank credit to be supplemented by saving because, in the case shown, workers are willing to invest in non-owned assets (save) at interest rates *below* the prevailing bank rate $i_0$. The critical rate $r^*$ is less than $i_0$ and, therefore, if the capital productivity curve does not fall too sharply, an intersection with the savings schedule is possible in the range $BS$. In Figure 18-2, the effective productivity curve after bank credit has been utilized is $uK'$; thus, when the origin of the diagram is moved from $O$ to $w$, curve $BS$ shifts to $bS'$ and the self-finance solution emerges as $wM$.

If the rate of interest charged by the banks were lower than $r^*$, however, things would be quite different. Then, no savings would be made by the collective for investment in the firm. For example, assuming the ruling interest rate is $i_1$, it follows that *credit will be substituted completely for savings* and that total investment will be $Ou'$ instead of $OM$. But, here too, no larger investment sum than $Ow'$ can be attained by violating the sequence rule. The strategy of credit-first insures the greatest rate of capital accumulation, and the most favorable income stream over time. For, as Figure 18-1 indicates, larger capital stocks are associated with the higher opportunity loci (e.g., $RR'$, $YY'$) and, in general, the higher the position of a locus the greater is the collective's possible satisfaction.

## III

The preceding analysis leads to a conclusion of some importance. It appears that the availability of bank credit exerts a markedly adverse effect on self-finance activity and is very likely to cause workers to *stop all personal investment in the firm*.[29] If the members of a Yugoslav collective are rational and truly free to seek their own best interests without governmental interference, they should tend to allocate funds in accordance with the pattern of incentives present in the

29. Compare Pejovich (1969a).

Table 18-1.   The Allocation of Profits (in Percentages)

|  | Wage Fund (Gross of Taxes Paid from the Wage Fund) | Other Funds |
|---|---|---|
| 1964 | 69 | 31 |
| 1965 | 70 | 30 |
| 1966 | 72 | 28 |
| 1967 | 76 | 27 |
| 1968 | 77 | 23 |
| 1969 | 81 | 19 |
| 1970 | | |

Sources. *Podatci Zavrsnih Racuna Privrednih Organizacija, 1964-68,* and *Statisticki Godisnjak Jugoslavije,* 1970.

system. But the incentives are unfavorable to self-finance.[30] In what may be considered the typical case, the bank rate of interest ($i$) is almost certain to be less than the critical rate of return on non-owned assets ($r^*$). That is, unless the collective's planning horizon ($T$) is quite long, the adjustment for the property rights structure via equation (13) must lead to a relatively large value for $r^*$. The following examples suggest the dimensions of the problem.[31] If the horizon is short ($T = 3$) and the return on savings deposits modest[32] ($s = .05$), the value of $r^*$ turns out to be no less than .37. With $T = 5$, $s = .05$, the value of $r^*$ is .23. The implication of these figures is clear. Even assuming that the cost of credit is substantial (say, $i = .20$), $r^*$ is still greater than $i$ and, as Figure 18-2 illustrates, this means that the free choice solution calls for bank credit to be used exclusively (zero self-finance).

Viewing the situation from another side, we see that when $i$ has the plausible value .10 and $s = .05$, the collective's planning horizon must be about seventeen years if $i$ is to be greater than $r^*$ by 1 percent; and the horizon must equal twenty years for a 2 percent gap to appear. Moreover, these calculations are based on the assumption that *all* of the increased profit attributable to capital expansion is paid out each period in the form of wage increases; if only a fraction of the productivity improvement is devoted to raises, still longer time horizons are necessary. In general, then, there can be no doubt that the $T$ value is critical to the functioning of the labor-managed firm. In order for there to be *any possibility*[33] that the collective will invest its savings in the firm voluntarily (i.e.,

30. The information in Tables 18-1 and 18-2 tends to confirm the predictions of the idealized model. Note that the 1965 reform marks the beginning of substantial freedom of choice for the firm.

31. The calculations are based on the annuity tables reproduced in Cox (1967, p. 193).

32. Ceteris paribus, the smaller the value of $s$, the greater the incentives for self-finance.

33. Even if $i > r^*$, the shape and position of the firm's marginal efficiency of investment schedule can be such that no intersection with the savings schedule is possible in the range above $r^*$

Table 18-2.  Sources of Gross Investment in Fixed Assets (Percentages)

| | 1964 | 1965 | 1966 | 1967 | 1968 | 1969 | 1970 | 1971 |
|---|---|---|---|---|---|---|---|---|
| Business firms | 26 | 28.9 | 39.3 | 32.7 | 31.2 | 28 | 27 | 27 |
| Banks (including investment in housing) | 31 | 36.6 | 38.9 | 44.9 | 47.1 | 49 | 51 | 51 |

Sources. *Statisticki Bilten SDK*, No. 6, 1970, and *Statisticki Bilten SDK*, No. 8, 1970, and No. 9, 1972.

choose to acquire non-owned assets), the members of the collective must acquiesce to very long planning horizons.

The obvious question that arises is whether workers can be expected to operate with planning periods of twenty or more years. It is, of course, hazardous to attempt a definitive answer, but we know that for a long-term arrangement to be feasible the employees of the firm must be willing to remain with the firm over the requisite $T$ periods, and must have confidence that the terms of the original "agreement" about the stream of wage improvements will be honored. Practically, the chances for these conditions being met do not seem good. Older workers who foresee retirement before the full payout period (1, 2, ..., $T$) is completed will be disposed to vote against commitments involving long time horizons. Similarly, any worker contemplating a move from one firm to another in the future will tend to vote so that he does not have to make sacrifices for non-owned assets that will never yield him adequate benefits.[34] Risk calculations can also influence the length of the time horizon workers will accept. As time elapses, there is danger that the national government may alter the rules under which the firm operates, the membership of the collective may change in such way as to generate new voting patterns and revised payoff policies, etc. Indeed, since risks and uncertainties tend to increase as the length of the planning period is extended, there are many forces that push the collective in the direction of a relatively short planning horizon. This general result means, in turn, that $r^*$ is almost certain to be greater than $i$ and that the incentive to invest in non-owned assets is virtually nil.

There is, then, an inherent flaw in the structure of the pure labor-managed firm.[35] Troubles appear because the new socialist organization has its own form of "internal contradiction." On the one hand, the law gives each collective significant decision-making powers and allows workers to reject economic alternatives that are unfavorable to their interests. On the other, the system enforces a structure of property rights that permits individuals only the right of use of capital goods and, thus, limits severely the incentives for investment in the firm. What can be expected from this arrangement is, unfortunately, *the retardation of voluntary saving in the economy as a whole*. Failing the special conditions that lead to $i > r^*$ and the possibility of self-finance activity, each collective is effectively cut off from investment alternatives promising higher rewards than the rate of interest ($s$) paid on savings deposits. Relative to Figure 18-2, if the interest on savings deposits is a modest $s_0$ and the loan rate is $i_1$, the collective will save and acquire *owned* assets only to the extent $OA$. In short, given the structure of incentives implied by the labor-managed firm and the existence of

34. If most workers had long planning horizons and intended to remain with their original firms for twenty or more years, labor mobility in the economy as a whole would be reduced to an alarming degree.

35. Compare Vanek (1969).

an elastic supply of bank credit, *consumption becomes the most attractive alternative open to workers.*

From the narrow viewpoint of any individual collective, saving does not seem to be a necessary precondition to economic progress. To workers, high consumption and rising incomes appear mutually compatible as long as the firm is able to finance new investment opportunities through the banking system.[36] And, ceteris paribus, the banking system in a growth-oriented socialist state like Yugoslavia will tend to be accommodating. Presumably, there is a desire on the part of the government to maintain decentralization and, at the same time, stimulate the expansion of firms so that national investment objectives can be reached. In other words, credit will tend to be forthcoming as an offset to limited self-finance. The trouble is, however, that too much new money is likely to be put into the system—causing total investment to become larger than total saving at full employment and generating inflation.[37] Although any emerging economy struggling to develop is susceptible to major price movements, the case under consideration is special because the structure of the labor-managed firm, as such, contributes significantly to the process of inflation. The labor-managed firm may permit a socialist nation to escape the inefficiencies of central planning but creates new problems of its own.

The line of criticism developed above can, perhaps, be stated in a different way by saying that the Yugoslav economy has been unable to find a fully satisfactory method for financing industrial expansion. The lack of a comprehensive system of capital markets is crucial; for, without the varied array of financial instruments found in the West, voluntary savings are more difficult to mobilize. At the same time, the existing property rights structure prevents the labor-managed firms from engaging in much self-finance activity. Thus, major responsibility for progress falls on bank-lending and/or operations by the central government. But this situation means, in turn, that business firms tend to accumulate large contractual obligations to the banks and, in general, become less independent in their policy formation. The fundamental problem remains one of discovering an institutional matrix that can provide an equilibrium volume of investment funds to firms while preserving the efficiency and flexibility of decentralized decision making.

It can be objected, of course, that the picture painted above is too black. Indeed, there is empirical evidence to indicate that the labor-managed firm in Yugoslavia does save and usually follows investment policies that are somewhat more in keeping with the social interest than has been suggested so far. But

---

36. In terms of Figure 18–1, the collective is not condemned to point $X$ if no savings are made, but can move to $Y$, and beyond $Y$ to even more favorable positions provided technological change shifts the opportunity locus $YY'$ outward.

37. The banks themselves are labor-managed enterprises and have some interest in expanding their own profits by placing loans.

these conditions hold largely because the government does not allow the collective the freedom of action the idealized model of the firm calls for. In practice, the Yugoslav firm does not have the privileged position that is implied by the bare legal structure; the firm's actual decisions result from an interplay of economic and political forces. The central authorities are forced to use both direct and indirect means in the attempt to guide the behavior of the firm and induce it to act in "socially approved" ways. Optimization by a firm, then, goes forward subject to a set of special constraints[38] imposed by outside agencies. It is also true that the development of an appropriate set of such constraints raises serious problems that have not yet been solved, and are not likely to be solved without a return to a more rigid system of administrative controls.[39] In any event, the central point should be clear. While tax policy, credit-rationing, and other control devices can be invoked to pressure the collective into investing in non-owned assets, the inherent characteristics of the labor-managed firm remain poorly adapted to the needs of a society that wishes to encourage *voluntary* restriction of consumption.

38. For example, the government may have a conception of what constitutes a "fair" wage in a given industry, and departures from this norm may invoke strong reaction calling for change. Further, if allocations to the Business Fund are accepted as evidence of patriotic spirit or political reliability, investment in the firm can possess a special appeal beyond its capacity to convey financial gain.

39. The model of section I can be extended to consider these problems, but such analysis lies beyond the objectives of the present study.

# The Less Developed Economy

Chapter Nineteen

# Controlling Corruption in Africa and Latin America

N. Sanchez
A. R. Waters

Paper presented at the Southern Economic Association Meetings, 1973.
Printed by permission of the authors.

Corruption is like sex was in Victorian England: it absorbs intense activity and is the subject of much speculation, but it is seldom considered a suitable topic for serious economic analysis.[1] The typical reaction to the discovery of corruption in one of the more developed countries is a quick enactment of laws which increase the degree of government supervision of economic activity; while a similar discovery in one of the less developed nations may also lead to anguished debate about the need to improve the moral fiber of politicians, to widespread feelings of moral indignation, and ultimately even to conflict and repression. Every revolution in the less developed world has been at least partially inspired by the desire to drive out corrupt rulers and officials, replacing them with honest men and raising the moral tenor of society. But the process is never completed. One regime replaces another, and the corruption appears again.[2]

The purpose of this chapter is to show how the reactions just described are inefficient methods of dealing with corruption; they do not attack its roots. We emphasize, first of all, that corruption decreases social welfare *not* because it leads to nonoptimal resource allocation but because it serves

---

[1] Political scientists and sociologists have tried to explain the emergence of corruption by analyzing the historical forces that have affected different societies, and by making *change* the leaven of corruption; for a summary and refinement of the modern view see Smelser (1971, pp. 7–29). Economists have done little research in this area, but their literature on property rights can easily be applied to the problem; this is our aim. For a summary of the recent literature on property rights see Furubotn and Pejovich (1972c); also, for an elementary treatment of the property rights approach to economic theory see Alchian and Allen (1972).

[2] The thirty-eight nations of Africa have averaged two-and-a-half revolutions each since their independence in the 1960s.

to redistribute a society's wealth in a way that generates social tension.[3] We will show that the strongest reaction will come precisely from those groups in society whose wealth is most affected by corruption: a fact which seems sufficient to explain the periodic outbursts by succeeding generations of students in the less developed world. Our analysis explores not only the causes of corruption but it also attempts to explain the particular problems which individual officials and bureaucrats face as corrupt decision-makers, thus leading to a clearer understanding of the behavior of the government structure as a whole. We conclude with the pessimistic assertion that although we know how to control corruption, and the necessary means exist, there may be historical forces at work which do not favor the implementation of the necessary policies.

This chapter is divided into four sections. The first section indicates briefly the extent of corruption in the less developed countries of Africa and Latin America; it suggests why corruption decreases social welfare. The second section discusses the immediate causes of corruption at two levels of government: the bureaucracy and the rulers, be they elected or self-appointed. The second section also establishes the necessary conditions which must exist for corruption to appear. The third section examines the behavior of corrupt officials and bureaucrats; also it explores the more distant causes of corruption and examines the factors which affect the stability of corrupt systems. The final section sets forth our conclusions.

Our analysis is inspired by the recognition that corruption exists in Africa and Latin America, and a belief that the resulting social tension and social conflict sap the strength of less developed nations in these areas. Furthermore, we believe that revolution is an inefficient remedy for corruption and that the usual attempts to impose *higher* moral standards upon a society are not only bound to fail but must also lead to an expansion of corrupt practices. Moral indignation is not bound to solve the problem of corruption; understanding and perhaps compassion may.

## THE NATURE AND EXTENT OF CORRUPTION

Although we could quote at length from official inquiries, legal proceedings, newspaper reports, or scholarly studies on the extent of corruption in Africa and Latin America, we prefer to draw our examples from a single source: the studies by Stanislaw Andreski. We have chosen this source because Andreski has lived and taught in both Africa and Latin America, because his examples are

---

[3] A number of studies have attempted to determine the effect of corruption upon economic development, stressing the *allocative* consequences of corruption; for a summary of the propositions in the literature see Park (1969). Our paper is concerned with the *distributional* consequences of corruption, a problem which the literature seems to have ignored.

succinctly stated, and because his explanation of corruption differs markedly from our own. Andreski describes the Latin American situation thus:

> Customs inspectors derive most of their incomes from bribes taken for conniving at evasion. Porters, who may be able to charge an arriving passenger more than a factory worker earns in a week or even two, have to pay big bribes to officials who issue permits to work within the harbour. In Chile, where other branches of administration are less ridden with graft than in other countries of Latin America, customs officials are conspicuous for their dishonesty: in addition to taking bribes, they help themselves to the goods which they are inspecting or enter into collusion with bands of thieves organized among the porters and shunters.
>
> All sales and purchases effected by the government are liable to be decided by graft. There are many examples of lands belonging to the state having been sold to plenipotentiaries of the favorites of men in power, or to buyers who gave bribes, at prices many times lower than the market value. Obversely, land required for government installations or roads has often been bought from similar persons at grossly exaggerated prices; and decisions about locating roads, railways and other installations have often been guided solely by the aim of enlarging the profits of such individuals.
>
> Licenses of various kinds and exemptions from import duties on articles which can be sold at great profit are frequently given to the favorites of the government or in exchange for bribes. Fabulous sums were obtained by the Venezuelan dictators for granting concessions to oil companies, and in other countries great fortunes were made from sales to mining or agricultural companies of lands belonging to the state. (1966, pp. 64–67)

Speaking about the African situation, Andreski has stated:

> After only a few years in office the top politicians have amassed fortunes worth a hundred times the sum of salaries received. Many of them have simply transferred big sums from the treasury to their private accounts, but the practice of getting cuts on government contracts constitutes the chief fount of illegal gains. . . . People like municipal councillors and district officers or provincial commissioners can make substantial gains on local contracts and awards of licenses for market stalls. Scarcely a waste paper basket is bought for an office without somebody getting a tip from the seller, who then gets it back from the public funds by charging a higher price than he could get from a private buyer.
>
> I have known hospitals in West Africa where the patients had to pay nurses to bring them a chamber pot; where the doctors (who were receiving a salary from the state and were supposed to treat

the sick free of charge) would look only at those patients who had given them money, and saw those first who had paid most, regardless whose condition was most urgent.

Teachers' salaries are sometimes embezzled by the headmasters or higher officials. Moreover in the same way as people in other public services, many teachers had to pay for getting appointed, and continue to pay ransom for being kept on the payroll.

The police are among the worst offenders against the law: they levy illegal tolls on vehicles, especially the so-called mammy-wagons (heavy lorries with benches and roofs) which usually carry many more passengers than they are allowed and transgress a variety of minor-regulations. They are allowed to proceed regardless of the infractions of the law if they pay the policeman's private toll. (1968, pp. 95–98)

All of these examples, which should be familiar to any development economist who has lived in Africa or Latin America, emphasize the misuse of *public* power for private profit, and because of this they should be labelled as acts of "political corruption." There is a danger, though, in emphasizing acts of political corruption; the conclusions of any study of the effects of corrupt practices in different countries or even within the same country at different periods of time, may be biased if attention is paid only to political corruption. This point has been stressed by James C. Scott, who argues that present analysis fails to specify the behavior being compared, and that therefore the comparative findings derive only from the particular definition of corruption used. Scott then points out that the definition used refers almost without exception to illegal activities by private individuals in the public sector, and that the outcome is therefore determined by the legal environment at a point in time (Scott 1969).

Scott illustrates the disparity of standards that exist in judging public and private corruption:

The president of a business firm may appoint his inept son-in-law assistant vice-president and, although he may regret the appointment from a financial point of view and be accused of poor taste, he remains quite within the law. Similarly, if he lets an overpriced supply contract to a close friend in return for a percentage of the excess profit, the market may punish him, but not the law.
(P. 320)

Should we study, then, all acts of corruption or only those which affect the public sector? And why do the people in general, the news media, and scholars place such a strong emphasis on the mores of the public sector? To answer the second question we do not need to postulate the existence of different ethical standards of judgment; we only need to observe the *alternatives* which are open to an individual who is confronted with corruption at any (public or private) level of decision-making.

Suppose, to use the example offered by Scott, that a person finds out about the hiring of an inept son-in-law by a firm's president. If the person has no property rights in the hypothetical firm, he will consider the problem none of his business. If the person has ownership rights in the firm and there exists an *inexpensive* way of making his displeasure known to other owners of the business, the likelihood that the firm's president may be fired has been increased, as the president is not pursuing maximization of wealth for the owners of the firm; the president's increased welfare will not compensate the owners for their loss of wealth. Finally, if ownership rights in the firm are very dispersed and if the costs of informing other owners of the expected decrease in future earnings is prohibitive (because of annual stockholders meetings in faraway places), the person who has the information has at least the option of transferring his property rights over the firm to other people who either do not have the information or who are willing to bear the risk that the new hiring has brought on the firm. In other words, he can sell his stock. And, if the firm's profits are ultimately reduced by mistaken policies, the firm's president will have to account for his behavior to the firm's owners.

The point that we make is that even in the worst of situations, where an owner's control over a firm is minimal, the owner can transfer his property rights to other individuals and reduce his private risks. Furthermore, if widespread dissatisfaction with managerial policies occurs (as a result of corrupt private practices), "the more shares relative to their total number will be sold and the lower will be the price of the company's stock relative to that of other companies. The latter condition, of course, presents a clear danger to management" (Furubotn and Pejovich 1972c, p. 1150). As long as there are private property rights over a firm, there will be self-policing forces which will restrain the extent of corruption by officials or employees.

What is the situation of a person who confronts political corruption? The individual does not need to own shares in the corporate state to realize that he receives benefits from the state (e.g., subsidized education, police and fire protection, the services of roads, etc.) and that he must bear the costs of state activities. Hence, the discovery of corruption in public places must make a person aware that either his benefits will be reduced or his costs will be increased, a situation which amounts to nothing else but a reduction in his wealth. (Alternatively, a person may feel that without corruption, and with a different pricing policy, the state could increase his benefits and reduce his costs, more will be said about this later). It may of course be true that corrupt practices lead to an optimal resource allocation and even to economic growth (Leff 1964; Bayley 1966), but this is not what is important to the discoverer of corrupt practices; what matters to him is that a redistribution of wealth from the community as a whole, of which he is a member, to a small and select group of individuals (the bureaucracy or the elected officials) has taken place. Corruption decreases social welfare not because it leads to sub-optimal resource allocation but because it redistributes wealth from the many to the few and gives rise to social tension. We can only ignore the problem of corruption if we are willing to accept the risk of conflict and chaos.

An individual who is confronted with public corruption and who is unable to sell his property rights in public organizations (for short, public property rights) will turn to an alternative: political participation. If he is lucky, the individual will be able to cast a ballot for the politician of his choice; if he is less lucky, he will only be able to express anger and discontent with the managers of the state in negative ways. The proverb "that which is everybody's business is nobody's business" is patently false: political activity is proof to the contrary. People do care about reductions in their wealth, but only their options (and the prices of those options) will determine their behavior. If property rights are nontransferable, as in the case with most public property rights,[4] the appearance of corruption will only serve to raise the general level of political tension.

Since the benefits and costs of state services are not equally dis-tributed among the population, different poeple will react to corruption at different degrees and levels of participation. At one extreme the subsistence farmer who is by-passed by government activities will remain apathetic to charges and counter-charges of corrupt behavior; his indifference and cynicism are rooted in economic considerations. At the other extreme the students in less developed countries, who are heavily subsidized by the state and dependent upon it for their subsequent careers, will react strongly to corruption. It is not difficult for students to perceive that the funds which corruption transfers to the bureaucracy could very well be used for further subsidies, perhaps to raise the quality of education. The relative conservatism of students in the pri-vate schools of these countries needs no involved sociological explanation: it can be explained by the limited net reward these students must expect from an honest government.

In the light of these arguments we conclude that the literature on corruption has been correct in placing its emphasis on political corruption. Even when political corruption leads to economic growth and development, it sets in motion forces which are bound to create social tension and conflict, and this is the real cost of corrupt practices.

## THE CAUSES OF CORRUPTION

The property of the community as a whole (e.g., schools, roads, armaments, etc., and the sources of community revenues) is not controlled directly, but

---

[4] This point is discussed by DeAlessi (1969, p. 17).

by "representatives of the people" (the elected officials or by employees
of the state, the bureaucracy). The elected officials and the bureaucracy
stand with respect to the community as a whole as the board of directors
(which we will call managers) and the employees of a corporation stand with
respect to the owners of a corporation. The policies of the managers of the
state will help determine the wealth of the community, just as the policies
of the directors of a corporation will help determine the wealth of the corporation owners. We now ask, what are the factors which will lead to corruption
in the public sector?

Corruption may arise either with the managers of the state or
with the employees of the state. We begin our analysis by assuming that the
managers of the state are incorruptible and that they establish an accounting
system which allows them to supervise every transaction which the bureaucracy makes in the name of the state. The managers need not participate in
every transaction, since that is an impossibility, but supervision could effectively require that the bureaucrats deposit into a government fund the amount
established by law for the good or service which the bureaucrat provides. In
other words, if the bureaucrat sells a government license, he must deposit into
a government account the license fee which was established by law.

Corruption may now arise, and will only arise, under the following
circumstance: if the managers of the state establish sale and purchase prices
for government goods and services which differ from the private valuation of
those goods and services. Let us take as an illustrative example the sale of
offices or government appointments in Africa. The salaries for the government
posts are above the alternative salaries which the prospective employees can
command in private employment; in other words, the managers of the state
have placed a higher value on the services of an individual with some specific
qualifications than the public is willing to pay for those qualifications in private
employment. The difference between private and government valuation for
the particular service will mean that in order to obtain the job the prospective
employee can use part of his salary as some form of payoff to the bureaucrat
who has the right to make the appointment, and that the remaining salary will
still be worth at least as much as the employee would require to take the job.

By overvaluing the services of a person with some given qualifications, the managers of the state have provided a given bureaucrat with a free
gift. Hence, the managers of the state have been able to redistribute wealth
from the community as a whole to the particular bureaucrat, since the payoff
to the bureaucrat could have been used to increase the services provided by
the state. Or, if the government had valued the services of the new employee
at market clearing prices, the public could have reduced its tax outlays.

It should be emphasized that the right to choose or appoint a government employee is not a sufficient condition for the appearance of corruption. If the salary that the government offers is equal to the alternative salaries
which prospective employees can command elsewhere, the bureaucrat who is

responsible for the appointment will not be able to extract a payoff from the prospective employee. The *necessary* condition is the divergence between private and government valuation of an item or activity. This line of argument can be extended to a large number of corrupt practices; however, it should be understood that our analysis does not include outright theft. Theft involves an abrogation or appropriation of property rights rather than a distortion of the value of those rights.

Corrupt practices are quite evident in transactions which involve foreign exchange. The problem begins with a situation where the domestic currency is overvalued because the official exchange rate, set by the managers of the state, does not represent the private valuation of the worth of foreign currencies. A private person will be willing to pay a bribe to the controlling government official in order to obtain the foreign currency, say, to bring an imported good or to travel abroad. The payoff to the official may consist of a direct money payment, but it may also be indirect or even in kind. When customs officials consistently take some of the goods which they inspect, as mentioned by Andreski, we may suspect that those officials must in turn pay bribes to the higher officials who allowed the importation of those goods, and who had de facto control over the allocation of foreign currencies; this suspicion is based on the general proposition that people attempt to maximize their wealth, and if the higher officials do not require bribes they are giving up pecuniary or nonpecuniary gains. That the public continues to import goods under such calamitous procedures seems to indicate that the public's monetary payments for the imported goods, in the domestic currency, are below the public's valuation of the goods; only under these conditions would they be willing to put up with expected graft by the customs officials. A government official could not extract a bribe from a would-be importer or tourist if the official exchange ratio represented the private valuation of foreign currencies.

Let us analyze several other examples provided by Andreski. He mentions that porters, who are able to charge arriving passengers a fee which is above what the porters could earn in alternative lines of employment (Andreski does not use this terminology, but his meaning is obvious), must pay bribes to the officials who issue work permits within the harbor. The porters are able to charge such high fees because they lack competition from other workers who would surely prefer to work in the harbor than in lower-paying jobs. The competition is lacking because harbor officials are restricting entry into the porters' profession, and since the officials are the ones who decide who can work in the harbor, the officials are in a position to receive at least part (if not all) of the monopoly profits which accrue to the porters due to contrived scarcity.

The award of licenses for market stalls in Africa creates a situation similar to the one described above. Since the price which the government sets on the market stalls is below the private valuation of those stalls, the local official has an opportunity to extract a bribe from the would-be merchant. We are not arguing in this case, nor in the previous example, that it is desirable or undesirable to limit the number of participants in a particular market; what we argue is that once the decision is made to limit those participants, unless a market clearing price is established corruption is likely to appear. It does not matter whether the government official is rich or poor; if he sees an opportunity to increase his wealth, he will do so, and to believe any other general hypothesis is wishful thinking. Andreski is therefore guilty of moralizing to no useful purpose in his analysis when he says:

> There are extenuating circumstances for the corruption of minor officials: most of them receive salaries on which they cannot feed their families, so it is not surprising that they take bribes whenever they can. . . . There is no excuse, however, for the big profiteers who already have much more than they need for living in luxury, but who nevertheless make use of every opportunity for criminal gain. (1966, p. 67)

The divergence between the government's valuation of governmental services and the private valuation of those services is nowhere more evident than in the case of patients who tip the nurses and doctors in public hospitals of Africa. Those patients who are willing to tip the nurses and doctors should have been charged higher entrance fees into the hospitals. Neither the doctors nor the patients are to blame for corruption in the system: we must only blame an admissions policy that allows the divergence of valuation to exist.

The cases which we have discussed deal with the employees of the state, but we must not forget that corruption can also arise with the managers of the state. So far we had assumed that the managers were incorruptible, but we must now question the motives which lead the managers to the establishment of laws which redistribute wealth from the community to the bureaucracy. Suppose that, contrary to usual assertion, the goal of each and every manager were the maximization of his personal wealth. If this were the case, every alternative confronting a manager would be weighed by the benefits and costs which it brings to the manager *as an individual.* The costs involved would have to include the risks of losing future elections or even getting overthrown by competing managers.

Since it may be difficult for the managers to increase the tax revenues of the state and assign themselves huge salaries, they can decide to generate sources of revenues for themselves by purposely creating a divergence between the private and government valuation of public goods and services. Since the managers will assign different bureaus in the state the task of enforcing government regulations, they will be able, in various ways, to take a cut in the monopoly gains that accrue to the bureaucrats who administer the law.

If laws are passed in order to favor some special interest in the community, the managers of the state may also expect some direct or indirect reward from the special interests which they have favored. The indirect payments may even take the form of campaign contributions by the special interests, a behavior which is, in some nations, sanctioned by the law.

Any policy which increases a politician's wealth will also increase the risks of his losing power, since the added wealth will attract additional and more forceful competition. As we have noted repeatedly, any divergence which the politician creates between the government and private valuation of public goods is bound to lead to a redistribution of wealth from the society to the bureaucracy and elected officials, and this will always be a source of conflict. There may be, however, an additional source of conflict: since the monopoly situation of the bureaucracy is contrived, the people who must acquire the goods and services produced by the state may become aware of the advantage that a competitive situation would bring them. This situation would be particularly important for a firm that confronts a downward sloping demand curve, in other words, a firm which is not in a competitive market. If this firm could lower the costs of one of its major inputs (which is produced by the government), it would be able to increase its wealth. Hence it is important for the government to avoid the production of intermediate goods which are major inputs to a restricted number of firms since those firms are bound to organize opposition against the present managers of the state.

This analysis suggests that politicians will tend to resort to market restrictions which affect each of many individuals by a small amount, since it can easily be assumed that the costs of organizing large numbers of people into political opposition are much higher than the costs of organizing few firms (especially firms which have at stake a vital interest in lowering their input costs). Hence, even in those situations where the government comes into the open and grants monopolies, it will prefer to do so where the goods are sold directly to consumers or are a minor part of business expenditures. Monopolies on salt, matches, and the mail, which are quite common in underdeveloped countries, are good examples of the kind of monopolies which our analysis predicts.

If the government takes over the production of a major intermediate product which is to be sold to a limited number of firms in the internal market, government officials must resort to a different strategy to buy off competition from the affected firms. One possible strategy may be to grant the affected firms monopoly rents in their markets, by restricting the competition which they have to face. For example, if the government takes over the production of steel, creating a monopoly in this commodity, it is likely that the government will restrict the competition faced by car manufacturers who must buy the steel by imposing high tariffs on imported cars. The car manufacturers will, of course, realize that they could increase their profits if steel were sold under competitive conditions, but they now have a vested interest in maintaining the government's protection of their market.

Let us now go back to the original aim of this section: to pinpoint the causes of corruption. The immediate cause of corruption is contrived scarcity. Contrived scarcity, in turn, appears whenever the government sets a price for a good or service which is not a market clearing price, and then insists that the bureaucrats sell or purchase the good or service at such a price. Two other conditions are necessary for corruption to appear One is that both the bureaucrat and the prospective giver of a bribe are allowed to possess transferable property rights; if the bureaucrat, for example, is part of a commune which provides for all of his needs and with which he must share all of his possessions, he will have little interest in acquiring a bribe which is not likely to directly or even indirectly change his individual welfare.

The other condition is that the bureaucrat must consider his behavior toward others as affecting his own welfare in a minimal way (aside from the bribe which he is able to receive). A policeman who allows transgressors of minor regulations to carry on their activities must feel that his own welfare would not be affected much if he changed his behavior; if the policeman were a religious zealot and believed that any transgression of a law on his part would bring him divine punishment and damnation, he would, of course, carry on his duties according to the letter of the law. Within this framework of analysis, it is not difficult to incorporate a more traditional view of bribery. Bribery is fairly easy if the enforcing authorities are being asked to overlook something which is not thought to be wicked by the bulk of the community (including the authorities); whereas bribery to overlook something which the bulk of the community does think is wicked, such as murder, is likely to be more difficult.

The bureaucrat's estimate of the effect that his behavior toward others has on his own welfare indicates one possible way to combat corruption: to inculcate the bureaucracy with predetermined ethical and moral standards by means of education, propaganda, or other forms of reinforcement. However, the general success in this respect of such systems as Christianity, Communism, or, more recently, Skinnerian psychology leaves too much in doubt, and we will prefer to concentrate our attention on alternative policies which are familiar to the economist: the changing of constraints.

## BUREAUCRATIC BEHAVIOR AND THE PERSISTENCE OF CORRUPTION

Although it may in practice be impossible to separate the problems which confront the managers of the state from those which confront the bureaucracy proper, especially where the bureaucracy has gained complete ascendency in the management of the state, we will continue to make the distinction for purposes of analysis. One major problem confronting the managers of the state is the invention of laws and regulations which increase the managers' personal wealth but which do not increase the risk of their losing political power. We noted in the last section that it would be characteristic of such laws that they would affect large numbers of people in a minimal way, and when laws do not possess this attribute, the government must buy off political opposition from the most affected individuals. Now, as long as the government allows private property rights in the business and industrial sector, we would expect that an increase of interdependence among economic activities will make it more difficult for the government to restrict political opposition. The point may be best explained with an illustration.

Suppose that the government decides to create a monopoly on steel production (this can be done directly or indirectly, by means of licenses). If most of the steel is sold to car manufacturers, the government can buy off political opposition from car producers by restricting the number of car imports and thereby granting the affected firms monopoly rents. But if a high degree of interdependence has been reached in the economy, with a large number of firms using steel as a major input, and still other firms using the output of the steel consuming firms as inputs in their own production processes, protection from political opposition becomes an almost impossible task. First, it will become difficult for the government to determine all of the effects that its actions will produce, so that political opposition may develop before the government is able to buy it off. Second, even when the government is able to buy off opposition from the firms which are directly affected by the price of steel, a high degree of interdependence will mean that additional firms will be hurt by the second round of protective practices. Third, even when the government is willing to take on the added administrative costs of expanded protection, it opens up the door to political opposition from potential importers. As protection becomes an all encompassing government activity, then, the potential profits from trade will rise, and forces will develop in a country to open up the channels of trade. And finally, the potential gains from trade may be so great that illicit traffic will develop, increasing once again the administrative costs of policing the government regulations.

The argument just presented suggests that political competition is more likely to develop in societies where there exists a higher degree of internal economic interdependence; such societies may, in time, expect greater political responsiveness to the wishes of the mass of the population. The arguments may thus explain why the less developed African and Latin American states are prone to be governed by single dominant political parties and also why many of these countries' governments insist upon economic self-sufficiency despite the facade of regional cooperation, specialization, and interdependence.

The managers of the state must also convince the civilian populations that the government's policies exist to benefit the people. Although we are all familiar with the arguments which are used to protect domestic firms from foreign competition, it may be worth to recall that most of the regulations of the state are imposed "to protect" the consumers from "inferior" goods (e.g., "unsafe" standards in mammy-wagons), "unethical" buyers (e.g., employers who would be willing to hire additional help but only at wages which the law calls "unfair"), "unethical" sellers (e.g., bankers who would charge "unethical" interest rates), "disorderly" markets (e.g., those where government controls are imposed to avoid price fluctuations), or even social "disorder" (e.g., the dangers that would occur if police did not know the whereabouts of people).

It is in the interest of the managers of the state to convince people that they can get something for nothing: that the promulgation of laws which restrict exchange will make the higher costs of producing "superior" goods vanish. Just because the government decrees an increase in the value of one peso so that it is now equal to one dollar, making everybody believe that his purchasing power has risen, it does not mean that foreign goods can be bought at cheaper prices. Such a decree must only mean that part of the payment for the foreign good will reach the pocket of some bureaucrat. Since the alternative to distortion of valuation was the payment of the true price of the foreign good into the national treasury, the decree is nothing else but a way of redistributing wealth from the community as a whole to the bureaucracy.

The more able the manager of the state is in convincing people that they should use moral judgment in establishing the price of economic goods, the more likely is the bureaucrat to redistribute wealth towards himself. This we call the paradox of morality: as the public becomes convinced that the value of additional goods and services should be established by norms which are independent of personal and individual valuation, or as those norms are raised higher and higher, the sources of corruption will expand in the society. If society could become convinced that their own personal and individual norms were good enough to determine the value of goods, and that those values could be established under competitive conditions, corruption would disappear.

Let us now turn to the problems facing the bureaucracy proper. For the purposes of our analysis we will assume that well-established channels exist between the bureaucracy and the managers of the state, and that these channels are used to transfer throughout the bureaucracy some part of any gains which accrue to the system. The immediate problem which confronts an individual bureaucrat is similar to that facing any individual firm: how to price the goods and services which he controls. Since the bureaucrat is unable to sell his property rights in an open market, he is in the enviable position of being able to use discriminatory pricing. The bureaucrat is not confronted with a single aggregate demand function but with a host of them. His pricing policy will lead to a reduction in the consumer surplus which each individual will derive in his dealings with the bureaucrat, and even if the result is an optimal allocation of resources, there is a likelihood of discontent among those consumers who realize that they could increase their welfare in an open market.

If the bureaucrat sells his goods or services to a business enterprise which is itself noncompetitive, the firm will resent the reduction in wealth which is forced upon it by the bureaucrats' pricing technique. Discriminatory pricing will allow the bureaucrat to extract larger sums of money for the goods and services which he controls than could an open monopoly (assuming that the illegality of bribery does not drive away a substantial number of customers).

An individual bureaucrat is also faced with the problem of preventing other bureaucrats from offering for sale the goods or services which he is supposed to control. We must not be surprised if many bureaus claim jurisdiction over the limited number of goods and services offered by the government: each bureau is trying, understandably, to maximize its control over property rights and the potential wealth that it can acquire through bribes. Competition among bureaucrats will increase in the short-run if growth is uneven, and if some bureaucrats act in the belief that others are taking a disproportionate share of the increasing scope for corruption. However, economic growth, whether even or uneven, provides a growing arena for the exploitation of existing property rights, and frequently new areas are also being brought under bureaucratic control. Thus the safety valve of expansion is available to mitigate the danger of conflict between bureaucrats. It will, of course, be true that competition among elements of the bureaucracy for poorly defined property rights within government may lead to destruction of the whole bureaucratic apparatus.

In both the short and long run, the greatest problem faced by the individual bureaucrat is the risk involved in conducting illegal activities. The bureaucrat must fear that knowledge about his activities may be gained by the political opposition and the press. The bureaucrat should expect that information leaks are a function of time and the extent of his activities. As time proceeds, random pieces of information will fall into the hands of unfriendly groups, and given enough time, the unfriendly groups will be able to recognize the pattern of activity and organization of corrupt bureaucrats. The bureaucrat can attempt to minimize the extent of this problem by changing the regulations and procedures of government at short intervals of time: in this way any information that reaches the opposition will tend to be outdated. Even if the opposition gains full knowledge of bureaucratic corruption, the individual bureaucrat can admit that things were not working properly under the old system but that he has demonstrated his concern for the problem by changing the regulations.

The risks of bureaucratic expansion are more difficult to deal with. Each bureaucrat has a vested interest in expanding his activities, but his risks will increase as he does so. When the bureaucrat takes on subordinates, his costs are also bound to increase, as he must now police the services of his subordinates. Since we do not see how the risks of expansion can be avoided, we will assume that each bureaucrat will expand his activities to the point where his estimate of marginal cost, based on his estimate of the risk involved, is equal to his expected marginal return.

What are, in fact, the long-run sources of instability for the whole bureaucratic apparatus? We can think of two major sources: the "dual" position of the bureaucracy and economic stagnation. Since the members of the bureaucracy are also members of the national community, they have a vested interest in honest government; this interest is only offset by the direct income which the individual bureaucrats may derive from corruption. Self-interest may convince a bureaucracy that it should forsake the present managers of the state and turn to the political opposition in the hope of attaining an increase in wealth as individual citizens in an honest state; it can happen, but it is unusual: Fidel Castro won in Cuba, and the old bureaucracy found out too late where its true interest lay. Stagnation means a contraction in the demand for a whole range of government functions. For example: a reduction in the rate of expansion in the education system will lead to a reduced demand for school building permits, and fewer exports and imports mean less scope for corruption at every level from underhand foreign exchange transactions to petty graft.

With stagnation and reduced scope for corruption, segments of the bureaucracy will become aware that they can only continue to obtain monopoly gains from their activities by encroaching on the property rights of other bureaucrats. Competition and conflict will ensue. The pressure is accentuated because stagnation causes a reduction in the present value of the wealth which accrues to property rights as it alters expectations about future returns. Therefore, stagnation is likely to produce accelerated and expanded corrupt activity as bureaucrats attempt to retain their absolute position. This increased overt competition has often led to a military bureaucracy taking over the civilian functions of the state. It is ironic that to the extent that economic development leads to peace within the different factions of the bureaucracy it may also be a factor in perpetuating corruption in government.

If what we define as corruption is widely accepted by society as part of its normal way of life, and if there are no pressures for change, the system may endure. There must, however, be no change in the pattern of control over property rights, and the existing distribution of wealth and income must be widely accepted. But such a system, widespread and traditional and accepted, would amount to a new and de facto legal system replacing the written but unenforced laws which existed before or laws which were introduced with no intention of being enforced. However, though their ability to adapt to change may be limited and the lifespan of individual regimes may be short, corrupt regimes do survive.

## CONCLUSIONS

Three conditions seem necessary for the existence of corruption: contrived scarcity, transferability of property rights, and the belief by each member of the bureaucracy that his own actions as part of the bureaucratic structure will not have a significant negative effect upon his personal wealth and well-being. We have stressed contrived scarcity in our analysis because we do not think that in the near future the majority of African and Latin American countries are willing to abolish private property rights and the transferability they entail; also, we believe that all efforts to indoctrinate the bureaucracy with high standards of honesty have failed in the past, and that this experience should indicate to the African and Latin American countries that further effort in this direction alone would be fruitless.

The reader who accepts that contrived scarcity is the *immediate* cause of corruption may still wonder what the factors are that bring about policies of contrived scarcity; since our analysis has not answered this question, the reader may claim that we have not solved the problem of corruption. Two points should be made. First, we have implied in this chapter that our hypothetical reader is asking the wrong question. It is improper to ask, "What forces lead to policies of contrived scarcity?" The reader should ask instead, "What forces *prevent* the appearance of such policies?" Policies of contrived scarcity are bound to appear if public officials have a free rein in pursuing their self-interest; it is naive to believe that people in power will not use that power to increase their wealth and well-being.

Second, we have tried to shed some light upon the conditions that will prevent the policies of contrived scarcity from appearing. We have stated that political competition will tend to serve the interests of the mass of the people and that such competition is more likely to appear when economic interdependence develops within a country. Economic interdependence is important because it raises the costs to the government structure of compensating those whose interests are affected adversely by government policy.

Following the hypothesis of the last paragraph, we could suggest that capitalistic-democratic societies developed by historical accident, as economic interdependence developed faster than the tentacles of government. The slow growth of government could be attributed to its lack of effective information networks, a deficiency which was later made up by technological discoveries. Hence, it may be possible that the situation which nurtured capitalistic-democratic societies is never again to reappear and that historical necessity will force the African and Latin American countries to develop along different lines.

Knowledge about the immediate cause of corruption should help us determine the policies that must be pursued to control corruption. The general policy prescription is rather simple: the government must make sure that its goods, services, and job opportunities are offered at market clearing prices. Whenever the government restricts the output of a commodity or service it must be aware that it creates monopoly rents which someone is bound to capitalize. We do not even argue about the desirability of such restrictions, but once the restrictions are introduced, the government should increase the Treasury's funds and not those of the bureaucracy.

Our policy prescription should be briefly compared to one which advocates greater policing of the economic activities of the state. Even though we recognize that some policing of those activities is necessary in order to make the bureaucracy accountable for its activities, we also recognize that if contrived scarcity leads to large sources of gain, the government officials and the bureaucracy will have the necessary power to buy off the members of the policing force. The introduction of additional policing force in a situation where the root cause of corruption has not been eradicated is only bound to redistribute wealth in favor of the increased policing force. It may be possible, of course, to introduce successive levels of supervision and regulation to the point where the offers from the lower levels are not sufficient to compensate the higher officials for the risks they take; thus corruption could be controlled. This is not, however, solving the problem of corruption but merely internalizing its costs. Society as a whole has not redistributed wealth back from the bureaucracy to itself; it has simply shifted resources to an activity (policing) which could have been avoided if the appropriate laws had been in effect.

The policy which we advocate does not serve the interest of government officials; throughout this chapter we have stressed that these officials have no *incentives* to advocate such policies. The solution to the problem, then, is to restrict the scope of government activities both to those where transactions costs, such as the cost of excluding "free riders," make it impossible for private enterprise to provide the goods or services, and to those where the amount of use of the good or service by any one person does not reduce the amount available to others. This policy proposal is a lonely cry in our modern times, but it is precisely the cry that must be heard if the underdeveloped countries of Africa and Latin America want to avoid the world which Frantz Fanon (1967) foresaw: a world in which "privileges multiply and corruption triumphs, while morality declines" (p. 138).

Part IV

# Property Rights and the Construction of a More General Theory of Production and Exchange

## Chapter Twenty

# Some General Observations

Certainly, the property rights approach offers a fresh and useful way of looking at economic problems; indeed, there are those who would say that the new analysis represents one of the most important advances in economic thinking that has appeared in the post-war period. The basic objective of the property rights literature is to achieve a generalization of the standard theory of production and exchange, and it accomplishes this with the construction of an analytical model that is both simple and flexible. By placing emphasis on the interconnectedness of ownership rights, incentives, and economic behavior, the theory promises to explain a wider class of real events, to demonstrate the mutual interdependence of the legal system and economic phenomena, and to provide a series of testable propositions about economic behavior. Because the basic optimization model here is more general, the property rights approach permits a much greater range of institutional data to be considered and, for the first time, eliminates the need for developing special ad hoc theories to account for business activity taking place in different socio-economic environments. In general, then, it seems clear that substantial contributions have been made to economic understanding; moreover, the literature shows continuing vitality and promises significant future accomplishments.

To say all this, however, is not to suggest that the property rights analysis is without its own special problems and deficiencies. A great many questions remain to be explored. Within a certain framework of assumptions, the new theory has been able to establish the general implications of alternative property rights assignments and their effects on the use of resources. But even in the context of this basic model, formal equilibrium conditions have yet to be worked out for numerous cases. The lack of a rigorous and fully developed analytical treatment can be troublesome; more important, however, is the issue of how far the process of theoretical generalization should be carried. While the existing property rights approach has gone a certain distance in enlarging the applicability of conventional microeconomic theory, still further extensions are conceivable.

The truth of this last statement is, prhaps, obvious, but an example drawn from the area of comparative systems can be used to underscore the problem. Traditionally, theories of the capitalist firm, the Soviet firm, and the labor-managed firm have been based on highly specialized behavioral assumptions. That is, a separate theory was constructed for each type of firm in the conviction that each pursued its own simple and distinctive objective—respectively, profit maximization, bonus maximization, and wage maximization. The insights provided by property rights analysis, however, permit a more satisfactory solution to be obtained. As Moore has argued in Chapter 22 that follows, the three separate theories of the firm can be deduced from a more general economic theory of utility maximization. The gain in understanding here is real. Nevertheless, it remains true that still more general theories lie behind the basic utility maximization model. For example, the latter can be interpreted as the *static* counterpart of static profit, bonus, and wage maximization models; and insofar as this is so, utility maximization represents only a special case of a more general *dynamic theory* capable of considering optimization over time.

In point of fact, a number of extensions of the analytical framework normally used in the property rights literature could be introduced so as to broaden the scope of the theory.[1] Movement from static to dynamic analysis represents one avenue that should be explored more fully. But greater attention might also be given to the existence of decision makers operating at different levels within the firm, and to the consequences of interaction among such individuals. Further, discussion need not be limited to completely deterministic models; formulations involving *uncertainty* would seem particularly well suited to the problems considered. Game-theoretic models go beyond conventional maximization procedures, but are otherwise compatible with the fundamental conceptions of the property rights approach. The conclusion, then, is clear. Property rights research has taken a first step in a generalization process that can be expected to continue.

Ideally, pure theories are supposed to give insight into economic processes and to guide applied studies. Relative to this standard, the property rights analysis can be said to perform reasonably well, but it is useful to consider some of the strengths and weaknesses of the approach. One possible difficulty arises because of the subjective cast of the new theory. When the focus shifts to the individual manager or decision-maker and to the problem of utility maximization, the analysis runs the danger of losing its operational character. Indeed, by placing the burden of explanation on utility maximization, it is at least conceivable that the theory will yield nothing more than ex post rationalizations for any outcomes observed. In other words, with this type of model, it may always be

---

1. The literature is, of course, constantly growing, and a few examples of these analytical extensions can already be found.

possible to attribute empirical results to the peculiarities of a utility function whose form has not been predesignated precisely.[2]

Whatever its limitations, the neoclassical model of the firm has some scientific appeal in that it is based on objective data. Given perfect competition and the other standard assumptions, managerial behavior is highly circumscribed. Thus, in principle, knowledge of existing technical and market information is sufficient to determine the firm's output level, input mix, etc. By contrast, the property rights model represents a much more open construction. And once the relatively straightforward theory based on profit maximization is abandoned, there is need for a great deal more empirical input into the model of the firm. Precise specification must be made of the decision-maker's utility function and of the ruling institutional constraints;[3] and, of course, such particularization can be very difficult to accomplish in practice.

Following the property rights logic, it is plausible to say that as long as the costs of monitoring managerial behavior are positive, some scope exists for the manager to appropriate personal benefits from the firm. But just how far the manager will go in availing himself of the opportunities present is an open question. Departures from "ideal" behavior or the behavior desired by the owners of the firm may be larger or smaller and thus the firm's input-output plan will show larger or smaller departures from the neoclassical position. In general, the manager can pursue any of various different strategies depending on the background data and such things as his willingness to take risks, his ability to secure information, etc. No simple analytical formula can be employed to say anything very significant about the firm's equilibrium solution; rather, if the optimization model is to be useful, detailed information must be available concerning the technical and institutional characteristics of the particular system considered.

Correctly applied, the property rights analysis does not lead to empty formalism. In fact, its subjective character can serve to alert the theorist to the dangers of limiting discussion to a consideration of abstract marginal conditions.

As the articles reprinted here suggest, however, a little empirical input can often go a long way when introduced into an appropriate property rights framework. The writings presented are all concerned with attempts to extend conventional theory. Alchian and Demsetz examine an absolutely fundamental question and seek to explain how the firm emerges as a separate and distinct organization. The central hypothesis proposed is that the problems of

2. Boulding's early comment on this point is worth noting. See Boulding (1960, p. 4).

3. Alchian (1965) summarizes the situation succinctly as follows: "The utility maximizing theory is applicable if and only if (1) we can identify some of its components beside direct pecuniary wealth, and if (2) we can identify circumstances that involve differences in the cost of each of the various types of non-pecuniary goods. By satisfying these two conditions we can deduce the relative extent of such activities in each of these circumstances. One important circumstance is the type of ownership of the firm."

contract enforcement under conditions of team production make a centralized organization economically beneficial to the parties concerned. Moore demonstrates that a general theory of managerial behavior can be developed for business firms operating in quite different socioeconomic environments when analysis is cast in terms of a constrained utility maximization model. In the final chapter, Pejovich considers another aspect of generalization and shows that different property rights structures can be expected to exert significanctly different effects on the community's (voluntary) allocation of income between current consumption and investment.

In view of the diversity of the articles in this book, no simple summary statement can be made concerning them. In a sense, it is somewhat artificial to think of the property rights contributions as falling into a distinct area of specialization. Ultimately, property rights analysis must penetrate all subdivisions in economics. If the objectives of the new approach are to be realized, property rights analysis has to build on and merge with the traditional theory so that, in the end, only one integrated body of microeconomics will exist.

## Chapter Twenty-one

# Production, Information Costs, and Economic Organization

A. Alchian
H. Demsetz

Reprinted from the *American Economic Review* 62 (December 1972): 777–795, by permission of publisher and authors.

The mark of a capitalistic society is that resources are owned and allocated by such nongovernmental organizations as firms, households, and markets. Resource owners increase productivity through cooperative specialization and this leads to the demand for economic organizations which facilitate cooperation. When a lumber mill employs a cabinetmaker, cooperation between specialists is achieved within a firm, and when a cabinetmaker purchases wood from a lumberman, the cooperation takes place across markets (or between firms). Two important problems face a theory of economic organization—to explain the conditions that determine whether the gains from specialization and cooperative production can better be obtained within an organization like the firm, or across markets, and to explain the structure of the organization.

It is common to see the firm characterized by the power to settle issues by fiat, by authority, or by disciplinary action superior to that available in the conventional market. This is delusion. The firm does not own all its inputs. It has no power of fiat, no authority, no disciplinary action any different in the slightest degree from ordinary market contracting between any two people. I can "punish" you only by withholding future business or by seeking redress in the courts for any failure to honor our exchange agreement. That is exactly all that any employer can do. He can fire or sue, just as I can fire my grocer by stopping purchases from him or sue him for delivering faulty products. What, then, is the content of the presumed power to manage and assign workers to various tasks? Exactly the same as one little consumer's power to manage and assign his grocer to various tasks. The single consumer can assign his grocer to the task of obtaining whatever the customer can induce the grocer to provide at a price acceptable to both parties. That is precisely all that an employer can do to an employee. To speak of managing, directing, or assigning workers to various tasks is a deceptive way of noting that the employer continually is involved in renegotiation of contracts on terms that must be acceptable to both parties. Telling an employee to type this letter rather than to file that document is like my telling a grocer to sell me this brand of tuna rather than that brand of bread. I have no contract to continue to purchase from the grocer, and neither the employer nor the employee is bound by any contractual obligations to continue their relationship. Long-term contracts between employer and employee are not the essence of the organization we call a firm. My grocer can count on my returning day after day and purchasing his services and goods even with the prices not always marked on the goods—because I know what they are—and he adapts his activity to conform to my directions to him as to what I want each day—he is not my employee.

In what way, then, is the relationship between a grocer and his employee different from that between a grocer and his customers? It is in a *team* use of inputs and a centralized position of some party in the contractual arrangements of *all* other inputs. It is the *centralized contractual agent in a team productive process*—not some superior authoritarian directive or disciplinary power. Exactly what is a team process and why does it induce the contractual form, called the firm? These problems motivate the inquiry of this article.

## THE METERING PROBLEM

The economic organization through which input owners cooperate will make better use of their comparative advantages to the extent that it facilitates the payment of rewards in accord with productivity. If rewards were random and without regard to productive effort, no incentive to productive effort would be provided by the organization; and if rewards were negatively correlated with productivity, the organization would be subject to sabotage. Two key demands are placed on an economic organization—metering input productivity and metering rewards.[1]

Metering problems sometimes can be resolved well through the exchange of products across competitive markets, because in many situations markets yield a high correlation between rewards and productivity. If a farmer increases his output of wheat by 10 percent at the prevailing market price, his receipts also increase by 10 percent. This method of organizing economic activity meters the *output directly*, reveals the marginal product and apportions the *rewards* to resource owners in accord with that direct measurement of their outputs. The success of this decentralized, market exchange in promoting productive specialization requires that changes in market rewards fall on those responsible for changes in *output*.[2]

---

1. Meter means to measure and also to apportion. One can meter (measure) output and one can also meter (control) the output. We use the word to denote both; the context should indicate which.

2. A producer's wealth would be reduced by the present capitalized value of the future income lost by loss of reputation. Reputation, i.e., credibility, is an asset, which is another way of saying that reliable information about expected performance is both a costly and a valuable good. For acts of God that interfere with contract performance, both parties have incentives to reach a settlement akin to that which would have been reached if

The classic relationship in economics that runs from marginal productivity to the distribution of income implicitly *assumes* the existence of an organization, be it the market or the firm, that allocates rewards to resources in accord with their productivity. The problem of economic organization, the economical means of metering productivity and rewards, is not confronted directly in the classical analysis of production and distribution. Instead, that analysis tends to assume sufficiently economic—or zero cost—means, as if productivity automatically created its reward. We conjecture the direction of causation is the reverse—the specific system of rewarding which is relied upon stimulates a particular productivity response. If the economic organization meters poorly, with rewards and productivity only loosely correlated, then productivity will be smaller; but if the economic organization meters well productivity will be greater. What makes metering difficult and hence induces means of economizing on metering costs?

## TEAM PRODUCTION

Two men jointly lift heavy cargo into trucks. Solely by observing the total weight loaded per day, it is impossible to determine each person's marginal productivity. With team production it is difficult, solely by observing total output, either to define or determine *each* individual's contribution to this output of the cooperating inputs. The output is yielded by a team, by definition, and it is not a *sum* of separable outputs of each of its members. Team production of $Z$ involves at least two inputs, $X_i$ and $X_j$, with $\partial^2 Z/\partial X_i \partial X_j \neq 0$.[3] The production function is *not* separable into two functions each involving only inputs $X_i$ or only inputs $X_j$.

---

such events had been covered by specific contingency clauses. The reason, again, is that a reputation for "honest" dealings—i.e., for actions similar to those that would probably have been reached had the contract provided this contingency—is wealth.

Almost every contract is open-ended in that many contingencies are uncovered. For example, if a fire delays production of a promised product by $A$ to $B$, and if $B$ contends that $A$ has not fulfilled the contract, how is the dispute settled and what recompense, if any, does $A$ grant to $B$? A person uninitiated in such questions may be surprised by the extent to which contracts permit either party to escape performance or to nullify the contract. In fact, it is hard to imagine any contract, which, when taken solely in terms of its stipulations, could not be evaded by one of the parties. Yet that is the ruling, viable type of contract. Why? Undoubtedly the best discussion that we have seen on this question is by Stewart Macaulay.

There are means not only of detecting or preventing cheating, but also for deciding how to allocate the losses or gains of unpredictable events or quality of items exchanged. Sales contracts contain warranties, guarantees, collateral, return privileges, and penalty clauses for specific nonperformance. These are means of assignment of *risks* of losses of cheating. A lower price without warranty—an "as is" purchase—places more of the risk on the buyer while the seller buys insurance against losses of his "cheating." On the other hand, a warranty or return privilege or service contract places more risk on the seller with insurance being bought by the buyer.

3. The function is separable into additive functions if the cross partial derivative is zero, i.e., if $\partial^2_Z /\partial X_i \partial X_j = 0$.

Consequently there is no *sum* of $Z$ of two separable functions to treat as the $Z$ of the team production function. (An example of a *separable* case is $Z = aX_i^2 + bX_j^2$ which is separable into $Z_i = aX_i^2$ and $Z_j = bX_j^2$, and $Z = Z_i + Z_j$. This is not team production.) There exist production techniques in which the $Z$ obtained is greater than if $X_i$ and $X_j$ had produced separable $Z$. Team production will be used if it yields an output enough larger than the sum of separable production of $Z$ to cover the costs of organizing and disciplining team members—the topics of this article.[4]

Usual explanations of the gains from cooperative behavior rely on exchange and production in accord with the comparative advantage specialization principle with separable additive production. However, as just suggested, there is a source of gain from cooperative activity involving working as a *team*, wherein individual cooperating inputs do not yield identifiable, separate products which can be *summed* to measure the total output. For this cooperative productive activity, here called "team" production, measuring *marginal* productivity and making payments in accord therewith is more expensive by an order of magnitude than for separable production functions.

Team production, to repeat, is production in which (1) several types of resources are used and (b) the product is not a sum of separable outputs of each cooperating resource. An additional factor creates a team organization problem—(c) not all resources used in team production belong to one person.

We do not inquire into why all the jointly used resources are not owned by one person, but instead into the types of organization, contracts, and informational and payment procedures used among owners of teamed inputs. With respect to the one-owner case, perhaps it is sufficient merely to note that (a) slavery is prohibited, (b) one might assume risk aversion as a reason for one person's not borrowing enough to purchase all the assets or sources of services rather than renting them, and (c) the purchase-resale spread may be so large that costs of short-term ownership exceed rental costs. Our problem is viewed basically as one of organization among different people, not of the physical goods or services, however much there must be selection and choice of combination of the latter.

How can the members of a team be rewarded and induced to work efficiently? In team production, marginal products of cooperative team members are not so directly and separably (i.e., cheaply) observable. What a team offers to the market can be taken as the marginal product of the team but not of the team members. The costs of metering or ascertaining the marginal products of the team's members is what calls forth new organizations and procedures. Clues to each input's productivity can be secured by observing *behavior* of individual inputs. When lifting cargo into the truck, how rapidly does a man move to the

---

4. With sufficient generality of notation and conception this team production function could be formulated as a case of the generalized production function interpretation given by our colleague, E.A. Thompson (1970).

next piece to be loaded, how many cigarette breaks does he take, does the item being lifted tilt downward toward his side?

If detecting such behavior were costless, neither party would have an incentive to shirk, because neither could impose the cost of his shirking on the other (if their cooperation was agreed to voluntarily). But since costs must be incurred to monitor each other, each input owner will have more incentive to shirk when he works as part of a team than if his performance could be monitored easily or if he did not work as a team. If there is a net increase in productivity available by team production, net of the metering cost associated with disciplining the team, then team production will be relied upon rather than a multitude of bilateral exchange of separable individual outputs.

Both leisure and higher income enter a person's utility function.[5] Hence, each person should adjust his work and realized reward so as to equate the marginal rate of substitution between leisure and production of real output to his marginal rate of substitution in consumption. That is, he would adjust his rate of work to bring his demand prices of leisure and output to equality with their true costs. However, with detection, policing, monitoring, measuring, or metering costs, each person will be induced to take more leisure, because the effect of relaxing on *his realized* (reward) rate of substitution between output and leisure will be less than the effect on the *true* rate of substitution. His realized cost of leisure will fall more than the true cost of leisure, so he "buys" more leisure (i.e., more nonpecuniary reward).

If his relaxation cannot be detected perfectly at zero cost, part of its effects will be borne by others in the team, thus making *his* realized cost of relaxation less than the true total cost to the team. The difficulty of detecting such actions permits the private costs of his actions to be less than their full costs. Since each person responds to his private realizable rate of substitution (in production) rather than the true total (i.e., social) rate, and so long as there are costs for other people to detect his shift toward relaxation, it will not pay (them) to force him to readjust completely by making him realize the true cost. Only enough efforts will be made to equate the marginal gains of detection activity with the marginal costs of detection; and that implies a lower rate of productive effort and more shirking than in a costless monitoring, or measuring, world.

In a university, the faculty use office telephones, paper, and mail for personal uses beyond strict university productivity. The university administrators could stop such practices by identifying *the* responsible person in each case, but they can do so only at higher costs than administrators are willing to incur. The extra costs of identifying each party (rather than merely identifying the presence of such activity) would exceed the savings from diminished faculty "turpitudinal peccadilloes." So the faculty is allowed some degree of "privileges, perquisites,

---

5. More precisely: "if anything other than pecuniary income enters his utility function." Leisure stands for all nonpecuniary income for simplicity of exposition.

or fringe benefits." And the total of the pecuniary wages paid is lower because of this irreducible (at acceptable costs) degree of amenity-seizing activity. Pay is lower in pecuniary terms and higher in leisure, conveniences, and ease of work. But still every person would prefer to see detection made more effective (if it were somehow possible to monitor costlessly) so that he, as part of the now more effectively producing team, could thereby realize a higher pecuniary pay and less leisure. If everyone could, at zero cost, have his reward-realized rate brought to the true production possibility real rate, all could achieve a more preferred position. But detection of the responsible parties is costly; that cost acts like a tax on work rewards.[6] Viable shirking is the result.

What forms of organizing team production will lower the cost of detecting "performance" (i.e., marginal productivity) and bring personally realized rates of substitution closer to true rates of substitution? Market competition, in principle, could monitor some team production. (It already *organizes* teams.) Input owners who are not team members can offer, in return for a smaller share of the team's rewards, to replace excessively (i.e., overpaid) shirking members. Market competition among potential team members would determine team membership and individual rewards. There would be no team leader, manager, organizer, owner, or employer. For such decentralized organizational control to work, outsiders, possibly after observing each team's total output, can speculate about their capabilities as team members and, by a market competitive process, revised teams with greater productive ability will be formed and sustained. Incumbent members will be constrained by threats of replacement by outsiders offering services for lower reward shares or offering greater rewards to the other members of the team. Any team member who shirked in the expectation that the reduced output effect would not be attributed to him will be displaced if his activity is detected. Teams of productive inputs, like business units, would evolve in apparent spontaneity in the market—without any central organizing agent, team manager, or boss.

But completely effective control cannot be expected from individualized market competition for two reasons. First, for this competition to be completely effective, new challengers for team membership must know where and to what extent shirking is a serious problem, i.e., know they can increase net output as compared with the inputs they replace. To the extent that this is true, it is probably possible for existing fellow team members to recognize the shirking. But, by definition, the detection of shirking by observing team output is costly for team production. Secondly, assume the presence of detection costs,

6. Do not assume that the sole result of the cost of detecting shirking is one form of payment (more leisure and less take home money). With several members of the team, each has an incentive to cheat against each other by engaging in more than the average amount of such leisure if the employer can not tell at zero cost which employee is taking more than average. As a result the total productivity of the team is lowered. Shirking detection costs thus change the form of payment and also result in lower total rewards. Because the cross partial derivatives are positive, shirking reduces other people's marginal products.

and assume that in order to secure a place on the team a new input owner must accept a smaller share of rewards (or a promise to produce more). Then his incentive to shirk would still be at least as great as the incentives of the inputs replaced, because he still bears less than the entire reduction in team output for which he is responsible.

## THE CLASSICAL FIRM

One method of reducing shirking is for someone to specialize as a monitor to check the input performance of team members.[7] But who will monitor the monitor? One constraint on the monitor is the aforesaid market competition offered by other monitors, but for reasons already given, that is not perfectly effective. Another constraint can be imposed on the monitor: give him title to the net earnings of the team, net of payments to other inputs. If owners of cooperating inputs agree with the monitor that he is to receive any residual product above prescribed amounts (hopefully, the marginal value products of the other inputs), the monitor will have an added incentive not to shirk as a monitor. Specialization in monitoring plus reliance on a residual claimant status will reduce shirking; but additional links are needed to forge the firm of classical economic theory. How will the residual claimant monitor the other inputs?

We use the term monitor to connote several activities in addition to its disciplinary connotation. It connotes measuring output performance, apportioning rewards, observing the input behavior of inputs as means of detecting or estimating their marginal productivity and giving assignments or instructions in what to do and how to do it. (It also includes, as we shall show later, authority to terminate or revise contracts.) Perhaps the contrast between a football coach and team captain is helpful. The coach selects strategies and tactics and sends in instructions about what plays to utilize. The captain is essentially an observer and reporter of the performance at close hand of the members. The latter is an inspector-steward and the former, a supervisor manager. For the present all these activities are included in the rubric "monitoring." All these tasks are, in principle, negotiable across markets, but we are presuming that such market measurement of marginal productivities and job reassignments are not so cheaply performed for team production. And in particular our analysis suggests that it is not so much the costs of spontaneously negotiating contracts in the markets among

---

7. What is meant by performance? Input energy, initiative, work attitude, perspiration, rate of exhaustion? Or output? It is the latter that is sought—the *effect* or output. But performance is nicely ambiguous because it suggests both input and output. It is *nicely* ambiguous because as we shall see, sometimes by inspecting a team member's input activity we can better judge his output effect, perhaps not with complete accuracy but better than by watching the output of the *team*. It is not always the case that watching input activity is the only or best means of detecting, measuring or monitoring output effects of each team member, but in some cases it is a useful way. For the moment the word performance glosses over these aspects and facilitates concentration on other issues.

groups for team production as it is the detection of the performance of individual members of the team that calls for the organization noted here.

The specialist *who receives the residual rewards* will be the monitor of the members of the team (i.e., will manage the use of cooperative inputs). The monitor earns his residual through the reduction in shirking that he brings about, not only by the prices that he agrees to pay the owners of the inputs, but also by observing and directing the actions or uses of these inputs. *Managing or examining the ways to which inputs are used in team production is a method of metering the marginal productivity of individual inputs to the team's output.*

To discipline team members and reduce shirking, the residual claimant must have power to revise the contract terms and incentives of *individual* members without having to terminate or alter every other input's contract. Hence, team members who seek to increase their productivity will assign to the monitor not only the residual claimant right but also the right to alter individual membership and performance on the team. Each team member, of course, can terminate his own membership (i.e., quit the team), but only the monitor may unilaterally terminate the membership of any of the other members without necessarily terminating the team itself or his association with the team; and he alone can expand or reduce membership, alter the mix of membership, or sell the right to be the residual claimant-monitor of the team. It is this entire bundle of rights: (a) to be a residual claimant; (b) to observe input behavior; (c) to be the central party common to all contracts with inputs; (d) to alter the membership of the team; and (e) to sell these rights, that defines the *ownership* (or the employer) of the *classical* (capitalist, free-enterprise) firm. The coalescing of these rights has arisen, our analysis asserts, because it resolves the shirking-information problem of team production better than does the noncentralized contractual arrangement.

The relationship of each team member to the *owner* of the firm (i.e., the party common to all input contracts *and* the residual claimant) is simply a quid pro quo contract. Each makes a purchase and sale. The employee "orders" the owner of the team to pay him money in the same sense that the employer directs the team member to perform certain acts. The employee can terminate the contract as readily as can the employer, and long-term contracts, therefore, are not an essential attribute of the firm. Nor are "authoritarian," "dictational," or "fiat" attributes relevant to the conception of the firm or its efficiency.

In summary, two necessary conditions exist for the emergence of the firm on the prior assumption that more than pecuniary wealth enter utility functions:

1. It is possible to increase productivity through team-oriented production, a production technique for which it is costly to directly measure the marginal outputs of the cooperating inputs. This makes it more difficult to restrict shirking through simple market exchange between cooperating inputs.

2. It is economical to estimate marginal productivity by observing or specifying input behavior. The simultaneous occurrence of both these preconditions leads to the contractual organization of inputs, known as the *classical capitalist firms* with (a) joint input production, (b) several input owners, (c) one party who is common to all the contracts of the joint inputs, (d) who has rights to renegotiate any input's contract independently of contracts with other input owners, (e) who holds the residual claim, and (f) who has the right to sell his central contractual residual status.[8]

### Other Theories of the Firm

At this juncture, as an aside, we briefly place this theory of the firm in the contexts of those offered by Coase (1952) and Knight (1965).[9] Our view of the firm is not necessarily inconsistent with Coase's; we attempt to go further and identify refutable implications. Coase's penetrating insight is to make more of the fact that markets do not operate costlessly, and he relies on the cost of using markets to *form* contracts as his basic explanation for the existence of firms. We do not disagree with the proposition that, ceteris paribus, the higher is the cost of transacting across markets the greater will be the comparative advantage of organizing resources within the firm; it is a difficult proposition to disagree with or to refute. We could with equal ease subscribe to a theory of the firm based on the cost of managing, for surely it is true that, ceteris paribus, the lower is the cost of managing the greater will be the comparative advantage of organizing resources within the firm. To move the theory forward, it is necessary to know what is meant by a firm and to explain the circumstances under which the cost of "managing" resources is low relative to the cost of allocating resources through market transaction. The conception of and rationale for the classical firm that we propose takes a step down the path pointed out by Coase toward that goal. Consideration of team production, team organization, difficulty in metering outputs, and the problem of shirking are important to our explanation but, so far as we can ascertain, not in Coase's. Coase's analysis insofar as it had heretofore been developed would suggest open-ended contracts but does not appear to imply anything more—neither the residual claimant status nor the distinction between employee and subcontractor status (nor any of the implications indicated below). And it is not true that employees are generally employed on the basis of long-term contractual arrangements any more than on a series of short-term or indefinite length contracts.

The importance of our proposed additional elements is revealed, for example, by the explanation of why the person to whom the control monitor is responsible receives the residual, and also by our later discussion of the implica-

---

8. Removal of (b) converts a capitalist proprietary firm to a socialist firm.
9. Recognition must also be made to the seminal inquiries by Silver and Auster (1969) and by Malmgren (1961).

tions about the corporation, partnerships, and profit-sharing. These alternative forms for organization of the firm are difficult to resolve on the basis of market transaction costs only. Our exposition also suggests a definition of the classical firm—something crucial that was heretofore absent.

In addition, sometimes a technological development will lower the cost of market transactions while, at the same time, it expands the role of the firm. When the "putting out" system was used for weaving, inputs were organized largely through market negotiations. With the development of efficient central sources of power, it became economical to perform weaving in proximity to the power source and to engage in team production. The bringing in of weavers surely must have resulted in a reduction in the cost of negotiating (forming) contracts. Yet, what we observe is the beginning of the factory system in which inputs are organized within a firm. Why? The weavers did not simply move to a common source of power that they could tap like an electric line, purchasing power while they used their own equipment. Now team production in the joint use of equipment became more important. The measurement of marginal productivity, which now involved interactions between workers, especially through their joint use of machines, became more difficult though contract negotiating cost was reduced, while managing the *behavior* of inputs became easier because of the increased centralization of activity. The firm as an organization expanded even though the cost of transactions was reduced by the advent of centralized power. The same could be said for modern assembly lines. Hence the emergence of central power sources expanded the scope of productive activity in which the firm enjoyed a comparative advantage as an organizational form.

Some economists, following Knight, have identified the bearing of risks of wealth changes with the director or central employer without explaining why that is a viable arrangement. Presumably, the more risk-averse inputs become employees rather than owners of the classical firm. Risk averseness and uncertainty *with regard to the firm's fortunes* have little, if anything, to do with our explanation, although it helps to explain why all resources in a team are not owned by one person. That is, the role of risk taken in the sense of absorbing the windfalls that buffet the firm because of unforeseen competition, technological change, or fluctuations in demand are not central to our theory, although it is true that imperfect knowledge and, therefore, risk, in *this* sense of risk, underlie the problem of monitoring team behavior. We deduce the system of paying the manager with a residual claim (the equity) from the desire to have efficient means to reduce shirking so as to make team production economical and not from the smaller aversion to the risks of enterprise in a dynamic economy. We conjecture that "distribution-of-risk" is not a valid rationale for the *existence* and organization of the *classical* firm.

Although we have emphasized team production as creating a costly metering task and have treated team production as an essential (necessary?) condition for the firm, would not other obstacles to cheap metering also call forth the same kind of contractual arrangement here denoted as a firm? For example, suppose a farmer produces wheat in an easily ascertained quantity but with subtle and difficult to detect quality variations determined by how the farmer grew the wheat. A vertical integration could allow a purchaser to control the farmer's behavior in order to estimate productivity more economically. But this is not a case of joint or team production, unless "information" can be considered part of the product. (While a good case could be made for that broader conception of production, we shall ignore it here.) Instead of forming a firm, a buyer can contract to have his inspector on the site of production, just as home builders contract with architects to supervise building contracts; that arrangement is not a firm. Still, a firm might be organized in the production of many products wherein no team production or jointness of use of separately owned resources is involved.

This possibility rather clearly indicates a broader, or complementary, approach to that which we have chosen.

1. As we do in this article, it can be argued that the firm is the particular policing device utilized when joint team production is present. If other sources of high policing costs arise, as in the wheat case just indicated, some other form of contractual arrangement will be used. Thus, to each source of informational cost there may be a different type of policing and contractual arrangement.

2. On the other hand, one can say that where policing is difficult across markets, various forms of contractual arrangements are devised, but there is no reason for that known as the firm to be uniquely related or even highly correlated with team production, as defined here. It might be used equally probably and viably for other sources of high policing cost. We have not intensively analyzed other sources, and we can only note that our current and readily revisable conjecture is that the first approach is valid, and has motivated us in our current endeavor. In any event, the test of the theory advanced here is to see whether the conditions we have identified are necessary for firms to have long-run viability rather than merely births with high infant mortality. Conglomerate firms or collections of separate production agencies into one owning organization can be interpreted as an investment trust or investment diversification device— probably along the lines that motivated Knight's interpretation. A holding company can be called a firm because of the common association of the word firm with any ownership unit that owns income sources. The term firm as commonly used is so turgid of meaning that we can not hope to explain every entity to which the name is attached in common or even technical literature. Instead, we seek to identify and explain a particular contractual arrangement induced by the cost of information factors analyzed here.

## TYPES OF FIRMS

### Profit-Sharing Firms

Explicit in our explanation of the capitalist firm is the assumption that the cost of *managing* the team's inputs by a central monitor, who disciplines himself because he is a residual claimant, is low relative to the cost of metering the marginal outputs of team members.

If we look within a firm to see who monitors—hires, fires, changes, promotes, and renegotiates—we should find him being a residual claimant or, at least, one whose pay or reward is more than any others correlated with fluctuations in the residual value of the firm. They more likely will have options or rights or bonuses than will inputs with other tasks.

An implicit "auxiliary" assumption of our explanation of the firm is that the cost of team production is increased if the residual claim is not held entirely by the central monitor. That is, we assume that if profit sharing had to be relied upon for *all* team members, losses from the resulting increase in central monitor shirking would exceed the output gains from the increased incentives of other team members not to shirk. If the optimal team size is only two owners of inputs, then an equal division of profits and losses between them will leave each with stronger incentives to reduce shirking than if the optimal team size is large, for in the latter case only a smaller percentage of the losses occasioned by the shirker will be borne by him. Incentives to shirk are positively related to the optimal size of the team under an equal profit-sharing scheme.[10]

The preceding does not imply that profit-sharing is never viable. Profit-sharing to encourage self-policing is more appropriate for small teams. And, indeed, where input owners are free to make whatever contractual arrangements suit them, as generally is true in capitalist economies, profit-sharing seems largely limited to partnerships with a relatively small number of *active*[11] partners. Another advantage of such arrangements for smaller teams is that it permits more effective reciprocal monitoring among inputs. Monitoring need not be entirely specialized.

Profit-sharing is more viable if small team size is associated with situations where the cost of specialized management of inputs is large relative to the increased productivity potential in team effort. We conjecture that the cost of managing team inputs increases if the productivity of a team member is difficult to correlate with his behavior. In "artistic" or "professional" work, watching a man's activities is not a good clue to what he is actually thinking or doing with his mind. While it is relatively easy to manage or direct the loading of trucks by a team of dock workers where input activity is so highly related in an obvious way to output, it is more difficult to manage and direct a lawyer in the preparation and presentation of a case. Dock workers can be directed in detail without the monitor himself loading the truck, and assembly-line workers can be monitored by varying the speed of the assembly line, but detailed direction in the preparation of a law case would require in much greater degree that the monitor

10. While the degree to which residual claims are centralized will affect the size of the team, this will be only one of many factors that determine team size, so as an approximation, we can treat team size as exogenously determined. Under certain assumptions about the shape of the "typical" utility function, the incentive to avoid shirking with unequal profit-sharing can be measured by the Herfindahl index.

11. The use of the word active will be clarified in our discussion of the corporation, which follows.

prepare the case himself. As a result, artistic or professional inputs, such as lawyers, advertising specialists, and doctors, will be given relatively freer reign with regard to individual behavior. If the management of inputs is relatively costly or ineffective, as it would seem to be in these cases, but nonetheless if team effort is more productive than separable production with exchange across markets, then there will develop a tendency to use profit-sharing schemes to provide incentives to avoid shirking.[12]

### Socialist Firms

We have analyzed the classical proprietorship and the profit-sharing firms in the context of free association and choice of economic organization. Such organizations need not be the most viable when political constraints limit the forms of organization that can be chosen. It is one thing to have profit-sharing when professional or artistic talents are used by small teams. But if political or tax or subsidy considerations induce profit-sharing techniques when these are not otherwise economically justified, then additional management techniques will be developed to help reduce the degree of shirking.

For example, most, if not all, firms in Yugoslavia are owned by the employees in the restricted sense that all share in the residual. This is true for large firms and for firms which employ nonartistic, or nonprofessional, workers as well. With a decay of political constraints, most of these firms could be expected to rely on paid wages rather than shares in the residual. This rests on our auxiliary assumption that general sharing in the residual results in losses from enhanced shirking by the monitor that exceed the gains from reduced shirking by residual-sharing employees. If this were not so, profit-sharing with employees should have occurred more frequently in Western societies where such organizations are neither banned nor preferred politically. Where residual sharing by employees is politically imposed, as in Yugoslavia, we are led to expect that some management technique will arise to reduce the shirking by the central monitor, a technique that will not be found frequently in Western societies since the monitor retains all (or much) of the residual in the West and profit-sharing is largely confined to small, professional-artistic team production situations. We do find in the larger scale residual-sharing firms in Yugoslavia that there are employee committees that can recommend (to the state) the termination of a managers' contract (veto his continuance) with the enterprise. We conjecture that the workers' committee is given the right to recommend the termination of the manager's contract precisely because the general sharing of the residual increases "excessively" the manager's incentive to shirk.[13]

12. Some sharing contracts, like crop-sharing or rental payments based on gross sales in retail stores, come close to profit-sharing. However, it is gross output sharing rather than profit-sharing. We are unable to specify the implications of the difference. We refer the reader to Cheung (1969b).

13. Incidentally, investment activity will be changed. The inability to capitalize the investment value as "take-home" private property *wealth* of the members of the

### The Corporation

All firms must initially acquire command over some resources. The corporation does so primarily by selling promises of future returns to those who (as creditors or owners) provide financial capital. In some situations resources can be acquired in advance from consumers by promises of future delivery (for example, advance sale of a proposed book). Or where the firm is a few artistic or professional persons, each can "chip in" with time and talent until the sale of services brings in revenues. For the most part, capital can be acquired more cheaply if many (risk-averse) investors contribute small portions to a large investment. The economies of raising large sums of equity capital in this way suggest that modifications in the relationship among corporate inputs are required to cope with the shirking problem that arises with profit-sharing among large numbers of corporate stockholders. One modification is limited liability, especially for firms that are large relative to a stockholder's wealth. It serves to protect stockholders from large losses no matter how they are caused.

If every stock owner participated in each decision in a corporation, not only would large bureaucratic costs be incurred but many would shirk the task of becoming well informed on the issue to be decided, since the losses associated with unexpectedly bad decisions will be borne in large part by the many other corporate shareholders. More effective control of corporate activity is achieved for most purposes by transferring decision authority to a smaller group, whose main function is to negotiate with and manage (renegotiate with) the other inputs of the team. The corporate stockholders retain the authority to revise the membership of the management group and over major decisions that affect the structure of the corporation or its dissolution.

As a result of a new modification of partnerships is induced—the right to sale of corporate shares without approval of any other stockholders. Any shareholder can remove his wealth from control by those with whom he has differences of opinion. Rather than try to control the decisions of the management, which is harder to do with many stockholders than with only a few, unrestricted salability provides a more acceptable escape to each stockholder from continued policies with which he disagrees.

Indeed, the policing of managerial shirking relies on across-market competition from new groups of would-be managers as well as competition from members within the firm who seek to displace existing management. In addition to competition from outside and inside managers, control is facilitated by the temporary congealing of share votes into voting blocs owned by one or a few contenders. Proxy battles or stock-purchases concentrate the votes required to displace the existing management or modify managerial policies. But it is more

firm means that the benefits of the investment must be taken as annual income by those who are employed at the time of the income. Investment will be confined more to those with shorter life and with higher rates or payoffs if the alternative of investing is paying out the firm's income to its employees to take home and use as private property. For a development of this proposition, see Furubotn and Pejovich (1970a) and Pejovich (1969a).

than a change in policy that is sought by the newly formed financial interests, whether of new stockholders or not. It is the capitalization of expected future benefits into stock prices that concentrates on the innovators the wealth gains of their actions if they own large numbers of shares. Without capitalization of future benefits, there would be less incentive to incur the costs required to exert informed decisive influence on the corporation's policies and managing personnel. Temporarily, the structure of ownership is reformed, moving away from diffused ownership into decisive power blocs, and this is a transient resurgence of the classical firm with power again concentrated in those who have title to the residual.

In assessing the significance of stockholders' power it is not the usual diffusion of voting power that is significant but instead the frequency with which voting congeals into decisive changes. Even a one-man owned company may have a long term with just one manager—continuously being approved by the owner. Similarly a dispersed voting power corporation may be also characterized by a long-lived management. The question is the probability of replacement of the management if it behaves in ways not acceptable to a majority of the stockholders. The unrestricted salability of stock and the transfer of proxies enhances the probability of decisive action in the event current stockholders or any outsider believes that management is not doing a good job with the corporation. We are not comparing the corporate responsiveness to that of a single proprietorship; instead, we are indicating features of the corporate structure that are induced by the problem of delegated authority to manager-monitors.[14]

14. Instead of thinking of shareholders as joint *owners*, we can think of them as investors, like bondholders, except that the stockholders are more optimistic than bondholders about the enterprise prospects. Instead of buying bonds in the corporation, thus enjoying smaller risks, shareholders prefer to invest funds with a greater realizable return if the firm prospers as expected, but with smaller (possibly negative) returns if the firm performs in a manner closer to that expected by the more pessimistic investors. The pessimistic investors, in turn, regard only the bonds as likely to pay off.

If the entrepreneur-organizer is to raise capital on the best terms to him, it is to his advantage, as well as that of prospective investors, to recognize these differences in expectations. The residual claim on earnings enjoyed by shareholders does not serve the function of enhancing their efficiency as monitors in the general situation. The stockholders are "merely" the less risk-averse or the more optimistic member of the group that finances the firm. Being more optimistic than the average and seeing a higher mean value future return, they are willing to pay more for a certificate that allows them to realize gain on their expectations. One method of doing so is to buy claims to the distribution of returns that "they see" while bondholders, who are more pessimistic, purchase a claim to the distribution that they see as more likely to emerge. Stockholders are then comparable to warrant holders. They care not about the voting rights (usually not attached to warrants); they are in the same position in so far as voting rights are concerned as are bondholders. The only difference is in the probability distribution of rewards and the terms on which they can place their bets.

If we treat bondholders, preferred and convertible preferred stockholders, and common stockholders and warrant holders as simply different classes of investors—differing not only in their risk averseness but in their beliefs about the probability distribution of the firm's future earnings, why should stockholders be regarded as "owners" in any sense distinct from the other financial investors? The entrepreneur-organizer, who, let us assume,

## Mutual and Nonprofit Firms

The benefits obtained by the new management are greater if the stock can be purchased and sold, because this enables *capitalization* of anticipated future improvements into present *wealth* of new managers who bought stock and created a larger capital by their management changes. But in nonprofit corporations, colleges, churches, country clubs, mutual savings banks, mutual insurance companies, and "coops," the future consequences of improved management are not capitalized into present wealth of stockholders. (As if to make more difficult that competition by new would-be monitors, multiple shares of ownership in those enterprises cannot be bought by one person.) One should, therefore, find greater shirking in nonprofit, mutually owned enterprises. (This suggests that nonprofit enterprises are especially appropriate in realms of

---

is the chief operating officer and sole repository of control of the corporation, does not find his authority residing in common stockholders (except in the case of a take over). Does this type of control make any difference in the way the firm is conducted? Would it make any difference in the kinds of behavior that would be tolerated by competing managers and investors (and we here deliberately refrain from thinking of them as owner-stockholders in the traditional sense)?

Investment old timers recall a significant incidence of nonvoting common stock, now prohibited in corporations whose stock is traded on listed exchanges. (Why prohibited?) The entrepreneur in those days could hold voting shares while investors held nonvoting shares, which in every other respect were identical. Nonvoting share holders were simply investors devoid of ownership connotations. The control and behavior of inside owners in such corporations has never, so far as we have ascertained, been carefully studied. For example, at the simplest level of interest, does the evidence indicate that nonvoting shareholders fared any worse because of not having voting rights? Did owners permit the nonvoting holders the normal return available to voting shareholders? Though evidence is prohibitively expensive to obtain, it is remarkable that voting and nonvoting shares sold for essentially identical prices, even during some proxy battles. However, our casual evidence deserves no more than interest-initiating weight.

One more point. The facade is deceptive. Instead of nonvoting shares, today we have warrants, convertible preferred stocks all of which are solely or partly "equity" claims without voting rights, though they could be converted into voting shares.

In sum, it is the case that the stockholder-investor relationship is one emanating from the *division* of *ownership* among several people, or is it that the collection of investment funds from people of varying anticipations is the underlying factor? If the latter, why should any of them be thought of as the owners in whom voting rights, whatever they may signify or however exercisable, should reside in order to enhance efficiency? Why voting rights in any of the outside, participating investors?

Our initial perception of this possibly significant difference in interpretation was precipitated by Henry Manne (1967). A reading of his article makes it clear that it is hard to understand why an investor who wishes to back and "share" in the consequences of some new business should necessarily have to acquire voting power (i.e., power to change the manager-operator) in order to invest in the venture. In fact, we invest in some ventures in the hope that no other stockholders will be so "foolish" as to try to toss out the incumbent management. We want him to have the power to stay in office, and for the prospect of sharing in his fortunes we buy nonvoting common stock. Our willingness to invest is enhanced by the knowledge that we can act legally via fraud, embezzlement, and other laws to help assure that we outside investors will not be "milked" beyond our initial discounted anticipations.

endeavor where more shirking is desired and where redirected uses of the enterprise in response to market-revealed values is less desired.)

### Partnerships

Team production in artistic or professional intellectual skills will more likely be by partnerships than other types of team production. This amounts to market-organized team activity and to a non-employer status. Self-monitoring partnerships, therefore, will be used rather than employer-employee contracts, and these organizations will be small to prevent an excessive dilution of efforts through shirking. Also, partnerships are more likely to occur among relatives or long-standing acquaintances, not necessarily because they share a common utility function but also because each knows better the other's work characteristics and tendencies to shirk.

### Employee Unions

Employee unions, whatever else they do, perform as monitors for employees. Employers monitor employees, and similarly employees monitor an employer's performance. Are correct wages paid on time and in good currency? Usually, this is extremely easy to check. But some forms of employer performance are less easy to meter and are more subject to employer shirking. Fringe benefits often are in nonpecuniary, contingent form; medical, hospital, and accident insurance, and retirement pensions are contingent payments or performances partly in *kind* by employers to employees. Each employee cannot judge the character of such payments as easily as money wages. Insurance is a contingent payment—what the employee will get upon the contingent event may come as a disappointment. If he could easily determine what other employees had gotten upon such contingent events, he could judge more accurately the performance by the employer. He could "trust" the employer not to shirk in such fringe contingent payment, but he would prefer an effective and economic monitor of those payments. We see a specialist monitor—the union employees' agent—hired by them and monitoring those aspects of employer payment most difficult for the employees to monitor. Employees should be willing to employ a specialist monitor to administer such hard-to-detect employer performance, even though their monitor has incentives to use pension and retirement funds not entirely for the benefit of employees.

## TEAM SPIRIT AND LOYALTY

Every team member would prefer a team in which no one, not even himself, shirked. Then the true marginal costs and values could be equated to achieve more preferred positions. If one could enhance a common interest in nonshirking in the guise of a team loyalty or team spirit, the team would be more efficient.

In those sports where team activity is most clearly exemplified, the sense of loyalty and team spirit is most strongly urged. Obviously the team is better, with team spirit and loyalty, because of the reduced shirking—not because of some other feature inherent in loyalty or spirit as such.[15]

Corporations and business firms try to instill a spirit of loyalty. This should not be viewed simply as a device to increase profits by *over*working or misleading the employees, nor as an adolescent urge for belonging. It promotes a closer approximation to the employees' potentially available true rates of substitution between production and leisure and enables each team member to achieve a more preferred situation. The difficulty, of course, is to create economically that team spirit and loyalty. It can be preached with an aura of moral code of conduct—a morality with literally the same basis as the ten commandments—to restrict our conduct toward what we would choose if we bore our full costs.

## KINDS OF INPUTS OWNED BY THE FIRM

To this point the discussion has examined why firms, as we have defined them, exist? That is, why is there an owner-employer who is the common party to contracts with other owners of inputs in team activity? The answer to that question should also indicate the kind of the jointly used resources likely to be

15. *Sports Leagues*: Professional sports contests among teams is typically conducted by a *league* of teams. We assume that sports consumers are interested not only in absolute sporting skill but also in skills *relative* to other teams. Being slightly better than opposing teams enables one to claim a major portion of the receipts; the inferior team does not release resources and reduce costs, since they were expected in the play of contest. Hence, absolute skill is developed beyond the equality of marginal investment in sporting skill with its true social marginal value product. It follows that there will be a tendency to overinvest in training athletes and developing teams. "Reverse shirking" arises, as budding players are induced to overpractice hyperactively relative to the social marginal value of their enhanced skills. To prevent overinvestment, the teams seek an agreement with each other to restrict practice, size of teams, and even pay of the team members (which reduces incentives of young people to overinvest in developing skills). Ideally, if all the contestant teams were owned by one owner, overinvestment in sports would be avoided, much as ownership of common fisheries or underground oil or water reserve would prevent overinvestment. This hyperactivity (to suggest the opposite of shirking) is controlled by the league of teams, wherein the league adopts a common set of constraints on each team's behavior. In effect, the teams are no longer really owned by the team owners but are supervised by them, much as the franchisers of some product. They are not full-fledged owners of their business, including the brand name, and can not "do what they wish" as franchises. Comparable to the franchiser, is the league commissioner or conference president, who seeks to restrain hyperactivity, as individual team supervisors compete with each other and cause external diseconomies. Such restraints are usually regarded as anticompetitive, antisocial, collusive-cartel devices to restrain free open competition, and reduce players' salaries. However, the interpretation presented here is premised on an attempt to avoid hyperinvestment in team sports production. Of course, the team operators have an incentive, once the league is formed and restraints are placed on hyperinvestment activity, to go further and obtain the private benefits of monopoly restriction. To what extent overinvestment is replaced by monopoly restriction is not yet determinable; nor have we seen an empirical test

owned by the central-owner-monitor and the kind likely to be hired from people who are not team-owners. Can we identify characteristics or features of various inputs that lead to their being hired or to their being owned by the firm?

How can residual-claimant, central-employer-owner demonstrate ability to pay the other hired inputs the promised amount in the event of a loss? He can pay in advance or he can commit wealth sufficient to cover negative residuals. The latter will take the form of machines, land, buildings, or raw materials committed to the firm. Commitments of labor-wealth (i.e., human wealth) given the property rights in people, is less feasible. These considerations suggest that residual claimants—owners of the firm—will be investors of resalable capital equipment in the firm. The goods or inputs more likely to be invested than rented by the owners of the enterprise will have higher resale values relative to the initial cost and will have longer expected use in a firm relative to the economic life of the good.

But beyond these factors are those developed above to explain the existence of the institution known as the firm—the costs of detecting output performance. When a durable resource is used, it will have a marginal product and a depreciation. Its use requires payment to cover at least use-induced depreciation; unless that user cost is specifically detectable, payment for it will be demanded in accord with *expected* depreciation. And we can ascertain circumstances for each. An indestructible hammer with a readily detectable marginal product has zero user cost. But suppose the hammer were destructible and that careless (which is easier than careful) use is more abusive and causes greater depreciation of the hammer. Suppose in addition the abuse is easier to detect by observing the way it is used than by observing only the hammer after its use, or by measuring the output scored from a hammer by a laborer. If the hammer were rented and used in the absence of the owner, the depreciation would be greater than if the use were observed by the owner and the user charged in accord with the imposed depreciation. (Careless use is more likely than careful use—if one does not pay for the greater depreciation.) An absentee owner would therefore ask for a higher rental price because of the higher *expected* user cost than if the item were used by the owner. The expectation is higher because of the greater difficulty of observing specific user cost, by inspection of the hammer after use. Renting is therefore in this case more costly than owner use. This is the valid content of the misleading expressions about ownership being more economical than renting—ignoring all other factors that may work in the opposite direction, like tax provision, short-term occupancy, and capital risk avoidance.

---

of these two competing, but mutually consistent interpretations. This interpretation of league-sports activity was proposed by Thompson (1970) and formulated by Canes (1970). Again, athletic teams clearly exemplify the specialization of monitoring with captains and coaches; a captain detects shirkers while the coach trains and selects strategies and tactics. Both functions may be centralized in one person.

Better examples are tools of the trade. Watch repairers, engineers, and carpenters tend to own their own tools especially if they are portable. Trucks are more likely to be employee-owned rather than other equally expensive team inputs because it is relatively cheap for the driver to police the care taken in using a truck. Policing the use of trucks by a nondriver owner is more likely to occur for trucks that are not specialized to one driver, like public transit buses.

The factor with which we are concerned here is one related to the costs of monitoring not only the gross product performance of an input but also the abuse or depreciation inflicted on the input in the course of its use. If depreciation or user cost is more cheaply detected when the owner can see its use than by only seeing the input before and after, there is a force toward owner use rather than renting. Resources whose user cost is harder to detect when used by someone else tend on this count to be owner-used. Absentee ownership, in the lay language, will be less likely. Assume momentarily that labor service cannot be performed in the absence of its owner. The labor owner can more cheaply monitor any abuse of himself than if somehow labor-services could be provided without the labor owner observing its mode of use or knowing what was happening. Also his incentive to abuse himself is increased if he does not own himself.[16]

The similarity between the preceding analysis and the question of absentee landlordism and of sharecropping arrangements is no accident. The same factors which explain the contractual arrangements known as a firm help to explain the incidence of tenancy, labor-hiring, or sharecropping.[17]

---

16. Professional athletes in baseball, football, and basketball, where athletes having sold their source of service to the team owners upon entering into sports activity, are owned by team owners. Here the team owners must monitor the athletes' physical condition and behavior to protect the team owners' wealth. The athlete has *less* (not, *no*) incentive to protect or enhance his athletic prowess since capital value changes have less impact on his own wealth and more on the team owners. Thus, some athletes sign up for big initial bonuses (representing present capital value of future services). Future salaries are lower by the annuity value of the prepaid "bonus" and hence the athlete has *less* to lose by subsequent abuse of his athletic prowess. Any decline in his subsequent service value would in part be borne by the team owner who owns the players' future service. This does not say these losses of future salaries have no effect on preservation of athletic talent (we are not making a "sunk cost" error). Instead, we assert that the preservation is reduced, not eliminated, because the amount of loss of wealth suffered is smaller. The athlete will spend less to maintain or enhance his prowess thereafter. The effect of this revised incentive system is evidenced in comparisons of the kinds of attention and care imposed on the athletes at the "expense of the team owner" in the case where atheletes' future services are owned by the team owner with that where future labor service values are owned by the athlete himself. Why athletes' future athletic services are owned by the team owner rather than being hired is a question we should be able to answer. One presumption is cartelization and monopsony gains to team owners. Another is exactly the theory being expounded in this paper—costs of monitoring production of athletes; we know not on which to rely.

17. The analysis used by Cheung (1969b) in explaining the prevalence of sharecropping and land tenancy arrangements is built squarely on the same factors—the costs of detecting output performance of jointly used inputs in team production and the costs of detecting user costs imposed on the various inputs if owner used or if rented.

### Firms as a Specialized Market Institution for Collecting, Collating, and Selling Input Information

The firm serves as a highly specialized surrogate market. Any person contemplating a joint-input activity must search and detect the qualities of available joint inputs. He could contact an employment agency, but that agency in a small town would have little advantage over a large firm with many inputs. The employer, by virtue of monitoring many inputs, acquires special superior information about their productive talents. This aids his *directive* (i.e., market hiring) efficiency. He "sells" his information to employee-inputs as he aids them in ascertaining good input combinations for team activity. Those who work as employees or who rent services to him are using him to discern superior combinations of inputs. Not only does the director-employer "decide" what each input will produce, he also estimates which heterogeneous inputs will work together jointly more efficiently, and he does this in the context of a privately owned market for forming teams. The department store is a firm and is a superior private market. People who shop and work in one town can as well shop and work in a privately owned firm.

This marketing function is obscured in the theoretical literature by the assumption of homogeneous factors. Or it is tacitly left for individuals to do themselves via personal market search, much as if a person had to search without benefit of specialist retailers. Whether or not the firm arose because of this efficient information service, it gives the director-employer more knowledge about the productive talents of the team's inputs, and a basis for superior decisions about efficient or profitable combinations of those heterogeneous resources.

In other words, opportunities for profitable team production by inputs already within the firm may be ascertained more economically and accurately than for resources outside the firm. Superior combinations of inputs can be more economically identified and formed from resources already used in the organization than by obtaining new resources (and knowledge of them) from the outside. Promotion and revision of employee assignments (contracts) will be preferred by a firm to the hiring of new inputs. To the extent that this occurs there is reason to expect the firm to be able to operate as a conglomerate rather than persist in producing a single product. Efficient production with heterogeneous resources is a result not of having *better* resources but in *knowing more accurately* the relative productive performances of those resources. Poorer resources can be paid less in accord with their inferiority; greater accuracy of knowledge of the potential and actual productive actions of inputs rather than having high productivity resources makes a firm (or an assignment of inputs) profitable.[18]

18. According to our interpretation, the firm is a specialized surrogate for a market for team use of inputs; it provides superior (i.e., cheaper) collection and collation of knowledge about heterogeneous resources. The greater the set of inputs about which knowl-

## SUMMARY

While ordinary contracts facilitate efficient specialization according to comparative advantage, a special class of contracts among a group of joint inputs to a team production process is commonly used for team production. Instead of multilateral contracts among all the joint inputs' owners, a central common party to a set of bilateral contracts facilitates efficient organization of the joint inputs in team production. The terms of the contracts form the basis of the entity called the firm—especially appropriate for organizing team production processes.

Team productive activity is that in which a union, or joint use, of inputs yields a larger output than the sum of the products of the separately used inputs. This team production requires—like all other production processes—an assessment of marginal productivities if efficient production is to be achieved. Nonseparability of the products of several differently owned joint inputs raises the cost of assessing the marginal productivities of those resources or services of each input owner. Monitoring or metering the productivities to match marginal productivities to costs of inputs and thereby to reduce shirking can be achieved more economically (than by across market bilateral negotiations among inputs) in a firm.

The essence of the classical firm is identified here as a contractual structure with: (a) joint input production; (b) several input owners; (c) one party who is common to all the contracts of the joint inputs; (d) who has rights to renegotiate any input's contract independently of contracts with other input owners; (e) who holds the residual claim; and (f) who has the right to sell his central contractual residual status. The central agent is called the firm's owner and the employer. No authoritarian control is involved; the arrangement is simply a contractual structure subject to continuous renegotiation with the central agent. The contractual structure arises as a means of enhancing efficient organization of team production. In particular, the ability to detect shirking among owners of jointly used inputs in team production is enhanced (detection costs are reduced) by this arrangement and the discipline (by revision of contracts) of input owners is made more economic.

---

edge of performance is being collated within a firm the greater are the present costs of the collation activity. Then, the larger the firm (market) the greater the attenuation of monitor control. To counter this force, the firm will be divisionalized in ways that economize on those costs—just as will the market be specialized. So far as we can ascertain, other theories of the reasons for firms have no such implications.

In Japan, employees by custom work nearly their entire lives with one firm, and the firm agrees to that expectation. Firms will tend to be large and conglomerate to enable a broader scope of input revision. Each firm is, in effect, a small economy engaging in "intranational and international" trade. Analogously, Americans expect to spend their whole lives in the United States, and the bigger the country, in terms of variety of resources, the easier it is to adjust to changing tastes and circumstances. Japan, with its lifetime employees, should be characterized more by large, conglomerate firms. Presumably, at some size of the firm, specialized knowledge about inputs becomes as expensive to transmit across divisions of the firms as it does across markets to other firms.

Testable implications are suggested by the analysis of different types of organizations—nonprofit, proprietary for profit, unions, cooperatives, partnerships, and by the kinds of inputs that tend to be owned by the firm in contrast to those employed by the firm.

We conclude with a highly conjectural but possibly significant interpretation. As a consequence of the flow of information to the central party (employer), the firm takes on the characteristic of an efficient market in that information about the productive characteristics of a large set of specific inputs is now more cheaply available. Better recombinations or new uses of resources can be more efficiently ascertained than by the conventional search through the general market. In this sense inputs compete with each other within and via a firm rather than solely across markets as conventionally conceived. Emphasis on interfirm competition obscures intrafirm competition among inputs. Conceiving competition as the *revelation and exchange* of knowledge or information about qualities, potential uses of different inputs in different potential applications indicates that the firm is a device for enhancing competition among sets of input resources as well as a device for more efficiently rewarding the inputs. In contrast to markets and cities which can be viewed as publicly or nonowned market places, the firm can be considered a privately owned market; if so, we could consider the firm and the ordinary market as competing types of markets, competition between private proprietary markets and public or communal markets. Could it be that the market suffers from the defects of communal property rights in organizing and influencing uses of valuable resources?

Chapter Twenty-two

# Managerial Behavior in the Theory of Comparative Economic Systems

J. Moore

Paper presented at the Southern Economic Association Meetings, 1972.
Printed by permission of the author.

Theories of managerial behavior in capitalist and socialist economic systems usually employ simplifying assumptions about the motivation of the managers. These are commonly based on profit, bonus, and net income per worker maximization in the capitalist, centrally directed socialist, and Illyrian socialist cases respectively.[1] Recently, the capitalist theory has been subjected to criticism under some circumstances, and a more general theory, based on constrained utility maximization, is emerging in its place.

This chapter argues that the objections to the capitalist theory are equally applicable to the socialist theories. Furthermore, all three can be derived from the more general theory of constrained utility maximization, and the derivation in each case involves assuming away the same factor, the costs of monitoring managerial behavior. In this way, analysis based on the more general theory, as developed in recent work in property rights analysis, seems broadly applicable to the study of comparative economic systems. Finally, useful insights into problems of the socialist economies are gained by use of this approach.

## MANAGERIAL BEHAVIOR IN CAPITALIST ORGANIZATIONS

An idealization of a theory is derived from it by allowing certain variables to take on extreme values. As an example of this relation in the physical sciences, Richard Rudner gives the Boyle-Charles law of perfect gases, an idealization of the more general kinetic theory. In the idealization, molecular volume and intermolecular attraction are variables given the extreme values of zero.[2] A similar relation

---

1. In Rudner's terms, these "theories" are idealizations which, in principle, can be derived from more general theories by assigning extreme values to certain variables. See Rudner (1966).

2. The methodological points draw heavily on Rudner's (1966) work. Rudner argues (pp. 61–62) that idealizations in the social sciences have not been as fruitful as those in the physical sciences for three reasons:

a. There is no general theory of social action by means of which the applicability of particular idealization can be assessed.

seems to exist between the general economic theory of utility maximization and the theory of the firm, in which profit maximization is assumed. Individuals as consumers are assumed to be utility maximizers, seeking a multitude of personal satisfactions, given the resources and opportunities effectively open to them. But as managers of firms, they are assumed to seek only profit, even though they may have resources and opportunities effectively available which would permit seeking other ends. If profit maximization is an idealization of utility maximization, it is natural to raise the question of how it is derived from the more general theory, i.e., what are the variables assumed to take on extreme values?

Recent work in the theory of the firm, focusing on property rights, has suggested a partial answer: the costs of monitoring managerial behavior are implicitly assumed to be zero. Property rights analysis is based on the view that behavior depends on the appropriability of income streams; i.e., on the *effective* rights to various kinds of incomes. These streams may be pecuniary or non-pecuniary, and they may be negative (i.e., costs), but the key concept is appropriability. Rights seen in this way are actually rights to control the use of resources and to enjoy the benefits arising from their use; for that reason, it seems more suggestive to use the term resource rights. This avoids creating the incorrect impression that the analysis is limited to questions of formal legal arrangements and suggests that the analysis is generally applicable to individual behavior. Among other things, consumer behavior in waste disposal, noise production, congestion, auto exhaust emission, and other forms of environmental pollution can be usefully analyzed from the standpoint of effective rights to or appropriability of income streams.

In the case of managerial behavior, appropriability of income streams, pecuniary and nonpecuniary, is determined by the set of constraints faced by the manager. His behavior is subject to monitoring by some individual or group of persons—the owners, in the case of for-profit firms, a board of trustees in not-for-profit organizations, and so forth. Monitoring requires assessing managerial performance in achieving the organization's putative goals relative to its potential, given its resource constraints. It also involves enforcing the peak coordinator's

---

b. Idealizations in physical sciences are deduced from more general theories by assigning extreme values to certain variables, which permits specification of the extent of deviations from the ideal.

c. Concepts in idealizations in the physical sciences have operational clarity, i.e., they have relatively precise meanings in their observed forms. Rudner advocates a general theory of social behavior from which rational economic behavior (or utility-maximizing behavior) could be deduced by assigning extreme values to certain variables. Economists have, of course, recognized the limitations of economic analysis in just this sense; for one example, see Knight (1965, pp. 171 and 175). From this standpoint, utility-maximizing behavior is itself an idealization of social behavior, in which certain (unspecified) variables have, in principle, extreme values. The contribution of property rights analysis lies within the realm of economic behavior, specifically in establishing one link between the general theory of economic behavior and the idealization of that theory for managerial behavior in the firm.

sanctions in cases of detected deviant behavior. Both of these activities are costly, and hence managers will be able to seek personal satisfactions through use of the firm's resources.[3] Of course, all such activity bears some risk of sanctions, and over time, the manager may find his opportunity set shrinking unless he takes corrective steps.[4]

Of course, if monitoring were costless, managers would find it difficult to deviate from the ends of the peak coordinators, assumed to be profit in the case of capitalist firms. Thus, resource rights analysis leads to the conclusion that zero monitoring costs are a necessary (but not sufficient) condition for profit-maximizing behavior, in the absence of further qualifications about the manager's utility function.[5] This aspect of resource rights analysis gives concrete meaning to such vague terms as "separation of ownership and control" or "large" firms with "diverse" ownership. In situations characterized by these terms, monitoring costs are positive.

But when, one might well ask, are monitoring costs not positive? In the real world, where owners almost always hire managers, it is hard to give examples, for there are always positive monitoring costs in such situations. It is arguable that the owner-operated firm is a case in which the costs are zero, and, from that aspect, the profit maximizing theory is per se applicable. Even here, however, the further qualifications are required (at least) that the market is characterized by competition and that there are no legal or ethical constraints (or threat thereof) on competitive behavior.[6] Otherwise, owners managing their own firms would be expected to seek nonmarket ends by using their resources in different ways than those leading to maximum (expected) profits.

In a capitalist economy, appropriability and monitoring costs are affected by the capital market.[7] Incentives may be tied to managerial performance in generating profits by stock option plans or insider trading. Besides this kind of carrot, there is the stick: poor profit performance, which is reflected in share prices, may provide signals to outsiders that potential gains exist for a take-over and displacement of an inefficient management. In the same way, the capital market transmits information about managerial performance to firm owners,

---

3. These arguments owe a good deal to Alchian's work. See, inter alia, Alchian (1965).

4. This point is suggested in another context by Furubotn and Pejovich (1972b).

5. It is conceivable that some managers, by chance or through astute selection by peak coordinators, would have utility functions such that their interests coincide with those of the peak coordinators. If so, profit-maximizing behavior in the firm would not require zero monitoring costs. Careful selection seems to correspond to Knight's view of the situation. See Knight (1965, pp. 291–312).

6. This is necessarily vague, since there is no way to specify precisely the degree of competition sufficient for profit maximizing behavior. It is suggestive of why profit-maximizing behavior might not be observed in societies where competitive behavior is socially disapproved, even though monopoly is not observed.

7. See Williamson (1970, Ch. 6) for a summary of this discussion.

alerting them to poor performance and stimulating direct monitoring. While the information is noisy and imputation of performance difficult, the messages conveyed are not empty, and the existence of this extra-firm policing device is valuable to firm owners.

Once constrained utility maximization is accepted as the basis for a theory of managerial behavior in a large organization, it is clear that its applicability is not limited to for-profit capitalist firms. Indeed, the very ease of specification and measurement of the putative goal of such firms is a major reason why monitoring costs are lower than in organizations with more complex and less easily specifiable ends, such as not-for-profit private organizations and, perhaps especially, government units. Moreover, managerial constraints emanating from the capital market are less effective in these latter situations. Consequently, one would expect greater latitude for managers to seek their own ends, ceteris paribus, in these organizations than in for-profit firms.[8] Thus logical developments in the theory of the firm, stimulated by the theorizing and empirical evidence offered by Alchian (1955) lead to a more general theory of organizational behavior, in which appropriability and monitoring costs play key roles. It is from this point of view that it is useful to apply property rights analysis to the theory of management of socialist producer organizations.

## MANAGERIAL DISCRETION AND THE SOVIET-TYPE ENTERPRISE

In the case of Soviet-type state enterprises, practically all existing theory is based on the idealizing assumption that managers act so as to maximize bonuses;[9] in most variants, this implies output-maximizing behavior. This amounts to a bonus-maximizing theory of the enterprise, and is formally equivalent to the profit-maximizing theory of the for-profit capitalist firm. Given a maximand such as bonuses or profits, working out equilibrium conditions is a matter of routine in both cases, and empirical predictions can be derived.[10] Finally, like profit maximization, bonus maximization can be derived from a more general theory of behavior, utility maximization, by letting some variables take on extreme values.

---

8. It is worth noting that the fact that tastes differ causes empirical predictions to be hazardous. For example, to predict that, *on the average*, managers of regulated monopolies will have plusher offices or more beautiful secretaries than managers of profit-maximizing firms requires the auxiliary assumption that most managers have a taste for comfortable surroundings. Even without this assumption, one would predict greater variability in resource allocation patterns among organizations where there is latitude for managerial discretion; for the contrast between for-profit and not-for-profit hospitals, see Clarkson (1972).

9. The main exception to this is the article by Furubotn and Pejovich (1972b).

10. These predictions are often vague, commonly taking the form of comparing optimal equilibrium conditions for the bonus-maximizing enterprise with those for the profit-maximizing for-profit firm; such comparisons are not really amenable to test. See Ames (1965, especially pp. 54–57) for examples.

Bonus maximization has been valuable in extending understanding of state enterprises in centrally directed economies. It has provided a point of comparison between operation of those enterprises in an ideal situation and their similarly idealized counterparts in a capitalist free enterprise economy. But if property rights analysis leads to questions about the applicability of the profit-maximizing idealization to "large" capitalist firms, it must raise similar questions in the analysis of managerial behavior in state enterprises. The point may be put most clearly by noting what seems obvious: monitoring costs are not zero. Furthermore, there is reason to suppose that the deviation is significant.

Enterprise managers can presumably appropriate all bonuses which they earn in their work, but such pecuniary benefits are not the only returns they can realize through their allocation of enterprise resources. Even though monetary income is undoubtedly important, there are reasons to believe that managers seek other sources of satisfaction as well. First, the performance of the enterprise depends on more than just the manager's efforts; supply problems, uncontrollable forces of nature, political events that affect worker morale, and so forth affect plan fulfillment. In other words, imputation of enterprise performance is not clear-cut. This fact has two implications. On the one hand, it means that evaluation of a manager's performance is more difficult (i.e., costly) for his bureaucratic superiors. On the other hand, since managers know that bonus income does not depend solely on their efforts, their incentive to work within the set of rules leading to maximum bonuses is blunted. The uncertainty about earning bonuses arises not only from production uncertainties faced by any manager but also from a host of other sources (e.g., supply irregularities, unforeseen changes in plans). This suggests that the marginal bonus accruing to any managerial action should be converted to an expected gain by a probability of less than one, which means that the relative bonus cost of seeking other forms of satisfactions within the enterprise is less than it would otherwise be. The probability would vary with the tautness of the plan and with the particular environment in which the manager finds himself, but in any case the uncertainty about meeting plans suggests that tradeoffs will take place between bonuses and other internally obtained benefits.

Related to this, but different from it, is the notorious tendency not to overfulfill plans by amounts that managers expect will cause undesirable target increases in the next plan. If the manager believes that more output now (and more current bonus income) will lead to higher targets later, the cost of trading some current bonus income for nonpecuniary satisfactions obtained through the enterprise will seem lower. This consideration involves balancing current and future bonus income as well as current bonus and nonbonus income, and its effect on incentives in the current period is similar.[11]

11. The similarity to Williamson's "moving equilibrium" problem in capitalist firms (1970, p. 92) is obvious, as is the connection with the argument in Furubotn and Pejovich (1972a).

Besides these two arguments, there is abundant verbal evidence in the literature on Soviet managerial behavior that managers in fact seek other ends, and there seems to be no reason to suppose that they would not have interests similar to those of capitalist managers, as far as nonpecuniary income flows are concerned.[12] For at least these reasons, then, single-minded pursuit of bonuses by enterprise managers would not be expected.

At the same time, appropriability of benefits arising from use of enterprise resources for unplanned purposes could not take place if monitoring costs were zero, just as managers of capitalist firms could not deviate from profit-maximizing behavior in similar circumstances. With zero monitoring costs, the manager's superiors would have complete information about his activities and, moreover, would be able to impute enterprise performance perfectly to his behavior. They would also be able to enforce desired behavior patterns on the manager. Indeed, in these circumstances, bonuses linked to plan fulfillment could be replaced by a simple salary, since only a general incentive would be required. It hardly need be emphasized that monitoring costs are not zero in a real-world bureaucracy like that of the industrial sector of the Soviet Union. Again, no precise way exists to measure monitoring costs, but they are surely large relative to those in even large corporations with diversified ownership.

In addition to observing the sheer complexity of the system, this assertion is supported by the absence of a capital market to provide an outside source of information about managerial performance. The Soviet enterprise manager is in a position to control the flow of information about his own activities to his superiors. This has often been noted in connection with problems of measuring output, but it has clear applicability to monitoring costs as well. Furthermore, the existence of the wide variety of policing organizations and methods—Gosbank, Gosplan, Gossnab, TsSU, the ministries, and the CPSU itself—suggests strongly that in actual situations the bonus structure provided is inadequate for securing the desired performance.

For state enterprises, then, the developments of resource rights analysis with its emphasis on monitoring costs imply deviations from bonus-maximizing behavior. Thus, in the property rights framework, managers of state enterprises can be viewed as constrained utility maximizers.

Some useful insights have resulted from this analysis. In a departure from the conventional wisdom, Furubotn and Pejovich (1972a) have shown that there is incentive for enterprise managers to introduce cost-saving innovations, because doing so preserves their range of opportunity for attaining nonbonus rewards even though plan targets are generally raised over time.

Another slant on optimal plan tautness emerges from the analysis as well. Plan tautness acts to some extent as a substitute for direct monitoring, since it is plan slackness that provides the fat in resource availability from which

---

12. Citations to the literature seem superfluous since this assertion amounts to common knowledge. A standard source is Berliner (1957).

managers extract nonbonus satisfactions. Some tautness is therefore desirable, even in the absence of a policy of forced-draft industrialization. On the other hand, as output demands on a given allocation of resources rise, the probability of fulfillment begins to fall, and therefore so does the expected bonus return from managerial efficiency (relative to the plan). As mentioned earlier, this reduces the relative cost of using resources for other purposes, ceteris paribus, and therefore would tend to lessen incentives for plan fulfillment.

In a more general way, the focus on resource rights ties in with other phenomena observed in states like the Soviet Union, in particular the currently well-known environmental problems. One fairly obvious conclusion from resource rights analysis is that policing of rights will be undertaken only if the value of the rights to the enforcer exceeds the cost to him of policing (Demsetz 1964). In a recent article, Goldman argues that the absence of private property rights in the Soviet Union removes a potential barrier to pollution or "overuse" of natural resources, citing the example of the removal of sand and pebbles from Black Sea beaches by Georgian state contractors (1972, p. 324). The value of the pebbles and sand as beach are, apparently, not accounted for, in part because no private interest exists to place such a value. In principle, the state itself could make such decisions (the problem of socialist calculation assumed away), and it might be that the sand and pebbles would be valued more highly made into concrete than as beach. On the other hand, policing costs are clearly high, and even though the regime valued them more as beach than as concrete, the sum of their value as concrete plus policing costs to insure they remain as beach might well be greater than their value as beach, in which case they would be used as concrete. Even though (or perhaps especially because) private property in the means of production is abolished under socialism, property rights analysis is an important tool for understanding the operation of these systems.

## PROPERTY RIGHTS AND THE ILLYRIAN
## WORKER-MANAGED FIRM

The theory of managerial behavior in the Illyrian firm that corresponds to profit and bonus maximization is based on the assumption that enterprise directors seek to maximize net income per worker.[13] As in the case of the bonus-maximizing theory of the state enterprise, this theory has been helpful in providing comparisons of the optimal positions of the corresponding worker-managed firm and the profit-maximizing capitalist firm. However, little has been done by way of specifying how this theory can be deduced from the broader one of constrained utility maximization. On the other hand, more work has been done on developing the implications of the broader theory than in the case of the state enterprise (Furubotn 1971; Furubotn and Pejovich 1970b, 1972a).

13. See, for example, Ward (1958), Domar (1966), and Vanek (1970).

Despite the difference in property relations,[14] and the significant contrast in the bureaucratic organization, the reasons for questioning the idealization are the same in this case as in that of the state enterprise. Even though managers may be members of the cooperative, sharing in net income, there are still numerous reasons why their objectives will, in general, differ from maximization of net income per worker. Even though the firm may be an autonomous entity with fewer bureaucratic entanglements than the Soviet state enterprise, monitoring costs are still positive, thus extending the director's opportunity set. Furthermore, the deviations of the variables from the extreme values presumed in the net-income-per-worker maximization theory are arguably large. Consequently, here as elsewhere, the more general idealization of constrained utility maximization holds promise in understanding managerial behavior.

With nonzero monitoring costs, managers may seek to use firm resources to seek their own ends, i.e., they may seek to appropriate personal benefits from the firm. If they share in enterprise net income, why then would they not seek to maximize per worker net income? Why should their interests diverge from those of the other members of the collective?

In the first place, it is by no means obvious that rank-and-file workers would support policies that single-mindedly sought maximization of net income per worker. Some, at least, might prefer managerial policies that provided other sources of satisfaction. For example, risk-averse members of the collective presumably would value high variance, high expected return (per worker) investments less highly than more adventuresome members. Some members might have preferences for on-the-job nonpecuniary income flows, such as pleasant working conditions, longer coffee breaks, and so forth, in excess of levels that raise productivity.[15] The existence of such preferences would imply tradeoffs at some rates between these and pecuniary income.[16] One group of workers might favor policies that benefited them directly, even though the overall effect might be to reduce average net income per worker. These examples could be multiplied, but the point seems clear enough. It suggests that one variable implicitly assumed

14. The Yugoslav "right to use" seems to be a severely limited property right, since a cooperative member enjoying such rights in the property of the firm never acquires the right to remove his share. His right is restricted to enjoying the income from "his" share of the capital, a fact which, as Furubotn and Pejovich (1970) have pointed out, implies a reluctance to reinvest enterprise earnings.

15. Over some range, expenditures on such factors is profitable for capitalist firms and should be expected to raise net income per worker in Illyrian firms. See Williamson (1970, Ch. 4).

16. This is analogous to owners of capitalist firms who seek to use firm resources for nonmarket purposes, and market competition would tend to eliminate such behavior in either case. The actual situation in Yugoslavia [see Dirlam (1967)] gives reason to be skeptical about the degree of market competition. It should also be noted that to the extent that agreement on matters of nonpecuniary income cannot be reached, pecuniary income streams will be favored, as Furubotn (1971) has suggested.

zero in the idealization is interpersonal differences in preferences,[17] an assumption that is hard to countenance.

But even if all such conflicts among rank-and-file members of the collective are resolved so that they agree on maximization of net income per worker as their joint objective, it does not follow that managerial behavior would be such as to maximize it, as long as the managers' utility functions include arguments other than pecuniary income. In part, the reasons are parallel to those just given for the Soviet-type enterprise. Firm directors, even though they are sharing in net income as members of the collective, have attenuated rights in the residual generated by their efforts since the residual is divided among all members. Such dilution of return to managerial input means that the opportunity cost of pursuing other ends is less than it would otherwise be. By comparison, the owner-manager of a ("small") capitalist firm gives up the entire increment of profits arising from additional effort, so that his opportunity cost is relatively high. Egalitarian limitations on income differentials (as apparently exist in Yugoslavia) would compound this problem by putting an upper limit on the opportunity cost of nonmaximizing behavior. Furthermore, imputation is a problem in the Illyrian firm as well as in any other organization, and again it has two aspects. One is that the enterprise director knows that the outcome for the enterprise depends on the conjuncture of many factors, some of which he cannot control. In seeking a higher residual, he must discount the returns, both direct pecuniary gains (his share of net income) and incremental gains in his security and reputation, by some estimated probability of success, a function, to repeat, of many variables. As this probability falls, the opportunity cost of nonmaximizing behavior perceived by the director also falls, in general. The other aspect is that imputation difficulties raise the costs of monitoring managerial behavior by the other members of the collective.

The attenuation of rights in net income, then, reduces the costs of seeking other satisfactions, of which the variety is very large. On the one hand are what might be termed "Alchianesque" satisfactions—the perquisites of office, congenial colleagues, vacation spas, the quiet life, and so forth. On the other hand, there may exist other pressures on directors, as has been the case in Yugoslavia. Pressures from the local government to pursue particular employment practices, pressures to reinvest earnings for the sake of the industrialization programme, pressures from the Communist Party[18] to implement centrally determined policies, all combine with internal pressures for net-income-per-worker maximization to put the director in the position of trying to meet a be-

17. Vanek (1970) comes close to making this assumption explicit when he assumes away all other motives (pp. 2–3). Dubravcic has noted some of these interpersonal conflicts in a recent article (1970).

18. Dirlam (1967) notes that enterprise directors have almost always been party members.

wildering multitude of ends. If anything, this fact suggests that maximization of the *total*, rather than the *per worker*, residual, would be more appropriate in an idealization of the Yugoslav enterprise. But the very diversity of goals, resulting from both internal wants and external pressures, provides both problems and opportunities for the director. The problems are obvious; the opportunities exist because the diverse claims make it possible to play one claimant off against another.[19]

Of course, in these circumstances the director's position would be "impossible" if monitoring costs were zero, since it would be painful indeed to resolve the conflicting claims. But once again, reason exists to suppose that monitoring costs are sufficiently different from zero to warrant substitution of constrained utility maximization for its idealization. There is no Illyrian worker-managed counterpart of the owner-managed capitalist firm; even in relatively small Illyrian firms, then, monitoring costs must differ from zero. From the point of view of information, the strategic advantage the director enjoys by virtue of his position is compounded by the absence of a capital market and the problem of imputation of enterprise performance to managerial efforts. Without a capital market, workers must rely for a basis for judging managerial performance on comparisons of their incomes with those received in similar situations elsewhere, a costly process in any case which is rendered more costly by inclusion of non-pecuniary satisfactions in their incomes (vacations, working conditions, joint insurance programs, and so forth). The imputation problem raises the costs for workers to assess results achieved, a fact known to directors and one which they can exploit. Information costs such as these are likely to rise with the size of the organization, and Yugoslav experience shows that worker-managed firms become large, as do capitalist firms. Even in relatively small firms, however, these costs seem likely to be important.

Furthermore, the attenuation of the rights of collective members themselves in the income stream reduces the opportunity cost of failing to monitor managerial behavior, and thus reduces their willingness to incur costs in obtaining information. A comparison to capitalist firms is useful here. In closely held firms with hired managers, incremental profits accrue to relatively few persons; to each the opportunity cost of failing to police management would be correspondingly high. Direct monitoring would not be surprising in such cases. Where ownership is diverse, however, incremental total profits are diluted over all owners; to each, on the average, the corresponding opportunity cost is thus smaller. Less direct policing and greater reliance on other factors (the information conveyed by the capital market, the possibility of takeovers, policing by owners with relatively large blocks) would be expected. Workers in a worker-managed

19. Recent domestic tendencies seeking so-called "corporate responsibility" would have the same effect on managers of U.S. corporations. Casual perusal of statements by corporate executives is consistent with this thesis. It should not be surprising if managers welcome this trend since it provides opportunities for them as well.

firm are, in this limited sense, in a position similar to that of small shareholders of a capitalist firm. Their willingness to incur monitoring costs depends on the expected increment in their incomes; but any increment in the net income of the enterprise must be shared with all other members of the collective, which has the effect of reducing the opportunity cost to an individual of not monitoring.

One can go further. Policing can usefully be regarded as a public good for members of the collective, since no worker can capture all the benefits of his own policing activities; therefore, free rider behavior should be expected. This is, perhaps, the principal reason for the existence of the works' council, since the actual operation of the enterprise is carried out by the hired director and not directly by the works' delegates. Perhaps it also explains why the workers are prepared to tolerate special privileges and perquisites for members of the workers' council, who are, to the extent that they execute their assignments faithfully, providing a valuable service to the other members.[20]

The foregoing discussion has raised some logical difficulties in the standard theory of the Illyrian firm. In addition to the logical problems, some empirical evidence exists that is consistent with predictions of the resource rights theory and that tends to contradict the theory of maximization of net income per worker. Space permits only brief reference to this evidence.

Although it is usually heavily qualified, a significant conclusion from the income-per-worker idealization is that supply elasticities should be low or, possibly, negative.[21] One should then expect to see increases in industry supply accounted for principally by entry of new firms; however, a test of this hypothesis by Sacks (1972) is not consistent with the hypothesis. Specifically, Sacks found no correlation between changes in industry output and changes in the number of enterprises in the industry, thus suggesting that the supply response of existing enterprises was sufficiently elastic to account for changes in industry output. While apparently contradicting the hypothesis of maximization of net income per worker, this result is not inconsistent with constrained utility maximization.

A recent article by Wachtel (1972) contains evidence bearing generally on resource rights analysis. In testing various hypotheses about the Yugoslav inter-industry wage structure, he finds that average labor productivity is statistically significant in 1958 and thereafter, but not before. It is important to note that Wachtel's regressions involve the *full* wage, which includes bonuses paid from individual income. Both the net-income-per-worker and the managerial utility-maximization hypotheses imply that the demand for labor is a function of labor productivity; the lack of significance of that variable before 1958 requires explanation. Before 1957, bonus payments to workers could be made

---

20. Public good aspects similarly apply to policing by small shareholders in capitalist firms but are alleviated where concentrations of ownership make failure to police relatively costly for some individuals.

21. See Vanek [1970, pp. 46, 49, 55–56 (" ... the low supply elasticities are the main weak point of the decentralized labor-managed situation")].

only with the approval of the local commune and the trade union.[22] Beginning
in 1957, however, there was a gradual shift in effective property rights in enterprise net income in favor of the enterprise:[23] specifically, the right to determine
the share of net income accruing to workers as wages shifted gradually from local
government authorities to the enterprise. One would expect the wage structure
to reflect economic criteria more clearly after this change, an expectation with
which Wachtel's data seem to be in accord. The important point here is not which
of the two idealizations is appropriate, but rather to observe the impact of a
change in property rights.

An example of how changing property rights affect behavior is taken
from a recent article by Furubotn and Pejovich (1972a, especially pp. 283-287).
Since 1957, enterprise net income has been devoted to four principal funds
(other than taxes): wage payments, the business fund, the collective consumption
fund, and the reserve fund. In an earlier article applying property rights analysis
to the Yugoslav firm (Furubotn and Pejovich 1970), these authors had shown
that the legal institution of "right to use" had the result that relatively high
expected rates of return would be required to induce voluntary reinvestment of
enterprise earnings by workers. Furthermore, the appeal of collective consumption through that fund of the enteprise would be restricted by the range of
agreement possible among members of the collective with their varying tastes.
(Payments to the reserve fund have been obligatory and are of little interest here.)
Before 1965, the proportion of the residual that could be paid to workers as
wages was constrained by various legal requirements governing payments to the
various funds (Pejovich 1966); after the 1965 economic reform, according to
Milenkovitch, ". . . total profits were placed at the disposal of workers (*sic*)
council" (Pejovich 1966, pp. 30-32). Property rights analysis would predict an
increase in the share of net profits going to the wage fund after this change;
Furubotn and Pejovich (1972a) report an increase from 69 percent to 81 percent
between 1964 and 1969. While not providing direct evidence for or against either
idealization, this evidence suggests the importance of property rights in the
analysis of the Yugoslav enterprise, and thus can be argued to provide indirect
evidence supporting the property rights theory.[24]

## CONCLUSIONS

Three theories commonly used in analyzing managerial behavior in differing
economic systems—profit maximization, bonus maximization, and maximization
of net income per worker—can be deduced from the more general economic
theory of utility maximization. A key variable, implicitly assumed to be zero in
each theory, is the cost of monitoring managerial behavior. If this cost is not

---

22. See Pejovich (1966, p. 30) and Milenkovitch (1971, p. 106).
23. See Paj (1970, pp. 72-82) for discussion.
24. See De Alessi (1971, p. 869).

zero, the manager can appropriate streams of income or nonpecuniary satisfactions which may result from his use of the enterprise's resources. Under these circumstances and to the extent that such returns are appropriable, deviations from the behavior predicted by the idealizations should be expected.

It was argued that certain institutional features, notably the lack of a capital market and attenuation of rights in the net income of enterprises in the noncapitalist systems in question, make monitoring costs relatively high in the Soviet-type and Illyrian enterprises. Furthermore, the complexity of the bureaucracy in the former case and the existence of large firms in both cases would lead one to conclude that monitoring costs are at least as high as in capitalist firms where the profit maximization theory has been rejected. In the case of Yugoslav worker-managed enterprises, and to a lesser extent in the case of Soviet enterprises, empirical data suggest that an analytical approach based on property rights analysis, which embodies a return to the more general idealization of constrained utility maximization, is potentially more fruitful in understanding managerial behavior in each of the systems.

## Chapter Twenty-three

# Towards a General Theory of Property Rights

S. Pejovich

Reprinted from *Zeitschrift für Nationalökonomie*, Band 31 (Heft 1-2, 1971): 141-155, by permission of the publisher.

The literature in the field of comparative economics contains only passing references to the role and importance of property-rights structures. This is not to say that the differences in property relations have not been appreciated by the economics profession at large. The point is that the fundamental role of the property-rights structures as a specification of the set of opportunity choices about resource uses has yet to be formally incorporated into the theory of economic systems.

The purpose of this article is to demonstrate that the effects of various property-rights structures on the pattern of human behavior can be incorporated into traditional economic analysis and that in the process the scope of economic analysis is broadened.[1] This article is intended to be a contribution to the pure theory of human behavior under various property-rights arrangements, which (property arrangements) are, it is asserted, a powerful and possibly necessary condition for the very existence of different economic systems.

The study will concentrate on the problem of short-run adjustments in the rate of real income *voluntarily* diverted to gross investment under four different forms of ownership in capital goods. Those adjustments in the rate of investment will be ascertained via the effects of various ownership rights in capital goods on the equilibrium rate of interest. The latter is taken to be the rate which brings into equality: the rate of increase of wealth per marginal unit of the rate of investment; the community's valuation of future income relative to current consumption; the return on government bonds; and the interest rate implicit in relative prices of capital goods.

In order to observe the effects of the various forms of ownership in capital goods on the community's rate of income diverted to gross investment, let us assume that (a) the community's income is *given* and defined as the maximum that its members can consume per unit of time without reducing their

1. See Bajt (1968) and Pejovich (1969b).

wealth; (b) all capital goods are of the same kind; (c) the return corresponding to each rate of investment is known; (d) the rate of interest paid by banks on savings deposits is regulated by the government; (e) the consumption of non-pecuniary goods is a source of utility; (f) profit-maximizing behavior is taken to mean the maximization of the firm's net worth; (g) the form of ownership in capital goods is uniform throughout the community.

The article begins with consideration of a private property capitalist community and proceeds to the subsequent analysis of the effects of the attenuated private property rights, the attenuated state ownership (usus fructus), and the non-attenuated state ownership (usus) in the means of production on the community's allocation of income between current consumption and investment.

## PRIVATE PROPERTY CAPITALIST COMMUNITY

Fundamental characteristics of private property are taken to be *exclusivity* of right of use of a thing and voluntary *transferability* of that right. The institution of private property and the desire for more (a behavioral characteristic common to all men in all human societies) establish the basis for two major propositions in traditional economic theory: (a) scarce resources tend to be allocated to those uses where they are expected to be most productive, and (b) the extent of exchange (trade) depends upon the initial amount of goods held by individuals and their marginal rates of substitution. In other words, each and every individual in a private property capitalist community is free, given his time preference and personal evaluation of monetary, physical, and human assets, to convert his current income to wealth or to sell his nonhuman assets in the open market.

Let us now turn to the short-run equilibrium in the capital market. The $(SS)$ curve in Figure 23-1[2] shows the assumed supply of the stock of existing capital in the community. The demand curves $(DD)$ relate the stock demand for capital to hold to the price of capital; this price is defined as the present value of the flow of expected earnings from the existing capital stock discounted at the relevant rate of interest $(r_0 > \bar{r}_0 > \bar{\bar{r}}_0)$. Given the rate of interest, the current price at which the public is willing to hold the existing stock of capital emerges. This price is determined in the capital market where the rate of interest is equated to the percentage return from the capital stock.

Should personal preferences change toward a greater desire for future income, the price of both the stock of existing physical assets and bonds would increase and the rates of return from nonhuman assets would fall. The stock demand curve for capital would shift to $(\bar{D}_0\bar{D}_0)$, and rate of interest implicit in relative prices of capital goods would fall. The equilibrium rate of interest $(r_0)$ falls to $(\bar{r}_0)$. In other words, all the various rates of interest would be brought into equality by switching activity among different markets.

2. The model was developed by Clower (1954) and Witte (1963).

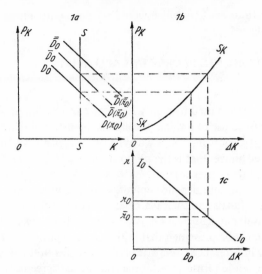

**Figure 23–1.** Short-Run Equilibrium in the Capital Market

The assumed production market for capital goods is shown in 1b of Figure 23–1. The $(S_k S_k)$ is the flow supply curve of capital goods. Given this schedule, the rate of output of new capital goods by capital producing industries is determined for each given market price on the vertical axis. The producers are assumed to equate the marginal supply price to the market price of capital goods. The rate of investment decision becomes the rate of output decision of supplying firms. The important underlying assumption is that "the annual flow of new capital goods adds such a small quantity to the stock of capital goods that the rate of return is unaffected" (Witte 1963, p. 450). This is a convenient assumption which permits us to assume that the flow demand for new capital goods is perfectly elastic at the level of the current price. Thus, *new capital goods can be sold at the going price.* It must also be noted that the scales on horizontal axes in 1a and 1b are different.

In Figure 23–1, 1c shows the rate of output of new capital goods as a function of the rate of interest. The investment function $(I_0 I_0)$ is a market equilibrium curve and not a demand curve for investment. Its shape and position depend upon the slope and position of the supply curve of new capital goods. Moreover, the rate of interest and the marginal efficiency of investment are equal at each given point on the $I_0 I_0$ curve.

The rate of real income diverted to gross investment is $(OB_0)$ in 1c. The equilibrium rate of interest $(r_0)$ brings into equality the rates of return from capital goods and bonds, the community's valuation of future income relative to current consumption and the interest rate implicit in relative prices of capital goods. A change in any of these four rates would result in switching activity among all the various markets which would continue until a new common rate of interest is established.

## ATTENUATED PRIVATE PROPERTY CAPITALIST COMMUNITY

The term attenuation is used to signify the degree of restriction on the owner's right to the exclusive use of a thing. It can be demonstrated that the attenuation of private property rights interferes with the two major propositions in economic theory mentioned above, that is the propositions that (a) scarce resources tend to be allocated to those uses where they are expected to be most productive, and (b) the extent of exchange depends upon the initial amount of goods in the possession of individuals and their marginal rates of substitution.

Consider an agreement between two parties to exchange some goods and services. It must be presumed that both parties expect to be better off, that is reach a higher indifference curve after the contract is fulfilled. Otherwise one or both of them would refuse to enter the contractual agreement. Since every contract means an exchange of some bundle of property rights, the attenuation of private property rights reduces the set of opportunity choices of the contracting parties and affects the allocation of resources. For example, a minimum wage law attenuates the person's property rights over his own labor by forbidding him from transferring it to consumers (via an intermediary, the firm) below certain price. That is, the law prevents some people from entering into contractual agreements which attain for them the most preferred position.

The attenuation of private property rights in a capitalist community can ordinarily be traced to the laws and regulations such as price controls, production quotas, licensing, etc.[3] For simplicity we shall consider only one type of the attenuation of private property rights. The government in our hypothetical community issues a decree announcing that the profits of business firms are to be controlled and limited to some maximum set by the state. Public utilities in the USA operate under similar conditions. Our objective is to determine the effects of profit control on resource allocation, other things in the community remaining the same. It could also be demonstrated that all other forms of the attenuation of private property would lead to similar results.

Let us now briefly review our assumption that consumption of nonpecuniary goods is a source of one's utility. The term nonpecuniary goods is used to emphasize an important analytical difference between the general and the specific consumption. The former is defined as consumption out of one's income, while the latter is taken to represent consumption of some specified goods, the

---

3. Another form of the attenuation of private property might arise from an increase in the stockholders costs of controlling the managers. In everyday parlance this case is referred to as a divorce of ownership from management. For an excellent analysis of this case see Alchian (1969).

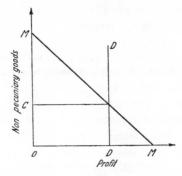

**Figure 23-2.** Effect of Profit Control on the Behavior of Managers

nonconsumption of which would not affect the person's income. For example, a free vacation in Florida which an individual had never contemplated represents an increase in his consumption of specific goods. Should he choose not to take it, his general consumption out of his given income would not change. General and specific consumption will, therefore, yield the same satisfaction to an individual only when the extra money income which happens to equal the price of a specific good would be used by that person for consumption of that particular good. In other words, consumption of specific goods is inferior to an equivalent increase in money income since the latter offers a greater range of choices.

The managers of business enterprises can purchase nonpecuniary goods such as beautiful secretaries, monthly conferences in Las Vegas, employment of less efficient but more desirable employees, etc., via a reduction in their respective firms' earnings. In a private property capitalist society, the manager's rate of consumption of nonpecuniary goods depends on the owners' cost of control. Moreover, competition among the managers would tend to reduce the owners' cost of control (Alchian 1959). The resulting pattern of the managers' behavior justifies the traditional profit-maximizing hypothesis.

Figure 23-2, which is based on the work done by Alchian, Becker, Kessell, and others,[4] shows the effect of profit control on the behavior of the managers. Let $(OM)$ be the profits the firm was earning prior to the imposition of profit control, $(MM)$ the rate at which the managers can exchange profits for their consumption of nonpecuniary goods (where linearity is assumed for convenience), and $(OD)$ the allowed profit. The managers will have incentives to pursue the profit-maximizing behavior inspite of the legal ceiling because they should be able to conceal higher profits from the state and capture them. The higher profits are absorbed into higher costs via the purchase of nonpecuniary goods such as plush offices, more "desirable" colleagues, shorter hours, etc. (Alchian and Kessell 1962; Becker 1967). From the point of view of stockhold-

4. See Alchian and Kessel (1962) and Becker (1967).

ers the attenuation of private property in capital goods induces them to tolerate management behavior which in a private property capitalist community would reduce the stockholders' wealth. More specifically, the managers will find the $(OC)$ rate of consumption of nonpecuniary goods virtually costless. The conclusion is that the managers (and not the consumers) will appropriate the major if not the entire share of the stockholders' loss of wealth.

The attenuation of private property rights in capital goods results, as we have seen, in a decrease in the net earnings from the stock of existing capital goods, other things remaining the same. Given the rate of interest $(r_0)$, the stock demand curve for capital shifts downward ($D_1 D_1$ in Figure 23-3), and the market price of capital goods falls. In the process of reaching the general equilibrium, a related increase in the demand for human and monetary assets occurs. The net effect is to reduce the rate of interst, and shift the demand curve back to, say, $\bar{D}_1 \bar{D}_1$ in 3a, where $r_1 < r_0$.

Given the flow supply schedule of capital-producing industries $(S_k S_k)$, the social investment function shifts from $(I_0 I_0)$ to $(I_1 I_1)$ indicating a lower rate of gross investment at each given rate of interest. That the $(I_1 I_1)$ schedule lies below the original schedule *must not* be taken to reflect a change in the gross marginal product of capital or the inefficient use of resources. The shift in the social investment function reflects the redistribution of wealth from those who own property to those who do not which, to recall, is attributable to the attenuation of private property rights in capital goods.

If the rate of interest falls to $(r_2)$ in the Figure's 3c, the market price of capital goods and the rate of gross investment would be just about the same as in the nonattenuated private property case. However, there is no reason for this rate to arise. The owners' loss from the attenuation of private property rights in capital goods is in the form of a loss of general wealth. The consumers' gain, if any, is also in the form of general wealth. However, the managers' gain is in the form of current consumption of some specific goods. The managers are obviously better off than they would be in the nonattenuated private property case. However, they are not as well off as they would be if they received an equivalent increase in their incomes; for the possibility that *all* of them would use that income to purchase precisely the same bundle of goods can be ruled out. It follows that the loss of wealth and income to the owners of capital is in excess of the consumers' and managers' gains and the community's wealth is correspondingly reduced. Given the community's propensity to save, the rate of income diverted to nonconsumption falls at each given rate of interest. Consequently, an increase in the demand for monetary and human assets will not be strong enough to reduce the rate of interest down to $(r_2)$. Thus, the common rate of interest which brings into equality all the various rates will be found somewhere between $(r_0)$ and $(r_2)$. In our case we assume it to be at $(r_1)$ in Figure 23-3.

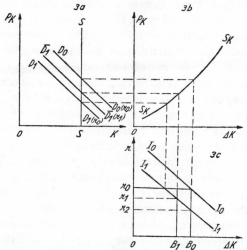

**Figure 23-3.** Attenuated Private Property Rights and
Short-Run Equilibrium in the Capital Market

## ATTENUATED STATE OWNERSHIP;
## USUS FRUCTUS

Usus fructus is a form of property ownership defined as the user's right to use an
asset belonging to someone else (the state in a socialist community) and to
appropriate its yield, but not to sell it nor to change its quality. The last point
implies that business firms must generate and invest sufficient depreciation funds
indefinitely. Yugoslavia is the only socialist country in which this specific type
of property rights applies to capital goods.[5] In fact, the property rights in capital
goods are somewhat broader in Yugoslavia. The Yugoslav firm can sell its physical
assets to another firm. However, if the asset is sold for less than its book value
the firm must invest the difference in another asset, i.e. the firm must maintain
the book value of its fixed assets. Thus usus fructus category of property rights
in capital goods applies to the Yugoslav firm.

    The attenuation of public property rights in capital goods implies a
transfer of some specified rights in capital goods from the state to the firm. To
follow the Yugoslav example, we assume that the entire firm's profit belongs to
its employees. The employees may choose to exchange their current consumption for higher future income via leaving a part of the profit with the firm for investment in additional capital goods. Their property rights to new assets acquired
by the firm would, however, be limited to increased profits and only for as long

5. See Pejovich (1966, ch. 1.).

as they remain employed by the enterprise. The firm, on the other hand, must maintain indefinitely the value of those additional assets.

The set of opportunity choices available to the members of the community with respect to the accumulation of wealth is reduced compared to the private property capitalist case. Indeed, all persons who are not employed by business firms have no reason to invest their nonconsumed income in physical assets (although they *can* do it via gifts to business firms). The employees of business enterprises, on the other hand, can increase their wealth by leaving a part of the profit with the firm for investment in additional capital goods. Yet, their set of opportunity choices is also reduced (relative to the private property capitalist case) for at least two reasons: (a) when an employee leaves the firm, he loses all claims on the future earnings of the capital—even though his sacrifice of present consumption has helped to finance the new stock; and (b) the employee's decision to invest in the additional capital stock is irreversible; for he cannot, at some later date, choose to recoup the market value of his original investment.

With respect to the first point just raised, assume that the majority of employees of a firm expect to remain employed by *that* firm for ten years, and further that the rate of interest $(r_0)$ in Figure 23-1, which is also redrawn in Figure 23-4, is 10 percent.

The time horizon being specified, an investment of one dollar of the firm's profit (i.e., one dollar of foregone current consumption by the employees) in capital goods must yield at least sixteen cents a year over the period of ten years. To put it differently, the present value of a stream of income of sixteen cents a year for ten years, discounted at the rate of interest of ten percent is one dollar. Given the firm's obligation to maintain indefinitely the value of its capital stock, the rate of return from investment must be at least 16 percent; otherwise the investment would be submarginal.

The $\bar{r}\ \bar{r}$ curve shows the rate of return which makes one dollar invested in *nonowned* assets just as attractive to the workers as one dollar invested

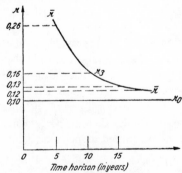

**Figure 23-4.** Tradeoffs Between Returns from Investment Alternatives Available to Employees of Yugoslav Firms

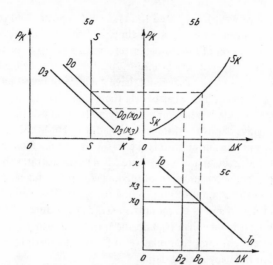

**Figure 23-5.** Attenuated State Property Rights and Short-Run Equilibrium in the Capital Market

in *owned* assets at 10 percent, for each given length of employment expected by the majority of employees. The difference between the points on $(\bar{r}\ \bar{r})$ schedule and $(r_0)$ indicates the effects of a change in the form of ownership in capital goods from the nonattenuated private ownership to the attenuated state ownership (usus fructus) in capital goods, all other things remaining the same. The stock demand curve for capital goods $(D_3 D_3)$ in Figure 23-5's 5a reflects the adjustment in the rate of return $(r_3)$ for a change in the form of ownership in capital. It follows that the rate of gross investment by the community is $(OB_2)$ in 5c.[6]

So far we have seen that the *employees'* personal valuation of current consumption relative to future income, the rate of marginal productivity of capital, and the interest rate implicit in relative prices of capital goods are brought into equality at $(r_3)$. However, we have yet to show that the entire *community's* valuation of current consumption relative to future income is brought into equality with the rate of interest $(r_3)$. To put it differently, we must show that the community's saving schedule in effect cuts the $(I_0 I_0)$ schedule at a rate of interest higher than $(r_0)$.

Consider those members of the community who are not employed by business firms. The set of opportunity choices open to them with respect to

6. The following statement translated from a Yugoslav weekly supports this analysis: "Workers of a very successful enterprise in Slovenia wish to renounce a good part of what they have earned in order to help build a new workshop. But they say they would like, in turn, a paper which would indicate what they have given and what rights they would have to the future income of the enterprise" (D. Boskovic, from *Vjesnic v Srijedu*, 23 November, 1966).

the accumulation of wealth is limited to (a) savings deposits, and (b) investment in human capital. Given the community time preference, the rate of income diverted to accumulation of nonhuman assets by this group of people is perfectly inelastic above the regulated rate of interest paid on savings deposits. The employees of business firms, on the other hand, have a choice of investing nonconsumed income (or part of it) in physical assets via their respective firms. Thus, the community's saving schedule is less than perfectly inelastic above the regulated rate of interest on savings deposits. Moreover, the adjustment in the employees' valuation of current consumption relative to future income from investment in *nonowned* physical assets (shown in Figure 23-4) demonstrates that each given rate of saving (i.e., nonconsumption of income) requires a higher rate of interest, all other things in the community remaining the same. The community's saving schedule shifts upward and in effect cuts the $(I_0 I_0)$ schedule at a rate of interest such as $(r_3)$ which is higher than $(r_0)$. In the process, it brings the community's valuation of present consumption relative to future income into equality with other rates, given the background data.

If the banks were organized along the same line as business firms the bank rate would also be brought into equality with other rates at $(r_3)$. Otherwise, the government would have to use either the cost-benefit method or some other criteria to ration the existing funds among the competing firms.

The conclusion reached will be reinforced if the effects of a change in property relations on the demand for human assets are incorporated into the analysis. A basic similarity exists between investment in physical and human assets, given the postulated property relations (usus fructus): the investor cannot recoup the market value of his original investment. He irreversibly substitutes the flow of future income from a specific asset for current consumption. However, a basic difference also exists between the two types of investment in a socialist community: human assets are owned by the person in whom the investment is made, while the capital goods are not. Thus the relationship between the rate of interest $(r_3)$ and the internal rate of return from human assets becomes the relationship between the expected income streams from two nonsellable assets of which only one is privately owned. It is quite likely that some people might consider investment in *owned* human assets to be a source of greater utility. If this were true, a change in the relative demand for nonhuman and human assets would occur in the community, and the rate of income diverted to gross investment in nonhuman assets would be further reduced.

## NON-ATTENUATED STATE OWNERSHIP; USUS

This specific category of the general concept of property rights is dominant in the USSR and other east European countries. The direct users of capital goods, i.e., the employees (including the managers) of business firms, have only the

right to use an asset belonging to the state, but not appropriate its yield nor to
sell it nor to change its quality.

　　Once again the analytical problem is to incorporate the effects of a
change in the form of ownership into our standard model. The demand for the
stock of existing as well as additional capital goods is limited to the state, or more
precisely to the ruling group. Unlike the potential investors in the three cases just
discussed, the ruling group can purchase one dollar's worth of new capital goods
without any appreciable decrease in its current consumption. The cost is borne
by the community at large. Moreover, the ruling group, by the virtue of its right
of ownership, determines the allocation of returns from the capital stock. This
power to decide *who gets what* is obviously a source of utility. From the point
of view of the ruling group, the cost of purchasing additional capital has fallen
while the benefits, pecuniary as well as nonpecuniary, have risen. Economic
logic thus suggests that the ruling group would increase its demand for additional
capital goods beyond the rate $(OB_0)$ established for the nonattenuated private
property case.

　　Each additional dollar invested beyond this rate increases the community's dissatisfaction (via violating its time preference). This dissatisfaction is,
of course, a real cost to the ruling group. Presumably, the ruling group will
increase the rate of gross investment up to the point such as $(B_3)$ where *its* gains
from the last dollar invested is just equal to *its* costs from increasing other
people's costs.

　　Given the rate of investment $(OB_3)$ in 6b and 6c of Figure 23–6 and
the rate of interest $(r_4)$, we can postulate the implicit price of the stock of exist-

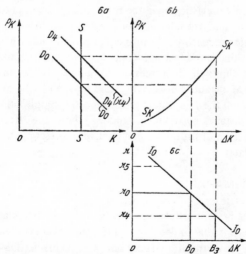

**Figure 23–6.** State Ownership and Short-Run Equilibrium in the Capital Market

ing capital to the state in 6a. It is approximated by the $(D_4 D_4)$ curve. The rate of interest $(r_4)$ brings into equality marginal productivity of capital and the ruling group valuation of future income relative to current consumption. The $(B_0 B_3)$ distance in 6c shows the effect of a change in the form of ownership in capital goods, from the nonattenuated private property rights to usus, on the rate of income diverted to gross investment, other things remaining the same.

The rate of interest $(r_4)$ does not, however, reflect the community's valuation of future income relative to current consumption. The set of opportunity choices open to the members of the community for converting their current incomes into wealth is limited to savings deposits and investment in human assets. Given the community's time preference and the regulated rate of interest on savings deposits, the demand for knowledge and skill must increase relative to the private property capitalist case, all other things remaining the same. For example, the importance which the average youngster in Russia attaches to education reflects not necessarily his greater desire for knowledge but the simple fact that human capital is the only type of earning assets he can own and earn a rate of return over and above the bank rate on savings deposits. The citizen of the Soviet Union does not possess the option of investing his non-consumed income in a pizza place.

The property relations being specified, the community's saving schedule, i.e., the rate of income voluntarily diverted to investment in nonhuman assets, is perfectly inelastic above the regulated rate of interest. It follows that the saving schedule in effect cuts the $(I_0 I_0)$ curve at a rate of interest such as $(r_5)$ in 6c of Figure 23-6, which must be above the $(r_3)$ rate in 5c. It must be so because the saving schedule in the attenuated state ownership case was shown to be less than perfectly inelastic above the bank rate on savings accounts.

To conclude, the community's valuation of future income relative to current consumption is *not* brought into equality with the rate of interest $(r_4)$ in Figure 23-6. Thus the state must use its discretionary powers to generate forced savings in order to eliminate the forces of disequilibrium that underscore the system. The vertical distance between $(r_4)$ and $(r_5)$ shows the difference between the owners' of capital (i.e., the ruling group) and the people's time preference. Also, the vertical distance between $(r_0)$ and $(r_5)$ shows the effect of usus on the community's valuation of future income relative to present consumption, given the background data.

## CONCLUDING REMARKS

The analysis of the present article leads to the following two major conclusions:

1. It is *possible* to develop an integrated theory of economic systems around the valid core of traditional economics by incorporating into the analysis the effects of various property-rights structures on the pattern of human behavior.

2. It seems *desirable* to develop an integrated economic theory around the concept of property-rights structures because the unifying theme provided by

property rights makes possible deeper and fuller understanding of the economic processes in countries operating under widely different political and social schemes. Such a theory would provide a common denominator for the analysis, comparison, and evaluation of different economic systems.

The analysis also suggests that a reduction in the scope of private property rights tends to change the community's pattern of behavior in favor of a greater preference for current consumption. Thus a growth-oriented socialist state, which most of them are, must rely on a number of administrative measures to increase its rate of economic growth.

We conclude the analysis with a quote which has inspired this paper: "The utility maximizing theory is applicable if and only if (1) we can identify some of its components beside direct pecuniary wealth, and if (2) we can identify circumstances that involve differences in the cost of each of the various types of non-pecuniary goods. By satisfying these two conditions we can deduce the relative extent of such activities in each of these circumstances. One important circumstance is the type of ownership of the firm" (Alchian 1965, pp. 30–41).

# References

Alchian, Armen A. *Some Economics of Property.* RAND P-2316. Santa Monica, Calif.: RAND Corporation, 1961.

———. "The Basis of Some Recent Advances in the Theory of Management of the Firm." *Journal of Industrial Economics* 14 (1965): 30–41.

———. "Corporate Management and Property Rights. In *Government Policy and the Regulation of Corporate Securities,* edited by H. Manne. Washington, D.C., 1969.

Alchian, Armen A., and Allen, William R. *University Economics.* 3rd ed. Belmont, Calif.: Wadsworth Publishing Company, 1972.

Alchian, Armen A., and Demsetz, Harold. "Production, Information Costs, and Economic Organization." *American Economic Review* 62 (1972): 777–795.

Alchian, Armen A., and Kessel, R.A. "Competition, Monopoly, and the Pursuit of Pecuniary Gain." In *Aspects of Labor Economics.* Princeton, N.J.: Princeton University Press, 1962.

Ames, Edward. *Soviet Economic Processes.* Homewood, Ill.: Richard D. Irwin, 1965.

Andreski, Stanislaw. *Parasitism and Subversion, The Case of Latin America.* London: Weidenfeld and Nicolson, 1966.

———. *The African Predicament, A Study in the Pathology of Modernization.* New York: Atherton Press, 1968.

Arrow, Kenneth J. "Economic Welfare and the Allocation of Resources of Invention." In *The Rate and Direction of Inventive Activity.* National Bureau of Economic Research. Princeton, N.J.: Princeton University Press, 1962.

Bain, J.S. *Barriers to New Competition.* Cambridge, Mass.: Harvard University Press, 1962.

Bajt, A. "Property in Capital and in the Means of Production in Socialist Economies." *Journal of Law and Economics* 11 (1968): 1–4.

Baker, J.C. *Executive Salaries and Bonus Plans.* New York: McGraw-Hill, 1938.

Ball, Stuarts. "The Vertical Extent of Ownership in Land." *University of Pennsylvania Law Review* 76 (1928): 631–689.

Barnard, C.I. *The Functions of the Executive.* Cambridge, Mass.: Harvard
  University Press, 1962.
Bator, Francis M. "The Simple Analytics of Welfare Maximization." *American
  Economic Review* 47 (1957): 31.
——. "The Anatomy of Market Failure." *Quarterly Journal of Economics* 72
  (1958): 351.
Baumol, W.J. *Business Behavior, Value and Growth.* New York: Harcourt,
  Brace, 1959.
——. "On the Theory of Expansion of the Firm." *American Economic Review*
  52 (1962): 1078–1087.
——. "On the Performing Arts." *American Economic Review Proceedings*
  55 (1965): 495–502.
Bayley, David H. "The Effects of Corruption in a Developing Nation." *West-
  ern Political Quarterly* 19 (1966): 719–732.
Becker, Gary S. *The Economics of Discrimination.* Chicago: University of Chi-
  cago Press, 1957.
——. "Competition, Monopoly, and the Pursuit of Pecuniary Gain: Comment."
  In *Aspects of Labor Economics.* Universities–National Bureau,
  Committee for Economic Research. Princeton, N.J.: Princeton
  University Press, 1962. (a)
——. "Irrational Behavior and Economic Theory." *Journal of Political
  Economy* 70 (1962): 1–13. (b)
Berle, A., and Means, G. *The Modern Corporation and Private Property.* New
  York: Macmillan, 1933.
Berliner, J. "The Informal Organization of the Soviet Firm." *Quarterly Jour-
  nal of Economics* 66 (1952): 342–365.
Blackman, J. "The Kosygin Reforms: New Wine in Old Bottles." In *The De-
  velopment of the Soviet Economy,* edited by V. Treml. New York:
  Praeger, 1968.
Blum, Walter J., and Kalven, Harry, Jr. *Public Law Perspective on a Private Law
  Problem: Auto Compensation Plans.* Boston: Little, Brown, 1965.
Boskovic, D. "The Self-Managing Shareholding Society." *Vjesnik u Srijedu,* 23
  November, 1966.
Bottomley, Anthony. "The Effect of Common Ownership of Land upon Re-
  source Allocation in Tripolitania. *Land Economy* 39 (1963): 91.
Boulding, Kenneth. "The Present Position of the Theory of the Firm." In
  *Linear Programming and the Theory of the Firm,* edited by K.
  Boulding and W. Spivy. New York: Macmillan, 1960.
Breckner, Norman V. "Government Efficiency and the Military 'Buyer-Seller'
  Device." *Journal of Political Economy* 68 (1960): 469–486.
Brown, R.S., Jr. "Character and Candor Requirement for FCC Licensees."
  *Law and Contemporary Problems* 22 (1957): 644.
——. *Loyality and Security: Employment Tests in the United States.* New
  Haven: Yale University Press, 1958.
Buchanan, James M. "Politics, Policy and the Pigovian Margins." *Economica*
  29 (1962): 17.

——. "An Economic Theory of Clubs." *Economica* 32 (1966): 1–14. (a)
——. "Joint Supply, Externality and Optimality." *Economica* 33 (1966): 404. (b)
——. *Public Finance in Democratic Process.* Chapel Hill: University of North Carolina Press, 1967.
Buchanan, James M., and Stubblebine, W. Craig. "Externality." *Economica* 29 (1962): 371–384.
Calabresi, Guido. "Does the Fault System Optimally Control Primary Accident Costs?" *Law and Contemporary Problems* 33 (1968): 429–463.
Caldwell, Louis G. "The Standard of Public Interest, Convenience or Necessity as Used in the Radio Act of 1927." *Air Law Review* 1 (1930): 295–296.
——. "Censorship of Radio Programs." *Journal of Radio Law* 1 (1931): 441–473.
——. "Freedom of Speech and Radio Broadcasting." *Annals* 177 (1935): 179–203.
Canes, M. "A Model of a Sports League." Ph.D. dissertation, University of California at Los Angeles, 1970.
Chafee, Z. *Free Speech in the United States.* Cambridge, Mass.: Harvard University Press, 1942.
——. *Government and Mass Communications.* Chicago: University of Chicago Press, 1947.
Cheung, Steven N.S. "Transaction Costs, Risk Aversion, and the Choice of Contractual Arrangements." *Journal of Law and Economics* 12 (1969): 23. (a)
——. *The Theory of Share Tenancy.* Chicago: University of Chicago Press, 1969. (b)
Childs, William Wallace. "Problems in the Radio Industry." *American Economic Review* 14 (1924): 520–523.
Christy, Francis T., Jr., and Scott, Anthony. *The Common Wealth in Ocean Fisheries.* Baltimore: Johns Hopkins, 1965.
Clarkson, Kenneth. "Some Implications of Property Rights in Hospital Management." *Journal of Law and Economics* 15 (1972): 363–384.
Clower, R.W. "An Investigation into the Dynamics of Investment." *American Economic Review* 44 (1954): 64–81.
Coase, Ronald H. "The Nature of the Firm." *Economica* 4 (1937): 386–405.
——. "The Nature of the Firm." In *Readings in Price Theory,* edited by George J. Stigler and Kenneth Boulding. Homewood, Ill.: Richard D. Irwin, 1952.
——. "The Federal Communications Commission." *Journal of Law and Economics* 2 (1959): 1.
——. "The Problem of Social Cost." *Journal of Law and Economics* 3 (1960): 1–44.
Codding, G.A., Jr. *The International Telecommunication Union.* Leiden: E.J. Brill, 1952.
——. "The International Law of Radio." *Federal Communications Board Journal* 14 (1955): 85.

Commission on Freedom of the Press. *A Free and Responsible Press.* Chicago: University of Chicago Press, 1947.

"Contracts in China Revisited, with a Focus on Agriculture, 1949–63." *China Quarterly* 28 (October–December 1966): 106.

Cowan, Thomas A. "Some Policy Bases of Products Liability." *Stanford Law Review* 17 (1965): 1094.

Cox, E.B., ed. *Basic Tables in Business and Economics.* New York, 1967.

Crutchfield, James A. "Common Property Resources and Factor Allocation." *Canadian Journal of Economics and Political Science* 22 (1956): 292.

Crutchfield, James, and Zellner, Arnold. "Economic Aspects of the Pacific Halibut Fishery." *Fishery Industrial Research* 1 (1962).

Cyert, R.M., and March, J.G. *A Behavioral Theory of the Firm.* Englewood Cliffs, N.J.: Prentice-Hall, 1963.

Dano, S. *Industrial Production Models.* New York: Springer-Verlag, 1966.

Davis, Otto A., and Whinston, Andrew. "Externalities, Welfare, and the Theory of Games." *Journal of Political Economy* 70 (1962) 241–262.

Davis, S. *The Law of Radio Communication.* New York: McGraw-Hill, 1927.

De Alessi, L. "The Short-Run Revisited." *American Economic Review* 57 (1967): 450–461.

——. "Implications of Property Rights for Government Investment Choices." *American Economic Review* 59 (1969): 13–24.

——. "Reversals of Assumptions and Implications." *Journal of Political Economy* 79 (1971): 867–877.

Demsetz, Harold. "The Exchange and Enforcement of Property Rights." *Journal of Law and Economics* 7 (1964): 11–26.

——. "Some Aspects of Property Rights." *Journal of Law and Economics* 9 (1966): 66.

——. "Information and Efficiency: Another Viewpoint." *Journal of Law and Economics* 12 (1969): 1.

Dill, C.C. *Radio Law.* Washington, D.C.: National Law Book Co., 1938.

Dirlam, Joel, "Report." *Year Book of the American Philosophical Society for 1967* (1967): 331–335.

Doerfer, John C. Address presented to the National Association of Broadcasters, Chicago, March 17, 1959.

Domar, E. "The Soviet Collective Farm as a Producer Cooperative." *American Economic Review* 56 (1966): 734–757.

Downs, Anthony. *Inside Bureaucracy.* Boston: Little, Brown, 1967.

Dubravcic, Drago. "Labour as Entrepreneurial Input: An Essay in the Theory of the Producer-Co-operative Economy." *Economica* 37 (1970): 297–310.

Dyer, J. Raymond. "Radio Interference as a Tort." *St. Louis University Law Review* 17 (1932): 125.

Edelman, J.M. *The Licensing of Radio Services in the United States, 1927 to 1947.* Urbana: University of Illinois Press, 1950.

"Expert Meeting on the Economic Effects of Fishery Regulations, Ottawa, 1961." In *Economic Effects of Fishery Regulation,* edited by R. Hamliseh. 1962.

Fanon, Frantz. *The Wretched of the Earth.* Harmondsworth: Penguin Books, 1967.

Federal Communications Commission. *Public Service Responsibility of Broadcast Licensees.* Washington, D.C.: U.S. Government Printing Office, 1946.

Federal Communications Commission, *Report of the Network Study Staff on Network Broadcasting.* Washington, D.C.: U.S. Government Printing Office, 1957.

Feezer, Lester W. "Tort Liability of Manufacturers and Vendors." *Minnesota Law Review* 10 (1925): 19–20.

Feldstein, M. *Economic Analysis for Health Service Efficiency.* Amsterdam: North-Holland Publishing Co., 1967.

——. "Hospital Cost Inflation: A Study of Nonprofit Price Dynamics." *American Economic Review* 61 (1971): 853–872.

Feldstein, P. "Research on the Demand for Health Care." *Millbank Memorial Fund Quarterly,* Pt. II (1966): 128–165.

Fellner, William. "External Economies and Diseconomies." In *Readings in Price Theory,* edited by George J. Stigler and Kenneth Boulding. Homewood, Ill.: Richard D. Irwin, 1952.

Fisher, Irving. *The Theory of Interest.* Clifton, N.J.: Kelley, 1961.

Fletcher, William Meade. "The Interstate Character of Radio Broadcasting: An Opinion." *Air Law Review* 11 (1940): 345–393.

Friedman, J.J. "Top Management Faces the Cost Challenge." *Dun's Review and Modern Industry* 77 (1961): 34–36.

Friedman, M. *A Theory of the Consumption Function.* Princeton, N.J.: Princeton University Press, 1957.

Friedman, M., and Savage, L. "The Utility Analysis of Choices Involving Risk." In *Readings in Price Theory,* edited by George J. Stigler and Kenneth Boulding. Homewood, Ill.: Richard D. Irwin, 1952.

Furubotn, E. "Investment Alternatives and the Supply Schedule of the Firm." *Southern Economic Journal* 31 (1964): 21–37.

——. "Toward a Dynamic Model of the Yugoslav Firm." *Canadian Journal of Economics* 4 (1971): 182–197.

Furubotn, E., and Pejovich, S. "Property Rights and the Behavior of the Firm in a Socialist State: The Example of Yugoslavia." *Zeitschrift für Nationalökonomie* 30 (1970): 431–454. (a)

——. "Tax Policy and Investment Decisions of the Yugoslav Firm." *National Tax Journal* (1970): 335–348. (b)

——. "The Role of the Banking System in Yugoslav Economic Planning, 1946–1969." *Revue Internationale D'Histoire De La Banque* 4 (1971).

——. "The Formation and Distribution of Net Product and the Behavior of the Yugoslav Firm." In *Jahrbuch der Wirtschaft Osteuropes,* edited by Franz-Lothar Altmann. Munich: Gunter Olzog Verlag, 1972. (a)

——. "Le Chef d'Entreprise Sovietique el l'Innovation." *Revue de l'Est* 3 (1972): 29–46. (b)

——. "Property Rights and Economic Theory: A Survey of Recent Literature." *Journal of Economic Literature* 10 (1972): 1137–1162. (c)

Gaffney, M. Mason. "Concepts of Financial Maturity of Timber and Other Assets." A.E. Information Series No. 62, North Carolina State College, 1960. Mimeographed.

Ginsburg, P. "Capital in Non-Profit Hospitals." Ph.D. dissertation, Harvard University, 1970.

Goldman, Marshall I. "Externalities and the Race for Economic Growth in the USSR: Will the Environment Ever Win?" *Journal of Political Economy* 80 (1972): 314–327.

Gordon, H. Scott. "The Economic Theory of a Common Property Resource: The Fishery." *Journal of Political Economy* 62 (1954): 124.

Gordon, M.J. *The Investment, Financing and Valuation of the Corporation.* Homewood, Ill.: Richard D. Irwin, 1962.

Gordon, R.A. *Business Leadership in the Large Corporation.* Berkeley: University of California Press, 1961.

Graaff, J. *Theoretical Welfare Economics,* Cambridge, England: Cambridge University Press, 1967.

Hadley, G. *Nonlinear and Dynamic Programming.* Reading, Mass.: Addison-Wesley, 1964.

Halm, C. *Economic Systems.* New York: Holt, Rinehart, and Winston, 1968.

Harberger, A.C. "Monopoly and Resource Allocation." *American Economics Review Proceedings* 44 (1954): 78–87.

Head, J.C. "The Welfare Foundations of Public Finance Theory." *Rivista Di Diritto Finanziario E Scienza Della Finanze* (1965): 3–52.

Herzel, Leo. "'Public Interest' and the Market in Color Television Regulation." *University of Chicago Law Review* 18 (1951): 802–809.

Hettinger, Herman S. "The Economic Factor in Radio Regulation." *Air Law Review* 9 (1939): 115–128.

Hoover, Herbert. Opening Address Before the Fourth Annual Radio Conference, 1925. Reproduced in Hearings on S.1 and S. 1754, Radio Control, before the Senate Committee on Interstate Commerce, 69th Cong., 1st Sess. 50, 1926.

Horvat, B. "Yugoslav Economic Policy in the Post-War Period: Problems, Ideas, Institutional Developments." *American Economic Review* (Supplement) (1971): 99–108.

Hsiao, Gene T. "The Role of Economic Contracts in Communist China." *California Law Review* 56 (1965).

"International Technical Conference on the Conservation of the Living Resources of the Sea." In *The Economics of Fisheries,* edited by Ralph Turvey and Jack Wiseman, 1956.

Jaeger, Walter H.E. "Privity of Warranty: Has the Tocsin Sounded?" *Duquesne University Law Review* (1963): 1.

Jome, Hiram L. "Property in the Air as Affected by the Airplane and the Radio." *Journal of Land and Public Utility Economics* 4 (1928): 257–272.

Kaysen, C. "The Corporation: How Much Power? What Scope?" In *The Corporation in Modern Society,* edited by E.S. Mason. Cambridge: Harvard University Press, 1960.

——. "Another View of Corporate Capitalism." *Quarterly Journal of Economics* 79 (1965): 43.

Keeton, Robert E., and O'Connell, Jeffrey. *Basic Protection for the Traffic Victim.* Boston: Little, Brown, 1965.

Kennedy, Walter B. "Radio and the Commerce Clause." *Air Law Review* 3 (1932): 16–26.

Knight, Frank H. "Some Fallacies in the Interpretation of Social Cost." In *Readings on Price Theory,* edited by George J. Stigler and Kenneth Boulding. Homewood, Ill.: Richard D. Irwin, 1952.

——. " 'What is Truth' in Economics." In *On the History and Method of Economics,* edited by Frank H. Knight. Chicago: University of Chicago Press, 1956.

——. *Risk, Uncertainty, and Profit.* New York: Harper Torchbooks Edition, 1965.

Koontz, H., and O'Donnell, C. *Principles of Management.* New York: McGraw-Hill, 1955.

Kuhn, H.W., and Tucker, C.W. "Nonlinear Programming." In *Proceedings of the Second Berkeley Symposium on Mathematical Statistics and Probability.* Berkeley: University of California Press, 1951.

*Kujigovodstvo.* Belgrade: Kujigovodstvo, 1968.

Lancaster, K. *Mathematical Economics.* New York: Macmillan, 1968.

Lange, Oskar. "On the Economic Theory of Socialism." *Review of Economic Studies* 4 (1936): 53–71.

Larner, R.J. "The 200 Largest Nonfinancial Corporations." *American Economic Review* 56 (1966): 779.

Leacock, Eleanor. "The Montagnes 'Hunting Territory' and the Fur Trade." *American Anthropologist* 56, Pt. 2.

Lee, M.L. "A Conspicuous Production Theory of Hospital Behavior." *Southern Economic Journal* 38 (1971): 48–59.

Leff, Nathaniel H. "Economic Development Through Bureaucratic Corruption." *American Behavioral Scientist* 8 (1964): 8–14.

Levine, H. "The Centralized Planning of Supply in Soviet Industry." In *The Soviet Economy,* edited by M. Bornstein and D. Fusfeld. Homewood, Ill.: Richard D. Irwin, 1966.

Liberman, Y. "The Plan, Profits and Bonuses." *Pravda,* 9 September, 1962.

Lindsay, C.M. "Supply Response in the Financing of Medical Care." Ph.D. dissertation, University of Virginia, 1968.

Lissner, ——. "Public Control of Radio." *American Journal of Economics and Sociology* 5 (1946): 552.

Long, M.F. "Efficient Use of Hospitals." In *The Economics of Health and Medical Care.* Ann Arbor, Mich., 1964.

Macaulay, S. "Non-Contractual Relations in Business: A Preliminary Study." *American Sociological Review* 28 (1968): 55–69.

McCain, James. "The Medium Through Which the Radio Wave is Transmitted as a Natural Channel of Interstate Commerce." *Air Law Review* 11 (1940): 144.

McDougal, Myres S., and Burke, William T. *The Public Order of the Oceans.* New Haven: Yale University Press, 1962.

McGuire, J.W., Chiu, J.S.Y., and Elbing, A.O. "Executive Incomes, Sales, and Profits." *American Economic Review* 52 (1962): 753–761.

McKean, Roland N. *Efficiency in Government Through Systems Analysis.* New York: Wiley, 1958.

——. "The Unseen Hand in Government." *American Economic Review* 55 (1965): 496–505.

——. *Public Spending.* New York: McGraw-Hill, 1968.

Malmgren, H.B. "Information, Expectations and the Theory of the Firm." *Quarterly Journal of Economics* 75 (1961): 399–421.

Manion, Clarence. *Law of the Air.* Indianapolis: Bobbs-Merrill, 1950.

Manne, H. "Our Two Corporation Systems: Law and Economics." *Virginia Law Review* 53 (1967): 259–284.

Marshall, Alfred. *Industry and Trade.* London: Macmillan, 1932.

Mason, E.S., ed. *The Corporation in Modern Society.* Cambridge, Mass.: Harvard University Press, 1960.

Meade, J.E. "External Economies and Diseconomies in a Competitive Situation." *Economics Journal* 62 (1952): 54.

Milenkovitch, Deborah O. *Plan and Market in Yugoslav Economic Thought.* New Haven: Yale University Press, 1971.

Mill, John Stuart. *Principles of Political Economy.* 4th ed. Baltimore: Penguin, 1857.

Mishan, E.J. "A Survey of Welfare Economics, 1939–1959." *Economics Journal* 70 (1960): 197–256.

——. "Reflections on Recent Developments in the Concept of External Effects." *Canadian Journal of Economics and Political Science* 31 (1965): 3–34.

Neuman, K. Sidney. "The Uniform Commercial Code and Greater Consumer Protection Under Warranty Law." *Kentucky Law Journal* 49 (1960–61): 240–269.

Newhouse, J. "Toward a Theory of Non-profit Institutions: An Economic Model of a Hospital." *American Economic Review* 60 (1970): 64–73.

——. "The Economics of Group Practice." *Journal of Human Resources* (1972).

Nichols, Alfred. "Stock Versus Mutual Savings and Loan Associations: Some Evidence of Differences in Behavior." *American Economic Review* 57 (1967): 337–346.

Niles, Emory H. "The Present Status of the Ownership of Airspace." *Air Law Review* 5 (1934): 132–156.

Niskanen, William A., Jr. *Bureaucracy and Representative Government.* Chicago: Aldine-Atherton, 1971.

Noel, Dix W. "Manufacturers of Products—The Drift Toward Strict Liability." *Tennessee Law Review* 24 (1957): 963–1018.

North, Douglass. "Sources of Productivity Change in Ocean Shipping 1600–1850." *Journal of Political Economy* 76 (1968): 953.

——. "The Creation of Property Rights in Western Europe 900–1700 A.D."
    Unpublished manuscript, 1972.
*Nove Mere Za Sprovodjenje Privredne Reforme.* Belgrade: Knjizevne Novine,
    1968.
Nove, Alec. "The Problem of Success Indicators in Soviet Industry." *Econom-
    ica* 25 (1958): 1–13.
——. *The Soviet Economy.* London: Allen & Unwin, 1961.
Nutter, W. "Markets Without Property: A Grand Illusion." In *Money, the
    Market, and the State,* edited by N. Beadles and A. Drewry. Athens:
    Georgia University Press, 1968.
Oi, W., and Clayton, E. "A Peasant's View of a Soviet Collective Farm." *Ameri-
    can Economic Review* 58 (1968): 37–59.
"Old Standards in New Context: A Comparative Analysis of FCC Regulation."
    *University of Chicago Law Review* 18 (1950): 78–83.
Olson, M. *The Logic of Collective Action.* Cambridge, Mass.: Harvard Univer-
    sity Press, 1962.
Paj, Ivan. "The Development of the System of Distribution of The Social Prod-
    uct and Net Income." *Yugoslav Survey* 11 (1970): 65–88.
Park, Rolla Edward. *Effects of Graft on Economic Development: An Examina-
    tion of Propositions from the Literature.* Santa Monica, Calif.:
    RAND Corporation, 1969.
Pauly, M. "Clubs and Cores." *Public Choice* 9 (1970): 53–65.
Pejovich, Svetozar. *The Market-Planned Economy of Yugoslavia.* Minneapolis:
    University of Minnesota Press, 1966.
——. "The Firm, Monetary Policy and Property Rights in a Planned Economy."
    *Western Economics Journal* 7 (1969): 193–200. (a)
——. "Liberman's Reforms and Property Rights in the Soviet Union." *Journal
    of Law and Economics* 12 (1969): 155–162. (b)
Perl, Martin L. "The Science Advisory System: Some Observations." *Science*
    (1971): 1211–1215.
Pfeffer, Richard M. "The Institution of Contracts in the Chinese People's Re-
    public." *China Quarterly* 14, 15 (April–June 1963, July–September
    1963): 153, 115.
Pigou, A.C. *The Economics of Welfare, Pt. 1.* London: Macmillan, 1920.
——. *The Economics of Welfare, Pt. 2.* 4th ed. London: Macmillan, 1932.
Plott, Charles R. "Externalities and Corrective Taxes." *Economica* 33 (1966):
    84.
Prosser, William L. *Handbook of the Law of Torts.* St. Paul, Minn.: West Pub-
    lishing Co., 1941.
——. "The Assault upon the Citadel (Strict Liability to the Consumer)." *Yale
    Law Journal* 69 (1960): 1099–1148.
"Radio and Television Station Transfers: Adequacy of Supervision Under the
    Federal Communications Act." *Indiana Law Journal* 30 (1955):
    351.
"Radio Program Controls: A Network of Inadequacy." *Yale Law Journal* 57
    (1947): 275.

Reder, M. "Some Problems in the Economics of Hospitals." *American Economics Review Proceedings* 55 (1965): 472–480.

Roberts, D.R. *Executive Compensation.* Glencoe, Ill.: Free Press, 1959.

Robinson, Joan. "Rising Supply Price." In *Readings in Price Theory,* edited by George J. Stigler and Kenneth Boulding. Homewood, Ill.: Richard D. Irwin, 1952.

Rogers, Walter S. "Air as a Raw Material." *Annals* 112 (1924): 251–254.

Rosenberg, Nathan. "Some Institutional Aspects of the Wealth of Nations." *Journal of Political Economy* 68 (1960): 557–570.

Rostow, E.V. "To Whom and for What Ends Is Corporate Management Responsible?" In *The Corporation in Modern Society,* edited by E.S. Mason. Cambridge, Mass.: Harvard University Press, 1960.

Rowley, Frank S. "Problems in the Law of Radio Communication." *University of Cincinnati Law Review* 1 (1927): 1–35.

Rudner, Richard S. *Philosophy of Social Science.* Englewood Cliffs, N.J.: Prentice-Hall, 1966.

Sacks, Stephen, R. *Entry of New Competitors in Yugoslav Market Socialism.* Berkeley: Institute of International Studies, in press.

Salsbury, Franklin C. "The Transfer of Broadcast Rights." *Air Law Review* 11 (1940): 113–143.

Samuels, W. "Interrelations Between Legal and Economic Processes." *Journal of Law and Economics* 14 (1971): 444.

Samuelson, P.A. "Evaluation of Real National Income." *Oxford Economic Papers* 2 (1950): 1–29.

——. *Foundations of Economics.* Cambridge, Mass.: Harvard University Press, 1958.

——. *Economics.* 7th ed. New York: McGraw-Hill, 1966.

Segal, Paul M., and Warner, Harry P. " 'Ownership' of Broadcasting 'Frequencies': A Review." *Rocky Mountain Law Review* 19 (1947): 111–122.

Schall, Lawrence. "Technological Externalities and Resource Allocation." Ph.D. dissertation, University of Chicago, 1969.

Schmeckebier, L.F. *The Federal Radio Commission.* Washington, D.C.: The Brookings Institution, 1932.

Schwartz, B. *The Professor and the Commissions.* New York: Knopf, 1959.

Schwartzman, D. "The Effect of Monopoly on Price." *Journal of Political Economy* 67 (1959): 352–362.

Scitovsky, Tiber. "Two Concepts of External Economies." *Journal of Political Economy* 62 (1954): 143.

Scott, Anthony. "The Fishery: The Objectives of Sole Ownership." *Journal of Political Economy* 63 (1955): 116.

——. "Optimal Utilization and the Control of Fisheries." In *The Economics of Fisheries,* edited by Ralph Turvey and Jack Wiseman, 1956.

——. "Economic Obstacles to Marine Development." Manuscript prepared for the Conference on Marine Aquaculture, Oregon State University, May 1968.

Scott, James C. "The Analysis of Corruption in Developing Nations." *Comparative Studies in Society and History* 11 (1969): 315–341.

Scott, M. Fg. "Relative Share Prices and Yields." *Oxford Economics Papers* 14 (1962): 218–250.

Siepmann, Charles A. *Radio, Television and Society.* New York: Oxford University Press, 1950.

Silver, M., and Auster, R. "Entrepreneurship, Profit, and the Limits on Firm Size." *Journal of Business of the University of Chicago* 42 (1969): 277–281.

Simon, Herbert Alexander. "The Compensation of Executives." *Sociometry* 20 (1957): 32–35.

——. *Administrative Behavior.* 2nd ed. New York: Macmillan, 1961.

——. "New Developments in the Theory of the Firm." *American Economic Review* 52 (1962): 1–15.

Sinclair, Sol. *License Limitation-British Columbia: A Method of Economic Fisheries Management.* Canada: Canadian Department of Fisheries, 1960.

Smead, E.E. *Freedom of Speech by Radio and Television.* Washington, D.C.: Public Affairs Press, 1959.

Smelser, Neil J. "Stability, Instability, and the Analysis of Political Corruption." In *Stability and Social Change,* edited by Bernard Barber and Alex Inkles. Boston: Little, Brown, 1971.

Smith, Vernon L. "On Models of Commercial Fishing." *Journal of Political Economy* 77 (1969): 181.

Smythe, Dallas W. "Facing Facts About the Broadcast Business." *University of Chicago Law Review* 20 (1952): 96.

Speck, Frank G. "The Basis of American Indian Ownership of Land." *Old Penn Weekly Review* (January 16, 1915): 491–495.

Spiljak, M. *The System of Remuneration in Yugoslavia.* Belgrade: Publishing House, 1961.

Spulber, N. *The Soviet Economy.* New York: Norton, 1962.

Stevens, C. "Hospitals Market Efficiency: The Anatomy of the Supply Response." In *Empirical Studies in Health Economics,* edited by H. Klarman. Baltimore: Johns Hopkins, 1970.

Stewart, Irvin. "The Public Control of Radio." *Air Law Review* 8 (1937): 131–152.

Stigler, George J. "Production and Distribution in the Short Run." *Journal of Political Economy* 47 (1939): 305–327.

——. "The Statistics of Monopoly and Merger." *Journal of Political Economy* 64 (1956): 33–40.

——. "The Economics of Information." *Journal of Political Economy* 69 (1961): 213.

——. *The Organization of Industry.* Homewood, Ill.: Richard D. Irwin, 1968.

Stigler, George J., and Boulding, Kenneth, eds. *Readings in Price Theory.* Homewood, Ill.: Richard D. Irwin, 1952.

Takekoshi, Yasoburo. *The Economic Aspects of the History of the Civilization of Japan.* 3 vols. New York: Paragon, 1967.
Taugher, James Patrick. "The Law of Radio Communication with Particular Reference to a Property Right in a Radio Wave Length." *Marquette Law Review* 12 (1928): 179–299.
Thompson, E.A. "Nonpecuniary Rewards and the Aggregate Production Function." *Review of Economic Statistics* 52 (1970): 395–404.
Thompson, E.T. "The Cost Cutting Urge." *Fortune* 57 (1958): 118–121.
Thompson, V.A. *Modern Organization.* New York: Knopf, 1961.
Tullock, Gordon. *The Politics of Bureaucracy.* Washington, D.C.: Public Affairs Press, 1965.
Turvey, Ralph. "Optimization and Suboptimization in Fishery Regulation." *American Economic Review* 54 (1964): 64.
Turvey, Ralph, and Wiseman, Jack, eds. *The Economics of Fisheries.* 1956.
Vance, L.L. *Theory and Technique of Cost Accounting.* Brooklyn, 1952.
Vanek, Jaroslav. "Decentralization Under Workers-Management: A Theoretical Appraisal." *American Economic Review* 53 (1969).
———. *The General Theory of Labor-Managed Market Economies.* Ithaca: Cornell University Press, 1970.
Viner, Jacob. "Cost Curves and Supply Curves." In *Readings in Price Theory,* edited by George J. Stigler and Kenneth Boulding. Homewood, Ill.: Richard D. Irwin, 1952.
Vojnich, D. *Aktuelni Problemi Ekonomske Politike i Privrednog Sistema Jugoslavije.* Zagreb: Informator, 1970. (a)
———. *Investicije i Fiksni Fondovi Jugoslavije.* Zagreb: Ekonomski Institut, 1970. (b)
Wachtel, Howard M. "Worker's Management and Inter-industry Wage Differentials in Yugoslavia." *Journal of Political Economy* 80 (1972): 540–560.
Wade, John W. "Strict Tort Liability of Manufacturers." *Southwestern Law Journal* 19 (1965): 5–25.
Ward, B. "Workers Management in Yugoslavia." *Journal of Political Economy* 65 (1957): 373–386.
———. "The Firm in Illyria: Market Syndicalism." *American Economic Review* 48 (1958): 566–589.
Warner, H.P. *Radio and Television Law.* Albany, N.Y.: M. Bender, 1948.
Weisbrod, B. "Some Problems of Pricing and Resource Allocation in a Non-Profit Industry—The Hospitals." *Journal of Business* (1965): 18–28.
Wellisz, Stanislaw. "On External Diseconomies and the Government Assisted Invisible Hand." *Economica* 31 (1964): 345.
"White Collar Cutback." *Wall Street Journal,* 3 January, 1963, p. 1.
Williamson, O.E. "Managerial Behavior: The Evidence from the Field Studies." Behavioral Theory of the Firm Working Paper No. 38. Pittsburgh, 1962.
———. "A Model of Rational Managerial Behavior." In *A Behavioral Theory of the Firm,* edited by R.M. Cyert and J.G. March. Englewood Cliffs, N.J.: Prentice-Hall, 1963. (a)

——. "Managerial Discretion and Business Behavior." *American Economic Review* 53 (1963): 1032–1057. (b)

——. "Selling Expense as a Barrier to Entry." *Quarterly Journal of Economics* 77 (1963): 112–128. (c)

——. *Corporate Control and Business Behavior.* Englewood Cliffs, N.J.: Prentice-Hall, 1970.

Williamson, Oliver E., Olson, Douglas G., and Ralston, August. "Externalities, Insurance, and Disability Analysis." *Economica* 34 (1967): 235–253.

Witte, J. "The Microfoundations of the Social Investment Function." *Journal of Political Economy* 71 (1963): 441–456.

Yett, D., Drabek, L., Intriligator, M., and Kimball, M. "A Macroeconomic Model for Regional Health Planning." *Economics and Business Bulletin* 24 (1971): 1–21.

Zaleski, E. *Planning Reforms in the Soviet Union, 1962–1966.* Chapel Hill: University of North Carolina Press, 1967.

Zoeteweij, H. "Fisherman's Remuneration." In *The Economics of Fisheries,* edited by Ralph Turvey and Jack Wiseman, 1956.

# About the Authors

**Eirik G. Furubotn** is currently Professor of Economics at Texas A & M University. Prior to joining the Texas A & M faculty he served as chairman of the department of economics at SUNY, Binghamton and did his graduate work at Columbia University. Dr. Furubotn's research interest is microeconomic theory, and in recent years he and Dr. Pejovich have collaborated in research on the Yugoslav economic system. He is the co-author of *The Evolution of Modern Demand Theory* and numerous journal articles.

**Svetozar Pejovich** is Professor of Economics at Ohio University and Adjunct Professor at the University of Dallas. Previously he taught at St. Mary's College, the University of Nevada at Las Vegas, and Texas A & M University. He is the author of *The Market-Planned Economy of Yugoslavia* and a member of the editorial boards of the *Review of Social Economy* and *Modern Age*.